Is Taiwan Chinese?

Given to my loving father for his 50th birthday on
August 23, 2004. Thank you for all that you do. I love
you.

Albert H. Shih
8/23/04

BERKELEY SERIES IN INTERDISCIPLINARY STUDIES OF CHINA

Published in collaboration with the Center for Chinese Studies

Wen-hsin Yeh, Editor

1. *The Lure of the Modern: Writing Modernism in Semicolonial China, 1917–1937,* by Shu-mei Shih

2. *Is Taiwan Chinese? The Impact of Culture, Power, and Migration on Changing Identities,* by Melissa J. Brown

3. *Positioning for Power: Beijing University, Intellectuals, and Chinese Political Culture, 1898–1927,* by Timothy B. Weston

Is Taiwan Chinese?

The Impact of Culture, Power,
and Migration on Changing Identities

Melissa J. Brown

UNIVERSITY OF CALIFORNIA PRESS
Berkeley · Los Angeles · London

University of California Press
Berkeley and Los Angeles, California

University of California Press, Ltd.
London, England

© 2004 by the Regents of the University of California

Library of Congress Cataloging-in-Publication Data

Brown, Melissa J.
  Is Taiwan Chinese? the impact of culture, power,
and migration on changing identities/Melissa J. Brown
      p. cm.—(Berkeley series in interdisciplinary
  studies of China; 2)
    Includes bibliographical references and index.
    ISBN 0-520-23181-3 (cloth : alk. paper).—
    ISBN 0-520-23182-1 (pbk. : alk. paper)
    1. Taiwan aborigines—Ethnic identity—History.
  2. Ethnicity—Taiwan—History.   3. Ethnicity—
  China—History—20th century.   4. Nationalism—
  Taiwan—History—20th century.   5. Nationalism—
  China—History—20th century.   6. Chinese reunification question, 1949–.   7. Tujia (Chinese
  people)—China—Enshi Tujiazu Miaozu Zizhizhou—
  Ethnic identity—History—20th century.
  8. Taiwan—Relations—China.   9. China—
  Relations—Taiwan.   10. Enshi Tujiazu Miaozu
  Zizhizhou (China)—Ethnic relations—History—
  20th century.   I. Title.   II. Series.

DS799.42.B76   2004
305.89'925—dc21   2003012763

Manufactured in the United States of America
13 12 11 10 09 08 07 06 05 04
10 9 8 7 6 5 4 3 2 1

The paper used in this publication is both acid-free
and totally chlorine-free (TCF). It meets the minimum
requirements of ANSI/NISO z39.48–1992 (R 1997)
(*Permanence of Paper*).

FOR
Ann Davis
and
Michael Kaplan

teachers at
Nichols Middle School
Evanston, Illinois

who first taught me how to think
about social theory and
about science

Contents

Illustrations

Preface

This book makes several bold theoretical claims. Moving from the more specific to the more general, they are: identity is based on social experience, not cultural ideas or ancestry; cultural meanings and social power constitute two distinct, though interacting, systems that affect human behavior and societies differently; demographic forces such as migration affect human behavior and societies in yet another way; and human cognition—both cognitive structure and decision-making processes—mediate the influences of culture, power, and demographic conditions. In arguing these claims, I weave together theoretical perspectives from across the postmodernism-science divide to produce a synthesis that, hopefully, provides a clearer picture of the processes shaping human behavior and societies.

These theoretical claims are grounded in empirical case studies of identity changes in Taiwan and China. In fact, the case studies take precedence until the concluding chapter, primarily because the theoretical claims are most easily explained with ethnographic illustrations. Chapter 1 introduces the context of Taiwan and the People's Republic of China (PRC), and more specifically the debate between them over Taiwan's identity and future. I do discuss some theoretical issues relating to identity here, primarily to alert readers to key issues to be examined in the case studies. Chapter 2 provides a historical sketch of Taiwan's political history, with particular attention to plains Aborigines. Chapter 3, the ethnographic heart of the book, contains the most detailed of the case studies.

It documents and analyzes the twentieth-century identity change of plains Aborigines to Han (the ethnic majority), which I call the "long route" to Han, and briefly discusses their recent reclassification as plains Aborigines again. Chapter 4 uses historical materials to reconstruct the seventeenth-century acquisition of Han identity by some plains Aborigines in Taiwan, which I call the "short route to Han."

For purposes of comparison, chapter 5 examines another group with a history of identity changes from non-Han to Han and back again: the Tujia in the PRC, specifically in the province of Hubei. Both plains Aborigines in Taiwan and Tujia in Hubei are very sinicized—that is, they have adopted many cultural ideas and practices of the Han majority. Also, they were historically subject to the same Confucian-based imperial regime (the Qing dynasty), yet they had different historical trajectories before coming under Qing rule and after 1895. Thus, they show sufficient similarities to warrant comparison and sufficient differences to allow us to evaluate the varying influences of culture, power, and migration.

Finally, in my concluding chapter, I turn to theory and politics. I first outline the theoretical synthesis that serves as my framework for analyzing the case studies in Taiwan and Hubei; then, using this framework, I analyze political implications of identity in Taiwan and China in a fashion that can inform policy decisions about Taiwan's future relations with the PRC.

The case study material presented here combines anthropological field research and historical reconstruction. In 1991–92, I interviewed in three plains Aborigine communities in Taiwan: thirty-five people over age 70 in Toushe, twenty-nine people over age 70 in Jibeishua, and fifteen people over age 60 in Longtian. (There were not very many people left in Longtian whose ancestors were Aborigines, making it difficult to find fifteen people to interview, even after broadening the age range.) I also interviewed neighboring Han—twelve people over age 70 in Danei and a few additional people in other communities—in order to learn about the larger social context and provide a local Han comparison. I revisited these areas in 1994 and 2000. In addition, Chinese colleagues and I interviewed thirty-three people who were not officials in one village in Hubei in 1996. We also interviewed five ritual specialists, three of whom lived outside the village. The interviews ranged in length from one hour to fifteen hours spread over five visits, averaging around three and a half hours each in Taiwan and two hours each in Hubei. I covered the same set of topics in open-ended fashion with all those people in Taiwan and a different set of topics with all those people in Hubei.

These numbers may seem small, especially to non-anthropologists, but more than ninety interviews in Taiwan and more than thirty interviews in Hubei constitute a substantial body of anthropological material. Not only do these numbers represent more interviews than many anthropologists perform, but more importantly, the people I interviewed are not a small sample of a larger population. They constitute almost every living person in 1991–92 whom local people could help me find from each targeted community who was over 70 years old (or over 60 in the case of Longtian) and who had once been considered plains Aborigine. In other words, I interviewed virtually the entire targeted population alive at the time. I am less certain of having approached the entire targeted population in Hubei, thus I give no tables in chapter 5.

Originally, I gave pseudonyms to all the villages in which I worked (see Brown 1995, 1996b, 1997, 1999, 2000, 2001, 2002). The pseudonyms—Jiashe, Yishe, Bingshe, and Dingcun for the Taiwan villages and Wucun for Hubei—are the Chinese equivalent of A, B, and C plains Aborigine villages (for the names ending in *she*) and D and E villages (for the names ending in *cun*). After much thought and discussion, I chose to use the real names of the Taiwan villages in this book: Toushe (Jiashe), Jibeishua (Yishe), Longtian (Bingshe), and Danei (Dingcun). The real names of all these communities have previously appeared in anthropological and historical literature in the U.S. and Taiwan and popular literature about plains Aborigines in Taiwan. Moreover, all these sites have become included in a large demographic project analyzing marriage patterns, fertility and mortality (e.g., Engelen and Wolf in press). At the urging of several colleagues, I decided to use the real names here, so that readers can compare my results and analyses with those of other scholars working with material from the same sites. Because the Hubei village is not part of the demographic project, I have retained the previously published pseudonym for it: Wucun, that is, E- or Fifth-Village.

Every work of such scope requires the assistance of many people, and I am pleased to acknowledge the contributions of others to my work. My gratitude for their help and insights does not make them accountable for the end product. Full responsibility for this book, and any remaining errors it may contain, is mine alone.

I want to thank a number of people for careful reading of the book, in whole or in part. My doctoral dissertation committee—Stevan Harrell, Donna Leonetti, and Eric Alden Smith—read early versions of chapters 2, 3, and 4. Steve Harrell also read part of chapter 5 as an article for *Asian Ethnicity* and read the entire manuscript when it was finished. My writing group at the University of Cincinnati—Elizabeth Brown Frierson,

Laura Dudley Jenkins, and Mona L. Siegel—read multiple drafts of the book with rigor, support, and good humor. As part of the review process for the University of California Press, Hill Gates, David Strand, Wen-hsin Yeh, and an anonymous University of California faculty member offered constructive suggestions and still gave me the leeway to convey all of my ideas as I chose. John R. Shepherd generously provided his thoughtful disagreement in writing and has remained cordial in spite of our differences. Three University of Cincinnati undergraduates—Elizabeth Royalty-Cantwell, Daniel White, and Stephanie A. Woebkenberg—offered a student perspective. My colleague at Cincinnati, Rhoda H. Halperin, made crucial organizational suggestions early on. My husband, James Truncer, listened to passages, organizational issues, and theoretical dilemmas with great patience and offered many substantive and calming suggestions. Elizabeth Royalty-Cantwell at the University of Cincinnati and Clarissa Smith, Elba Garcia, and Elaine Chao at Stanford University assisted greatly in production of the manuscript. Charles Roseman at Stanford produced the maps. Huang Yu-ching of the Fu Ssu-nien Library at the Institute of History and Philology at the Academia Sinica and Larry C. Huang of the Cheng Wen Publishing Company helped with the Qing-period illustration of Aborigines.

My debt to people who helped me in Taiwan and China is tremendous. Arthur Wolf provided crucial introductions to scholars in both places. In Taiwan, the Institute of Ethnology at the Academia Sinica (Minzuxue Yanjiusuo, Zhongyang Yanjiuyuan) made me a Visiting Research Associate. Many members of the Institute kindly gave me the benefit of their time and knowledge. Pan Inghai did even more: he formally sponsored my research, helped me select my field sites, introduced me to people there, and helped me navigate the social and cultural waters of my first fieldwork so that it was successful. For all his help, I am immensely grateful. Chuang Ying-chang, Arthur Wolf, and Pan Inghai allowed me to use the household registers which they had collected for my field sites. David Prager Branner, a linguist of Chinese languages, visited my field sites in 1992 and analyzed the local Minnan and secret language spoken there. In my field sites, the elderly people who allowed me to interview them—most if not all of whom are now dead—trusted me with stories about their lives and I have tried to honor both their accomplishments and their privacy. The families of Chen Jinhe, Duan Xintian, Chen Xiong, Chen Jiahe, Li Renji, and Lian Zhushan were all more than just patient with my intrusion into their lives; their genuine hospitality allowed my research to proceed. Five local women (listed here in the order in which I met them) made my research possible at the most fundamental level: Wu Difeng, Luo Huirong, Duan Liliu, Yang Yiling, and Chen Suimei. Four of them arranged interviews and translated for me between Mandarin and Taiwanese (Minnan) in those interviews, and one helped me find the first translator and also translated one lengthy formal interview herself. They shared with me their knowledge of the local community, their insights into local social and cultural processes, and their friendship. They helped shape the field data about plains Aborigines in Taiwan on which much of this book is based.

In China, the Department of Ethnology at the South-Central Nationalities College (Minzuxue Xi, Zhongnan Minzu Xueyuan) in Wuhan sponsored my research. A number of scholars at the college as well as scholars at the Institute of Ethnology at the Central Nationalities University (Minzuxue Yanjiuso, Zhongyang Minzu Daxue) in Beijing generously met with me and offered suggestions. It was Dong Luo, however, who made my research in China possible. She helped me select the Tujia as an appropriate comparison group, arranged all the necessary permissions for the field research, and accompanied me to the field, giving me the benefit of her insight and experience there. She even managed to win official permission for us to live in a farm family's home! Dong Luo brought Wu Xu, one of her graduate students, into the project, and he proved a very knowledgeable and able research assistant. Officials in the Enshi Tujia-Miao Autonomous Prefecture and scholars associated with the Tujia Research Center at the Hubei Nationalities College also generously shared their knowledge and experience. The farm family in "Wucun" where we lived provided very warm hospitality at a very cold time of year. The head of the household graciously accepted the village head's request that he accompany us on our interviews and provided much-needed translation between standard Mandarin and the local, rural version of Southwest Mandarin.

Finally, I am pleased to acknowledge the funding I have received. My field research in Taiwan was supported by an American Council of Learned Societies/Social Science Research Council Chiang Ching-kuo Foundation Dissertation Research Fellowship in Chinese Studies, a Pacific Cultural Foundation Research Fellowship, and a Visiting Research Associate position at the Institute of Ethnology, Academia Sinica. My field research in China was supported by a National Science Foundation International Post-Doctoral Fellowship (INT-9505686). The analysis and write-up phases were supported, in part, by the same NSF fellowship; by a postdoctoral fellowship at the Center for Chinese Studies at the University of California, Berkeley; by a Charles Phelps Taft Grant from the University of Cincinnati; and by provision of a research assistant from the Center for East Asian Studies and work-study student assistants at Stanford University.

M. J. B.
Stanford, California
January 30, 2002

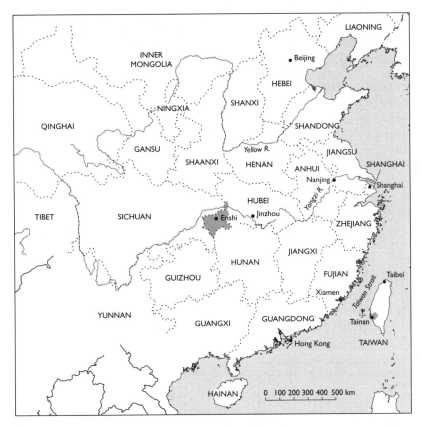

Figure 1. Map of China and Taiwan. China Historical GIS Dataset, Version: Pre-release (October 2001).

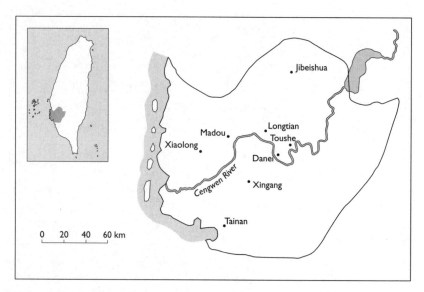

Figure 2. Map of Tainan County, Taiwan. China Historical GIS Dataset,
Version: Pre-release (October 2001).

Regimes in Taiwan		Regimes in China	
Dutch	1624–1661	Ming	1368–1644
Zheng	1662–1683	Qing	1644–1911
Qing	1683–1895		
Japanese	1895–1945	Republican	1911–1949
Nationalist, Martial Law	1945–1987	Communist	1949–present
Nationalist, Post-Martial Law (transitional period)	1987–1996		
Full electoral democracy	1996–present		

Figure 3. Regimes in Taiwan and China.

CHAPTER I

What's in a Name?

Culture, Identity, and the "Taiwan Problem"

At the turn of the twenty-first century, Taiwan is a global hot spot. The events and rhetoric surrounding Taiwan's second presidential election in March 2000 raised fears that tensions in the region might result in actual warfare among nuclear powers. Why is Taiwan—with a stable, democratic government and a strong economy—considered a threat to world peace? The People's Republic of China (PRC) disputes Taiwan's de facto sovereignty. The "one China" policy, officially supported by the PRC, the U.S., and many other countries, and formerly supported by Taiwan, asserts that there is only one China and that Taiwan is a part of it.[1] And yet, Taiwan is clearly no more a part of the PRC at the turn of the twenty-first century than, say, South Korea. So why does the PRC dispute Taiwan's sovereignty? Ultimately, the problem is one of identity—Han ethnic identity, Chinese national identity, and the relationship of both of these identities to the new Taiwanese identity forged in the 1990s.* The PRC

---

*Discussion of these issues is further complicated by problems in terminology. The English term "Chinese" can refer to ethnic identity (Americans of Chinese ancestry) or to national identity (citizens of the PRC). In Mandarin Chinese, the official language of both Taiwan and China, the distinction appears clear: *han ren* (lit., "Han person") refers to the Han ethnic majority, whom most Americans would think of as the ethnic Chinese. (Han are the ethnic majority both in China and in Taiwan.) *Zhongguo ren* (lit., "China person") refers to national citizenship and includes all 56 *minzu* (ethnic groups) officially recognized in China. However, the use of *zhongguo ren* in Taiwan is complicated by the term's earlier political uses: under the martial law rule of the Nationalist party (1947–1987), the term was used to support Taiwan's claims to ruling mainland China. For clarity, I use "Han" to refer to ethnic identity and "Chinese" to refer to national identification with China.

claims that Taiwan (unlike Korea) is ethnically Han and therefore should be part of the Chinese nation. Even though Taiwan acknowledges and honors its Chinese heritage, it now claims not to be Chinese. In the 1990s, this claim was made primarily on the basis of Aborigine contributions to Taiwanese culture and ancestry.[2] Since 1999, however, Taiwan has started to assert its claim to sovereignty in terms of the social basis of its identity. The complex ways in which identity underlies the political debate over Taiwan's future relationship with China are the subject of this book.

One of the most fundamental misunderstandings about identity is the widely accepted view that ethnic and national identities are based on common ancestry and/or common culture and therefore that identity is grounded in antiquity. Ancestry and culture are the ideological terms in which ethnic and national identities are claimed,[3] and as long as identity is discussed in these terms, antiquity seems a reasonable measure of its authenticity. However, culture and ancestry are *not* what ultimately unite an ethnic group or a nation. Rather, identity is formed and solidified on the basis of common social experience, including economic and political experience. When we realize that identity is really a matter of politics, and that it is no less authentic or "real" as a result—real in the sense of being meaningful and motivating to people—then we must examine identities and their implications very differently. We must untangle the social grounding of identities from the meanings claimed for those identities in the political sphere. We must also reveal where the claimed meanings run roughshod over the very personal, experienced-based meanings of individual members of identity groups.

Taiwan is a global political hot spot now because it is transforming its national and ethnic identities in ways that have unwelcome implications for the PRC's national identity and ethnic politics. Between 1945 and 1991, Taiwan's government portrayed Taiwan as ethnically Han and nationally Chinese, even claiming that it was the lawful government of mainland China. Since 1987, for the obvious political purpose of justifying their distance from the PRC, people in Taiwan have increasingly claimed Taiwanese identity to be an amalgam of Han culture and ancestry, Aborigine culture and ancestry, and Japanese culture (but not ancestry), in the making for almost 400 years, and separate from China for the entire twentieth century (cf. Chang 2000). (China disputes the length of separation.) Ironically, the PRC was more comfortable when Taiwan's government claimed legal authority over China, because at least then there was no questioning of whether Taiwan belonged within the Chinese nation. An independent Taiwan poses problems for China's national identity. First, it leaves out of the Chinese nation a territory that originally left China's authority due to colonial annexation: the PRC emphasizes this problem. Second, an independent Taiwan also raises issues for ethnic territories under Chinese authority: if Taiwanese are allowed to "leave" the nation because of ethnic differences, then why not Tibetans, or Turkic Muslims (such as the Uighur), or even Cantonese? Taiwan independence could have a domino effect that would break up the PRC, like the USSR or, worse, Yugoslavia. Given the political stakes involved, the rhetoric is emotional and often convoluted.

How can we get at the reality underneath the political rhetoric? How do we know what identities ordinary individuals in Taiwan and China have, and the basis on which these identities are actually built and claimed? Examining the borders of identities—how borders are drawn and how people cross them—helps to answer these questions. On the Taiwan side, three identity changes by descendants of plains Aborigines who intermarried with Han—one shift in the seventeenth century and two in the twentieth century—show the extent to which Taiwanese people and culture really are an amalgamation of Aborigine and Han contributions. These shifts also help us understand how identity changes can occur at all and how new identities come to be meaningful. Similar identity changes in China—among the ancestors of Tujia (an officially designated ethnic minority) in Hubei—shows that such changes in ethnic identity are not unique to Taiwan before 1949. Descendants of intermarried locals and Han immigrants in Hubei became the local Han. Although the fact of identity change in Hubei appears to raise questions for Taiwan's claims to nationhood, in fact it does not. Examination of subsequent identity change in Hubei after 1945 (to a non-Han minority), and PRC policies and actions affecting local identity and culture, shows that there *were* real differences in identity between Taiwan and Hubei at the end of the twentieth century. Moreover, the PRC's own policies and actions drove these differences. China's dismissal of the pre-1949 change to Han identity in Hubei contradicts its claims about Taiwan (where it emphasizes Han identity). That contradiction provides room for negotiating Taiwanese identity.

A CHINESE VIEW OF THE "TAIWAN PROBLEM"

People in China feel strongly that Taiwan is and should be a part of the Chinese nation. In March 1996, the PRC held war games in the strait between Fujian Province and Taiwan—effectively subjecting Taiwan to a military blockade. These war games were in response to actions that might eventually lead to Taiwan's declaring itself a nation, independent of China. Many Americans do not understand why tensions run so high on this issue, given that Taiwan functions independently of China and has done so for years. But to date, Taiwan does not *call* itself a nation independent of China. Its government officially calls itself "the Republic of China" (sometimes adding "on Taiwan") and has done so since Chiang Kai-shek (Jiang Jieshi) and his Nationalist (*guomindang* or GMD) followers fled the Chinese mainland in defeat in 1949. Both sides of the Taiwan Strait use the phrase *taiwan wenti*—translated variously as the "Taiwan problem" or "Taiwan question" or "Taiwan issue"—to refer to this impasse, but the phrase has slightly different meanings from these different vantage points. On the China side, the problem is how to bring Taiwan back into the Chinese nation. On the Taiwan side, the problem is how best to maintain comfortable economic and political trajectories without being swallowed up or bombed by China.

In July 1999, Taiwan's first democratically elected president, Lee Teng-hui (Li Denghui), said on German radio that future talks between Taiwan and China should be "state-to-state" talks, suggesting that Taiwan be *treated* as an independent country by the PRC. Beijing was furious and called Taiwan's president a "troublemaker." His move has been debated, with the PRC considering it a move toward independence and others, such as James Lilley (head of the U.S. mission to Taiwan under Reagan and U.S. ambassador to China under the elder President Bush), seeing the move as maintaining the status quo. Although one Taiwanese student in the U.S. suggested to me that Lee has a tendency to speak off the cuff without thinking, this move may not have been unplanned. In the summer of 1994, Lee publicly referred to his political party as the *taiwan guomindang*—the Taiwan Nationalist Party. The *"guo"* in *guomindang* refers to the nation, which since the party's founding has always meant the Chinese nation. Lee's usage as early as 1994 implied Taiwan's status as a nation. Moreover, Lee has publicly stated, "What the Republic of China [Taiwan] needs the most is an international affirmation of its sovereignty" (see *Free China Journal*, June 16, 1995:1 for the text of the speech).

This stance does not go over well in China. Traveling around southwestern Hubei in 1996 (before the war games, but when tensions were building), I frequently met local-level officials. Most of them would ask me about Taiwan when they found out I had done research there. Although each of these conversations began with questions about what Taiwan is like socially, economically, and culturally, they all turned sooner or later to the question of Taiwan's status as part of China. My responses—that most people I knew in Taiwan who had discussed the issue with me were not strong supporters of independence but were not enthusiastic about reuniting with China either—were invariably met with vehement assertions. Taiwan is part of China's territory, I was told, it is for China to decide Taiwan's fate, and the U.S. had better stay out of it. I always agreed, and still do, that the U.S. has no right to decide this issue. However, I pointed out that in Taiwan, people think they—the people of Taiwan—should decide their own future, not China. The international support sought by Taiwan, which China interprets as moves toward independence, can ensure this freedom for the people of Taiwan to decide for themselves. The problem with this position, from China's point of view, is that it assumes precisely what they want to question—that Taiwan is *sovereign*—for sovereignty is a right granted to *nations,* not to their constituent parts.[4]

NARRATIVES OF UNFOLDING

National identity and ethnic identity are commonly portrayed as fixed, with clear borders. Identity is seen as the product of a person's culture and/or ancestry, and there is no room for individual choice about belonging or departing. In order to "mobilize people behind their political agendas," governments and ethnic leaders "actively hide the fluidity and changeability of identity and group membership" (Harrell 1996a:5); they discuss identity in terms of purported common descent and/or purported common culture (including language), even though ultimately it is common sociopolitical experience which binds group identity. The concealment of fluidity is accomplished by constructing "narratives of unfolding" (Bhabha 1990:1, Harrell 1996a:4), origin myths (Keyes 1981:8, Williams 1989:429), or a reified "History" (Duara 1995:4) that portrays the group as having a long and unified history distinguished from other groups. These narratives draw heavily on selected historic sociopolitical events to galvanize support around claimed ancestry and/or culture.

I prefer the term "narratives of unfolding," bulky as it is, because of three conceptual advantages. First, the term clearly distinguishes between constructed narratives of the past and the totality of what is actually known about past events, in a way that the term "history"—capitalized or uncapitalized—does not.[5] I use "history" to refer to actual events that

occurred in the past, and I emphasize that we know about history imperfectly. Many events are completely unknown to us, many events are
known only through extremely biased perspectives, and many events are
so contradictorily reported that it is difficult to reconstruct even a chronological sequence of what occurred. Narratives of unfolding are not history, nor are they simply a biased interpretation of past events; they are
ideologies—"a conscious falsification, a conscious selection of some of the
available evidence" of the past over other evidence for political purposes
(Harrell 1996a:5–6n, emphasis in original). Thus, narratives of unfolding attempt to selectively shape our understanding of the past for political purposes. Their authors may call these narratives history, but they
are in fact constructed ideologies.

The second conceptual advantage of the term "narratives of unfolding" is that it captures the sense which these narratives attempt to convey of an inevitable unfolding of destiny from the primordial past. At
the same time, the term can refer to narratives about the "unfolding" of
different things—the unfolding of one's own nation, the unfolding of a
hostile nation, the unfolding of a disputed territory as part of one's own
nation. Although the anthropological concept of "origin myths" incorporates both an attempt to construct a primordial past and a notion of
a group charter, the term lacks the flexibility to refer to one group's version of the origins of another group and also lacks the sense of a destiny
which continues into the present. The relation of the past to the present
is crucial to narratives of unfolding. Although ostensibly about the past,
they are really about the present. They are attempts to justify, to natu-
ralize, to immortalize the present-day claims of a nation or an ethnic
group.

Finally, narratives of unfolding change as societies change, as present-
day political goals change, as international relations change. The terms
"history" and "origin myth" do not easily accommodate the concept of
a narrative that is constantly changing as people reformulate and transform their identities in the present. The term "narratives of unfolding,"
however, can be understood both as a purported unfolding of primordial
destiny and also as narratives that are themselves continually unfolding
and changing in relation to changing social contexts.

For example, consider China's narrative about the diversity of its population. China's Han imperialism *(da han zhuyi)* is glossed over in a narrative celebrating China's status as a united nation of diverse ethnicities
(tongyi duominzu de guojia) (cf. Harrell 1995b). Yet we can see, simply
in the classification of ethnicities, where the power lies. There are fifty-

six officially recognized ethnic groups *(minzu)* in China—the Han ethnic majority, constituting 91 percent of the population, and fifty-five ethnic minorities, together constituting 9 percent of the population.[6] However, there are also many unofficially recognized "regional" varieties of Han, and these so-called "regional" differences (or "subethnic" differences, as they are sometimes called) among the Han are really ethnic differences, both by the Stalinist criteria purportedly used to define ethnic groups in the PRC—common territory, common language, common economy, and common psychological make-up reflected in common culture—and by comparison to ethnic differences elsewhere in the world (as I discuss further below). Officially, all ethnic groups are determined according to the Stalinist criteria. However, the PRC government never considered variation within the Han ethnic group in terms of these criteria.[7]

Han were never subjected to classification into distinct minzu because of an older narrative of China's unfolding as a Han civilization. Han viewed themselves as a single group embodying Confucian civilization—the Middle Kingdom (*Zhongguo*, China) that stood between Heaven and the barbarian non-Han (cf. Ebrey 1996). In this older narrative, the great linguistic, cultural, social, and economic variation among the Han was irrelevant to their classification as part of a single Han civilization. In the PRC, classifying all Han as a single ethnic group both maintains the links of the present-day nation-state to past Han civilization and justifies Han political and demographic dominance as natural and predestined. If Han had been broken up into different ethnic groups, they would have competed with each other and none could have claimed to be the exclusive inheritors of the Confucian mantle. In spite of its dissonance with the older Han narrative, the very existence of a Chinese narrative about diversity (which I discuss below) shows that narratives of unfolding do change along with societies and their politics.

TAIWANESE IDENTITY

Because Taiwan's sociopolitical experience took a different path from China's, Taiwanese identity does not neatly correspond to any of these PRC identities—ethnic minority or "regional" Han. Before 1895, when Taiwan came under Japanese colonial rule, people in Taiwan did not think of themselves as a unified group (Chang 2000:53–54). Although Han in Taiwan undoubtedly viewed themselves as different from non-Han (both Aborigines and Europeans), there is no evidence of unity among the Han.

On the contrary, in the seventeenth century Han merchants warned the Dutch about an uprising of Han farmers and laborers, showing class rather than ethnic solidarity. From the seventeenth through the twentieth centuries, while some Han cheated Aborigines of their land and rents, other Han married Aborigines and helped them sue and even rebel against such abuse, showing solidarity along lines of personal connections and common economic interests rather than ethnic identity. Nevertheless, Han in Taiwan were surely as aware of European colonial incursions as Han on the mainland, and they may have begun to develop a single Chinese identity in reaction. Still, feuding *(xiedou)* based on ethnicity, lineage, and place of origin erupted frequently in Taiwan, with alliances crossing and re-crossing these identities as circumstances varied (e.g., Lamley 1981, Harrell 1990, Shepherd 1993:310–323), thus showing no signs of ethnic solidarity.

With the imminent arrival of Japanese troops came the first indications of a pan-Taiwanese identity, an identity limited to Han. James Davidson, an American war correspondent with the Japanese army, reported (1988 [1903]:257–370) that representatives of the various Han groups in Taiwan formed a short-lived "Republic of Taiwan" and organized a seven-year resistance to Japanese occupation of the island (cf. Harrell 1990, Ka 1995:83n1, 84n2). Thus, the first clear Taiwanese identity was a national one, linked to the unsuccessful formation of a nation-state.

Under Japanese colonial rule (1895–1945), peoples in Taiwan were classified by a notion of race which in practice, in the early Japanese household registers, looks a lot like today's ethnic classifications. Under the category of "race" *(zhongzu)*, the Japanese colonial government distinguished between Hoklo and Hakka—"regional" varieties of Han with mutually unintelligible "dialects" and some significantly different customs—and classified Hoklo as *fu* and Hakka as *fu* or *guang,* depending on their province of ancestral origin.[8] The Japanese government also distinguished Aborigines—called barbarians *(fan)*—as "raw" *(sheng)* or "cooked" *(shu),* depending on their relationship to Han culture. "Raw" or "wild" Aborigines—living in the high central mountains, on Taiwan's eastern plain, and on Orchid Island off Taiwan's southeastern coast—had adopted few or no Han customs. "Cooked" or "civilized" Aborigines—living on Taiwan's western plain and in the western foothills of the central mountains—had adopted much of Han culture, including language. Thus, the Japanese colonial government perpetuated classification terms from the Qing regime, perhaps concerned that feuding along ethnic lines might continue.

However, by 1915 or so, these distinctions were not particularly important and they were no longer entered in the registers. Much more important to the Japanese were the distinction between Japanese and everyone else, as well as so-called class *(zhongbie)* distinctions, which were really police reliability ratings (Wolf and Huang 1980:19). Among other things, these latter distinctions affected wages and the frequency of routine police visits (Davidson 1988 [1903]:600, Wolf and Huang 1980:19). By the 1930s, many "cooked" Aborigines, who are now more politely referred to as "plains" Aborigines, had assimilated to Hoklo identity, and the Japanese government brought "raw" or "mountain" Aborigines forcibly under their control, removing once and for all Han fears of them.[9] Efforts were made during the late 1930s and early 1940s to get people in Taiwan to think of themselves as loyal subjects of the Japanese empire, but people in Taiwan experienced clear categorical differences between themselves and Japanese which left them with a sense of non-Japanese identity (cf. Chang 2000:56–62).

In 1945, Taiwan was "gloriously returned" *(guangfu)* to Chinese rule. Control of Taiwan was given to the Chinese Nationalists (GMD) by the terms of a 1943 agreement among Franklin Roosevelt, Joseph Stalin, Winston Churchill, and Chiang Kai-shek. "There must have been a moment when, knowing they would soon be under Chinese rule again, Taiwanese [i.e., Han in Taiwan] could assume themselves simply to be Chinese. That moment lasted until shortly after the Mainlanders arrived" (Gates 1987:44, cf. Chang 2000:62). Corruption was rampant at all levels of government and the military, inflation skyrocketed, and the Mainlanders kept coming—some one to two million of them by the autumn of 1949. Tensions led to a Taiwanese uprising, referred to as the 2:28 Incident because of its start on February 28, 1947. The GMD brutally suppressed the uprising, executing thousands of Taiwanese within a few weeks and later hauling many more off to jail.[10] The GMD declared martial law, suspending constitutional rights for "security" reasons.

Under Nationalist martial-law rule (1947–87), Taiwanese identity became a strong "regional" identity. The term *taiwan ren* (Taiwanese) is often used in Taiwan today to refer to the Hoklo, who are the ethnic majority. Through the late 1980s, however, the term was generally synonymous with *bensheng ren* (lit., people from within the province), thereby including both Hoklo and Hakka whose ancestors came to Taiwan before 1895 when the Japanese colonial government suspended futher immigration from China. "Taiwanese" were thus mainly contrasted with *waisheng ren* (lit., people from outside the province), that

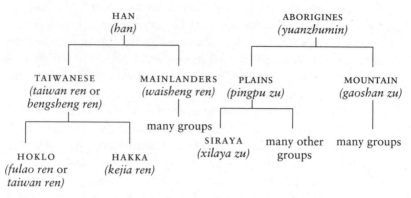

Figure 4. Relation of ethnic terms used for peoples in Taiwan.

is, Mainlanders who came to Taiwan with the Nationalists between 1945 and 1949 and their children and grandchildren born and raised in Taiwan.[11] "Cooked" Aborigines had disappeared (in the Japanese period) into the Taiwanese category, and "raw" Aborigines were classified separately as *gaoshan zu* (mountain tribes) but ignored in the political sphere until recently. (See figure 4.)

I suggest (contra Chang 1996:78n1) that the category "Mainlander" is an ethnic distinction in Taiwan (and hence should be capitalized, like "Han" and "Aborigine").[12] Mainlander identity is claimed on the basis of culture and ancestry—sometimes positively, in terms of language, culture, and recent ancestry from mainland China, and sometimes negatively, as simply not having Taiwanese language, culture, and ancestry. The fact that Mainlanders as a group do not share the *same* ancestry and culture should no more disturb their classification as a single ethnic group than the fact that Hoklo and Hakka do not share the same ancestry and culture disturbs their classification as Taiwanese, or the fact that Ami, Bunun, Atayal and other "mountain tribes" do not share the same ancestry and culture disturbs their classification as Aborigines. These differences emphasize the point made earlier: although group identity is *claimed* in terms of ancestry and/or culture, it is ultimately held together by common sociopolitical experience. "Taiwanese," for example, were largely (but not entirely) excluded from political power and national corporations in Taiwan during the period of martial law, and "Mainlanders," in turn, were largely (but not entirely) excluded from small and medium-sized businesses owned and operated by Taiwanese (cf. Gates 1981; Chang 1994, 2000; Corcuff 2000).

Taiwanese also excluded Mainlanders from their social spheres when they could. Political scientist Edward Friedman (1994, personal communication) tells a story of such exclusion from the 1970s. A Taiwanese-owned cafeteria that Friedman frequented near National Taiwan University had a sign in the window welcoming Japanese tourists. (In the 1970s, there were no Japanese tourists in Taiwan, in part because of the enmity with which Mainlanders viewed Japanese.) After some time, when Friedman knew the owner sufficiently to ask about the sign, the owner explained that he could not put a sign in the window telling Mainlanders to stay out but that this sign achieved the same results—no Mainlanders came in.

Martial law had important economic implications. The Nationalist government advertised Taiwan abroad as having a plentiful, cheap, and docile labor force that was forbidden to strike, and it established policies and special export zones favoring firms—both foreign and domestic—that exported all their products. Taiwan's economy grew more or less steadily from the late 1960s, faltering most seriously during the oil crisis of the mid-1970s but recovering thereafter. Indeed, the rapid economic development together with the social and political stability of the 1960s through the early 1980s is known as the "Taiwan miracle" (e.g., Gold 1986). Today, Taiwan has a fully developed economy and is quite wealthy, even with the economic downturns in 1997 and 2001.

Until 1986, political opposition to Nationalist Party rule and advocacy of Taiwan independence—meaning the declaration of Taiwan as a nation independent of China—was suppressed, often brutally. Unexpectedly, in 1986, then-president Chiang Ching-kuo (Jiang Jingguo, Chiang Kai-shek's son) tolerated the illegal formation of the Democratic Progressive Party (DPP), which made Taiwan independence part of its party platform. He lifted martial law in July 1987, six months before his death, and set in motion other changes leading to democratization (e.g., Chang 1994, Gold 1994). The people of Taiwan now directly elect the National Assembly (since 1991), the governor of Taiwan and the mayors of the cities of Taibei and Gaoxiong (since 1994), and the president and vice-president (since 1996).[13]

Further political liberalization has occurred since 1986 as well. Mainlanders, and later Taiwanese, were allowed to visit the PRC. Public demonstrations are legal and frequent. Newspapers have genuine freedom to investigate and report. The 2:28 Incident, once unmentionable, has been the subject of an international-prize-winning film *(A City of Sadness)*, numerous publications, a presidential committee investigation and report, an official presidential apology, monuments, and museum exhibits.

With the political and economic transformations of the 1980s and 1990s, Taiwanese identity has changed dramatically, becoming increasingly inclusive, proud, and nationalistic. During the 1998 Taibei mayoral campaign, Lee Teng-hui publically articulated the new Taiwanese identity as embracing both the ethnic Taiwanese and the Mainlanders.[14] The fact that Chen Shui-bian—the incumbent DPP mayor of Taibei running for re-election—started using this concept of an inclusive new Taiwanese identity as well shows how popular it is.

These politicians did not invent this identity; they merely articulated and emphasized a change in Taiwanese identity that had been developing over the previous decade. For instance, one person I know from Taiwan, whose parents had fled the mainland with the Nationalists in the 1940s, visited China in the mid-1980s, soon after such visits were allowed by Taiwan's government. After expressing shock at the standards of living, at the loss of Confucian civility and propriety in relationships, and at the apparent lack of work ethic which she found in China, she identified herself proudly as from Taiwan. Other "Mainlanders" from Taiwan have reported similar experiences and sentiments (cf. Hsiao and So 1996). Another anecdotal example of pride in Taiwanese identity dates from 1987, when I met a scholar wearing a knit hat which read "MIT." I asked if she had done her Ph.D. at the Massachusetts Institute of Technology, and she explained that to her it means "Made In Taiwan." She had bought the hat on a recent visit to Boston because she had been a student in the U.S. during the 1960s and 1970s, when "Made in Taiwan" was on so many labels (as "Made in China" is today), and Taiwan was associated with cheap products—inexpensive and not very well made. She had been ashamed to have Americans associate her with such cheap products. She said that now that Taiwan was known for its economic success, she would wear her MIT hat proudly. As a further example of the social basis of this new Taiwanese identity, another Taiwanese person, who had been bored by the American presidential campaigns she witnessed as a student in the U.S., recounted to me the unexpected captivation of Taiwan's first presidential campaign in 1996 and the strong sense of empowerment from voting in the election. These sentiments are probably not unique, and the people of Taiwan are not likely to forget such feelings of empowerment. The new, inclusive Taiwanese identity is born of such experiences.

Because it initially focused on including various Han identities, the new Taiwanese identity only recently began to explicitly include Aborigines. However, from the first, it implicitly included Aborigines as a result of the new narratives of Taiwan's unfolding constructing Taiwanese identity as an amalgam of Aborigine and Han ancestry (a major theme of this book). This new identity, with its basis in actual social experiences, contributes to the increasing numbers of Taiwanese who approve of the calculated risk of angering China in order to win international support for Taiwan's sovereignty.

FORMING IDENTITIES, NEGOTIATING CLASSIFICATIONS, DRAWING BORDERS

Identities must be negotiated; they are not simply a matter of choice, because identity formation in individuals and groups derives from their interaction with the social and cultural context in which they live (cf. Keyes 1981, Bentley 1987, Williams 1989, Harrell 1995a, Brown 1996a). ("Social context" here refers to the specific hierarchical organization of a society. By this broad definition, social context thus includes political and economic contexts.) Nevertheless, identity—a sense of who we are, in terms of how we fit into the world—is derived from how our minds process the world around us. Identities of individuals are socially constructed—formed and negotiated through everyday experiences and social interactions. Individuals understand these lived and social experiences in terms of the cultural meanings of the specific society in which they live (cf. Goffman 1963, Strauss 1992b, Strauss and Quinn 1994).[15] The experiential nature of identity is usually accepted for idiosyncratic identities associated with personality or achievement, such as Phi Beta Kappa members. However, as I have already discussed, identities of individuals as members of groups—especially national identity and ethnic identity—are portrayed by political leaders as fixed, with borders that are not based on individual experiences.

Our cognitive processing of the perceived identity choices available to us is influenced both by the biological structure of the human brain and its relation to mind and also by the cultural meanings and social processes we have experienced, which we rely on to make sense of the world around us (cf. Strauss and Quinn 1994). At the most fundamental level, identity is the way that a person classifies him- or herself, a mental representation or thought. This level of identity, however, is not what is generally discussed by scholars or political leaders, because we cannot know exactly what a person thinks, only what he or she reports thinking or what we interpret him or her to think based on statements or actions. In other words, we cannot know the actual mental representations of individuals, only their public representations (utterances or actions), which may or may not accurately reflect mental representations.[16] Individuals or groups of individuals may keep their mental representations concealed, for many possible reasons. Thus, what are actually discussed, in this book and in other discussions of identity, are the *public representations of identity* by individuals or groups.

How then can we compare what ethnic identity means to different individuals, let alone to people in different cultures and at different historical periods? Surely what it means to be Taiwanese is different than what it means to be American, and both of these identities were different in the seventeenth century than they are today. Of course the specific meanings of ethnic identities and their significance vary across individuals, across cultures and across time, but I suggest that the way that identity is formed does not vary. Moreover, I suggest that a universal process of identity formation means that the way that ethnic identity shapes the lives of individuals does not vary either. Because ethnic identity is based on *social* experience, Taiwan Aborigines in the seventeenth century and, for example, African Americans in the twentieth century both understood that being classified by these labels affected how other people treated them, their position in their local social hierarchy, and their ability (or inability) to negotiate a higher position.

A wide variety of factors influences which specific identities individuals will form: the meaning of particular identities in the culture(s) to which the individuals or groups are exposed, the social status or relative power of members of particular identities, and the various characteristics—cultural, social, and/or physical—used to mark or categorize particular identities.[17] Individuals may have limited choices about their identities, or may have no choice at all, because these factors affect the possibility of being classified as one or another identity. These factors also affect the benefits and disadvantages of being classified one way or another, and thereby affect which option people choose when choice is possible. There are also constraints on whether others accept the classification claimed by individuals or groups (cf. Yelvington 1991). Thus, the specific identities that form for individuals are the negotiated product of the interaction between what people claim for themselves and what others allow them to claim.

Identity formation occurs through the social experience of this interaction. People negotiate with others, both those who claim the same identity and those who claim different identities, and what these different groups of "others" allow one to claim often varies. For example, Gentiles and Jews often have different views about whether a person claiming Jewish identity is to be regarded as Jewish (that is, "allowed" to claim Jewish identity). There is variation within a group as well: Ultra-Orthodox, Reform, and secular Jews have different standards for judging claims to Jewish identity. *Identity formation, then, is the process of socially negotiating how to classify oneself in terms of the broader classifications of people existing in a particular social and cultural context* (cf. Barth 1969, Keyes 1981:7). Generally, such classifications (American, Taiwanese, Tujia) have social consequences, including political consequences—only U.S. citizens may run for Congress, non-Han minorities in China are given extra points on their college entrance examination scores, and so on.

Classification is a general human cognitive process. The physiological workings of human cognition interact with the socially and culturally constructed content of specific categorizations. Anthropologist Dan Sperber suggests that because of a human cognitive process which encourages essentializing classifications, cultural input which classifies people can be construed in the brain as signifying a larger, more essential distinction (cf. Boyer 1998):

> It is quite possible, then, that being presented with nominal labels for otherwise undefined and undescribed humans is enough (given an appropriate context) to activate the initialization of the *ad hoc* template. If so, then perception of physical differences among humans is indeed not the triggering factor in racial classification. (Sperber 1996:144)[18]

In other words, racial identities—and I would suggest other kinds of ethnic identities—are formed by a combination of social, cultural, and cognitive influences (I define a race as a special kind of ethnic group—an ethnic group with an *assumed* biological basis).[19] Telling a child that a man is black or white—or Han or barbarian, whichever terms are locally meaningful—may set up an essentialized cognitive difference for the child, which is later reinforced when the child finds differences in how black men and white men or Han and barbarians are treated in her society. Sperber's insight probably also extends to gender: we refer to someone as a man or a woman even more frequently than simply as a person.

Consider an example of classification which I discuss further in chapter 4. There were large numbers of Han men who migrated to southwestern Taiwan in the seventeenth century. Many of these men married local women—Aborigine women or women of mixed Han-Aborigine

parentage—and settled in "Aborigine" villages. Under Dutch rule of Taiwan, it would have been to the disadvantage of the "mixed" population
to be characterized as Han by the Dutch. In contrast, under the succeeding
Zheng regime, it was to the advantage of the "mixed" population to be
considered Han. Moreover, patrilineally derived surnames linked to written Chinese characters had long been markers of Han status (Ebery 1996).
This cultural classification scheme gave people of mixed heritage an opportunity to manipulate their own identities. If those who had been designated Aborigines under the Dutch had a Han father or paternal grandfather whose surname they could take with legitimacy in the eyes of other
Han, they were likely to do so and thereafter be categorized as Han by
the Zheng regime and later by the Qing regime.

In addition to changes in individual classification, many of the villages
where Han men intermarried were later reclassified as "Han" villages.
The designation of a village as Aborigine or Han had important social
ramifications for all the members of the village, regardless of their individual identities: the tax structure was based on the ethnic classification
of a village, for example. On what basis, then, was a village considered
Aborigine or Han? A very "interesting turning point . . . occurred when
the density of [Han] Chinese settlers [in a village] was such that people
no longer perceived [Han] Chinese men in an Aborigine village and instead began to perceive a [Han] Chinese community with Aborigines in
it" (Brown 1995:157, 1996b:67). I suggest that there is a cognitive threshold, related to critical mass, above which people perceive a public representation (here, an identity label of Han) as shared by the majority of
individuals in a group (here, a village), and thus apply that representation to the entire group (here, viewing the village as Han) (Brown 1997,
see also chapter 6 below).

From this example we can see several important aspects of classification as it relates to identity. Classification is influenced by demographic trends: without the migration of Han settlers, there would have
been no reclassification at any level. Demographic trends do not, however, determine classification contents and labels. The mixed population could negotiate between Han and Aborigine identities, and economic and political advantages strongly influenced which identity people
sought.

Identities are both fluid and changeable. The terms "fluidity" and
"changeability" are sometimes used interchangeably by other authors,
but I will use the two terms more specifically, to refer to two different
dynamics. Although the portrayal of identities as fixed found in narra-

tives of unfolding implies that there should be little problem in drawing an unambiguous border to classify different identities (that is, a border between individuals of one identity and individuals of another identity), in fact how the border is defined often shifts, across time and across space, allowing individuals and even entire groups to fall first on one side and then on the other side. I use "fluidity" to refer to this shifting of borders around individuals and groups who themselves do not necessarily change in cultural content (ideas and beliefs) or ancestry, the terms in which identity is claimed. The population of mixed Han-Aborigine heritage had the border to Han shift around them in the short span between the late Dutch period (1650) and the early Qing period (1685); similarly, the people in the villages of southwestern Taiwan where I conducted fieldwork had the border to Han shift around them in a short time span around 1930.[20] "Changeability," then, refers to the ability of individuals or groups to change the identity label under which they are classified: the border remains fixed—defined the same way as before—but individuals (and, rarely, groups) actively push across it. Individuals of mixed Han-Aborigine ancestry in the eighteenth and nineteenth centuries probably used patrilineal surnames to negotiate a reclassification of themselves as Han. People in the PRC use the minority status of a grandparent to change their own status from Han to minority. Although the portrayal of identities as fixed implies that people should not be able to change the identity classification by which they are labeled, in fact they can and do change it under certain conditions. Thinking of fluidity as involuntary relabeling by external sources and changeability as voluntary self-relabeling can help us analyze specific cases, as long as we realize that these two dynamics can interact with each other. Once an external source has started relabeling individuals, these individuals can act to speed up or further shape the process.

"Variability" as I use the term in relation to identity refers to changes in the *content* of an individual's or group's identity. Which social, cultural, and/or physical characteristics are considered or claimed as part of a particular identity can change over time and across geographic space. Variability is related to the multivocality of identity, which means that the people classified within any given identity are not homogeneous. The degree of accepted social, cultural, and physical variation can differ widely for different classifications—for example, the category "Han" encompasses a wider range of variation than "Japanese." However, even identities claiming a large degree of homogeneity tolerate *some* variation among their members. As we shall see, such variation creates the potential for changing from one identity label to another and for changing the content of a single identity classification. Variability (content change) is strongly related both to changeability (voluntary label change) and to fluidity (involuntary relabeling). When the content of an identity varies, individuals may have the opportunity to change their identity labels and, at the same time, the classification border dividing that identity from others may shift.

Just how easy is it for an individual or group to change identity labels, and how often does the content of a person's or a group's identity change? In this book, I examine two groups who *have* changed identity labels, crossing the border to Han: plains Aborigines and their descendants in Taiwan, and Tujia and their ancestors in Hubei. However, it is important to realize that these changes were difficult. Although the content—and especially the cultural content—of identities varies easily and frequently, it is very difficult for individuals and especially groups to change the identity labels under which they are classified. Such label changes require special social and demographic conditions, including migration, intermarriage, and changes in political regimes.

Why are identity labels so difficult to change when identity content is not? I suggest that the stubborn persistence of identity labels, even in the face of varying cultural, social, and physical characteristics used to classify people, is related to cognitive processing of the "primordial" aspect of identity: purported common descent. Across cultures, descent is formulated in kinship terms. In a matrilineal society, for example, one is descended from "mother," a term which conflates biological and social roles. The terminology of adoption makes this conflation clear: the terms "birth mother" and "adoptive mother" both incorporate "mother," though one indicates genetic relatedness and one a social role. Cognitively, kinship is one of the most basic classification schemes of any society: the categories of mother, sibling, and father (or mother's brother) are among the first classifications of other humans that an infant learns. Moreover, these relations are biologically fixed—one cannot change one's mother or siblings or father—and so kinship and descent may also be *perceived* as fixed or in some sense "primordial."[21] One can change these relations socially, for example, through adoption, but in many societies descent is re-asserted fictively, with an adopted child using the same terms that a biological child would.

Across cultures, kinship terms reflect social kinship relations, not actual genetic relatedness. For example, although American kinship terminology classifies all first cousins by the same term, corresponding to their similar degree of genetic relatedness, Han kinship terms do not. Patrilateral parallel cousins (one's father's brothers' children) have one set of kinship terms, are considered family, and have always been subject to the incest taboo applied to patrilineal relatives. Matrilateral parallel cousins and both types of cross cousins are grouped together under a different set of kinship terms, are considered more distant relatives ("relatives" versus "family"), and were formerly considered good marriage partners.[22] These differences between American and Han kinship classification terms reflect important social and cultural differences in kinship relations. In American society, which has long followed neolocal postmarital residence (newlyweds establishing their own independent house), a person is unlikely to grow up with any of his or her cousins in the same household; in Taiwanese society, which has only begun to depart from Han virilocal postmarital residence (newlyweds living in the husband's parents' household), a person might grow up in the same household with his or her patrilateral parallel cousins but would not usually grow up with any other category of first cousins.

One general observation about kinship helps clarify the difficulty in changing identity labels and helps identify the social conditions under which identity labels can change: kinship varies across cultures, or, more precisely, principles guiding social kinship relations vary across cultures (cf. Westermarck 1922 II:193, 1934:38; Wolf 1995:512–514). For example, seventeenth-century Dutch missionaries reported that, upon contact, Siraya plains Aborigines in southwestern Taiwan were matrilineal, calculating descent from the mother; Han immigrants from Fujian in China were patrilineal, calculating descent from the father. Where identity labels are linked to a single kinship principle, they are difficult to change, but when circumstances bring two differing kinship principles into the same society—as occurred in seventeenth-century southwestern Taiwan—identity labels can change more easily.

COMPETING NARRATIVES OF TAIWAN'S UNFOLDING

Certain aspects of the PRC's official narrative of Taiwan's unfolding as a Han and a Chinese domain are remarkably similar to the narratives used in Taiwan during the martial law period (based on PRC government white papers; see TAOIOSC 1999 [1993]:78–84). Taiwan is said to belong to China since antiquity, by asserting that the place names (Yizhou, Liuqiu) in third-century and later historical records refer to Taiwan, and by inflating the number of Han visits and size of the Han pop-

ulation in Taiwan prior to the seventeenth century. Both the older Taiwan narratives and the PRC narrative minimize the presence and significance of the many Aborigine groups who lived on Taiwan when the Han
arrived, although the PRC narrative departs from older Taiwan narratives when it construes Aborigines as "Chinese people" (TAOIOSC 1999
[1993]:78) in accordance with the present-day rhetoric of China as a multiethnic nation. Expansion of the Han population in Taiwan in the seventeenth century is attributed to the efforts of Han pioneers, with no mention made of Dutch colonial impetus for this expansion. The PRC goes
further than older Taiwan narratives ever did, in portraying Dutch control of Taiwan from 1624 through 1661 as an immoral invasion and occupation of Chinese territory (TAOIOSC 1999[1993]:79). However, both
regard the Zheng invasion as restoring, rather than establishing, a Han
rule which proceeds unproblematically through 1895; both gloss over
the war between the Zheng regime and the ruling Qing dynasty in China.
Both emphasize the initial Taiwanese opposition to Japanese colonial rule,
but narratives used by the GMD government emphasized it especially
strongly, minimizing later Taiwanese acceptance of Japanese rule and
Japanese contributions to the economic development of Taiwan. Older
Taiwan narratives ended with the "glorious return" of Taiwan to "China,"
meaning the start of GMD control, but the PRC narrative goes on to
assert the PRC's authority over Taiwan and to implicate the U.S. for maintaining the division between China and Taiwan.

The PRC government gives its narrative of Taiwan's unfolding further
importance by embedding it within its narrative of China's unfolding as
a modern nation-state.

> The modern history of China is a record of subjection to aggression, dis
> memberment, and humiliation by foreign powers. It is also a chronicle of
> the Chinese people's valiant struggles for national independence and in
> defense of their state sovereignty, territorial integrity, and national dignity.
> The origin and evolution of the Taiwan question are closely linked with
> that period of history. For various reasons Taiwan is still separated from
> the mainland. Unless and until this state of affairs is brought to an end, the
> trauma of the Chinese nation will not be healed and the Chinese people's
> struggle for national reunification and territorial integrity will continue.
> (TAOIOSC 1999 [1993]:77)

China's larger narrative of national unfolding focuses on its nineteenth-
and twentieth-century political history, emphasizing the colonial annexations of territory and people by Western and Japanese powers, including the cession of Taiwan to Japan by the Qing imperial government in

1895. This national narrative of colonial humiliation—sometimes referred to as the "Century of Humiliation" *(bainian guochi)*—explains
the tremendous symbolic importance to China of the return of Hong
Kong in 1997 and Macao in 1999. It also construes Taiwan's de facto
independence as further imperialism against the Chinese people.

Taiwan's new narratives of unfolding, however, distance Taiwanese
identity from the Chinese nation by incorporating Aborigines in ways
that acknowledge Aborigine cultural influence and even matrilineal ancestral contributions. The poem *Island Nostalgia: The Epic of Taiwan*
(Liu 1991) emphasizes the cultural blending of Aborigine and Han
peoples in Taiwan and imagines the island of Taiwan and migration to
it as symbolic of Taiwan's distinctness from China (cf. Ren 1996). It starts
with mythic stories of six mountain Aborigine groups—groups who were
not only different from the ones whom the Han colonists faced on the
southwestern plains but who actually had little contact with the Han until the twentieth century—implicitly claiming the cultural origins of these
mountain Aborigine groups on Taiwan as part of Taiwanese origins. In
accordance with older narratives, the poem presents a Han immigrant
outraged by Dutch colonial efforts to "occupy our land" (Liu 1991:41)
before considering the plains Aborigines perspective, thereby ignoring
that Taiwan was Aborigine and not Han upon Dutch contact in the early
seventeenth century. Moreover, plains Aborigines disappear into the category of Han:

> Our women,
> their men
> have become an unseparated part of the island. . . .
>
> We covered up our history,
> afraid of disappointing their 5,000 year culture. . . .
>
> We eventually cannot find ourselves
> on the island where we have lived for thousands of years. . . .
>
> In this unpredictable cycle of life
> the plains Aborigine is the beginning
> and the Taiwanese the ending.[23]

Aborigine contributions of culture and matrilineal ancestry are presented
both as sufficiently present to make Taiwanese different from Chinese and
as sufficiently hidden to allow Taiwanese to claim continuity with narratives about 5,000 years of "Han" culture. Thus, plains Aborigines produce a tension even within variations on the new Taiwanese narrative—
Aborigine contributions are necessary to further the argument that

Taiwanese are not Chinese, but their contributions raise the uncomfortable topics of Han colonialism and non-Han barbarism. This tension is
best elucidated in terms of the border between Han and non-Han.

CHINESE IDENTITY, CULTURE, AND THE BORDER TO HAN

Through 1999, both Taiwan and the PRC apparently accepted the idea
that if Taiwan's people are culturally Han, they should be part of the nation of China. Lee Teng-hui's remark in July 1999 that Taiwan would
continue negotiations only on a "state-to-state" basis prompted further
clarifications from the Taiwan government, which suggested that Taiwan
may no longer officially accept the link between Han culture and Chinese national identity. (I discuss these remarks further in chapter 6.)
Nevertheless, it is important to understand this link in order to understand both China's and Taiwan's rhetorical positions prior to 1999 and
to understand the lingering influences of this idea upon ordinary people
in both China and Taiwan. Thus, several assumptions about Han ethnic
and Chinese national identities that are built into this idea need to be examined. First, Han ethnic identity is linked to Chinese national identity.
Second, Chinese national identity is linked to Han culture. Third, Chinese national identity has a clear border, and a person or group is located on one side of it or the other; that is, a person or group is definitively Chinese or not Chinese, Han or non-Han. All of these assumptions
are problematic.

Han ethnic identity and Chinese national identity are conflated by
people within China, both Han and non-Han, and by academics within
and outside of China. This conflation can most easily be seen linguistically. The term *zhonghua minzu* is used by the PRC (as it was by the
GMD) to refer to all the people of the Chinese nation, even though *hua*
is a term associated with ethnic Han, and even though usage of the same
term outside of China refers primarily to Han (Borchigud 1996:160).[24]
Additionally, the national language of the PRC is generally referred to
as *putonghua* (lit., "common speech"), but *hanyu* (lit., "Han language")
is considered a synonymous term. *Putonghua*—called "Mandarin Chinese" in English—is linguistically a Sino-Tibetan language and the first
language primarily for Han people, which justifies this conflation on one
level: it is a Han language. However, to refer to the national language
of a multiethnic country in terms of the dominant ethnic group implies
that this ethnic group is most properly associated with the nation as a

whole and that other ethnic groups have only a loose affiliation with the nation.[25]

The association of Han ethnic identity with Chinese national identity can also be seen in the frequent reminder that all ethnic groups are brothers and sisters in the officially multiethnic PRC, but the Han are Big Brother *(lao da)*, leading the way and offering guidance. The coincidence of Chinese usage with that of George Orwell is appropriate, because within Han kinship siblings are not equals—both sisters and younger brothers are subject to the authority of the oldest brother.[26] Before 1949, the Chinese imperial and republican states officially supported the hegemony of the oldest brother, as instituted morally in Confucian principles, just as these states supported the hegemony of parents (cf. Wolf 1995:95–96, 215–219). Since then, the Chinese communist state has implicitly supported the hegemony of the oldest brother through its promotion of a Han cultural model for the Chinese nation (Harrell 1995b).

The second assumption—that Chinese national identity is linked to Han culture—builds on the assumption that Chinese national identity is linked to Han ethnic identity, by adding the claim that Han ethnic identity is based on cultural practices, not on ancestry. The association of Han culture with Chinese national identity derives from a historic narrative of unfolding which links China as a political entity *(zhongguo)* and Han (or Hua or Xia, as it was sometimes called) *wenhua* (culture, civilization, education). In simplified form, this narrative says that the essential elements of wenhua—writing, a state system, a code of ritualized hierarchical relations *(li)* including patrilineal ancestor worship—developed in the historic Shang and legendary Xia dynasties three to four thousand years ago in the Yellow River valley, while peoples in the rest of what is today China were illiterate and tribal "barbarians" *(man)*.[27] These elements of wenhua spread to neighboring areas, creating a number of small states on the north China plain. In the third century B.C.E., these states were first united briefly under the ruler of the state of Qin. Rule of the largest part of that empire eventually passed to the state of Han, which held power for some 400 years. These early states are claimed as direct "ancestors" of modern Chinese states—imperial, republican, and communist—passing on writing, a state bureaucratic system, ritual, and ancestor worship largely intact, even though the actual "line" is rather circuitous in terms of territory, ruling powers, and actual cultural practices. Today, these essential elements of wenhua are referred to as Han, not Hua or Xia (e.g., Ebrey 1996:19n).[28] The full narrative is more complex than this outline indicates, and the actual events that accumulated to create the Chinese empire were even messier than the narrative recounts. However, we can see even from this sketch that aspects of "Han" culture are inextricably linked with statehood and the creation of China as a single political entity.

Ethnic identities are generally claimed in terms of ancestry, or in terms of ancestry and culture. However, the link between Han ethnic identity and specific cultural practices, such as the rituals of ancestor worship, is special. The link derives from a set of Confucian principles referred to as "culturalism," and it suggests that a person or group can be considered Han as a result of their cultural practices *regardless of their ancestry.*

> Confucius and his followers over the centuries saw [Han] Chinese culture as superior to any other culture; they also saw that culture as something outsiders could acquire. To them the Chinese state and the [Han] Chinese family were perfect forms of social organization because they were based on the truest moral principles, universal principles such as loyalty and filial piety; adherence to these forms and principles were what made China [Han] Chinese and what made China superior to other places. Confucianism thus offered little grounds for erecting barriers against absorption of outsiders and indeed saw expansion of China through transformation or assimilation of non-Chinese [non-Han] as the natural state of affairs. (Ebrey 1996:20)

This is not to say that Confucian culturalism explains the *actual* assimilation processes that non-Han experienced. Indeed, historian Patricia Ebrey (1996) discusses at length how ancestry, as construed by surname, was terribly important to actual claims of Han ethnic identity. Rather, Confucian culturalism served as an ideological explanation of assimilation and justification for expansion of Han political control. As ideology, it still influences people's view of how the world works. Specifically, it suggests that Han identity is most importantly based on culture—shared meaningful ideas, in this case Confucian moral principles. Thus, Confucian culturalism makes the link between Han ethnic identity and cultural practices, a crucial link underlying some of the problematic assumptions embedded within the idea that if Taiwan's people are culturally Han they should be part of the nation of China.

The third assumption built into the idea that if Taiwan's people are culturally Han they should be part of the nation of China is that the borders of Chinese and Han identities are clear. The borders of contemporary Chinese national identity may seem unambiguous enough—everyone legally and permanently within its borders is part of the nation—but even ignoring disputed areas such as Tibet, these borders are actually far from clear. For example, before the return of Hong Kong to the PRC in 1997, Great Britain and China argued over what would happen to the ethnic Indian population of Hong Kong. In the view of the PRC government, the presence of this population in Hong Kong for several generations did not entitle it to Chinese national identity. Moreover, there is the issue of so-called Overseas Chinese or *huaqiao*—people of Han (or Hua) ancestry who reside outside of China or Taiwan. Some huaqiao families are recent emigrants; some lineages, especially in Southeast Asia, have resided outside of China for centuries. Chinese Americans include both recent immigrants and families who have been in the U.S. for over 150 years. Sociopolitical treatment of huaqiao creates problems for defining the border to Chinese national identity because they have legal rights, in both China and Taiwan, which other foreigners do not have. For example, there are quotas that designate spots for huaqiao in Taiwan's universities, and huaqiao have been welcomed by both China and Taiwan after Indonesian unrest targeted Han there in massacres in the mid-1960s and in looting in 1998. Throughout the Maoist era, huaqiao in the PRC were "allowed" to buy new private homes in cities and to select burial rather than cremation (Whyte 1987:296n).

The border to Han ethnic identity is even less clear. Analysis of this border takes up the bulk of this book. However, for a brief example, consider whether a third-generation Chinese American who is Christian and neither speaks nor writes Chinese is Han. Based strictly on his or her cultural practices, we would say no. However, in both China and Taiwan, such Chinese Americans are frequently classified as huaqiao and "ABCs" (American-born Chinese). Furthermore, during the 1992 and 1994 Olympics, both China and Taiwan proudly covered the performances of U.S. athletes Michael Chang (tennis) and Michelle Kwan (figure skating) as Chinese or Taiwanese athletes. These actions suggest that Chinese Americans are considered fundamentally Han and Chinese on the basis of ancestry.

The U.S. goverment also periodically buys into this ancestry-based classification. Spy scares in both the 1950s and 1990s led U.S. officials to target Chinese Americans working in government and military labs for scrutiny on the basis of unproven allegations that they leaked sensitive information to the PRC. Ironically, in the 1950s, American willingness to disgrace Qian Xuesen, a U.S. Air Force colonel honored for his contributions to the development of Titan Intercontinental Ballistic Missiles, even though no evidence has ever been found against him, led to Qian's returning to the land of his birth and creating the Chinese Ballistic Missile System (Nelson 1999:6, 10). Treatment of Wen Ho Lee, a scientist at Los Alamos National Laboratory, in the 1990s was not much better. Stripped of his security clearances because he stored top-secret information on an unsecured personal computer, Lee endured almost a year of scrutiny and public allegations without any charges being brought against him. Eventually arrested and charged, he was denied bail in February 2000 for a trial set for November, and held in solitary confinement, even though European American John M. Deutch, a former CIA director who had downloaded far greater quantities of top-secret information onto an unsecured personal computer, was never charged with any crime. In spite of stern rebukes by the judge presiding over the case, the Justice Department continued to pursue the Lee case. Lee's lawyers finally negotiated a plea bargain in which Lee pled guilty to one charge of inappropriate handling of classified material and all the other charges were dropped. At the hearing for his release, the judge apologized to Lee for his treatment by the U.S. government. Prejudice because of ancestry-based classifications is also blatant in the 1999 Cox Report on Chinese spying:

> [This report] most irresponsibly . . . suggests that every Chinese visitor to this country, every Chinese scholar, every Chinese student, every Chinese permanent resident, and even every Chinese-American citizen is a spy, a potential spy, or "sleeper agent," merely waiting for the signal to rise up and perform some unimaginable act of treachery. (Nelson 1999:6)

Here we can see how readily ancestry-based classifications cross the line to racism.

How is someone who has only one parent of Han ancestry classified? Given Han patriarchal practices, someone with a Han father and non-Han mother was historically classified as Han; someone with a Han mother and non-Han father was not. Today, however, he or she *may* be classified on the basis of physical characteristics—whether he or she looks Han. However, physical characteristics are neither reliable nor consistent indicators of ethnic classification. Consider Tiger Woods, whom the media often identified as Asian American until he won big, and thereafter classified as African American. (Woods himself has tried to deflect such labeling, publicly calling himself "cablinasian"—meaning caucasian, black, Indian, and Asian—on Oprah Winfrey's talk show. The mixed category has gotten some press but the media continues to portray Woods as a prominent African American, often shown with his friend Michael Jordan.)

Social experience and how someone is treated in social interactions are always more important to actual identity than looks. Although Taiwanese Americans look Taiwanese, their experience in Taiwan often sets them apart from both Taiwanese and Americans. As a beginning language student in Taibei, my minimal Mandarin abilities were once lavishly praised by a Taiwanese shopkeeper who then berated my Taiwanese American friend's much better language skills as inadequate. Nevertheless, the potential to use surnames to organize Han identity across the usual markers of identity elsewhere—physical characteristics, language, culture, territory, a state—is exactly Ebrey's (1996:30) point when she argues that "imagining the linkage among [Han] Chinese as a matter of patrilineal kinship [as construed by surnames] differed in interesting ways from other ways of imagining group identities."

These assumptions leave loopholes in the argument that if Taiwan's people are culturally Han then they should be part of the nation of China. This argument could be challenged by questioning the link between Han ethnic identity and Chinese national identity. Most Americans would probably consider this challenge the most important, given that at the time of the American Revolution, American culture and English culture were not that far apart. Interestingly, however, this form of challenge has not been made by those advocating Taiwan's independence. The idea could also be challenged by revealing the actual role, as opposed to the ideologically claimed role, of culture in determining identity, or by revealing the ambiguities of the borders to Han and the Chinese nation. All of these challenges, however, require stepping outside of a Han cultural perspective.

Ironically, although people in Taiwan distance themselves from Chinese national identity, they often do so from within a Han cultural perspective. New narratives of Taiwan's unfolding accept the assumptions that borders to Han and Chinese identities are clearly defined and that these identities are inextricably linked to each other. They argue that Taiwanese fall outside the border because of the degree of Aborigine and Japanese influence on Taiwanese culture. This position takes Confucian culturalism to its logical conclusion: if non-Han can become Han, then Han can become non-Han. The irony here is that these narratives use a Han perspective to claim a non-Han identity and thus to challenge Taiwan's relation to the Chinese nation. Given Taiwan's emphasis on its wealth and political freedom relative to the PRC (e.g., MAC 1999[1994]: 97–98), this viewpoint also implies that Aborigine and Japanese cultural ancestors are as worthy as Han ancestors. Since 1999, politicians in Taiwan have begun to distance Taiwan from the Chinese nation on the basis of actual social experience—Taiwan has been governed separately from China since 1949—but the rhetoric of different culture and ancestry has not been repudiated.

Policies within the PRC have left the Chinese communist state in a position where logically they must accept the possibility that Han who emigrated to Taiwan have, over generations, changed culturally enough to be categorized as something else. Consider the following PRC policies. (1) Individuals can only claim a single identity, even if their parents have different ethnic identities. That is, a person is officially Han or Mongol or Tujia, *not* part Han and part something else. (People can petition to change their ethnic identities but only once.) This policy implies that ethnic identities and their borders are unambiguous. (2) China is a multiethnic country, but (3) the Han are Big Brother who lead the way to modernization and economic development for their "younger brothers and sisters." The introduction of Han political and economic practices is usually accompanied by the introduction of Han social practices and cultural ideas, linking Chinese national identity to Han culture and thus to Han ethnic identity (cf. Harrell 1995b). Linking Chinese national identity to Han ethnic identity in an officially multiethnic state poses a problem. If ethnic minorities in China are to be considered part of the Chinese nation by anything other than fiat, and with no ideological room left for separatist arguments, then the Chinese communist state must accept the possibility of non-Han becoming Han (sinicization), an idea derived from Confucian culturalism. Indeed, as we shall see in chapter 5, the official classification of people in southwestern Hubei as Tujia (a non-Han ethnic group) is based on an assumption that with intermarriage and sufficient time Han can be transformed into non-Han. The articles in Harrell's (1995a) edited volume argue that the Chinese communist state has undertaken a "civilizing project" that incorporates many of the assumptions and methods of the Confucian civilizing project. Given these current policies, the PRC is left arguing with Taiwan's distancing strategy in terms of the cultural character of Taiwan's people: how Han are Taiwanese?

The focus on whether Taiwanese are culturally Han diverts attention from the question of whether Chinese in the PRC are still culturally Han.

If we were to use Confucian criteria related to ancestor worship to classify people as Han, Taiwanese would turn out to be more Han than people classified as Han in post–Cultural Revolution China. Tu Wei-ming (1991) argues that in defining Chineseness as a Han identity, the "periphery"—that is, Han areas outside of China such as Taiwan, Hong Kong, Singapore, and Overseas Chinese communities in places like Bangkok and San Francisco—has been more important, because it is more Confucian than the PRC. These arguments support the claim of narratives such as Liu's poem *Island Nostalgia* that the new Taiwanese identity is both Han and non-Han.

Although the potential for de-sinicization (becoming non-Han) is a logical consequence of the principle of Confucian culturalism, it is a consequence of such extreme impropriety that it is not explicitly discussed. In Taiwan, at least two types of attempt soften the very radical claim that Taiwan's people have become so culturally different that they are no longer Han. First, the claim is often stated indirectly—that Taiwan's people have become so culturally different that they are no longer Chinese *(zhongguo ren)*. However, acceptance of the assumption that Han culture is linked to Chinese national identity implies the more radical underlying claim. Second, the claim is made primarily in terms of culture. Discussions of the Aborigine ancestry of Taiwanese people generally acknowledge the existence of intermarriage between Han men and Aborigine women but give little or no consideration to rates of intermarriage. As we shall see in chapter 4, there is evidence that the rates of intermarriage in the early seventeenth century were so high that about half the population under Dutch control may have had mixed Han and Aborigine ancestry. Aborigine ancestry, where mentioned, actually plays a rhetorical role contrary to that of culture because of the emphasis that Aborigines were matrilineal ancestors. Ebrey (1996) argues persuasively that, in spite of Confucian ideology, most historically documented claims to Han identity relied on patrilineal ancestry not cultural practices. Thus, while culture is used legitimately in terms of Confucian rhetoric to make the radical claim that Taiwanese are not Han and thus not part of the Chinese nation, an emphasis on matrilineal Aborigine ancestry and thus patrilineal Han ancestry is used to indicate that Taiwanese are "really" Han, in terms of a different Confucian rhetoric which promotes patrilineal kinship ties. As we shall see for the Tujia (in chapter 5), this strategy of acknowledging non-Han matrilineal ancestors is used by others at the border to Han.

SINICIZATION: IDEOLOGY VERSUS ACTUALITY

Sinicization, or *hanhua,* as an ideological narrative of unfolding is important to our understanding of social, cultural, and identity changes within Han-dominated territories. By exposing hanhua ideology as the justification for power that it is, we can begin to understand how it shaped and, I suggest, continues to shape the views and arguments of Han and non-Han regarding the expansion of Han cultural and sociopolitical hegemony. The ideological aspect of narratives of the past is crucial to Han hegemony, because hegemony implies not only the existence of a social power hierarchy but also cultural justification for this hierarchy which is accepted by people in both dominant and subordinate positions of the hierarchy (cf. Gramsci 1992). Thus, "Han cultural and sociopolitical hegemony" refers to the *accepted* dominant position of Han cultural ideas, social practices, and political authority.

Historian Pamela Crossley (1990:2) has rightly pointed out that the concept of hanhua long held by Han literati and adopted rather uncritically by Western scholars as "sinicization" is "a bundle of assumptions regarding the reasons for and the manifestations of cultural change throughout a very broad expanse of Asia." She criticizes this conception of hanhua, because it "implied that through nothing much more subtle than the sheer charisma of Chinese culture, people were attracted to China and its society from elsewhere and, no great obstacle withstanding, were consumed in the flames of *hanhua.*" However, we should not dismiss the conception of hanhua or sinicization as merely a biased description of historical events. It was and is a functioning Han *ideology,* intended to shape what people perceive about how assimilation occurs, and to ignore this ideology obscures the past just as much as accepting it at face value. The actual historical processes of assimilation to Han identity and acculturation to Han cultural models worked very differently from the way this ideology asserts, and so it is crucial to distinguish what we know of how these processes actually worked from the ideology of how they purportedly worked. In order to do so, there are three implications of the ideological conception of sinicization which we need to recognize.

First, the ideology implies that there was no obstacle to becoming Han—that it was easy to take on a Han identity. There is ample historical evidence to contradict this implication. For example, Ebrey (1996:25) cites a 1370 edict by the founding Ming emperor against Mongols who took single-character surnames that could lead to their being mistaken for Chinese (here using the term *huaren*). She concludes, "Cross-surname adoption bothered a lot of people, so it is not surprising that cross-ethnicity transformations would as well." As we shall see, people did take on a Han identity, but such transformation was not easy. It required specific social and political circumstances.

A second implication of this ideology is the concept of Confucian culturalism—that culture was the key to becoming Han. This ideological implication was not true in practice because people did not claim Han identity on the basis of culture. Rather, they claimed Han identity on the basis of ancestry. Ebrey (1996:23) reminds us:

> [The] genealogies compiled in great profusion from the Song period on . . . [overwhelmingly] tell a story of Han Chinese migration, sometimes in the Han but most often in the Tang, Song, or Yuan [periods]. Rather than say they became Chinese the Confucian way, by adopting Chinese culture, they wanted to say they were Chinese by patrilineal descent. If Chineseness was actually something one could acquire by learning, why were so few willing to admit that they had learned it?

There is a tension, then, between the ideology of sinicization and the ideology of patriliny, both of which derive from Confucianism. Sinicization links identity change to cultural change; patriliny links identity change to ancestry. The fact that people used the ideology of patriliny to make their claims to Han identity does not, in itself, mean they saw no link between identity and culture, but they did view it as less important than ancestry and thus certainly not the key factor. How could culture be the key to becoming Han, as the ideology of sinicization suggests, if Han themselves apparently did not believe it? As we shall see, there is a further problem with this idea: identity change and cultural change do not necessarily occur at the same time.

Third, the ideology of sinicization implies that assimilating non-Han had no cultural impact on the Han, and therefore that the non-Han became exactly like those who were already Han. This implication fuels the notion of Confucian culturalism, because it suggests that there is a single model of Han culture whose core aspects (at least) are unchanging and eternal, which in turn justifies including an extraordinary number of people in a single ethnic category—over a billion worldwide, including Han in the PRC and overseas Chinese (huaqiao) and, depending on who is counting, Han in Taiwan (cf. Ebrey 1996:19). This apparent cultural unity is emphasized in spite of "regional" diversity within the Han that is as great or greater than that between different nations in Europe. Linguists (e.g., Ramsey 1987) generally classify Chinese into seven mutually unintelligible regional language varieties (but Norman 1988 suggests eight). Work by John Lossing Buck (1937), Arthur P. Wolf and Huang Chieh-shan (1980), Chuang Ying-chang and Arthur P. Wolf (1995), Burton Pasternak (1985), Janice Stockard (1989), and others have examined the tremendous regional variation in forms of marriage across China and Taiwan. Hill Gates' (1996a) book *China's Motor: A Thousand Years of Petty Capitalism* lays out the regional variation in the relations between market economy and state power in her analysis of the tributary and petty capitalist modes of production. Moreover, this "regional" diversity is often labeled with the names of the non-Han peoples associated with those geographic locations prior to Han annexation— for instance, Yue in Guangdong, Min in Fujian, and Wu in Jiangsu and Zhejiang. Here is a problem for the ideology of sinicization: if assimilating non-Han had no cultural impact on the Han, then why is there so much cultural, linguistic, and social (including political and economic) differentiation among Han regions?

The modern diversity of the Han also contradicts the idea implicit in the ideology of sinicization, that there is and/or was a static or invariant model of the cultural content required to be Han. Linguist Edwin G. Pulleyblank (1983) and anthropologist Arthur P. Wolf (1989) have suggested that substrate influences of different non-Han peoples may explain the regional variation of the Han. This suggestion is, I believe, similar to historian David Johnson's (1985:62–63) argument that women in late imperial China played an important role in transmitting popular culture and that, given the tendency for Chinese men to marry women of a lower class, this transmission was "one of the basic mechanisms of cultural integration in China, one whose effects ran directly counter to the effects of that other important agency of integration, gentry hegemony."[29] Thus, there are a number of scholars looking at broad empirical evidence who conclude that many non-Han peoples took on a Han identity over time and appear to have contributed—albeit in different ways and to different degrees—to changes in local models of what it means to be Han. In other words, crossing the border to Han identity yet maintaining non-Han cultural and linguistic continuities has happened many times in China's history.

What implications does sinicization have for Taiwanese identity? As already discussed, the *ideology* has been used to argue that Taiwanese are no longer culturally Han: if non-Han can sinicize, according to this ideological model, then Han can de-sinicize, and they did in Taiwan. Thus, it is argued, Taiwanese identity should not be subsumed under Chinese national identity as, for example, Fujianese identity is. The *actual* historical processes of acculturation of practices and assimilation of identity which are masked by the ideology, however, pose difficulties for this particular distancing strategy.

First, this strategy ignores the obstacles to becoming Han—and by logical extension as well as empirical evidence, there are similar (though not the same) obstacles to becoming non-Han. When Taiwanese classify Chinese Americans as "ABCs" rather than American, they acknowledge the difficulties of identity change and thereby undermine their own claims to being non-Han. Second, this strategy ignores a more popular, competing ideology emphasizing patrilineal ancestry as more important to identity change than culture. Thus, cultural claims to a Taiwanese identity independent of Han and Chinese identities fail to counter competing claims to Han identity via patrilineal ancestry in their own narratives. As long as Taiwanese accept that Han patrilineal ancestry means Han identity, they undermine their own claim to being non-Han and non-Chinese. Finally, if the process of crossing the border to Han identity yet maintaining non-Han social, cultural, and linguistic continuities has happened many times in China's history, then what makes Taiwan different from Fujian or Guangdong or elsewhere?

The integrity of attempts to establish an independent Taiwanese identity are influenced in part by how sinicization and de-sinicization are resolved in claims to Taiwanese identity within Taiwan. In particular, while the new Taiwanese identity includes all varieties of Han—Hoklo, Hakka, and Mainlanders—inclusion of Aborigines has been more problematic. Descendants of Aborigines who assimilated to Hoklo identity in the 1930s were reclassified as Aborigine in the 1990s, after discovery and publication of their ancestry. This reclassification means that Taiwanese question the very transformation process which they embrace in their own bid for ethnic and national independence. Can such descendants be embraced as Taiwanese? In October 2000, several self-proclaimed plains Aborigines *(pingpu zu)* told me that they, not the Hoklo, are the "real" *(zhenzheng)* Taiwanese. They are making a bold bid for quintessential Taiwanese status, but this strategy could backfire and create a bitter dichotomy of indigenous peoples against colonizers if the Han Taiwanese do not welcome them into the new Taiwanese identity they are constructing. (The elderly people I interviewed in 1991–92 feared the return of such a dichotomy.) If, however, Han embrace Aborigines and their descendants as Taiwanese, then Taiwanese can make the Confucian argument that, in Taiwan at least, it truly is culture that matters. Thus, Taiwan could legitimately make the apparently contradictory claims of being quintessentially Han and at the same time non-Han, both on the basis of Confucian principles.

One legacy of the ideology of sinicization—specifically the assumption of total assimilation without substrate influence—is the acceptance of a strong link between ethnic identity and national identity. In China, this legacy ensures close government monitoring of minorities' political activities for anything which resembles separatism. It fuels the continuation of the government's "civilizing project," which encourages sinicization as part of modernization, and it highlights how important it is that Taiwan not call itself a separate nation, despite its de facto status as one. In Taiwan, the legacy of the ideology of sinicization comes into conflict with the reclassification of people as Aborigine based on evidence of how they actually sinicized. While debate rages over the "Chineseness" of Han descendants in Taiwan, the legacy of the ideology of sinicization led both China and Taiwan to accept for a long time this *cultural* debate as synonymous with the *political* question of whether Taiwan should be part of the Chinese nation. Taiwan's recent attempts to insert actual social experiences into the political rhetoric do not appear to have changed China's position.

CHAPTER 2

Where Did the Aborigines Go?

Reinstating Plains Aborigines in Taiwan's History

Variations of Taiwan's previous narrative of unfolding as a Han domain promoted Taiwanese identity as a Han identity. Thus these narratives open in the seventeenth century, when Han immigration to Taiwan began in earnest, and minimize the presence and significance of the many Aborigine groups who lived on Taiwan when the Han arrived. They tell of Han from Fujian leaving behind famine and poverty to bravely seek out a new life in Taiwan. Folk tales erroneously say that these Han colonists pushed the Aborigines who lived on the western plains into the mountains, and that the mountain Aborigines are the descendants of these displaced plains peoples.[1] Other, more scholarly versions of these older narratives view plains Aborigines who did not flee to the mountains as becoming completely sinicized, without influencing in any way the Han society into which they assimilated (e.g., Lamley 1981:282, Meskill 1979: 253–55).

As part of the construction of new narratives of Taiwan's unfolding, then, it has been necessary to reinstate Aborigines in Taiwan's history. The 1990s saw great interest, both scholarly and popular, in Taiwanese history. Not only did articles and books on the topic abound—e.g., Chen Gengjin (1986), Shi Wanshou (1990), Duan (1992), Pan Ying (1993), Shepherd (1993), and Chen, Chuang, and Huang (1994)—but the Academia Sinica (Zhongyang Yanjiuyuan), Taiwan's national consortium of research institutes, expanded Taiwanese history from a small program within the Institute of History and Philology into its own Institute of Tai-

wan History. Many of these various historical projects explored the inclusion of plains Aborigines in the formation of Taiwanese culture and
society.

The goal of this chapter is to provide a historical overview of Taiwan
that includes plains Aborigines from the early seventeenth century
through the end of the twentieth century. This overview serves two main
functions. First, at a general level, it provides a background of what is
reliably known about plains Aborigines, against which we can examine
the new narratives of the unfolding of Taiwanese identity. Nationalistic
narratives notoriously select historical events that serve their own purposes, sometimes distorting them in the process, and ignore those which
might undermine their nationalist agendas. Thus, it is helpful to review
a fuller account of what is known of Taiwan's past before examining narratives of unfolding about that past.

The second, and more important, function of this historical overview
is to highlight the disappearance of plains Aborigines in the historical
record. From seventeenth-century Dutch records, we know a great deal
about the plains Aborigines of southwestern Taiwan, but Zheng- and
Qing-period Han records say increasingly little about them, and Japanese records say even less. Where did these Aborigines go? In chapters 3
and 4, I argue that people once considered plains Aborigine changed their
identity labels several times—at least once in the seventeenth century and
twice in the twentieth century. Plains Aborigines "disappear" from the
historical record, therefore, because they became included in the "Hoklo
Taiwanese" category. Full consideration of these identity changes requires
an understanding of the context in which they occurred. In particular,
we must examine how the unequal exploitation of Han and Aborigines
shifted under the three regimes that ruled Taiwan in the seventeenth century, how plains Aborigines decreased in political importance from the
nineteenth through the early twentieth century, and how a new national
Taiwanese identity lauding plains Aborigine heritage arose at the end of
the twentieth century.

UNDER THE DUTCH (1624–61)

The Dutch period is the earliest era in Taiwan for which we have detailed
historical records, most written by Dutch merchant-officials or missionaries involved in colonization. These records indicate that Dutch colonial policies capitalized on, and indeed augmented, ethnic tensions (cf.
Shepherd 1993). Although Dutch colonizers encouraged Han immigra-

tion, they used Aborigine militia to supplement Dutch forces in controlling the rapidly increasing Han population.

Although Taiwan is only 100 miles off the southeastern coast of China and has been inhabited for thousands of years, the Dutch appear to have been the first to attempt to take political control of the entire island. The Dutch East India Company (*Vereenigde Oost-Indische Compagnie* or VOC) established a base in southwestern Taiwan in 1624 in order to contest the Portuguese and the Han Chinese of Fujian as middlemen in the lucrative but prohibited trade between China and Japan (Campbell 1903:457, Blussé 1990:254–55). During the Dutch period, Aborigines traded primarily deer parts—skins, meat, antlers, and penises (used in Chinese medicine)—but also rattan, medicinal herbs, and, later in the north, sulphur for explosives and coal (Shepherd 1993:37–38). They traded for salt, iron, porcelains, and cloth, and, later, tobacco, among other things (Shepherd 1993:14, 35–37). Aborigines living on the southwestern plain near present-day Tainan city, an area generally referred to as the "core" area of contact, were involved in commercial trade since at least 1547 (e.g., Shepherd 1993:35, 47). (See the map in figure 2, at the beginning of the book.)

The population in the southwestern core of Dutch control was ethnically diverse. Han Chinese traders, merchants, fishermen, and some farmers were present, as well as Japanese traders, Dutch missionaries, VOC officials, Dutch and Portuguese mercenaries working for the VOC, and African slaves in the service of Dutch officials and missionaries (e.g., Campbell 1903:241, 326).[2] Throughout their occupation, the Dutch population never reached more than 1,200 (Campbell 1903:386, Huber 1990:269n8). In the 1620s, Aborigines were the ethnic majority, and most in the immediate area shared the same Austronesian language, Siraya. In 1637, the Dutch established a "Pax Hollandia" among previously warring Aborigine villages (Campbell 1903:130–31, Shepherd 1993:54–55), bringing a diversity of Aborigines into their area of control. A Dutch census of the Aborigine population in 1650 estimates between 64,000 and 68,000 people islandwide (Nakamura 1936, Brown 1996b:48).

Aborigine agricultural practices did not exploit the land as fully as the VOC wanted. Prior to contact by the Dutch, they practiced shifting, swidden (slash-and-burn) agriculture and may also have used a type of permanent dry-field cultivation since they lived in permanent villages (cf. Thompson 1964:173, Ferrell 1969:10, Shepherd 1993:32–33). Aborigines did not produce an agricultural surplus, an issue of particular consternation to the Dutch, who wanted a surplus both to provision themselves and for colonial export. In late June of 1628, the first Dutch missionary, Candidius, reported "Though they possess such abundance of excellent and fertile land that those seven villages [in the southwestern core] could easily support an additional hundred thousand souls, they do not cultivate any more than is absolutely necessary" (translated in Campbell 1903:10). Traditionally, farming was done by Aborigine women and older men, who had already finished their age-grade service in village hunting and warring (Blussé and Roessingh 1984:68, Campbell 1903:21, Shepherd 1995:26–31). Thus, it seems likely that these Aborigines did not believe agricultural labor to be appropriate work for young men.

Although the VOC tried to persuade the Aborigines to produce surpluses throughout its regime (e.g., Campbell 1903:248–49), by the 1630s the VOC was already encouraging the immigration of Han men (Hsu Wen Hsuing 1980a:16–17; Huber 1990:265–68n3, 274n25; Shepherd 1993:85–86, 466–67n214; Ka 1995:11–12). Han farmers increased the local supply of provisions through surplus rice cultivation and the profitable cash crop of sugarcane for export (cf. Shepherd 1993:85). Because Han were coming from a highly commercialized economic system where surplus agricultural production and cash cropping were standard (cf. Gates 1996), they could be relied upon to produce the desired surplus. In 1636, the Dutch advanced cash to "some [Han] Chinese living in Sinkan and the surrounding [Aborigine] villages, who seem[ed] willing to cultivate rice" (Campbell 1903:155). By 1648, the VOC used missionaries as middlemen to purchase rice from Soulang and Mattau, two Aborigine villages in this area. It is not clear whether Aborigines or Han living in the villages produced the rice.[3]

Han farmers and laborers were subject to officially sanctioned exploitation by the Dutch and by wealthy Han merchants. In 1640, the Dutch started applying a poll tax or head tax to the Han residing within their military control (Huber 1990:274; Shepherd 1993:85, 86, 89). All Han, unless they received an exemption, had to have a poll tax receipt stamped every month upon payment of the tax (Huber 1990:281). Dutch missionaries commonly, though apparently unofficially, received these payments and issued stamps (Campbell 1903:267, 272). Dutch missionaries were also empowered to impose fines and punishments on Aborigines and Han alike,[4] and they were responsible for selling licenses to Han (Campbell 1903:149, 160, 167, 174–76, 180, 540; Shepherd 1993:62, 75, 84). Han too poor to pay for licenses often borrowed the money, from other Han or from Dutch clergy who were appalled at Han interest rates (Campbell 1903:187; Shepherd 1993:84–85). Some Dutch clergy and VOC officials lined their own pockets by exploiting Han (Campbell 1903:282–83, 290; Huber 1990:84; Shepherd 1993:78).

Nevertheless, over time, the Han population grew tremendously. In 1640, some 3,568 Han male settlers paid poll taxes to the Dutch; in 1650, VOC governor Verburg estimated that there were 15,000 Han in Taiwan, based on 10,811 Han men paying the poll tax and adding a number exempt from the tax and a few thousand tax evaders (Huber 1990: 274; see also Hsu Wen-hsiung 1980a:17, Shepherd 1993:86). Dutch were ambivalent about the increasing Han population. Missionaries, in particular, viewed them with great suspicion, because they felt that Han undermined their authority in the Aborigine villages (where many Han lived) by scoffing at Christianity.

Initially, the Dutch extracted profits from the Aborigines through the deer trade. However, annual tribute by Aborigine villages was mandated in 1642 (Shepherd 1993:76) and was in practice by 1647, although the amount of tribute is not clear (Campbell 1903:222). In 1644, the VOC decided to auction monopoly trade rights for each Aborigine village to the highest bidder—Han or Dutch not employed by the VOC. In 1645, the Dutch discontinued licensing Han to hunt deer, so the position of monopoly merchant or village leaseholder replaced that of deer hunter (Shepherd 1993:77). Competitive bidding was effective in exploiting the Han merchants. In 1650, the Han merchants paid out so much more than the amount they could earn that the VOC had to remit one-fifth of the contracted payments to save them from bankruptcy (Shepherd 1993:79).

Dutch taxes on agriculture were primarily aimed at Han, who produced a surplus (e.g., Huber 1990:276, Shepherd 1993:85, 87). Historian Johannes Huber (1990:274–75, 279) estimates that in 1652 four to five thousand hectares (roughly ten to twelve thousand acres) of land were under cultivation around the Dutch core area of Saccam, of which roughly 80 percent was rice and 20 percent was sugarcane. There was a 10 percent tax on the rice harvest, which was farmed out. Some of this tax went directly to missionaries as part of their pay (Campbell 1903:249, 298–99). The VOC and wealthy Han merchants sponsored reclamation—they supplied capital for draft oxen, seed, and building irrigation works (Shepherd 1993:87, 467n232)—and newly reclaimed land was not taxed. Han merchants, however, apparently directed most of their capital toward the cultivation of sugarcane.[5] Although land devoted to the cultivation of sugarcane was not directly taxed, the VOC monopoly on sugar purchases effectively taxed farmers' income from sugarcane. There was also, apparently, some kind of land tax, which Shepherd (1993:87–88) suggests came from land whose reclamation was financed by VOC capital. Numerous commercial taxes—such as taxes on butcher shops, liquor and distilleries, and market weighmasters, as well as import and export duties—were also added in the early 1640s and farmed out to private collectors (Shepherd 1993:88, cf. Ka 1995:12).

In September 1652, there was a rebellion against the Dutch by some 4,000 to 5,000 Han farmers and laborers, led by Guo Huaiyi.[6] Han merchants warned the Dutch of the rebellion in advance, which gave the Dutch time to organize a company of 120 professional soldiers, armed with muskets, and 2,000 Aborigines from several villages. They put down the rebellion in a few days, killing some 2,000 to 3,000 Han (see Huber 1990:270–73). What relations were like between the surviving Han farmers and both the Han merchants and the plains Aborigines—who, according to Dutch records, did most of the indiscriminate killing—is not recorded. Huber (1990:291), however, points out that it was probably not a coincidence that Zheng Chenggong's invading army landed in 1661 at the village where the 1650 rebellion began. According to Dutch sources, there were Han (no doubt farmers, not merchants) waiting on the beach with carts to help haul supplies and ammunition for Zheng's forces.

UNDER THE ZHENG (1661–83)

The ethnic balance of power in Taiwan changed dramatically in 1661 with the invasion of 30,000 mostly Han Chinese under Zheng Chenggong, of whom 20,000 to 25,000 are estimated to have been soldiers (Campbell 1903:413; Chen Shaoxing 1964:117; Jiang 1960[1704]:244, 258; Huber 1990:291; Shepherd 1993:96).[7] Another 6,000 or 7,000 Han, of whom 4,000 were soldiers, arrived in 1664 (Jiang 1960 [1704]:244, Shepherd 1993:96). Under Zheng rule, Han in Taiwan were mobilized for war (Ka 1995:13, 39n2). Their primary use for Aborigines was as exploitable labor, not as allies.

With Zheng Chenggong's invasion, the politics of mid-seventeenth-century China unavoidably enters Taiwan. In 1644, after peasant rebellion broke the Ming dynasty in China, Manchu forces (which had already declared a Qing dynasty in Manchuria in 1636) crossed the border into China unopposed and took Beijing, beginning a decades-long struggle to control the rest of China (see the list of regimes in figure 3, at the beginning of the book). Zheng Chenggong's father was a Han trader/pirate from Fujian who had spent some time working for the Dutch and had turned Ming navy commander (Blussé 1990). Zheng Chenggong continued his father's international maritime trade and his loyalty to the Ming dynasty even after his father defected to the new Qing dynasty in 1646 (Cheng 1990). He fought the Qing forces in southeastern China throughout the 1650s. It was not until 1659 that Qing forces gained the upper hand, driving Zheng back to Fujian and eventually off the mainland entirely in 1661. That same year, under Qing orders, a "coastal removal" policy was enacted along the southeast coast, which required the entire population to move twenty miles inland in order to deprive Zheng Chenggong and his forces of local support. "In Fujian province ... 8,500 farmers and fishermen were reported to have died between 1661 and 1663 as a direct result of this order" (Spence 1990:44). Zheng Chenggong died in 1662, and after some internal fighting his son, Zheng Qing, seized control of Zheng Taiwan and the Zheng maritime trade.

The Zheng regime continued the Dutch taxation system and, needing as much revenue as possible for its continuing war with the Qing dynasty on the mainland, extended it further (Shepherd 1993:95). According to Article VII of the treaty outlining the terms of the Dutch surrender in February 1662:

> The names of all [Han] Chinese debtors or lease-holders in Formosa [as the Dutch called Taiwan], with particulars of claims against them, shall be copied out from the Company's books, and handed to Lord Koxinga [as the Dutch called Zheng Chenggong]. (Translated in Campbell 1903:455)

The Zheng regime continued to apply the village monopoly tax to Aborigines, though it eliminated the auctioning process for middlemen and substituted fixed tax quotas (Shepherd 1993:97). It continued the Han poll tax, although the amount was substantially reduced (Huber 1990:275, Shepherd 1993:101), and continued to levy the commercial taxes of the Dutch, adding these to their substantial profits from international trade (Shepherd 1993:97, 100; see also Cheng 1990). Additionally, the Zheng regime imposed a new tax on Aborigines: corvée or forced labor service. The extent of corvée service under the Zheng regime is unknown, although the 1682 revolt by Aborigine porters in northwestern Taiwan suggests it was onerous (Shepherd 1993:102, 103).

The Zheng regime, following Han practice, taxed agriculture by cultivated acreage (Shepherd 1993:97). It placed all land previously "reclaimed" or "opened" (converted to agricultural fields) under state ownership *(wang tian* or *guan tian)* and maintained taxes for it at the Dutch levels (Shepherd1993:470n46). Most land cultivated in the Zheng period, however, was newly reclaimed by military colonization. Military and civil officials and local strongmen used retired soliders primarily to open land categorized as private *(si tian),* which was taxed at about 25 percent of the rate of crown lands; the standing army also opened land (*yingpan tian,* land of the armed forces), which was tax exempt (Ka 1995: 13–14). The Zheng regime, however, extracted further tribute from military officials and required them to supply soldiers from among their tenants in wartime.

Given the number of troops and other refugees, it is no surprise that, by late in the Zheng period, the total area under cultivation was two to three times the greatest cultivated area under the Dutch (Shepherd 1993:99). Sugarcane was largely abandoned in favor of rice to feed the population, but rice still had to be imported from Southeast Asia; it was made duty-free to encourage import (Shepherd 1993:99–100). With the shift in agricultural focus from sugarcane to rice came a concurrent drop in Taiwan sugar exports and the profit from it. The export of deerskins continued (Shepherd 1993:100). The Zheng regime appears to have earned less revenue from agriculture than the Dutch, even though it extracted more labor.[8]

Beyond the increasing financial obligations to a state regime, there must have been substantial changes in the nature of social relations between Han and Aborigines. Under the Dutch regime, Aborigines were allies of the ruling power, much needed to control the growing Han population. Under the Zheng regime, although the Aborigines were taken seriously as a military force (e.g., Shepherd 1993:91), it was as a potential threat not as crucial allies. The Zheng forces were sufficient, in numbers and skill, to control the local population, Han and Aborigine, as their suppression of Aborigine uprisings in 1661 and 1665 demonstrated (Shepherd 1993:93–94).

In July 1683, Admiral Shi Lang—a former Zheng admiral turned Qing admiral—led 300 war vessels to a crushing victory over Zheng forces in the Pescadores Islands, about 50 kilometers off Taiwan's western coast. Zheng forces on Taiwan were weakened by food shortages, troop defections after promises of amnesty by Qing officials, and a fire which destroyed 1,600 homes and shops in the Zheng capital at Tainan City. Shi Lang promised there would be no retribution if the Zhengs surrendered peacefully, which they did in September 1683. Qing forces landed in Taiwan the following month.

UNDER THE QING (1683–1895)

Han-Aborigine relations changed again, as they would several more times under Qing administration of Taiwan. In broad terms, the early and middle Qing periods were characterized by ethnic tensions among the Han and between Han and Aborigines. However, during the early Qing period (1683 through the 1730s), plains Aborigines were in good standing with the Qing government both because of their military service in suppressing Han rebellions and because of their contributions to Qing revenues through the deer trade. Thus, the Qing government made some attempts to protect Aborigine lands and livelihoods. The middle Qing period (1730s through 1860s) saw a change in Aborigine status. Although plains Aborigines were still useful in controlling unrest among the Han population, they no longer contributed significant revenues due to the extinction of deer and to the increasing Han population. Qing attempts at protecting Aborigine lands were notoriously unsuccessful, and some southwestern plains Aborigines and their descendants occasionally migrated away from areas of Han incursion. In the late Qing period (1860s through 1895), Aborigines lost their status as reliable militia, probably due to mass conversions to Christianity in the 1860s and 1870s, and became suspect to the Qing government. Although they were used to fight mountain Aborigines, they were no longer trusted to control the Han population. Tax restructuring in the 1880s substantially reduced the income from Aborigine lands, removing the last possible benefits to an Aborigine identity and making Aborigines completely subordinate to Han socially, economically, and politically.

The Early Qing Period (1683–1730s)

The Qing regime, like the Dutch before them, exploited ethnic tensions in Taiwan to their advantage. Plains Aborigine militia were used by the Qing at least twelve times between 1683 and 1800: four campaigns each against Han, mountain Aborigines, and other plains Aborigines (Huang Huanyao 1986:144, 192–93; Shepherd 1993:309). Upon taking control of Taiwan, the Qing oversaw an immediate reduction in the Han population (Shepherd 1993:106–107, 137, 472n6–7; Shi 1958[1685]:67, 69; Zhuang 1964:1–2). Zheng military forces were either sent back to their home communities on the mainland or incorporated into Qing armies; Han colonists without wives, property, or a trade also had to return home. At the beginning of 1684, Shi Lang estimated Taiwan's total Han population at 100,000; eight months later he estimated that half the Han population had left.

During this time, Qing officials debated what to do with Taiwan. Some advocated repatriating all Han and abandoning the island. Shi Lang argued strongly that for reasons of maritime security Taiwan had to be incorporated into the empire. The emperor decided to annex Taiwan and, in 1684, Taiwan was made a prefecture of Fujian Province. In order to foster economic recovery on the southeast coast of the mainland and to attempt to control a potentially rebellious population in Taiwan, the Qing regime imposed a partial quarantine on Taiwan—regulating the immigration of males to the island, preventing the immigration of families so that male migrants remained dependent on access to the mainland to see their families, and restricting rice exports (Shepherd 1993:107).

Qing officials and gazetteers (government-sponsored local histories) frequently criticized plains Aborigine agricultural practices. As a result of seventeenth-century Dutch and Han colonialism, Aborigines had adopted Han agricultural methods—first, simply the use of a plow and draft oxen; later, wet-paddy rice agriculture; finally, cash-crop agriculture—although it is difficult to say exactly when they did so. Dutch missionaries introduced draft oxen and plows (Campbell 1903:248–49), but the earliest evidence that Aborigines in substantial numbers may have used Han agricultural techniques dates from the Zheng period.[9] Eight villages from Fengshan, south of present-day Tainan, which were designated Aborigine, paid their head taxes in grain rather than cash. Such payment suggests that they were more active in plow or possibly even wet-paddy agriculture— some form that produced a surplus—than in deer hunting or trade (Shepherd 1993:102).

Further evidence of widespread use of the plow by Aborigines in the core southwestern area is found in the Qing era.[10] Reports from 1685 and 1697 suggest that oxcarts, if not plows and Han-style agriculture, had already been incorporated into Aborigine communities (Thompson 1964:182, 185). An early-eighteenth-century drawing (from ca. 1717) shows women in the fields with a man at an oxcart (see figure 5). None of the "Aborigine Scenes" in this collection includes a plow (see Shepherd 1993:368–69), though one drawing depicts a man and a woman in a wet-paddy rice field. Imperial Censor Huang Shujing reported that in 1722 the plains Aborigines were using agricultural tools like those of the Han, with some villages even using wet-paddy agriculture (Huang Shujing 1957 [1736]; translated in Thompson 1969:54–55, 102–103, 116, 122). In a 1746 painting of Aborigines "Cultivating and Planting," there

Figure 5. Aborigine scene, ca. 1717.

are Han-style tools: a plow, drawn by a water buffalo and guided by a
woman, and a hoe, used by a man in a nearby field (painting published
in Shepherd 1993:177 ff.).

However, even when Aborigines did adopt plow agriculture, they still
did not generally produce a surplus for commercial sale. The market-

oriented Dutch (Campbell 1903:10) and early Qing observers did not understand Aborigine reluctance to adopt cash-crop agricultural practices. Local Han gazetteers, for example, praised a variety of rice grown by the Aborigines in dry fields, suggesting it was an obvious cash crop that the Aborigines failed to develop: "each year [the Aborigines] plant only enough of this [type of rice] for their own consumption during the year. They do not market it; even though its value is several times higher [than that of ordinary rice], they will not sell it" (Huang 1957 [1736], translated in Thompson 1969:116, Shepherd 1993:366). Such gazetteer writers apparently believed that Aborigines should see the benefits they could gain from such cash-cropping and adopt it.

I suggest that the persistent contention by Han in gazetteers that Aborigines were bad farmers (see, e.g., Shepherd 1993:349–50) referred to Aborigines' resistance to the cash-cropping and surplus production of intensive commercialized agriculture. This resistance was seen by Qing officials as "a moral failure reflecting both laziness and irresponsibility toward family obligations. 'Knowing to lay up savings' was considered a sign of advancement, and the spread of civilization required teaching the [A]borigines 'the way to save against want'" (Shepherd 1993:380). However, I question the ability of Aborigines to profit from a surplus since they were subject to the oppressive Qing taxation system in Taiwan. Aborigine choices not to participate in commercial agriculture may reflect realistic calculations that surplus production would benefit people other than themselves and thus reflect resistance to Han ideology.[11]

Like the Zheng regime before it, the Qing regime took over the tax system of the previous regime. It continued to apply the Aborigine head tax, which still had to be paid through the village monopoly system that originated under the Dutch, as well as the corvée labor tax that originated under the Zhengs. The Qing granted across-the-board reductions of 30 or even 40 percent from the Zheng village tax quotas, then fixed these quotas until 1737. Han colonists continued to pay both a head tax and a land tax (Shepherd 1993:108–109, 111). While Han colonists had a clear claim to the land on which they paid taxes, Aborigine land rights were open to great variation in interpretation.[12]

Extortion of Aborigines under the early Qing was rampant and severe. In 1697, Yu Yonghe, a Hangzhou businessman on a trip from the southwestern port city of (present-day) Tainan to Danshui in the north seeking sulphur for export, wrote:

> In each administrative district a wealthy person is made responsible
> for the [Aborigine] village revenues. These men are called "village tax-
> farmers" [*sheshang*]. . . . The village tax-farmer in turn appoints inter-
> preters and foremen who are sent to live in the villages, and who record
> and check up on every jot and tittle [grown or brought in by hunting]
> of all the barbarians. . . . [The Aborigines] make a profit [from the sale
> of] both of these things [deer hides and dried meat] after paying their
> taxes. But these [interpreters and foremen] take advantage of the simple-
> mindedness of the barbarians and never tire of fleecing them, looking on
> whatever they have as no different than their own property. [In connection
> with] the activities of daily life, great and small, all of the barbarians—
> men, women, and children—have to serve in their homes without a day
> of respite. Moreover, they take the barbarian women as their wives and
> concubines. Whatever is demanded of them they must comply; if they
> make a mistake they must take a flogging. And yet the barbarians do
> not hate them greatly. (Translated in Thompson 1964:195–96; see also
> Shepherd 1993:116–17)

Officials knew about such abuses. In 1722, Zhou Zhongxuan, magis-
trate of Taiwan county,[13] estimated that the squeeze of such middlemen
interpreters more than doubled the tax burden to the Aborigines (Shepherd 1993:113). Some Aborigine villages avoided this added burden by
nominating their "own native" people as interpreters, but such nominations had to be confirmed by Qing officials, who frequently sought
bribes from interpreters and took bribes from those seeking to be licensed
as interpreters (Shepherd 1993:121–22).Whom the Aborigines considered their "own" people is ambiguous: was the son of a Han interpreter
and an Aborigine woman who was raised in an Aborigine village a "native" or not?

Corvée abuses were, if possible, worse. Official corvée services included
bearing officials in sedan chairs, delivering official documents, supplying oxcarts to transport lumber for shipbuilding, and serving as porters
for Qing troops; these duties were assigned by the tribal monopoly merchants and interpreters (Shepherd 1993:124). Abuse of the system came
at all levels. *Yamen* runners (low-level employees of Qing officials) and
soldiers regularly demanded of interpreters in the villages through which
they passed that oxcarts and drivers be provided, and interpreters demanded such service for their personal benefit as well. Historian Shi
Tianfu (1990) suggests that abuses were carried to such an extreme that
Aborigine hunting and farming suffered.[14]

Aborigines revolted against interpreter abuses and corvée services in the second month and the fifth month of 1699 (see Shepherd 1993: 125–32). Starting in 1710, Intendant Chen Bin tried to institute reforms, ordering that a fee be paid for every ten *li* (5.76 kilometers or roughly 3.33 miles) the oxcarts traveled, and that baggage porters be given money for food (Shepherd 1993:124). In 1724, bureaucrat Lan Dingyuan estimated that Aborigines, "by supplying carts, relieving troops by doing military service, providing countless labor services, and serving as postal carriers, did ten times more work than the [Han] Chinese settlers," yet he continues on to lament reductions in Aborigine corvée services and to warn against Aborigines considering themselves comparable to Han as a result of these reductions (Shepherd 1993:125).[15] Lan's remarks reveal the same ethnic prejudice against Aborigines that is shown in their categorization as barbarians *(fan)*. Exploitation of Aborigines continued and led to three more revolts in the 1730s.

By the end of the early Qing period, Aborigine-Han social relations had changed in a number of ways. The lucrative deerskin trade had all but ended, due to overhunting, so too had the revenue gained from that trade—hunting licenses, trading monopolies, and tax farms. The growth of the Han population and the spread of Han agricultural techniques had previously been limited to the southwest core and the sites of Zheng military farms, but with the extinction of the deer population, the area of Han incursion increased. Later colonists settled disproportionately in northern Taiwan, where there was more "available" land (i.e., land which had not already been turned into agricultural fields). The Qing regime lifted prohibition on family migration for eight years (1732–1740), bringing increased numbers of Han women to Taiwan. These changes transformed the fiscal basis of Qing rule (Shepherd 1993:134).

New Benefits to Aborigine Identity

Rebellion-inspired reforms in the 1730s led to two sets of policies. The first set exacerbated Han exploitation of Aborigines leading to a new rebellion, and the second set encouraged the maintenance of plains Aborigine identity by "mixed" descendants. The Taiwan frontier had a reputation for uprisings, both by Aborigines and by Han immigrants. In spite of earlier aid by plains Aborigine militia in controlling Han rebellions, the Qing regime paid little attention to Han exploitation of Aborigines until the plains Aborigine rebellions on the northern part of the western plain in 1731 and 1732, which sparked a brief Han uprising. These later uprisings (which required 6,000 reinforcements from Fujian to suppress) finally drew the attention of the Qing court both to Han oppression and extortion of plains Aborigines and to the real military threat to Qing control of Taiwan from allied plains Aborigines. In the aftermath of these rebellions, the Qing regime opened 20,000 to 30,000 *mu* (3,200–4,800 acres, 1,340–2,010 hectares) of Aborigine deer-hunting lands for Han "reclamation" on the northern plain, although the Aborigines still held the title and large-rent rights to the land.[16] It officially allowed the immigration of Han settlers' families, and it increased its military presence, especially in northern Taiwan. Moreover, 47 schools were founded in plains Aborigine villages to encourage sinicization (Shepherd 1993:128–32). These procolonization policies exacerbated the Han exploitation of Aborigines, leading to the next Aborigine uprising in 1736.

The two imperial censors charged with investigating the 1736 rebellion linked its causes to those of the 1731–32 rebellions and recommended changes that provided some benefits to plains Aborigines. One censor, focusing on the high rate of the tribal tax and the additional extortion squeezed from Aborigines by corrupt tax farmers and officials, recommended reducing the Aborigine head tax. The other censor, focusing on the hostility created by official extortion and Aborigine losses of land (and thus livelihood), recommended limiting Han reclamation of Aborigine land and establishing punishments for government soldiers who entered Aborigine settlements, extorted goods, or caused trouble (Shepherd 1993:133, 267). He also recommended prohibiting marriage between Han men and Aborigine women.

As a result of the censors' recommendations, the Qing regime enacted several policies that reduced Aborigine incentives to claim a Han identity. First, it lowered the Aborigine village tax quotas by 80 percent, to the same rate as the Han head tax in 1737 (Shepherd 1993:125, 133–34), which may have eliminated the incentive to change ethnic identity for tax purposes. However, ethnically differentiated taxes still existed. Aborigines remained subject to corvée labor service while Han were not, and new regulations against corvée abuses issued in 1752 and 1788 show that such abuse continued to be a problem.

Second, the Qing regime officially banned intermarriage (Shepherd 1993:133, 152, 267), making it impossible to legally change identities, because a man in an Aborigine-majority village claiming not to owe labor service because of a Han father would put his father at risk of arrest for intermarriage.[17] Qing officials said they supported intermarriage prohibitions in order to lessen antagonism between Han and plains Aborigines (e.g., Shepherd 1993:267), but sexual harassment and economic exploitation, not intermarriage, led to the 1731–32 Aborigine uprisings (e.g., Shepherd 1993:128–29). Even though the roots of all three rebellions lay in exploitation of plains Aborigines by Qing officials or their subordinates, the actual turn to violence in two of them was blamed on Han with connections in the villages fomenting rebellion—in the 1732 rebellion, these Han were actually sons-in-law of Aborigine rebels (Shepherd 1993:133, 477n96). Thus, the Qing regime probably wanted to discourage intermarriage between Han settlers and plains Aborigines because they were concerned about intermarriage leading to Han-Aborigine alliances. Such alliances could cost them plains Aborigine military support during a Han uprising and, at worst, could lead to a joint Han-Aborigine uprising which would be even more difficult and expensive to suppress than those they had already faced.

Third, in 1738, the governor-general ordered a land survey to clarify the "boundaries" between Han and Aborigine lands, which meant land contracts had to be officially inspected (Shepherd 1993:18, 267–68). Although the order ostensibly protected Aborigine land rights, by returning to the Aborigines land that Han had claimed by squatting and by forbidding future Han leases of Aborigine lands, it also allowed Han to remain on Aborigine lands where they had a lease contract. This acceptance of private lease contracts—which were not necessarily legal at the time they were written—probably undermined the prohibition on future lease contracts, intended to prevent Aborigine loss of lands. Anthropologist John Shepherd (1993:268–304) documents the outright sale of Aborigine lands in 1738 and subsequent government restatements of the ban on leasing or reclaiming Aborigine lands in 1744, 1746, 1750, and 1766. Although the government ordered Han settlers who had illegally lease-purchased Aborigine lands to pay what amounted to large-rent to the Aborigines (beginning in 1759, and again in 1760, 1767, 1768, and 1790), Shepherd cites numerous court suits showing the limitations and problems of the system. It was especially common for Han settlers to refuse to pay some or all of the rents due to Aborigines.

Fourth and finally, after crucial plains Aborigine assistance during the 1786–87 Lin Shuangwen rebellion—a major uprising that required 50,000 troops from the mainland and cost eight million taels (Chinese ounces of silver) to suppress—the Qing regime began to systematically rely on plains Aborigines as loyal militia for the suppression of Han uprisings, even institutionalizing this role in 1790 with the formation of Aborigine military colonies (Brown 1996b:59–60, Shepherd 1993:323–361). For the remainder of the period of Qing authority over Taiwan, the government regularly called on plains Aborigines for military assistance in the face of uprisings.

The Middle and Late Qing Periods (1730s–1895)

From the tax reform of 1737 through the late nineteenth century, the major aspects of Aborigine-Han social relations revolved around ethnic feuding and land rights.[18] The Taiwan frontier had a reputation for feuds *(xiedou)*—between Hoklo and Hakka, among Hoklo with different places of origin (e.g., Zhangzhou and Quanzhou), and among Quanzhou groups of Hoklo as well. Between 1782 and 1862, plains Aborigine militia were routinely used to quell Han ethnic feuds. From 1804 to 1862 alone, they were used nine times against Han Chinese (Huang 1986:194–96, Shepherd 1993:357).

After 1737, with the loss of the deer herds, the reduction in required taxes, and the much higher density of Han colonists all along the west coast, Aborigine villagers could earn their living as landlords, but only if they could circumvent extortion by officials and chicanery by Han colonists (cf. Ka 1995:40n6). Han sometimes "squatted" on Aborigine lands without any contract and refused to leave. Han sometimes contrived to get Aborigines to sign away their land rights without realizing it. More often, Han colonists signed contracts with Aborigines promising to pay large-rents and then either did not pay anything or paid less than they originally promised. Land disputes arose repeatedly between Aborigines and Han settlers, often among the same parties (Shepherd 1993, Chen 1994). Aborigines occasionally attempted to remove themselves from such Han harassment. Throughout the middle Qing period (1730s through 1860s), some southwestern plains Aborigines and their descendants migrated closer to and then into the foothills, away from areas of incursion by Han immigrants and Han cultures (mostly Hoklo, but with pockets of Hakka).[19]

After the 1858 Treaty of Tianjin, one of a series of treaties forced on the Qing government by Westerners in the Opium Wars, Aborigine-Han relations began changing once again. The treaty opened ports to Western trade, protected the open preaching of Christianity, and permitted travel by Westerners with valid passports anywhere inside China. In the 1860s and 1870s, plains Aborigines in Taiwan converted to Christianity whole villages at a time. Shepherd (1988) suggests that these mass conversions resulted from Aborigines' desire to ally themselves with foreign powers, which they perceived as stronger than the Han who cheated and abused them. Such alliance, however, may have made Qing officials suspicious of Aborigine militia. Plains Aborigine militia appear conspicuously absent from the forces used to fight the 1884–85 French invasion of Taiwan (a spillover of Sino-French tensions in Indochina).

After 1860, mountain Aborigines were also affected by increased contact with Westerners. With the introduction to northern Taiwan of tea, which is grown on mountain slopes, and the increasing world market for camphor (in demand for making celluloid and smokeless powder), the Qing government had financial and political incentives to overturn the long-standing policy of keeping Han out of the mountains. Financial incentives came in the form of export duties on camphor and land taxes on tea plantations, not to mention kickbacks from wealthy investors granted patent rights to these lands. Political incentives came not only from the fact that mountain Aborigines had never paid taxes (which would have granted them status under Qing law), but also from their 1871 massacre of shipwreck survivors, which caused a humiliating international incident with Japan (see Davidson 1988 [1903]:123–69). All nine mobilizations of plains Aborigine militia between 1875 and 1892 were to fight mountain Aborigines, not Han (Shepherd 1993:359–60, Huang 1986:194–96), although admittedly, after 1862, ethnic feuding among the Han had greatly subsided.

In 1886, the Qing regime elevated Taiwan to the level of a province. The first governor, Liu Mingchuan, pursued colonization of the mountains, in a series of very expensive campaigns from 1885 through 1891 (when he was withdrawn from Taiwan by the Qing court) that never wholly succeeded. In addition to the military campaigns, Liu had other expensive projects to finance. He established a temporary capital in Taibei in the north, for which he built a city wall, paved roads, and introduced electric lights for the official *yamen* and for lighting the streets. Liu also sponsored the introduction of rickshaws in Taibei and laid cable from Taiwan to the Pescadores and from Taiwan to Fujian, linking Taiwan to China's telegraphic system and thus to world communications.

To finance these projects, Liu conducted an island-wide cadastral survey, planning to increase his revenues by enrolling "hidden" land on the tax registers. Liu's survey quadrupled the taxed land area and more than tripled Taiwan's annual land-tax revenues, but it harmed the Aborigines (Shepherd 1993:360–61, Speidel 1976:453). As part of the survey, Liu shifted the land tax burden from large-rent holders to small-rent holders, simultaneously reducing the rents which the latter paid to the former in order to leave the large-rent holders' net income the same (Ka

1995:33–35, also see note 16). Aborigine lands, however, had not previously been subject to a direct land tax, so the reduction in the large-rents paid to them was not offset by a lowering of their tax burden. As a result, their net income was substantially reduced, though not completely eradicated. (The Qing government considered the Aborigine land tax to be included in the tribal tax.) It is not clear whether this reduction was directly caused by Qing suspicions of Aborigine connections to Westerners. However, the fact that plains Aborigine militia were not used to expel the French from Taiwan must mean that Aborigines were seen, at the very least, as not politically important so that their interests did not need to be taken into account in the tax restructuring. This income reduction removed the last potential benefits of Aborigine identity and completed the changes making Aborigines socially, economically, and politically subordinate to Han.

UNDER THE JAPANESE (1895–1945)

In the Treaty of Shimonoseki, which ended the Sino-Japanese War of 1894–95, China ceded Taiwan and the Pescadores to Japan. Japanese rule focused on making Taiwan a model colony, both to economically support Japan's then-growing imperialist ambitions and to demonstrate to Western nation-states that Japan was as capable an imperialist power as they were. The Japanese, however, did not take control of Taiwan without a fight—the local elite declared Taiwan a republic and mobilized "righteous armies" (yijun) which crossed the lines of ethnic feuding earlier in the century (Davidson 1988 [1903]:257–370, Harrell 1990b). The leaders of the republic surrendered at Anping in Tainan City on October 21, 1895, but organized guerilla resistance continued until 1902 (Ka 1995:83–84n1), when the Japanese finally achieved a lasting peace on the plains.

Once established, the Japanese colonial government announced a tax holiday of one year. Taxes resumed in 1897 at rates lower than the Qing rate. The three largest areas of revenue in 1900 were in land taxes, customs duties, and monopolies. In 1900, the Japanese held monopolies in camphor, salt, and opium (Ka 1995:52–57).[20] Later, monopolies were extended to include sugar and sulphur (Ka 1995:62–82). The Japanese government took these monopolies seriously. Sugarcane was a major crop in the south, and several people I interviewed in the region told me that if the Japanese police caught a farmer cutting as little as one stalk of cane from his own fields for personal use—to skin the cane and chew it to extract the juice—it was tantamount to theft and they would beat that farmer severely.

Aborigines did not fare well under Japanese colonial rule. The Japanese government ended the three-tier land cultivation system, expropriating the large-rent for the colonial government and making the small-rent holder the full legal owner (Ka 1995:58–62). This abolition completely wiped out most of plains Aborigines' remaining land rights claims as well as their livelihoods from landlordship, which were already greatly damaged by Liu Mingchuan's reduction of large-rents. The Japanese government also aggressively pursued "pacification" of the mountain Aborigines—subjugating them with modern artillery, forcing them to settle in lower elevations where they could be more easily observed and controlled, and even splitting up families in the course of relocating villages which had been particularly effective in their guerrilla warfare against Japanese forces.[21]

As one part of its strategy for monitoring and controlling its population, the Japanese colonial government instituted a household registration system which required that every person register with the police as a member of one, and only one, household (cf. Ka 1995:58–59). Because designation of the appropriate household in which to register was left to Taiwanese, the historic household registers from the Japanese period reflect a Taiwanese notion of family (*jia*; T., *ke*). The required registration information included name, age, sex, relation to the household head, marital status, educational level achieved, occupation, and, in the early years, "class" (*zhongbie*), "race" (*zhongzu*) as inherited from one's biological father, whether feet were bound (for females), which immunizations had been received, and whether addicted to opium (see Wolf and Huang 1980:16–33). "Race" was no longer recorded after 1915 or so, and the category was eventually removed from the form. Plains Aborigines were no longer officially distinguished from Han (though mountain Aborigines were). New information had to be registered with the police within 10 days, and police visited each household two or three times a year to ensure that all changes in the household had been registered. Penalties for failure to register were severe.

Between 1895 and 1930, Japan invested heavily in developing Taiwan's infrastructure, production, and population. Japan's revenues in Taiwan (excluding military costs) increased steadily from 1895 through 1900, with a concomitant decrease in expenditures (Davidson 1988 [1903]:615). (See Ka [1995: chapter 3] for a more detailed examination of Japanese revenues and expenses.) The Japanese government put in a railroad which ran the length of the island along the western plain and ran in segments along the eastern coast. It constructed bridges and roads islandwide and built hospitals, sewage systems, public wells, and dams for water reservoirs and irrigation systems. The Japanese introduced new agricultural varieties (such as Hawaiian sugarcane) and new processing techniques (e.g., for camphor), and built modern sugar mills (Ka 1995). They regulated the tea industry to ensure production of high-quality tea. Armed guards protected camphor workers against mountain Aborigine raids. Gold, coal, and sulphur were successfully extracted. Other plant products continued to be produced—rice, indigo, rattan, bamboo, sesame oil, tobacco, fruits. These public works and private industry projects had great effects on the population. Longtian (one of the places where I interviewed) had been a small community of a few dozen Aborigine households until the railroad went through and put in a station. Later, one of the major sugar mills was placed near there. Han came in large numbers, and Longtian became part of the small city of Guantian.

The Japanese government also invested in "developing" Taiwan's population. It began a public school system. The goal of compulsory education for all was never achieved, but schools reached an extraordinary number of pupils—mostly boys—in a very short time. The government made medical services, especially those of Japanese-trained midwives, more generally available. It instituted a criminal justice system in which the police and judges took no bribes. This incorruptibility was quite a departure from the Qing system—which was designed to keep people out of the courts, regardless of the legitimacy of their claims—and people flocked to raise old grievances (Davidson 1988 [1903]:609–610).

Despite the equality among Taiwanese before the law, the peoples of Taiwan were not accorded equality with Japanese. Day wages for skilled workers in 1903 were calculated on the basis of "race" and "class," with Japanese earning more than Taiwanese and first-class workers earning more than second-class workers (Davidson 1988 [1903]:600). In the 1920s and 1930s, Taiwanese activists, ranging from liberals to communists, worked for "home rule" (Chang 2000:54–62), but they had limited success in lessening the inequalities. In the early decades of Japanese rule, peoples from Taiwan were excluded from political participation and even from the study of law. Schools were segregated until 1922. Taiwanese were forbidden to marry Japanese. Such discrimination did ease somewhat in the 1930s, but there were other troubles then, related to Japan's imperialist expansions. In spite of these restrictions, many Taiwanese, especially the elite, became very "Japanized," particularly through education. Most Taiwanese who pursued education beyond elementary school were channeled into agricultural or medical studies. Some wealthy families sent their children to Japan for education. In later years, Taiwanese did come to be hired (in the lower ranks) by Japanese firms.

The Japanese did not radically alter most local cultural practices, though there were some exceptions. Japanese police enforced sanitation and hygiene measures—spitting in public was prohibited in cities, and police sometimes knocked holes in the walls of homes to "encourage" people to put in windows. The government officially discouraged foot-binding from 1905 onward, and banned it outright in 1915, with police ordering young girls' feet unbound and the practice stopped. The ban was effective, because local police made regular visits to homes as part of the household registration system. The Japanese colonial government did not generally interfere with local religious practices, although in one community where I interviewed a villagewide Aborigine rite involving nudity was forbidden by the Japanese after 1905 (Brown 1995:370–72). In the late 1930s, as part of the push to get civilians to gear up for war and be loyal subjects of the emperor, the Japanese suppressed traditional religious celebrations and ordered everyone to worship Shinto deities. In the communities where I interviewed, Japanese police destroyed all the deity images they could get their hands on. (Many images were saved, however, because the local people hid them, in one case in the nearby foothills.)

In virtually every interview I conducted, in every community, people told me that the Japanese police had come to every household and confiscated gold, silver, and Japanese money. No one was very certain of the year, but in relation to other local events, I believe this confiscation occurred around 1940. It made quite an impression on local people and certainly disillusioned many of them in their belief that the Japanese colonialists were strict but fair. The fate of Taiwanese men who served the Japanese Imperial Army during World War II further lowered the opinions of many of the people I interviewed about the Japanese.[22] The Japanese period in Taiwan ended after World War II: the terms of the Japanese surrender included the return of Taiwan to Chinese authority.

WAR IN CHINA

To understand why the Chinese Nationalists came to rule Taiwan at the end of World War II and the Nationalist attitude towards Taiwanese who had been part of the hated Japanese empire requires a brief look at events in China during the first half of the twentieth century. While Japan developed Taiwan as a model colony, Chinese and foreigners carved up China. In 1911 the Qing dynasty fell. The Republic of China was eventually formed in 1912 but was shaky from its beginnings. Warlords with their own personal armies held actual control over local territory. Opium production and addiction skyrocketed. Capitalizing on World War I, Japan made further incursions into China's territory and economy. The economic gap between rich and poor, landlords and tenants, and factory owners and workers grew exponentially. Foreign investments in China in industry and railroads remained high in spite of China's instability, and foreign profits at China's expense remained even higher.

Intellectuals formed political groups, including the Nationalist Party (*guomindang* or GMD) of Sun Yat-sen (Sun Zhongshan) and the Chinese Communist Party (CCP), in an effort to put China on a stable political course. Chinese warlords and foreign imperialists, especially the British, viciously suppressed strikes by workers and demonstrations by students. In 1922–23, advisors from the Soviet Union brokered an alliance between the GMD and the CCP, and in 1925, with troops led by Chiang Kai-shek, they began to rout the southeastern warlords. After Sun Yat-sen's death in 1925, Chiang took control of the GMD, and tensions between the GMD and the CCP grew. After 1927, the GMD and the CCP largely fought each other, although they periodically allied themselves against common enemies—first the warlords and then the Japanese. From 1931 to 1936, the GMD, which was focused on wiping out the CCP, largely accommodated Japanese military incursions into China. The Japanese took Manchuria and forced the Chinese to withdraw troops from Shanghai and part of Hebei Province, creating neutral zones favorable to Japan and leaving Beijing unprotected. While Chiang ordered GMD and allied troops to fight the Communists, Japanese incursions convinced many Chinese, including some of Chiang's generals, that the Japanese were the real enemy.

In the summer of 1937, a series of incidents culminated in full-scale war with Japan. Within a year, the Japanese captured all of eastern China, in particularly brutal warfare and appalling casualty rates that color Chinese opinions of Japanese to this day.[23] Chinese forces were isolated—the GMD in Sichuan, the CCP in Shaanxi. After a period of nominal alliance against the Japanese, relations between the GMD and the CCP again broke down into armed confrontations by early 1941. The entry of the United States into the war after Pearl Harbor changed the situation dramatically. Most U.S. aid went to the GMD, even as American military commanders grew more and more horrified by GMD corruption and forced "conscription." Like the wealthy landlords, financiers, industrialists, merchants, and foreign imperialists with whom the GMD had allied itself, many GMD officials amassed large personal profits. They took bribes, held up troops' pay to play the stock market, and stole outright. Ordinary soldiers stole from ordinary people to survive. The CCP, meanwhile, honed its guerrilla warfare techniques out of necessity and expanded its base of support among the ordinary people who made up the bulk of China's population—farmers and urban workers.[24]

The abrupt end of the war, with Japan's surrender in 1945, caught both the GMD and the CCP unprepared. Each rushed to accept surrenders from Japanese in strategic cities. With Soviet help, the CCP used Manchuria as a base to build up its military forces for the final confrontation with the GMD. Meanwhile the GMD—its troops demoralized and its leadership weakened by corruption and infighting—struggled to set up a government in the areas formerly controlled by Japan, including Taiwan. Inflation spiraled out of control, Communist-infiltrated unions called strikes, and Chiang insisted on fighting the Communists in Manchuria, in spite of repeated advice to pull his troops back behind the Great Wall and consolidate his power there. CCP victories accumulated, and they held all of northern China, including Beijing, by February 1949. Between April and October 1949, the Communists took the rest of China, with relatively little resistance as many GMD troops switched sides en masse. On October 1, 1949, Mao Zedong formally announced the founding of the People's Republic of China.

THE NATIONALIST MARTIAL LAW PERIOD (1947–87)

Nationalist troops landed in Taiwan in December 1945 to claim the island for China. Although Taiwanese initially welcomed the return to Chinese rule, and the troops which represented such rule, their sentiments soon changed (cf. Chang 2000:62–65). GMD troops had been feared on the mainland, where they had raped and looted, killed people and animals, and forced young men into service as soldiers or porters under the name of "conscription." Taiwanese, who had been part of the Japanese empire, were treated at least as badly, with little recourse for grievance or protection. GMD officials also continued their corrupt practices, seizing all Japanese property—public and private—and considerable Taiwanese property as well. Portable pieces of Taiwan's infrastructure left by the Japanese, including raw materials, equipment, and goods, were sold by Nationalist officials for personal profit in Hong Kong and Shang-hai. Inflation skyrocketed—the inflation rate was 3,400 percent in 1949 and was not reduced to 3 percent until 1961.[25]

The national language—required in schools, government offices, busi-nesses, and any public place—changed overnight from Japanese, which had been previously taught in schools, to Mandarin Chinese, which most people in Taiwan could neither speak nor understand. (Mandarin Chi-nese is mutually unintelligible with Minnan—also called Taiwanese—and Kejia, the Chinese languages spoken in Taiwan by Hoklo and Hakka, respectively.) Mainlanders who came to Taiwan knew Mandarin, hav-ing learned it at home, in school, or in the military. This change put Tai-wanese at a tremendous disadvantage. Teachers scrambled to find texts in Chinese and taught in Minnan (or Kejia) until they themselves had learned enough Mandarin to struggle through their classes. Teachers learn-ing the language in this fashion were naturally influenced by their native tongue, marking their speech as different than Mainlanders'. Even decades later, Taiwan Mandarin shows clear Minnan (Taiwanese) influence (e.g., Kubler 1985).

On February 28, 1947—known in Taiwan as "2:28"—rebellion broke out in Taiwan. At first, the Taiwanese gained the upper hand, seizing many of the important urban centers.

> Soon, however, military force and deceptive promises from the Nationalists [GMD] persuaded the Taiwanese to lay aside their arms and to open nego-tiations. As a participant told [Hill Gates] bitterly, "Under the Japanese, we learned to trust the word of the authorities. The Nationalists betrayed that trust; they will never have it again." Between ten and twenty thousand activists were rounded up and shot—by the sides of roads, from bridges, at a large open racetrack. The Nationalists hunted down survivors of this bloodbath during the following months, sending many more to torture and jail. In a few weeks, the liberal-minded, educated, and generally pro-Japanese middle class was virtually destroyed. People whose father, brother, or aunt had been implicated in the events of 2:28 were barred from gov-ernment work, including schoolteaching, and remained under a dangerous cloud of suspicion for decades. The government's violent response to the 2:28 uprising eliminated much of the potential Taiwanese leadership, ter-rorized the population, and left the Mainlanders firmly in control. (Gates 1987:45–46)

One Taiwanese person I know, whose brother was arrested in the round-up following the 2:28 Incident, told me that her father, a Japanese-trained medical doctor, burned his entire library of Japanese books at that time, afraid that possessing books in Japanese would be used against the family.

Ong Jok-tik (Wang Yude), a scholar who lost an older brother and was forced into exile in 1949, writes (1999:157):

> Only now [with the abuse by Chinese officials in Taiwan] did the Taiwanese begin to miss the Japanese period. The Taiwanese despised the Japanese and had called them "dogs." "Dogs" bark, but "dogs" will watch the door for you. Chinese are "pigs." "Pigs" are good for nothing except stuffing themselves. (Translated in Chang 2000:70n37)

In the context of such political, economic, and emotional upheaval, the Mainlanders kept coming. Between 1945 and 1949, an estimated one to two million Mainlanders, roughly half of them soldiers, came to Taiwan fleeing the Communist unification of China (Corcuff 2000:72). A purge followed, with Chiang Kai-shek eliminating those he suspected of disloyalty in the name of hunting Communists.

Expecting an immediate Communist invasion of Taiwan, the Truman Administration promised that the U.S. would *not* provide military aid or advice to the Nationalists. No invasion came, perhaps because of a realistic assessment of how difficult it would be to win the island. Then, in June 1950, North Korean troops crossed the thirty-eighth parallel and invaded South Korea. In response, Truman sent U.S. troops based in Japan to South Korea and ordered the U.S. Seventh Fleet to patrol the Taiwan Strait as a "neutralization" move, to prevent China from attacking Taiwan.[26] Thus, the Korean War saved the Nationalist Party and began an era of military and political alliance between Taiwan, bearing the title of the Republic of China, and the U.S.

Under pressure from the U.S., Chiang gave permission for land reform. Liberal members of the GMD, who had long advocated land reform on the mainland to no avail, managed it on Taiwan, buying land with government stocks and bonds—nearly worthless at the time but quite valuable by the end of the century—and reselling it with ten-year mortgages, which were lower than the previous tenancy rents. The government designated only three hectares (7.2 acres) as enough land for a family farm and forced people who owned more land than that to sell it to the government. They gave tenants the right of first purchase. The people I interviewed were all affected by this reform. It gave people who had been struggling all their lives to get enough to eat a little security and hope, but these benefits came at the expense of neighbors, some of whom had only had a little to begin with. Wealthy landlords, with vast holdings, were a small percentage of the population.

In addition to improving the standing of the Nationalists in much of

the countryside, land reform contributed to a shift in Taiwan's population from primarily rural to primarily urban. "By keeping landholdings
small, the policy meant that many farm children would have to leave the
land and go into other occupations. This created a pool of cheap labor
for industry when it began to expand" (Gates 1987:51). Since few farm
families even today can survive purely on agricultural production, most
have at least one family member engaged in wage labor. In Toushe, the
most remote of the villages in which I worked, this urban-rural split was
visibly apparent in 1991–92. Most of the eighteen- to forty-five-year-old
men in the village were gone during the week, living in or near an urban
area to work—at factories, as truck drivers, and so on. They returned
to the village only on the weekends to see their wives and families.

Industry expanded in the 1960s and 1970s, successfully exporting tex-
tiles, footwear, plastics, and electronics to the U.S. Taiwan's economic
growth followed a dual mode of industrialization, with a small number
of large state-owned enterprises—mostly monopolies such as Tai-Power,
China Petroleum, the banking industry, public transportation, and the
Monopoly Bureau of Wine and Tobacco—and a proliferation of private medium- and small-sized enterprises (Chang 1994, Gold 1986,
Greenhalgh 1984). These different modes are also linked to ethnicity
and politics—the state-owned enterprises are largely run and staffed by
Mainlanders, while the smaller private enterprises are owned, run, and
staffed by Taiwanese (Gates 1981, Chang 1994:118, Hsiao and So 1996).
Earnings from working for large enterprises often funded small-business
expansion.

Compulsory education was expanded so that now it is virtually universal, for girls and boys. By the late 1970s, over 90 percent of the population was literate (e. g., Chang 2000:66). Admission to high school and
university, which is (still) based on entrance exams, was once limited to
a small percentage of the population, but by 1991, 86 percent of middle
school students attended high school and 52 percent of high school students attended college as well (Bureau of Statistics 1992:22). Two years
of military service is required from all able-bodied males, and it is generally completed after schooling is finished. In the small villages where I
worked, this experience outside the home community had many social
effects, including a rise in men's choosing their own wives, often women
they met at the site of their military service. Medical care is also more
generally available to ordinary people than in the past, through public
health clinics in every subcounty unit. Mortality rates, especially for children, have dropped. Family planning nurses make the rounds, visiting

rural communities by motor scooter, and the average number of children per family has dropped. Most of the elderly people I interviewed saw only some siblings survive to adulthood, whereas most of their own (five to eight) children survived. Their children chose to limit their own off-spring to two or three.

With increasing prosperity, a consumer economy has taken off in Taiwan. By the early 1990s, the vast majority of households in Taiwan had refrigerators, color televisions, telephones, washing machines, and motor-cycles (Bureau of Statistics 1992:21). Ownership of VCRs, air conditioners, and cars was also on the rise. Traffic became a problem because so many people have private cars, and the government constructed a second north-south highway to alleviate traffic. Gambling—whether in one of the illegal lotteries or legally on the stock market—picked up, as did tourism and the degree of conspicuous consumption in weddings, funerals, and religious festivals. The increasing rate of reconstructing and expanding temples suggests that religious donations also increased.

In the midst of this "economic miracle," Taiwan's people faced strict political limitations (e.g., Gold 1986, Weller 1999, Chang 2000:65–69). The Nationalists continued a modified version of the Japanese household registration system as a means of monitoring the population (cf. Gates 1987:63); it is still in practice in Taiwan today. From the beginning of Nationalist rule in Taiwan until 1986, there was only one party—the Nationalist Party—headed by Chiang Kai-shek until he died in 1975 and then by his son, Chiang Ching-kuo. The central government was filled with Mainlanders, representing such mainland districts as Sichuan and Hubei, and focused for decades on winning back the mainland. Self-administration was granted at local levels of government, and local elections began in 1950. In spite of Taiwanese political participation at the local levels, Taiwanese were increasingly rare as one moved up the political ladder, because the Nationalist Party had the final say in the nomination and appointment process of local leaders.

Starting in the early 1970s, a "Taiwanization" process began in the Nationalist Party. In other words, the Nationalist ruling clique brought more of the Taiwanese elite into the party, including Lee Teng-hui, who would later become Taiwan's first Taiwanese president. Taiwanization, however, did not mean democratization (e.g., Chang 1994:115). People in Taiwan were allowed to elect some legislative representatives, due to the aging of lifelong representatives elected in the 1940s on the mainland, but these election processes were strictly controlled by the Nationalist Party. Political opposition of any form, but most especially advocacy of Taiwan independence, continued to be treated as sedition, punishable by imprisonment and even execution.

UNDER THE "TAIWAN NATIONALIST PARTY" (THE POST–MARTIAL LAW PERIOD)

World events in the mid-1980s leading to the liberalization and democratization of authoritarian regimes—such as the overthrow of Marcos in the Philippines, the retreat of South Korea's Chun Doo Hwan, and Gorbachev's program of *glasnost* in the USSR—were not lost on the GMD or on Taiwanese activists considered *dangwai* (lit., "outside the party," where *the* party was the GMD). In March 1986, dangwai activists organized a protoparty. Surprisingly, President Chiang Ching-kuo responded with tolerance, and on September 28, 1986, these activists formally and publicly established the Democratic Progressive Party (DPP). After a few tense days, Chiang accepted the new party, although the Legislative Yuan did not formally legalize political opposition parties until January 1989 (Gold 1994:56). In July 1987, shortly before his death, Chiang lifted martial law, setting the stage for democratization and the liberalization measures that fostered a Taiwanese identity (discussed in chapter 1). Lee Teng-hui, who had been Chiang's vice-president, became the first Taiwanese president in 1988, when he was appointed president after Chiang's death, and he became the first democratically elected president in 1996. When the opposition DPP candidate, Chen Shui-bian, became the second democratically elected president in 2000, Lee oversaw the peaceful transition of power from the GMD to the new ruling party.

In the late 1980s, the new ability to travel freely to the PRC led to huge rates of economic investment there by people from Taiwan. In 1990, Taiwan's investment there was second only to Japan's, with U.S. investment third (cf. Hsiao and So 1996:3). Economic downturns in 1997 and 2001 have led to increased concerns about Taiwan's degree of dependence on investment in and trade with the PRC. Nevertheless, high rates of investment in China continue, so people of Taiwan frequently travel there, creating personal experiences that shape their views.

Independence, another previously forbidden topic, also became part of public debate in the post–martial law period. Not only did the DPP make Taiwan independence part of its party platform, provoking anti-DPP statements from Beijing, but Lee Teng-hui appears to have been working towards an eventual declaration of Taiwan independence from China. In the summer of 1994, Lee publicly referred to the GMD as the

"Taiwan Nationalist Party" *(taiwan guomindang)* implying Taiwan's status as a nation *(guo)*.[27] In June 1995, Lee obtained a U.S. visa as a private citizen, as opposed to a head of state, to give the prestigious Olin Lecture at Cornell University, where he had obtained his Ph.D. in 1968. There, Lee emphasized that Taiwan peacefully became a democracy yet is still internationally isolated (see *Free China Journal,* June 16, 1995:7–8 for the text of the Olin Lecture). Upon his return to Taiwan, he went further, saying "What the Republic of China needs the most is an international affirmation of its sovereignty" (see *Free China Journal,* June 16, 1995:1 for the text of the speech). Sovereignty, of course, implies national status, since no one talks about the sovereignty of the state of Illinois or of Hubei Province. At the same time, Taiwan pressed for membership in the United Nations, arguing that "The 21 million people in the Republic of China on Taiwan [are] without due representation" (advertisement in *The New York Times,* June 26, 1995:A13), thereby implying that the PRC representative to the UN does not represent the people of Taiwan.[28] In the same vein, Lee's suggestion on German radio in July 1999 that further talks between Taiwan and China should be conducted on a state-to-state basis implies that Taiwan is a state which should be treated as China's political equal.

Such remarks gave Lee a reputation in the news media for speaking without thinking about the consequences, but Lee appears to have been engaged in a deliberate, if delicate, strategy of moving toward independence. After Lee's 1995 visit to Cornell, there was public speculation, for example, in the *Free China Journal* (June 16, 1995:2), that he would visit Japan under similar circumstances, since he attended Kyoto University as an undergraduate. Consolidating Japanese support makes sense, because Taiwan will need the support of both the U.S. and Japan to manage a declaration of independence. Such a trip did not materialize during his term of office, I suspect because Japan was not willing to give him a visa as a private citizen while he was still head of state. Retirement from office has put him in a unique position for international diplomacy—he is no longer a head of state, but as the elder statesman who presided over Taiwan's democratization, he has sufficient respect and experience to pursue unofficial diplomatic missions. Lee's (1999) book on democracy and identity in Taiwan appears calculated to place Lee in such a position. Chen Shui-bian, who became president in 2000, does not appear to have used Lee in such a capacity. Chen asserted, upon taking office, that Taiwan does not need to declare independence, since it already *is* independent. Speaking as the chair of the DPP in the summer of 2002, however, Chen raised the possibility of a referendum on reunification with China, something which the PRC strongly opposes. Party delegates were shown on Taiwan television cheering in response. Interesting political maneuvers undoubtedly lie ahead.

Plains Aborigines and Taiwanese Identity

Plains aborigines disappear twice from the historical discussion, only to reappear in the late twentieth century. These shifts relate to identity changes from plains Aborigine to Hoklo and back again. In chapters 3 and 4, I argue that sociopolitical and demographic changes drove these identity changes. In preparation for that argument, I want to place the identity changes in the historical context outlined above.

In the early twentieth century, a colonial intervention by the Japanese government altered social circumstances to such an extent that remaining descendants of plains Aborigines in southwestern Taiwan were able to take on a Hoklo identity. I refer to this change as the long route to Han, because identity change did not occur even after much cultural change. Throughout the martial law period, these long-route Han maintained a Hoklo or Taiwanese identity.

With the political changes beginning in the late 1980s, however, people began to reexamine the identity of the long-route Han. As part of the formation of a new Taiwanese identity, the long-route Han came to be seen, once again, as plains Aborigines. Chapter 3 examines these two twentieth-century changes.

CHAPTER 3

"We Savages Didn't Bind Feet"

Culture, Colonial Intervention, and Long-Route Identity Change

In villages along the edge of the foothills to the central mountains—Toushe, Jibeishua, and Longtian (see figure 2, at the beginning of the book)—descendants of plains Aborigines maintained an Aborigine identity in spite of some intermarriage with Hoklo men and significant cultural and linguistic changes.[1] They maintained this identity through the Qing period and did not finally cross the border to Han until after the Japanese colonial government mandated a ban on footbinding throughout Taiwan. Because footbinding was the last marker used to distinguish between Hoklo and Aborigines, its removal from the Han cultural repertoire allowed Toushe, Jibeishua, and Longtian to take on a Hoklo identity in the 1930s. I call this relatively recent identity change "the long route to Han" because so much cultural change occurred before the identity change. In other words, the substantial changes in their cultural practices did not induce the change in their identity classification. As we shall see, this case demonstrates the fluidity of identity I discussed in chapter 1, because the border to Han shifted around these villagers.

Toushe, Jibeishua, and Longtian are important to a consideration of the new narratives of Taiwan's unfolding because they are actual cases of the kind of identity change touted in these narratives. Moreover, the identity changes occurred recently enough that in the early 1990s, when I did my fieldwork, it was still possible to find out about the change from people who had experienced it in their lifetimes. Furthermore, the late

1990s witnessed another identity change, due to influence of the new narratives themselves.

In this chapter, I reconstruct when and how these identity changes occurred. After establishing that the villages' identity was Hoklo when I did my field research, I show that Toushe, Jibeishua, and Longtian were considered Aborigine at the beginning of the twentieth century. At that time, only the fact that residents did not bind women's feet visibly distinguished Toushe, Jibeishua, and Longtian from neighboring Hoklo villages. There were other differences in customs between these Aborigine villages and nearby Hoklo communities, as indicated by interview reports and observation of religious practices in Danei, a village near Toushe classified as Hoklo, and interview reports of other individual Hoklo in and near Toushe, Jibeishua, and Longtian.[2] As we shall see, these other differences were largely invisible and thus did not matter to classification of the villages. When and why these other differences disappeared, however, are crucial to understanding what allowed the identity change to occur at all. It was Japanese colonial intervention in banning footbinding that spurred identity change, not intermarriage and not cultural changes.

Having established when and how the identity change occurred, I turn to an analysis of the contributions that these long-route Han have made to Taiwanese culture: little or none, contrary to what the new narratives of unfolding suggest. Long-route Han adopted the pre-existing Hoklo culture of their neighbors, first practicing their customs and later beginning to accept the cultural ideas behind the customs. Finally, I examine effects of recent public interest in Toushe, Jibeishua, and Longtian on the villages themselves. As real examples of the new narratives of unfolding, their identity at the turn of the twenty-first century matters. It has shifted to plains Aborigine again, a shift with implications for the nationalist agenda of the very narratives of unfolding that prompted the shift.

LATE-TWENTIETH-CENTURY IDENTITY

From the beginning of my fieldwork, people made it very clear to me that the local identity in Toushe, Jibeishua, and Longtian was Han. In 1991, shortly after my arrival in Toushe, a young man who attended the prestigious National Taiwan University in Taibei came to talk to me about my research while he was home on a brief visit. Upon learning that my focus was cultural and identity changes, he assured me that 99 percent of the people in Toushe are Han. During the course of my research, I found that many young people were unaware of their Aborigine heritage until they heard their grandparents discussing it. Hoklo identity had been pervasive enough, at least since the 1970s, that young people had never had any reason to question their status as Hoklo.

Moreover, the people I interviewed made it very clear to me that they considered themselves Hoklo Taiwanese. When I first began interviewing people in Toushe, most of them readily responded that the local deity Thai Tsoo was Aborigine but that the village itself was no longer Aborigine. Thai Tsoo, they explained, is the deity of the place and whoever lives in Toushe must worship her. Some people referred to, but did not show me, patrilineal genealogies tracing an ancestor to Fujian Province, on the Chinese mainland, to verify that their own family was Hoklo.

When I asked what happened to the Aborigines who used to live there, they simply said that they were gone. On several occasions, when I pressed the question—Did they migrate? Were they killed?—people referred to a prominent, older man in the village with "black skin," darker than the other villagers; a "high nose," higher and more prominent than my Western nose, they pointed out; and "round eyes," like my Western eyes, they said.[3] They said that this man was the last Aborigine. Two of the people who described this man in this way were agnatically related to him, sharing the same surname, yet they insisted that he was Aborigine and they were not. They clearly perceived that the village had changed identities—become Hoklo—even though this man had not.

One man who told me that his village used to be considered Aborigine became nervous afterward. First, he denied the Aborigine identity he had just mentioned, and then he ended the interview shortly thereafter. I think part of villagers' discomfort in discussing their Aborigine past lay in the terminology. Elderly people in these communities had no ethnic term for their Aborigine ancestors except "savages" (T., *hoan-a*). Because of the polite terms in Mandarin, the national language—*pingpu zu* (lit., "plains tribes") and *yuanzhumin* (lit., "original inhabitants")—I initially did not believe my first translator when she said that there was no such polite term for Aborigines in Minnan, the local language.[4] She graciously humored me in one interview, using literal translations in Minnan of the polite Mandarin terms. The elderly couple being interviewed were bewildered about what she meant until she finally said "hoan-a." Then they understood. However, it was simply not possible to have conversations about people's Aborigine heritage when forced to ask "Were your ancestors savages?"

One day, by accident, I discovered an indirect way to ask about Aborigine heritage. During an early interview in Longtian, I was uncertain which of several topics to pursue next, so I asked a throwaway question—one I already knew the answer to—to buy time to think. I asked if the Longtian woman's mother or grandmother had had bound feet. I knew that they could not have—the Japanese household registers were quite clear that few women in Toushe, Jibeishua, and Longtian had bound feet—but I thought that by the time the question was translated into Minnan, answered in Minnan, and translated back into Mandarin, I would know what I wanted to ask next. The Longtian woman's response shocked me, her granddaughter who was present and my translator. She said, "We savages didn't bind feet" (T., *guan hoan-a bo pak-kha*). This throwaway question broke open my research because, in almost every subsequent interview, asking this question—whether the person's mother or grandmother had bound feet—elicited the term "hoan-a." By allowing the people I interviewed to bring up this pejorative term themselves, I was finally able to have direct and lengthy conversations about their Aborigine heritage.

I want to emphasize, however, that these people who so generously discussed their Aborigine past with me made it very clear that they did not think of themselves as Aborigines in the early 1990s when I interviewed them. They applied the term "hoan-a" to their parents and grandparents and those generations, and to their village in the past. They *never* applied the term to their children or grandchildren or to their contemporary community, other than to refer to the Aborigine status of their deity. In the present, they referred to themselves and their descendants as Taiwanese, which locally meant Hoklo. Most people were careful not to apply the term "hoan-a" to themselves, even in the past. Only a few people explicitly talked about having been called "hoan-a" themselves, and those who did relate such stories made it clear that such taunting occurred when they were very young, at a time when most Hoklo women still had bound feet.

EARLY-TWENTIETH-CENTURY IDENTITY AND INTERMARRIAGE

Historical records identify Toushe, Jibeishua, and Longtian as plains Aborigine in the early twentieth century, with the exception of one Han satellite settlement of Toushe (Zhang 1951, Lu 1956). As discussed in chapter 1, the ways in which people primarily claim identity—through ancestry and through culture—suggest that identity, culture, and ances-

try are closely linked. Similarly, the importance of patriarchy and the patrilineal inheritance of surnames in Han society suggests that people with
Han patrilineal ancestry would acquire Han identity relatively easily. Contrary to these expectations, some people in Toushe, Jibeishua, and Longtian *did* have patrilineal Hoklo ancestry yet they and their communities
were still socially categorized as plains Aborigine. Census records from
the Japanese period (1935) list the majority of village residents in Toushe (64.9 percent) and Jibeishua (76 percent) as plains Aborigine.[5] Longtian was a rural Aborigine village in the earliest memories of the oldest
people I interviewed there (ca. 1915); however, it rapidly became a small
Hoklo-majority city after the Japanese colonial government completed
the north-south railroad and put in a railroad station there.

The household register records, which begin in 1905 and which Japanese police kept with the aid of local men educated in Japanese, provide
documentary evidence that the distinction between the descendants of
Han and the descendants of plains Aborigines was difficult to identify
within these communities.[6] In the last years before the Japanese discontinued "racial" classifications, there were often "mistakes"—places
where someone originally wrote *"fu"* for Hoklo and later crossed it out
and wrote in *"shu"* for plains Aborigine. (See the genealogy in figure 6
for examples of such mistakes in one lineage.) I did not count all the
mistakes made, but in Toushe there were 15 people (1.3 percent of the
population of 1,126) in registers that were open between 1905 and 1910
whose classification was never clarified.[7] Ten people had both *"shu"* and
"fu" recorded and five people had both *"shu"* and *"guang"* (for Hakka)
recorded, even though people whom I interviewed reported that no
Hakka had lived in the village. My impression is that such mistakes occurred most often with newly registered individuals, such as newborns
and migrants. What these "mistakes" mean in human terms is that neither the Japanese policemen *nor their local interpreters* were able to distinguish people as Hoklo or plains Aborigines, even when the person was
standing in front of them! Interview reports agree with this documentary evidence but refine it to suggest that Hoklo and plains Aborigine
men were hard to distinguish. Men from Toushe, Jibeishua, and Longtian reportedly could pass for poor Hoklo in nearby market towns because of their Hoklo language, dress, and customs. Women, however,
could not pass as Hoklo because they did not have bound feet.

Toushe, Jibeishua, and Longtian were considered plains Aborigine
communities despite some intermarriage between village residents and
Hoklo. People I interviewed often reported Hoklo men who married ux-

orilocally into their families. In spite of Han preference for virilocal marriages (where a woman marries to her husband's household), a significant minority of Han men throughout Taiwan married uxorilocally (where a man marries to his wife's household) (e.g., Chuang and Wolf 1995, Wolf and Huang 1980, Wolf 1995). Generally, only Han men whose families were too poor to afford a brideprice married in this fashion. Interview reports suggest that uxorilocal marriages with Han men constituted virtually all the interethnic marriages (and a significant proportion of all the uxorilocal marriages) in Toushe, Jibeishua, and Longtian.

Unfortunately, the rate of intermarriage is difficult to estimate because interview reports and household register data yield different estimates. The Japanese-period household registers for Toushe (including the Han satellite settlement) from 1905 to 1910 yield an estimate that 3.3 percent of the population had "mixed" Hoklo and Aborigine ancestry (see table 1).[8] The people in the Hoklo category whose mothers were present in the register and listed as plains Aborigine constitute this low figure, because I use only marriages between Hoklo men and plains Aborigine women to calculate the intermarriage rate for the census data.[9] In other words, I do not include people in the plains Aborigine category with a Hoklo mother as part of the "mixed" population. These Hoklo women, although presumably of at least patrilineal Hoklo ancestry, were probably adopted and therefore not culturally Hoklo.[10] The registers defined identity in terms of biological fathers, but I define it in terms of the social parents.

Ethnic intermarriage, by definition, occurs only when the marital couple includes people of different ethnic identities. What is the real ethnic identity of a woman born to a Hoklo couple in a Hoklo village and given up for adoption as an infant to an Aborigine couple in a largely Aborigine village? Adopted daughters of plains Aborigines in Toushe, Jibeishua, and Longtian were exposed to the same cultural ideas as daughters of plains Aborigines. They experienced the same treatment by villagers and outsiders as daughters. For example, they did not have bound feet and were called "savages" by outsiders as a result. They appear to have been recognized as plains Aborigine by other villagers too, because interview reports of Hoklo women marrying plains Aborigine men (before 1930) were notably rare.

We cannot know, of course, whether the classifications in the household registers matched local classifications. There appears to have been a tendency in imperial historical records to refer to entire villages as "plains Aborigine" or "Hoklo" (e.g., Zhang 1951, Lu 1956). How do

TABLE I. ETHNIC IDENTITY
IN TOUSHE, 1905–1910

Plains Aborigine		
Mother Hoklo	9	(0.8%)
Mother plains Aborigine or not present	780	(69.3%)
Total plains Aborigine	789	(70.1%)
Hoklo		
Mother plains Aborigine	37	(3.3%)
Mother Hoklo or not present	285	(25.3%)
Total Hoklo	322	(28.6%)
Unclear classification	15	(1.3%)
Total village population	1,126	(100%)

NOTE: Figures come from hand-counted household registers for people alive 1905–1910.

we know the Japanese household registers do not merely reflect this bias, despite their efforts to identify individuals? It is not unreasonable to suppose that Hoklo men who married uxorilocally would not be remembered as Hoklo after two or three generations. If so, the 1905–1910 household registers reflect intermarriage rates for a generation, or at most two generations, since we would not know whether the "plains Aborigine" wives of uxorilocally married Hoklo men were themselves of mixed ancestry.

Interview reports suggest a higher rate of intermarriage than the household registers do.[11] For Toushe, Jibeishua, and Longtian combined, 11.8 percent of all reported marriages in their parents' and grandparents' generations were between plains Aborigine women and known Han men (table 2). This estimate is almost four times the estimate for Toushe from the household registers. For Toushe alone, 21.4 percent of all reported marriages in the parents' and grandparents' generations were to known Han men (table 3). This estimate is seven times the estimate for Toushe from the household registers! This difference is all the more striking because the interview data is biased toward the classification of plains Aborigines.[12]

The difference between the estimate based on household registers and the estimate based on my interviews may reflect, in part, a bias in the original classification in the registers. However, it may also reflect a higher probability of bringing in a Han son-in-law for marriage to an adopted daughter (who would almost certainly be registered as Hoklo), because one reason for adopting a child is that there were no surviving biological children (I discuss adoptions further below). The registers consider these marriages Hoklo-Hoklo marriages, but I classify them as plains

TABLE 2. ETHNIC ORIGIN OF SPOUSES IN
PARENTS' AND GRANDPARENTS' GENERATIONS
(Toushe, Jibeishua, and Longtian)

Form of marriage	# marriages	Plains Aborigine	Han	Unknown or mixed
Uxorilocal	43 (50.6%)	19 (22.4%)	10 (11.8%)	14 (16.5%)
Virilocal	42 (49.4%)	35 (41.2%)	2 (2.4%)	5 (5.9%)
Total	85 (100%)	54 (63.5%)	12 (14.1%)	19 (22.4%)

NOTE: Postmarital residence is within one of these communities. (Some column percentages are off due to rounding.)

Aborigine–Hoklo, because a child of whatever ancestry raised by Aborigine parents is socially and culturally Aborigine.

I think that the estimates of intermarriage based on interview reports are more reliable, which has an important implication for our understanding of identity change. If 11.8 percent of marriages in these villages were bringing in Hoklo men in each generation, then over several generations a significant proportion of the village populations would be patrilineally Han. This conclusion holds true even if there is some overlap in the families which brought in sons-in-law—that is, even if uxorilocally married Hoklo men showed a preference for Hoklo sons-in-law. Thus, plains Aborigines, Hoklo, and historical documents persistently classified Toushe, Jibeishua, and Longtian as plains Aborigine villages throughout the early twentieth century *in spite of actually increasing Hoklo patrilineal ancestry.*

I suggest that uxorilocally married Hoklo men were a primary means of cultural change for these long-route Han (cf. Brown 1995:140–43, 1996b:43–46). Thus, whatever the actual rates of intermarriage, the marriage of Hoklo men into the "plains Aborigine" communities is culturally significant because these men brought with them intimate knowledge of Hoklo culture. The increasingly Han society in which plains Aborigines and their descendants found themselves further introduced and reinforced sinicizing cultural change. Government decrees and economic structures—from basic market organization and schedules through taxation policies, schools, and so on—all used Han languages and operated on the basis of Han cultural ideas throughout the Qing period. The Japanese colonial government introduced changes in the economy and language in certain contexts but left undisturbed most Han cultural beliefs and values, and even language in most contexts.

At the beginning of the twentieth century, then, Hoklo patrilineal an-

TABLE 3. ETHNIC ORIGIN OF SPOUSES IN
PARENTS' AND GRANDPARENTS' GENERATIONS
(Toushe)

Form of marriage	# marriages	Plains Aborigines	Han	Unknown or mixed
Uxorilocal	19	9 (47.4%)	6 (31.6%)	4 (21%)
Virilocal	9	9 (100%)	0	0
Total	28	18 (64.3%)	6 (21.4%)	4 (14.3%)

NOTE: Postmarital residence is within Toushe.

cestry was actually increasing in Toushe, Jibeishua, and Longtian. How long such ancestry had been increasing is difficult to say. Some degree of intermarriage may have been going on since the seventeenth century. However, reductions in the benefits of Aborigine identity throughout the last half of the nineteenth century and the final loss of any remaining benefits with the transition to Japanese rule (see chapter 2) created a context in which Hoklo men may have been increasingly attractive as sons-in-law and husbands. Uxorilocally married Hoklo men could help mediate between villagers and the larger Han society, capitalizing on their personal contacts outside the village and their greater familiarity with Han social and cultural expectations. Nevertheless, the increasing presence of Han men in Toushe, Jibeishua, and Longtian did not change their status as Aborigine villages.

EARLY-TWENTIETH-CENTURY CULTURAL PRACTICES

Given that Toushe, Jibeishua, and Longtian were classified as plains Aborigine in the early twentieth century, it might be surprising to discover how closely these villages resembled poor Hoklo villages at that time. It is important to understand the social and cultural conditions common to the two kinds of villages, because the many Hoklo customs practiced in Toushe, Jibeishua, and Longtian show how persistent identity classifications can be and how little the adoption of cultural practices (including language) actually affected identity change.[13] What then were the similarities and differences between Hoklo villages and Toushe, Jibeishua, and Longtian? Poverty, although recognized as miserable, was not considered shameful in the same way that non-Han status was. Thus, throughout most of the twentieth century, people in Toushe, Jibeishua, and Longtian discussed their past differences from Han ideals as due to economic causes, not ethnic disparity. Moreover, many nearby Hoklo communities were just as poor, providing Hoklo infant girls for adoption and propertyless Hoklo men for uxorilocal marriages. Were the differences so pronounced as to justify a cultural basis for the identity distinction between Hoklo and plains Aborigines? I argue that differences other than footbinding were largely invisible to most Hoklo, because they resulted only in a somewhat higher or lower frequency of a particular custom, such as uxorilocal marriages; they did not result in the unexpected presence or total absence of a custom, as with footbinding. These invisible differences, however, aid our understanding of the process of identity change that did occur.

Practices Shared with the Hoklo

In spite of their non-Han identity, by 1915, the people in Toushe, Jibeishua, and Longtian were socially and culturally very similar to their poorest Hoklo neighbors.

Agriculture Toushe, Jibeishua, and Longtian were parts of Taiwan's capitalistic market economy.[14] Like their Han neighbors, residents of these communities practiced commercial agriculture by the end of the Qing period—growing primarily sugarcane in Toushe in the foothills and both rice and sugarcane in Jibeishua and Longtian on the plains. It is not clear exactly when these villages began practicing commercial agriculture. Officials in the early Qing period (e.g., Huang 1957 [1736] translated in Thompson 1969:116, Shepherd 1993:366) condemned Aborigines for not producing surplus rice for sale, seeing this behavior as a moral failure (Shepherd 1993:380). A 1752 gazetteer praised the farmers of Xingang, a village classified as Aborigine in the core area, implying their successful transition to commercial agriculture. Ancestors of some Toushe people reportedly came from Xingang.[15] They may have been migrating in part to avoid participating in commercial agriculture. Given current evidence, the most specific thing we can say about the transition to Han-style commercial agriculture in Toushe, Jibeishua, and Longtian is that it occurred sometime between 1750 and 1900.

Language By 1915, Toushe, Jibeishua, and Longtian residents spoke Minnan Chinese (or Taiwanese) as their first language, as did their Hoklo neighbors.[16] In the seventeenth century, upon contact with the Dutch, Aborigines spoke Austronesian languages.[17] The Dutch, Zheng, and Qing regimes all used Han interpreters and middlemen, suggesting that no Chinese language was in wide use in Aborigine villages through most, if not all of, the seventeenth century. Aborigines in the core area adopted Minnan much earlier than those in the foothills. A 1715 gazetteer, for instance, refers to core-area Aborigines circumventing their interpreter (Shepherd 1993:121, see also Brown 1995:438–439). By 1722, there were core-area Aborigine youths who could recite from the Confucian Analects (Thompson 1969:73, 85). But when did Minnan take over from Austronesian as Aborigines' first language? A Western missionary to Taiwan reported that in 1865 the sinicized descendants of plains Aborigines in Xingang "dress like the [Han] Chinese, and have forgotten their old language" (Pickering 1898:115). This report suggests that, by 1865, descendants of plains Aborigines in core areas had been Minnan-speaking for at least two or three generations, possibly from the 1790s.

The transition to Minnan occurred later among descendants of Aborigines in the foothills. William Pickering (1898:116) reports traveling in 1865 to a village in the foothills—possibly Toushe—to which some former Xingang villagers had migrated. There, he considered the people less sinicized and noted that "the old people retained a knowledge of the language spoken by their forefathers" (Pickering 1898:117). In other words, the young people spoke Minnan. The oldest people I interviewed reported that their parents and grandparents (who would have been born after Pickering's visit) could not speak any Aborigine language either. Thus, by the 1860s at the latest, Minnan was the standard language in these villages. By 1895, there were only a few elderly people in these areas "who remembered that [Austronesian] language and those [non-Han] customs" (Tsuchida et al. 1991:1).

Further confirmation that, by 1900, people in Toushe, Jibeishua, and Longtian had no knowledge of Austronesian languages lies in their use of "banana slang" (T., kin-chiu peh-a oe), a form of Minnan generated much like pig latin is generated from English.[18] The elderly people I interviewed reported that many of their parents knew this language and used it to respond to Han ethnic slurs and taunts, but none of them recognized banana slang as Minnan. In fact, some people thought it was an Aborigine language (T., hoan-a oe). Banana slang's primary reported usage—to respond to Han taunts—indicates that by the time the parents and grandparents of the people I interviewed were alive (circa 1870) there was no knowledge of Aborigine Austronesian languages. People told me that it was important not to let the Han understand precisely what was said, in order to avoid a fight, so they would probably have used Austronesian to respond to Han taunts had they been able to. Clearly, they were native speakers of Minnan, like their Hoklo neighbors.

Mortuary Practices   Another way in which the people of Toushe, Jibeishua, and Longtian were like their Hoklo neighbors is that they buried their dead rapidly, using the services of a Daoist priest unless they were Christian, and placed graves outside the community (Brown 1995: 388–89). These Han-style practices constitute significant changes from the practices described in early-seventeenth-century reports: dessicating corpses by fire and keeping them above ground for three years, with accompanying ritual observances, before burying them (see, for example, the 1603 report by Chen Di, translated in Thompson 1964:174, and a 1629 report by Candidius, a Dutch missionary, translated in Campbell 1903:21–22). When this shift occurred, however, is unclear.[19] People in Toushe, Jibeishua, and Longtian reported Daoist funerary rites with immediate burial for the earliest funerals that they could recall seeing—from the 1910s through the early 1930s. Their descriptions indicate that local funerary practices at that time generally followed the late-imperial standards described by Watson (1988), differing from the Han standards primarily by being simplified, less expensive versions, as one might expect in a poor area.

Marriage Form and Residence   By 1915, virilocal residence (the practice of living with the husband's family after marriage), prevalent among the Hoklo, was also common in Toushe, Jibeishua, and Longtian.[20] Virilocal residence represents a major departure from the postmarital residence at the time of Dutch contact. Early-seventeenth-century reports indicate that core-area Aborigines had matrilineally focused kinship relations—postmarital residence was first duolocal (husband and wife living apart) and then uxorilocal (living with the wife's family), and inheritance passed matrilineally (see Thompson 1964:173–74; Shepherd 1993:386; Blussé and Roessingh 1994:65, 68, 69, 73–74). By the early Dutch period, postmarital residence was reported as duolocal then neolocal (with husband and wife establishing a new home), although apparently inheritance remained matrilineal (Campbell 1903:19–21). After military victories over the Aborigines in1635 and 1636, the Dutch imposed changes in marital patterns, "encouraging" their "converts" to reside together immediately after marriage and to begin raising children at once (Campbell 1903:19–20, 162, 182–83, 186; Blussé and Roessingh

TABLE 4. UXORILOCAL AND
VIRILOCAL MARRIAGES, PARENTS'
AND GRANDPARENTS' GENERATIONS
(Toushe, Jibeishua, and Longtian)

	# marriages	Uxorilocal	Virilocal
Toushe	28	19 (67.9%)	9 (32.1%)
Jibeishua	39	17 (43.6%)	22 (56.4%)
Longtian[a]	18	7 (38.9%)	11 (61.1%)
Total	85	43 (50.6%)	42 (49.4%)

NOTE: Postmarital residence is within one of these communities. I use figures for within-village marriages because the people interviewed were not likely to know their parents' or grandparents' siblings
who married outside the village.
[a]The lower figure for Longtian could reflect the small sample size, or it could be due to the generally
younger age of the people interviewed there.

1994:70; Shepherd 1993:65–66, 1995:23–24). It is not clear whether the
Dutch encouraged uxorilocal, neolocal, or virilocal postmarital residence
among the Aborigines.[21] However, in 1722, Huang Shujing (a Qing Imperial Censor) reported both uxorilocal and virilocal postmarital residence as common in the plains Aborigines villages he visited (translated
in Thompson 1969:81, 83, 94, 101, 110, 119, 132–33).

Both uxorilocal and virilocal postmarital residence were still in practice in Toushe, Jibeishua, and Longtian at the turn of the twentieth century. However, there were differences—both among these villages and
between them and Hoklo communities—in the frequencies of different
forms of postmarital residence. First, consider the differences among Toushe, Jibeishua, and Longtian, based on the reports of people I interviewed
(see table 4). Uxorilocal marriages were very frequent in all three communities, but virilocal marriages were the majority in Jibeishua and
Longtian. Only in Toushe did uxorilocal marriages constitute a strong
majority of marriages.

Now consider the difference between Hoklo and plains Aborigine communities. Chuang and Wolf (1995:786, table 2), working from a database of Japanese-period household registers, report on the frequencies of
different types of marriage among plains Aborigine women and Hoklo
women in the same township *(xiang)* containing Toushe and Danei (see
table 5).[22] They suggest that, in the township as a whole, virilocal marriages were the majority for plains Aborigines but uxorilocal marriages
were still more than twice as frequent among plains Aborigines as they
were among the Hoklo. Unfortunately, Chuang's and Wolf's figures un-
dercount the percentage of uxorilocal marriages, because they catego-

TABLE 5. UXORILOCAL AND VIRILOCAL
MARRIAGES OF WOMEN IN DANEI TOWNSHIP

	# women	Uxorilocal marriages (%)	Virilocal marriages (%)	
			major	*minor*
Plains Aborigine	357	24.4	70.3	5.3
Hoklo	1,154	9.8	84.7	5.6

SOURCE: Chuang and Wolf (1995:786, Table 2).
NOTE: Only first marriages of women born 1881–1905 are included.

rized entire villages as Han or plains Aborigine, despite recognizing that
"[s]ome of these women [categorized by the authors as plains Aborig-
ine] were Han or at least identified themselves as Han" (Chuang and Wolf
1995:786).[23]

Minimally, the data from Chuang and Wolf (1995) and from my own
work indicate that, at the beginning of the twentieth century, both virilocal and uxorilocal postmarital residence were common among people
considered plains Aborigines in this area east of Tainan City where the
Jianan plain meets the foothills. Moreover, uxorilocal marriages were
more common among people classified as "Aborigines" than among
Hoklo in the same area. Given the limitations of the data from Chuang
and Wolf (1995), I rely on my data to suggest that, at the beginning of
the twentieth century, uxorilocal postmarital residence was at least an
acceptable alternative to virilocal marriages. It may even have been preferred in Toushe. (This difference from their Han neighbors is discussed
further below.)

Because it is relevant to our subsequent understanding of identity
change, let us examine postmarital residence by spouse's ethnicity. Interview reports indicate that in the early twentieth century, virilocal marriages of "plains Aborigines" were largely contracted with others classified as Aborigines (table 2 shows that 35 marriages, or 83.3 percent, of
42 total virilocal marriages occurred among plains Aborigines). Most of
the Han marrying into Toushe, Jibeishua, and Longtian were men marrying uxorilocally, although there were two reported virilocal marriages
to Han women. (These Han women were on their second or third marriage and brought one or more children with them to the marriage.)[24]
There may have been even more Han men marrying into the community, because many of the men whom I could not classify may well have
been Han. The reports for Toushe alone show even more clearly that

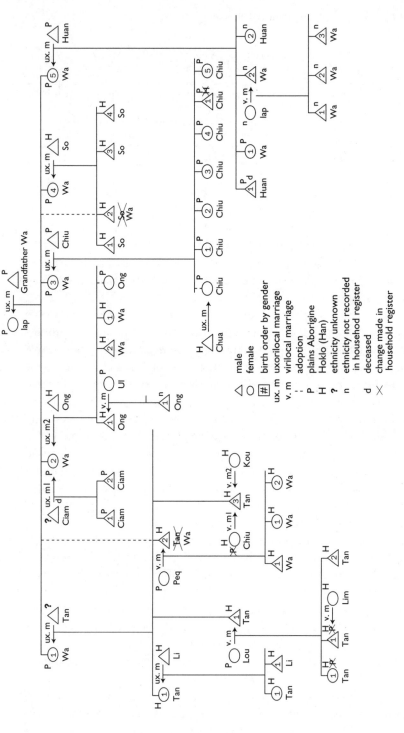

Figure 6. Wa family genealogy. The second sons of the first and third daughter were originally given their fathers' surnames, but they were later adopted by their grandfather and surnamed Wa. The children who received the Wa surname from birth did not need to be adopted.

in-marrying Han were men (see table 3). All of the virilocal marriages in Toushe were to other Aborigines, meaning that no Han women married in, while 31.6 percent of the uxorilocal marriages brought in men known to be Hoklo.

Consider the example of one prominent family in Toushe (see figure 6). It shows both that Hoklo men came in via uxorilocal marriage and that there was a trend toward virilocal marriage over time. In the 1880s, an Aborigine man, whom I will call Grandfather Wa, married uxorilocally in Toushe. His wife had at least five daughters who survived to adulthood.[25] By the time his daughters were ready to marry, Grandfather Wa was considered the richest man in town and owned a lot of land—everyone who mentioned him described him this way. He brought in sons-in-law for his five daughters—three Aborigine husbands and three Hoklo husbands, because one daughter remarried after her first husband died.[26] In the next generation, there are two uxorilocal marriages bringing in Hoklo men: for the oldest daughter's oldest daughter, and for the third daughter's adopted daughter. Although both uxorilocal and virilocal marriages were prominent among the earlier marriages, there is an increasing frequency of virilocal marriages later in time. (As we shall see, there was a trend across Toushe, Jibeishua, and Longtian for virilocal marriages to increase in frequency over the course of the twentieth century.)

There were, then, differences in the frequency of uxorilocal and virilocal marriages between Toushe, Jibeishua, and Longtian and their Hoklo neighbors. In spite of these frequency differences, I consider marriage form and postmarital residence to be largely shared by plains Aborigines and Hoklo at the beginning of the twentieth century, because, as I discuss further below, people at the time probably did not notice these frequency differences. Instead, they probably saw similar forms of marriage and postmarital residence existing in Toushe, Jibeishua, and Longtian, and Hoklo villages.

Surname and Property Inheritance   Uxorilocal postmarital residence included marriages that contracted a variety of rights and duties between the in-marrying husband and his wife's family. In Hoklo models of uxorilocal marriage, surname was closely linked to inheritance of property. By the early 1900s, surname and property were also linked in Toushe, Jibeishua, and Longtian, albeit not as tightly linked as among Hoklo in northern Taiwan.

Based on twentieth-century material from the predominantly Hoklo Haishan region of northern Taiwan (with some examples from nineteenth-century China), Wolf and Huang (1980:94–107) divide the continuous range of known uxorilocal marriages into three main categories, with "calling in a son-in-law for a specified time" (which was essentially a form of bride service) at one end of the continuum and "terminating the line" at the other. In between, there is a large "intermediate" category. In the "calling in a son-in-law for a specified time" and "intermediate" types, uxorilocally married husbands had no direct claim on their wife's family's property and, according to Wolf and Huang (1980:98–99), had the right to give some or all of their children their own surname. In the intermediate type, children who had their maternal grandfather's surname, and only those children, had rights to his property. How many and which specific children got which surname varied from marriage to marriage. In practice, the children's father—that is, the uxorilocally married man—often managed the property for his children, especially if they were still young when his father-in-law died. In "terminating the line," the third type, the uxorilocally married husband himself (in theory at least) had property rights, since he would drop his own surname and take his father-in-law's, thus accepting the rights and duties of a son.

Calling in a son-in-law for a specified time was the most common form of uxorilocal marriage among the people I interviewed and their relatives in Toushe, Jibeishua, and Longtian.[27] A son-in-law was needed for additional labor—most often to help cultivate rented land, since few people owned their own land, but frequently to bring in cash through outside wage labor. In Toushe, for example, one woman's family needed her uxorilocal husband to help them survive. She was the adopted daughter of her father's senior wife. (The junior "wife"—legally a concubine—had two daughters from her first marriage and a third daughter by this second marriage.) When the adoptive father died, the wives and their daughters had no property to split, only debts. In spite of the debts, the uxorilocally married man's wage earnings allowed them to provide a decent funeral. Often families called in a son-in-law for a specified time because the only surviving son was a boy when his older sister reached marriageable age and his aging parents needed help in the fields. In such cases, when the specified time was reached—when the son became old enough to take over responsibility for field labor—the son-in-law and his wife and their children would usually leave to establish their own home. They received no property when they left.

How families assigned surnames in uxorilocal marriages had implications for inheritance of property. Most children in Toushe, Jibeishua, and Longtian were assigned their father's surname (see table 6). In most

TABLE 6. ASSIGNMENT OF CHILDREN'S SURNAMES IN UXORILOCAL MARRIAGES
(Toushe, Jibeishua, and Longtian)

	# marriages	% of all marriages
All children given father's surname	30	63.8
2 or more children given father's and 1 child given mother's surname	6	12.8
2 or more children given father's and 2 or more children given mother's surname	4	8.5
1 child given father's and 1 child given mother's surname (only 2 children)	4	8.5
1 child given father's and 2 or more children given mother's surname	2	4.3
All children given mother's surname	1	2.1

NOTE: Figures are derived from marriages across all generations. Total number of uxorilocal marriages with information on children's surnames = 47.

families (63.8 percent), all the children received their father's surname, although in 34.1 percent of the families, there were children assigned to each of their parents' surnames. In all but one case there was at least one child reported with the father's surname. Nearly three-quarters of the cases for which I have property inheritance information demonstrate a Hoklo-style link between property and surnames (see table 7). In 54.3 percent of the cases, the children all had the father's surname and received no property. In seven of these cases, people explicitly stated that the children were all assigned their father's surname *because* there was no property to inherit. In another 20 percent, only those children with the mother's surname received property from her family. Most families in these villages, then, seem to have closely linked surnames with property inheritance, as did Hoklo.

However, there is evidence in the remaining 25.8 percent that people in Toushe, Jibeishua, and Longtian felt some ambivalence about not sharing property beyond the surname. That is, they appear ambivalent about a Hoklo-style link between surname and inheritance of property. Most of these families reportedly split the wife's family's property evenly among children with only the father's surname (in one case between two adopted daughters). In two cases, all children got shares, but those with the mother's surname got larger shares. In one case, a man—Grandfather Wa's second daughter's son by her first husband—was given his mother's surname but still did not get a share of her family's property. Grandfa-

TABLE 7. ASSIGNMENT OF MOTHER'S
NATAL FAMILY PROPERTY IN FAMILIES
WITH UXORILOCAL MARRIAGES
(Toushe, Jibeishua, and Longtian)

Assignment of surname	Property given only with mother's surname	Property shared: child(ren) with mother's surname get(s) larger share	Property shared equally regardless of surname	No property to share
All children given father's surname (no siblings with mother's surname)	–	–	5 (14.3%)	19 (54.3%)
1 or more children given mother's surname (1 or more siblings with father's)	7 (20%)	2 (5.7%)	1 (2.9%)	1 (2.9%)

NOTE: Total number of families with uxorilocal marriages for which information was available on children's surnames and assignment of property = 35. Percentages total 100.1 due to rounding.

ther Wa did not like him and refused to give him any property, splitting the property among the other cousins who had the Wa surname and the grandson surnamed Chiu who had no brothers. (The other grandsons who had their fathers' surnames only received shares of whatever property their fathers had earned themselves.) Finally, in one case, where there was no property to split, both parents' surnames were distributed among their children. Such variation is particularly important in analyzing how cultural practices and ideas spread across a community and how cultural and identity change are related (points I take up below). In spite of these (and other) minority cases of ambivalence (see Brown 1995:360–61 for further examples), people in Toushe, Jibeishua, and Longtian largely linked the actual distribution of property to surname by the early twentieth century, in accordance with a Hoklo cultural model.[28]

Adoption People in Toushe, Jibeishua, and Longtian were like their Hoklo neighbors in several aspects of how they practiced adoptions, as well as in their rationale for adopting boys, but they differed in their rationale for adopting girls. Frequencies of adoption in the generation of the people I interviewed (adoptions in their sibling sets, occurring roughly between 1890 and 1920) indicate that it was more exceptional and difficult to adopt boys than girls (compare tables 8 and 9).[29] Jibeishua is unusual in that there were more adoptions of boys than girls. Most adop-

TABLE 8. PLAINS ABORIGINE
FAMILIES ADOPTING BOYS

	Boys from plains Aborigines	Boys from Han	Boys from parents of unknown or mixed origin	Total per community
Toushe (N = 24)	2 (8.3%)	0	0	2 (8.3%)
Jibeishua (N = 22)	2 (9.1%)	0	1 (4.5%)	3 (13.6%)
Longtian (N = 11)	0	0	0	0
Total (N = 57)	4 (7.0%)	0	1 (1.8%)	5 (8.8%)

NOTE: Interviewees reported their own adoptions or those of individuals in their own generation (e.g., siblings). N = number of Aborigine families interviewed in each community.

TABLE 9. PLAINS ABORIGINE
FAMILIES ADOPTING GIRLS

	Girls from plains Aborigines	Girls from Han	Girls from parents of unknown or mixed origin	Total per community
Toushe (N = 24)	1 (4.2%)	4 (16.7%)	5 (20.8%)	10 (41.7%)
Jibeishua (N = 22)	0	0	0	0
Longtian (N = 11)	0	0	1 (9.1%)	1 (9.1%)
Total (N = 57)	1 (1.8%)	4 (7.0%)	6 (10.5%)	11 (19.3%)

NOTE: Interviewees reported their own adoptions or those of individuals in their own generation (e.g., siblings). N = number of Aborigine families interviewed in each community.

tions of boys occurred within the community (compare tables 8 and 10, where all of the adoptions from and to plains Aborigines occurred within the community). Moreover, as among Hoklo, most people adopted biologically-related boys (such as nephews). People reported a lack of sons as their motivation for adopting a boy. Adopting boys was difficult, though, because for both cultural and economic reasons few people—plains Aborigine or Hoklo—wanted to give up boys for adoption. Boys provided labor, carried on the surname, and worshipped ancestors. By contrast, it was easy to adopt girls and many people did—both Hoklo and plains Aborigines—although frequencies of adoption vary sharply

TABLE 10. PLAINS ABORIGINE
FAMILIES GIVING UP BOYS FOR ADOPTION

	Boys given to plains Aborigines	Boys given to Han	Boys given to parents of unknown or mixed origin	Total per community
Toushe (N = 24)	2 (8.3%)	0	0	2 (8.3%)
Jibeishua (N = 22)	2 (9.1%)	0	0	2 (9.1%)
Longtian (N = 11)	0	0	1 (9.1%)	1 (9.1%)
Total (N = 57)	4 (7.0%)	0	1 (1.8%)	5 (8.8%)

NOTE: Interviewees reported their own adoptions or those of individuals in their own generation (e.g., siblings). N = number of Aborigine families interviewed in each community.

TABLE 11. PLAINS ABORIGINE
FAMILIES GIVING UP GIRLS FOR ADOPTION

	Girls given to plains Aborigines	Girls given to Han	Girls given to parents of unknown or mixed origin	Total per community
Toushe (N = 24)	2 (8.3%)	0	0	2 (8.3%)
Jibeishua (N = 22)	0	0	0	0
Longtian (N = 11)	0	0	0	0
Total (N = 57)	2 (3.5%)	0	0	2 (3.5%)

NOTE: Interviewees reported their own adoptions or those of individuals in their own generation (e.g., siblings). N = number of Aborigine families interviewed in each community.

for Toushe, Jibeishua, and Longtian (see table 9). In Toushe, almost half of the families interviewed who were once considered "plains Aborigine" adopted girls, whereas in Longtian only one family did, and in Jibeishua none did.[30] Most of these girls came from outside the community, and many came from families known to be Han (compare tables 9 and 11, where all adoptions from and to Han and people of unknown origin—the majority of the unknown/mixed category—crossed community lines). Like Hoklo, many plains Aborigines did adopt girls, but unlike Hoklo they did not give up girls for adoption.

Why were girls brought into these communities? It appears that the underlying meaning of such adoptions was different for plains Aborigines than for Hoklo. In contrast to the Hoklo in the Haishan area of northern Taiwan, where it is clear that most families wanted to adopt daughters-in-law—girls they would raise to marry one of the family's sons, whether or not the son was born yet (Wolf and Huang 1980, Wolf 1995)—people in Toushe and Longtian adopted daughters. Unlike adopted daughters-in-law in northern Taiwan, these women born to Han couples and adopted by plains Aborigine families were treated like daughters. Families adopted girls because they had no children or because they had just lost a child. Childless couples expected their adopted daughter to care for them in old age and usually arranged a uxorilocal marriage for her.[31] Families with children adopted a girl upon the death of a child—not to assuage a mother's grief, as Pasternak (1985:122) suggests, but to protect the other children in the family. One woman in Toushe adopted a daughter because her biological daughter had died. She explained that when she was young the old people told her that if one child dies and you adopt another, then your other children, even those not yet born, will live. One Jibeishua woman, however, said that only if a woman *kept* having children die would she adopt a daughter.

Plains Aborigines appear to be similar to Hoklo, however, in terms of who actually made the decision to adopt. Wolf and Huang (1980:276–78) report that, for Hoklo in Haishan, a woman's mother-in-law usually made the decision about whether to give her daughter up for adoption (and replace her with an adopted daughter-in-law). In Toushe, Jibeshua, and Longtian, women were often reluctant to adopt. It was their mothers-in-law or mothers who usually made the decision to adopt. One Toushe woman who had been an adopted daughter herself considered her first husband to have treated her well because, among other reasons, he did not want to adopt even though they were childless (they were still young when he died). Another Toushe woman had an adopted daughter brought in for her by her mother-in-law, who was also her stepmother. The woman said that she had not wanted to raise an adopted daughter, but once her mother-in-law/stepmother went and got the girl and the child was actually there, what could she do?[32] A woman in Jibeishua also mentioned that she considered her parents-in-law good to her because, even though there were three years between her marriage and the birth of her first child, they never raised the issue of adoption. These women saw the adoption of a girl as an additional burden on them, not as comfort in their grief at losing a child.

On the whole, people of Toushe, Jibeishua, and Longtian were like their Hoklo neighbors in how they practiced adoption. They primarily adopted girls rather than boys, and when they did adopt boys, they were biologically related boys. Moreover, the senior generation—that is, a woman's mother or mother-in-law—usually made the decision to adopt a child or not. Differences in giving girls up for adoption and in why people chose to adopt show that not all Hoklo ideas about adoption had been embraced, but these differences were probably not particularly noticeable to neighboring Hoklo.

Practices Not Shared with the Hoklo

Toushe, Jibeishua, and Longtian were clearly different from their Hoklo neighbors in a number of customs related to gender, mortuary practices, and religious practices. Most Hoklo people probably noticed only the footbinding differences, but the other differences became more important later, after the identity change had occurred.

Footbinding   Most importantly, plains Aborigine women did not bind feet. Japanese-period household register data clearly indicates that women classified as "plains Aborigine" in Toushe, Jibeishua, and Longtian did not have bound feet. The 1905 islandwide census records only 0.5 percent of "plains Aborigines" as having bound feet *(Taiwan jinkō dōtai tōkei,* Shepherd 1993:527n134). Moreover, as I discussed above, interview reports consistently confirmed that not binding women's feet was the marker of Aborigine identity at the local level. This difference was highly visible and crucial to identification as plains Aborigine.

Use of Betel and Alcohol   Standards of beauty and behavior as dictated by notions of gender were generally linked to ethnic identity in 1915. Not only did most Hoklo women bind their feet, but they also did not chew betel (which dramatically stains the teeth) or drink alcohol (rice wine, *mijiu*). In contrast, most women in Toushe, Jibeishua, and Longtian, still chewed betel regularly.[33] A Longtian woman told me that when she was young, people said that women who chewed betel were savages (T., *hoan-a*).[34] According to interview reports, adult women often chewed betel through the mid-1920s and early 1930s, when the people I interviewed themselves became adults. Moreover, betel use by women dropped off rapidly in all three communities. Most people reported that their mothers, mothers-in-law, and grandmothers chewed betel but that women of their own generation did not. Interview reports suggest that rice wine consumption by women began dropping off earlier than chewing betel and did so at varying rates, so that by 1915 many women still drank in Toushe, some women drank in Longtian, and only a few women drank in Jibeishua. These gendered expectations became more pronounced with time. In the 1990s, women in Toushe, Jibeishua, and Longtian did not chew betel at all, and most did not drink alcohol either.[35]

Mortuary Practices   The adoption of Han-style mortuary practices occurred in stages, with funerals and timing of burials changing earliest, and thus being practices shared with the Hoklo by 1915. Use of gravestones—as well as tomb-sweeping rites and secondary burials—began later, and thus were practices not shared with the Hoklo by 1915. I take up each of these mortuary practices in turn. In order to understand the process of identity change, it is helpful to see not only where these practices differed from those of neighboring Hoklo, but also when and how these practices changed toward a Han cultural model.

In the early twentieth century, most graves were not marked at all in Toushe, Jibeishua, and Longtian.[36] Although more recent graves were marked by gravestones with writing, I also found some older graves in one Toushe cemetery marked by stones without writing and a few graves marked by broken bits of ceramic tile. A Toushe family whom I accompanied on the Qingming tomb-sweeping festival in 1992 reported that, a few years earlier, they had wanted to honor the senior man's mother with an expensive secondary burial and had made an extensive search for her grave but could not find it. Grandfather Wa himself had had no grave marker in 1987 before his grave was relocated.[37] In Jibeishua less than one in four people reported seeing a grave marked by a stone or rock (with no writing on it) in the first funeral they ever saw (1910s–1930s); in Longtian the numbers were less than one in seven.[38] No one said that gravestones were common in the past. One Jibeishua person explicitly said that local people had not bothered to mark graves with stones in the past. Recalling funerals of the early 1940s, a Longtian man said that only rich people had gravestones; most people had rocks, which were often pushed aside by grazing cattle, making it difficult to find a grave. Taiwan's lush environment also contributed so such difficulties, as plants could quickly cover a grave.

Assuming, then, that most people in the early twentieth century were not marking graves in these villages, we should not be surprised about reports that, in the past, most people neither tomb-swept—visiting the grave, clearing it of plants and debris, and making offerings—nor com-

missioned the exhumation and defleshing of bones for secondary burials, both common Hoklo practices. One Jibeishua woman said that there
was no tomb-sweeping at all when she was a child. She said that they
first started tomb-sweeping after her father's death (which occurred after her marriage in 1921) but only did it for three years. When asked
whether her family had given her father a secondary burial, she said that
they cannot *now* find any of her ancestors' graves, not even her father's,
which suggests that they did not consider secondary burial until recently.
Another Jibeishua woman also said that when she was young there was
no tomb-sweeping at all but that after 1945 people went occasionally—
if they brought in a daughter-in-law. (As we shall see, this link to postwar virilocal marriages connects mortuary practices with identity change.)
This woman also said that her family had not put a marker on her father's grave, although some other people had markers at that time. She
told me that she had never even heard of secondary burials and defleshing until later in her life.

Underlying these differences in mortuary practices, people's ideas
about the dead appear to have been quite different in Toushe, Jibeishua,
and Longtian than among Hoklo. While Hoklo honored and feared the
dead, people in early-twentieth-century Toushe, Jibeishua, and Longtian
appear to have seen the dead as irrelevant to the living.[39] One Jibeishua
woman who was in her nineties when I interviewed her in 1992 said, in
explaining that no one in the village used to tomb-sweep: "Once people
are dead they have no other use. They can't come back." She and her
son do not remember where her late husband, who died decades ago, is
buried. Her son, however, who was in his sixties, was embarrassed about
it, indicating a generational difference in this attitude.

We see, then, that in Toushe, Jibeishua, and Longtian mortuary practices—and apparently the ideas underlying them as well—differed significantly from those of the Hoklo. Over time, however, the people of Toushe, Jiebeishua, and Longtian adopted Hoklo-style practices. They first
began to mark graves, probably in the late 1930s, then began tomb-
sweeping in the late 1940s, and finally began performing secondary burials in the 1980s (Brown 1995:482ff). These changes in customs followed
identity change and, I will argue, occurred because of it.

Religious Practices   To a large extent, religious practices in Toushe,
Jibeishua, and Longtian in the early twentieth century were different than
those in Hoklo communities. Although some "plains Aborigine" families did worship deities in the Han pantheon, Han folk religion did not

predominate. For one thing, there was a sizable Christian minority in both Jibeishua and Toushe—one satellite settlement of Toushe was, and still is, predominantly Christian. Primarily, however, community worship focused on a deity explicitly acknowledged to be Aborigine. In the 1990s, this deity was called a variety of names: Thai Tsoo (Mandarin: Tai Zu) and Lau Kun (Mandarin: Lao Jun, short for Tai Shang Lao Jun) in Toushe and Longtian, A-li Tsoo (Mandarin: Ali Zu) as well in Longtian, and A-li Bu (Mandarin: Ali Mu) in Jibeishua.[40] Thai Tsoo means "first ancestor." Lau Kun means "venerable gentleman" and is a respectful title for Lao Zi, the founder of Daoism.[41] A-li Bu means "mother A-li," and A-li Tsoo means "ancestor A-li." A-li has no meaning in Taiwanese. The word is apparently from Siraya, the Austronesian language used by core-area plains Aborigines in the seventeenth century. The Dutch translation of the Gospel of Matthew into Siraya uses "Alit" as the term for God (Campbell 1888).

Religious practices dedicated to this deity were clearly different from Han religious practices in the early twentieth century, even to a casual observer.[42] Unlike in Han folk religion, which used anthropomorphic images, deities here were represented by vases or pots with plants in them. Temples (T., *kong-kai*) were walled only on three sides instead of four. Temples were located outside village living areas instead of lying within the community. Altars were low to or on the floor, not elevated. Pig skulls decorated the temple. The daily offerings were betel chaws and rice wine, not incense and food. The annual festivals included special songs— originally in Austronesian, later taught syllable by syllable among Minnan speakers—and a dance performed by villagers, although, like Han annual festivals, they also included entire pigs as offerings. At that time, according to interview reports, people believed the deity's spirit medium (T., *tang-ki*) should be a woman.

Very Like the Hoklo

Consider how Toushe, Jibeishua, and Longtian looked to Hoklo visitors around 1915. A visitor would have heard Minnan spoken and seen rice paddies and sugarcane fields. The only difference that would have been immediately apparent is that none of the women had bound feet. A visitor might also have noticed some women chewing betel, but the rest of the differences would not have been visible. Since uxorilocal marriages did not generally have marriage feasts, a visitor would only have noticed weddings for virilocal marriages, with accompanying feasts. If there happened to be a funeral, a visitor would probably have seen a Daoist priest presiding, as in a Hoklo village (because Christians were a minority). Hoklo visitors would have been unlikely at the Qingming festival, both because they had graves of their own to attend to and because of Hoklo religious taboos regarding other people's dead, so the lack of tomb-sweeping would likely have gone unnoticed. A visitor might have noticed that there was no Han-style temple, but that could have been explained by poverty—poor Han villages often rotated a focal deity through different households in the village. One Toushe satellite settlement did just that with the Hoklo deity Tsoo Su Kong. A visitor probably would not have noticed the temple for the Aborigine deity, because it was located outside of the village and was a simple, open-sided thatch-roof construction that would not have looked like a temple to Hoklo.

By the same token, a man from Toushe, Jibeishua, or Longtian going to a nearby market town would have looked and sounded like any poor Hoklo man. Only women from Toushe, Jibeishua, and Longtian were clearly recognizable as such. One woman I interviewed recalled that when she went to a neighboring market town in her youth she had been called a "Toushe savage," as people from Toushe were often called. When I asked how they knew where she was from, she said that they knew because her feet were not bound.

Except for the gendered practices of footbinding and chewing betel among women, Toushe, Jibeishua, and Longtian appeared culturally very like poor Hoklo villages. Thus, if Han identity were based primarily on cultural practices—as Confucianism culturalism and emphasis on orthopraxy suggests—we would expect these communities, by early in the twentieth century, to have been considered Hoklo, although perhaps somewhat coarse due to poverty.[43] As we have seen, however, Toushe, Jibeishua, and Longtian, continued to be labeled Aborigine in the most pejorative of terms: savages. That the adoption of the Hoklo language and many customs did not confer Hoklo identity upon the residents of Toushe, Jibeishua, and Longtian demonstrates that cultural practices were not enough to confer ethnic identity.

Moreover, there is evidence to suggest that changes in cultural practices did not directly correspond to changes in cultural ideas and meanings. In the early twentieth century, the underlying meanings, beliefs, and values of people in Toushe, Jibeishua, and Longtian still included many which were not the same as those of Hoklo. That is to say, just because these villagers adopted Hoklo practices does not necessarily mean that they attributed the same meanings to those practices as Hoklo did.

Most Hoklo visitors were probably not aware of the differences in meaning. Consider marital forms. A Hoklo visitor who became aware of the high rates of uxorilocal marriages might attribute this difference to poverty: high local mortality rates leading to the need to bring in sons-in-law for labor purposes. I suggest that, because the marital options available in Toushe, Jibeishua, and Longtian were apparently the same as those in Hoklo villages, a Hoklo visitor would presume that they indicated wholesale adoption of Hoklo culture (sinicization, *hanhua*). However, we need to remember that similar ideas, like similar practices, can become more or less common over time as an idea spreads through a population (Sperber 1996, Brown n.d.). Moreover, there is a great deal more variation within communities and societies than is often recognized for a single "culture." Some people in Toushe, Jibeishua, and Longtian in the early twentieth century may well have viewed these different forms of marriage in the same way as most Hoklo. I suggest that most people with such views probably had a Hoklo father or grandfather. Still, there would have been some who viewed these marital forms differently. The ethnographic problem, of course, is that practices are much easier to reconstruct than meanings, so although I can document the frequency of Hoklo practices among the Toushe, Jibeishua, and Longtian people I interviewed, I cannot document the frequency of Hoklo ideas.

Nevertheless, it does appear that practices spread through a population more quickly than ideas do. As we have seen, most people in Toushe, Jibeishua, and Longtian did link surname to inheritance of property in practice, but some people showed ambivalence about the idea of this link, including some people who conformed to Hoklo practice. Similarly, while Toushe, Jibeishua, and Longtian adoption practices appear much like Hoklo practices, their *reasons* for adopting girls differed from those of Hoklo.

As another example, there was one case of an uxorilocal minor marriage in Toushe; the rest of the few minor marriages I came across were virilocal, just as elsewhere in Taiwan. (In minor marriage, a form of marriage which no longer exists in Taiwan, a family adopted and raised a girl to become the wife of one of the sons in the family.) The woman in the uxorilocal minor marriage told me that, although she had initially been reluctant to marry the adopted "brother" who had been raised to be her elder sister's husband—a sentiment predicted for minor marriage partners by Arthur Wolf (e.g., 1995)—she was persuaded by neighbors to go through with the marriage. Her elder sister had died before the

marriage itself. The fact that neighbors accepted and encouraged an uxorilocal version of minor marriage indicates that local culture allowed
flexibility in adopting Hoklo practices, which in turn implies an underlying difference in the cultural meanings of marriage, adoption, and the
valuation of daughters. Although the same marital forms were considered options in Toushe, Jibeishua, and Longtian and in Hoklo villages,
they were not always applied in the same way, suggesting that the underlying ideational system of culture changed *after* practices were introduced. In other words, it appears that cultural meanings change more
slowly than cultural practices.

The elderly people I interviewed who remembered being called savages made it quite clear to me that footbinding was the marker—the single cultural practice—which, in the end, constituted the border to Han.[44]
Again and again, when I asked elderly people if their mothers or grandmothers had bound feet, they responded, "We savages didn't bind feet"
(T., *guan hoan-a bo pak-kha*). Thus, although footbinding was the only
clearly visible difference between people in these communities and their
Hoklo neighbors, people nevertheless consistently used this single difference to classify them as non-Han. The response "We savages didn't
bind feet" indicates the degree to which local people had accepted that
classification. They had internalized enough Han cultural ideas to believe that lack of footbinding proved them less than civilized, less than
Han. Thus, ironically, their very acceptance that this marker indicated
non-Han identity indicates how much they were culturally Han even if
they did not accept all Han cultural ideas.

What then can we say about the relationship between culture and identity in early-twentieth-century Toushe, Jibeishua, and Longtian? People
in these communities shared many of the same cultural practices as their
Hoklo neighbors. Of the few practices they did not share, only one was
highly visible—not binding women's feet. Clearly ethnic identity did not
follow cultural practices. The relationship between cultural ideas and ethnic identity does not appear strong either. Although some people in Toushe, Jibeishua, and Longtian maintained non-Han ideas about their Han
practices, there appears to be a range of variation in accepted cultural
meanings. Ethnic identity, by contrast, was clear-cut and explicitly marked
by the presence or absence of footbinding. Culture, then, did not determine ethnic identity. However, as we shall see, identity did drive further
cultural change. A change in identity was required in order to bring practices into full conformity with a Hoklo model and to bring the underlying system of cultural meanings in line with a Hoklo model as well.

THE COLONIAL FOOTBINDING BAN
AND LONG-ROUTE IDENTITY CHANGE

People in Toushe, Jibeishua, and Longtian were finally able to take on a Hoklo identity because the Japanese colonial government banned footbinding in 1915.[45] In a northern Hoklo community, where it had been common,

> the custom of footbinding was only eradicated by the tough-minded methods of the Japanese police. Elderly informants told [Arthur Wolf in the late 1950s] that the police were not content to simply record whether or not a woman's feet were bound. They insisted that children's feet be unbound and made period[ic] checks to make sure they were not rebound. One old man claimed that the police threatened to shoot him when they discovered that he had had his daughter's feet bound a second time. (Wolf 1995:53)

The ban did not merely remove the last ethnic marker distinguishing plains Aborigines and Hoklo identity. More importantly, it removed the marker in favor of the Aborigine model—no footbinding.

I argue that the footbinding ban finally spurred long-route identity change and thereby allowed increases in intermarriage between people of Toushe, Jibeishua, and Longtian and nearby Hoklo villages. Before the ban, it appears that marriage patterns in Toushe, Jibeishua, and Longtian followed a need to partner those stigmatized as "savages." After the ban, however, women from Toushe, Jibeishua, and Longtian were able to marry virilocally into nearby Hoklo villages. Moreover, Hoklo women also began marrying into Toushe, Jibeishua, and Longtian as first-time brides. For these virilocal intermarriages to have occurred, plains Aborigine identity must have disappeared with footbinding.

To understand the process of how the ban drove long-route identity change, and subsequent cultural change, we need to understand how changes in potential marriage partners ("the marriage market") and changes in actual marriage partners constitute changing social experience. Thus, I examine marriage partners before and after the footbinding ban, as well as the relationship of partners to social experience, cultural practices, and cultural ideas.

In Toushe, Jibeishua, and Longtian, as in the rest of Taiwanese society in the early twentieth century, virtually all women married. However, before the 1915 footbinding ban, Toushe, Jibeishua, and Longtian appear to have been limited to a smaller marriage market—that is, women stigmatized as "savages" had a narrower range of potential husbands than Hoklo women. Among the parents and grandparents of the generation

I interviewed, women considered plains Aborigine reportedly married within Toushe, Jibeishua, and Longtian, either virilocally within these villages or uxorilocally in their natal home. Most women married men who were considered plains Aborigine, although a significant minority uxorilocally married Han men (table 2). One Jibeishua man explicitly articulated why plains Aborigine women in his parents' and grandparents' generations could not virilocally marry Hoklo men:

> The old people all had dark skin and big [round] eyes. The women were all fierce. The men of surrounding villages [which were Hoklo] didn't want to marry them; they [the men from the other villages] called them [the Jibeishua women] *hoan-a-pho* [Mandarin: *fanzi po;* roughly "savage biddies"], so the [Jibeishua] village men had to marry them.[46]

That is, before the footbinding ban, marriages were arranged to find a partner for women stigmatized as "savages." Primarily, these women married plains Aborigine men. Only Hoklo men who had no other options for brides would marry these stigmatized women—their desperation being indicated by their agreement to marry uxorilocally, which Hoklo considered immoral (e.g., Wolf 1995:25–26), and also by their often arranging their own marriages, a sure sign of dire circumstances in a society where parents generally arranged marriages.

By the same token, plains Aborigine men also appear to have had access to a narrower range of potential brides. Most plains Aborigine men married plains Aborigine women—either uxorilocally (in or out of their natal village) or virilocally. A few men married Hoklo widows virilocally (table 2), and most such marriages described to me were secondary marriages for the man. Hoklo widows who married into these plains Aborigine communities were even more desperate than Hoklo men: not only were they willing to carry out the act of remarriage—immoral in Confucian terms–but they married men stigmatized as "savages" *and* married them as second wives, legally as concubines.

Toushe, Jibeishua, and Longtian would still have been visibly different for some time after the footbinding ban, because a visitor would have noticed that older women did not have bound feet. However, what apparently mattered for the marriage market was the feet of young women. In the 1930s, when there were no first-time brides with bound feet on the marriage market regardless of their ethnic identity, the range of potential partners for people formerly considered plains Aborigine opened up. Before the ban, when the people of Toushe, Jibeishua, and Longtian were labeled plains Aborigine, neighboring Han considered the men unacceptable marriage partners for their daughters and the women unacceptable daughters-in-law. After the footbinding ban, however, when even first-time Hoklo brides did not have bound feet, Hoklo apparently could no longer object to exchanging brides with communities formerly considered Aborigine because footbinding had been the local marker used to categorize people as Hoklo or Aborigines.

In Toushe, Jibeishua, and Longtian I found increased numbers of virilocal marriages overall, and virilocal marriages to Hoklo in particular. At the same time, there were decreases in the numbers of uxorilocal marriages overall, uxorilocal marriages to Hoklo, and marriages arranged among Toushe, Jibeishua, and Longtian. In short, the flow of marriage partners between Hoklo villages and Toushe, Jibeishua, and Longtian changed. Virilocal marriages to Hoklo did not start without some reservations. One woman who told me she was the first Han woman to marry into Toushe—meaning as a first-time bride—reported that it took three years for her husband's family to negotiate the marriage agreement with her parents, even though her father-in-law was a uxorilocally-married Han man.

Among the people I interviewed in Toushe, Jibeishua, and Longtian, these shifts took place beginning around 1925 to 1930. While people reported 30 to 60 percent of their plains Aborigine parents' and grandparents' marriages as virilocal, they reported 65 to 77 percent of the marriages in their own generation as virilocal, and even higher rates of virilocal marriages for their children's generation (see tables 4 and 12).[47] This trend was most pronounced in Toushe (see table 13).

Correlated to this general increase in virilocal marriage are two concurrent trends that, taken together, indicate a change in the flow of marriage partners: first, an increase in virilocal marriages *to Hoklo spouses*—many of them from nearby villages, and all from villages closer than the other villages formerly considered plains Aborigine in my study—and, second, a decrease in uxorilocal marriages *to Hoklo men*. People reported in interviews that, for married-out daughters, they preferred virilocal marriages to Hoklo men in nearby villages because it kept these daughters closer to their natal homes than if they married into other villages formerly considered plains Aborigine. Where daughters were closer, it was easier to visit, among other things.

The change in the flow of marriage partners constitutes a broad change in social experience. The increase in virilocal marriages to Hoklo women brought more Han women into Toushe, Jibeishua, and Longtian. Among the parents and grandparents of people I interviewed, Han men entered

TABLE 12. UXORILOCAL AND VIRILOCAL MARRIAGES, GENERATION OF PEOPLE INTERVIEWED
(*Toushe, Jibeishua, and Longtian*)

	# marriages	Uxorilocal marriages	Virilocal marriages
Toushe	44	10 (22.7%)	34 (77.3%)
Jibeishua	35	11 (31.4%)	24 (68.6%)
Longtian	20	7 (35%)	13 (65%)
Total	99	28 (28.3%)	71 (71.7%)

NOTE: Postmarital residence is within one of these communities.

TABLE 13. UXORILOCAL AND VIRILOCAL MARRIAGES ACROSS GENERATIONS IN TOUSHE

Generation with respect to person interviewed	# marriages	Uxorilocal marriages	Virilocal marriages
Parents and grandparents	28	19 (67.9%)	9 (32.1%)
Same	44	10 (22.7%)	34 (77.3%)
Children	43	5 (11.6%)	38 (88.4%)

NOTE: Postmarital residence is within Toushe.

the villages through uxorilocal marriage (tables 2 and 3). In fact, at that time, most Hoklo marrying into Toushe, Jibeishua, and Longtian were Han men marrying uxorilocally, not Han women marrying virilocally. In the generation of people I interviewed, by contrast, no known Hoklo men married uxorilocally (see table 14). Instead, some Han women started entering through virilocal marriages—at least 8.5 percent of virilocal marriages and possibly more whose identity is unknown. Although still a minority of virilocal marriages, this figure represents an increase from the 4.8 percent of virilocal marriages of plains Aborigine men who brought in Hoklo brides among the parents and grandparents of the people I interviewed (table 2). According to reports from the generation I interviewed, many of these Han women, marrying men who would have once been considered Aborigine, were first-time brides and they did not have bound feet. However, coming from Hoklo communities, they knew Hoklo culture, and they could talk about the practices of their husband's family to their natal family on home visits.

Women who would once have been considered plains Aborigine started marrying out virilocally to Han communities. This increase, although small, took women from Toushe, Jibeishua, and Longtian into

TABLE 14. ETHNIC ORIGIN OF SPOUSES IN THE GENERATION OF PEOPLE INTERVIEWED
(Toushe, Jibeishua, and Longtian)

Form of marriage	# marriages	Plains Aborigines	Han	Unknown or mixed
Uxorilocal	28	21 (75%)	0	7 (25%)
Virilocal	71	52 (73.2%)	6 (8.5%)	13 (18.3%)
Total	99	73 (73.7%)	6 (6.1%)	20 (20.2%)

NOTE: Postmarital residence is within one of these communities.

TABLE 15. ETHNIC ORIGIN OF SPOUSES IN THE GENERATION OF PEOPLE INTERVIEWED
(Toushe)

Form of marriage	# marriages	Plains Aborigine	Han	Unknown or mixed
Uxorilocal	10	7 (70%)	0	3 (30%)
Virilocal	34	24 (70.6%)	5 (14.7%)	5 (14.7%)
Total	44	31 (70.4%)	5 (11.4%)	8 (18.2%)

NOTE: Postmarital residence is within Toushe.

Hoklo villages and families, where they could observe Hoklo cultural practices and possibly describe them to their natal families. In the senior generation, there were no reports of plains Aborigine women marrying out virilocally to Hoklo men. In the generation I interviewed, seven women married outside the study communities to Han men.[48] These trends are even more remarkable in Toushe (where the data on the children's generation is more systematic). There, in the senior generation (the parents and grandparents of those I interviewed), uxorilocal marriages outnumbered virilocal marriages 67.9 percent to 32.1 percent (table 13). Within virilocal marriages, 100 percent were to other plains Aborigines (table 3). Also, no known Han women married virilocally into Toushe, and six known Han men married in uxorilocally—31.6 percent of uxorilocal marriages (table 3). In the Toushe generation I interviewed, there is a complete reversal of these trends. Virilocal marriages outnumbered uxorilocal marriages 77.3 percent to 22.7 percent (table 13). More Han women and fewer Han men married into Toushe. No known Han men married in uxorilocally, while five known Han women married in virilocally—14.7 percent of virilocal marriages (see table 15).

Correlated to the increases in both virilocal marriages overall and vir-

TABLE 16. COMMUNITY ORIGIN OF PLAINS
ABORIGINE WIVES IN VIRILOCAL MARRIAGES,
PARENTS' AND GRANDPARENTS' GENERATIONS
(Toushe, Jibeishua, and Longtian)

Community of postmarital residence	# marriages	Same community	Other study communities	Communities outside the study
Toushe	9	4 (44.4%)	3 (33.3%)	2 (22.2%)
Jibeishua	16	5 (31.3%)	6 (37.5%)	5 (31.3%)
Longtian	10	1 (10%)	7 (70%)	2 (20%)
Total	35	10 (28.6%)	16 (45.7%)	9 (25.7%)

ilocal marriages to Hoklo was a decrease in marriages among people from
Toushe, Jibeishua, and Longtian. In interviews, people often told me that
their mothers or grandmothers had married virilocally from one of the
other study communities, but I rarely came across a woman who had
done so herself (see tables 16 and 17). Information about the frequency
with which women married from other study communities is corrobo-
rated by anecdotal comments of women I interviewed (all of whom married after the footbinding ban): while Hoklo women generally did not
remark upon marrying out of their natal villages, the elderly women from
Toushe, Jibeishua, and Longtian who had married out of their natal villages to other communities in the study commented strongly upon it, especially upon how they had cried because they had not wanted to go so
far away. (Other plains Aborigine villages were significantly farther away
than nearby Hoklo villages for people on foot, oxcart, or bicycle.) The
fact that so many of their childhood friends married closer to home (see
tables 16 and 17) must have made their husband's community seem even
more distant—socially as well as geographically—and added to their dis-
tress. One woman, who was ninety-two in 1992 and who had married
from Jibeishua to Toushe, reported both that she had cried like a baby
every night for years after she was married and that her husband was
good to her.

This decrease in marriages among communities that had once been
considered plains Aborigine constituted a major difference in social experience, one that I suggest had implications for people's sense of identity. The decrease in marriages meant fewer of the intimate social contacts that accompany affinal ties (relations between in-laws), and, in
particular, less of a flow of the kind of intimate information that a woman
would share with her natal family. The decrease may also indicate a

TABLE 17. COMMUNITY ORIGIN OF PLAINS
ABORIGINE WIVES IN VIRILOCAL MARRIAGES
IN THE GENERATION OF PEOPLE INTERVIEWED
(*Toushe, Jibeishua, and Longtian*)

Community of postmarital residence	# marriages	Same community	Other study communities	Communities outside the study
Toushe	24	22 (91.7%)	1 (4.2%)	1 (4.2%)
Jibeishua	21	18 (85.7%)	2 (9.5%)	1 (4.8%)
Longtian	7	2 (28.6%)	4 (57.1%)	1 (14.3%)
Total	52	42 (80.8%)	7 (13.5%)	3 (5.8%)

broader deterioration of social ties among Toushe, Jibeishua, and Longtian. When I did my fieldwork in the early 1990s, there was relatively little interaction among these communities, even though access to motor-
ized transportation (primarily motor scooters, at the time) had effectively
shortened the distances between them. These differences in social experience raise the real possibility that any sense people of Toushe, Jibeishua
and Longtian may have had of these three communities being part of a
single larger "plains Aborigine" group deteriorated. At the same time,
each of these individual communities had increasing, and increasingly
intimate, contacts with geographically closer Hoklo communities. These
latter contacts may well have contributed to a shift in the sense of belonging, or identity, toward a Hoklo identity.

The change in the flow of marriage partners shown here occurred very
rapidly between 1925 and 1935. This change reflected a shift to Hoklo
postmarital residence patterns, where the vast majority of marriages are
virilocal. I suggest that, before the footbinding ban, the stigma of being
considered plains Aborigine limited the marital choices of people in Toushe, Jibeishua, and Longtian. Virilocal marriages, which they knew were
preferred in Han culture, were not often practicable options for parents
arranging marriages. Some fifteen years after the colonial intervention
of the footbinding ban occurred, however, the general lack of first-time
brides with bound feet gave parents in Toushe, Jibeishua, and Longtian
the opportunity to pursue virilocal marriages. Once they could, they did
so in increasing numbers.

The elderly people I interviewed themselves give circumstantial support to a causal link between identity change and increasing intermarriage to Hoklo. Those who talked with me about being called savages
by neighboring Hoklo recalled it from their childhood and early youth,

not from later in their lives. This taunting must have stopped at about the time that virilocal marriages to Hoklo increased. Hoklo must have realized the personal implications of calling someone a savage on the basis of not binding his or her daughters' feet, when Hoklo no longer bound daughters' feet themselves. Once virilocal intermarriages of first-time brides occurred in increasing numbers with Toushe, Jibeishua, and Longtian, neighboring Hoklo would probably not want to admit to the Aborigine heritage of their new in-laws.

This is the point at which the people and villages of Toushe, Jibeishua, and Longtian took on a Hoklo identity—after many shifts toward a Hoklo cultural model and after a crucial, colonial intervention that socially imposed a change in the cultural model of neighboring Hoklo. By banning footbinding, the Japanese colonial government allowed changes in social experience through widespread intermarriage. Thus, it was not the *descendants* of mixed marriages who came to be considered long-route Hoklo. It was *the intermarrying people themselves*—the people who had been called savages as children.

CONTRIBUTIONS OF LONG-ROUTE
HAN TO TAIWANESE CULTURE

What long-term contributions from Aborigine culture did long-route Han—as the residents of Toushe, Jibeishua, and Longtian must now be called—make to Hoklo cultural models in Taiwan? This question is important because the new narratives of Taiwan's unfolding portray Aborigine contributions as sufficiently present in Taiwanese culture and ancestry to render Taiwanese different from Chinese. Acquiring a new identity label itself both constitutes and spurs changing social experience and, as we shall see, can impact culture.

If we examine the customs that changed in Toushe, Jibeishua, and Longtian as a result of the increase in virilocal marriages with neighboring Hoklo, we find only two long-term contributions from Aborigine culture. First, older women maintained considerable authority in Jibeishua through the 1990s, which may not continue much longer because of the shift to virilocal marriages, and second, the Toushe spirit medium (T., *tang-ki*) and his assistant have been attempting to spread Thai Tsoo's influence.[49] The vast majority of the changes in customs that occurred after Toushe, Jibeishua, and Longtian took on a Hoklo identity—and changes in ideas, insofar as I can document them—were toward preexisting Hoklo cultural models. Even religious practices, the only customs in the early 1990s which still showed clear continuities with Aborigine culture, have become sinicized—more Han-like—although Toushe, Jibeishua, and Longtian differ in the degree to which their practices have been sinicized. I link the differences between the communities to gender issues, specifically to differences in women's reluctance to take on social roles of public authority in the context of a changing demographic pattern of marriage (see also Brown 2003).

Let us examine the cultural changes that occurred to see whether they constitute contributions of Aborigine culture to local Hoklo culture.

Gendered Expectations and Practices

We have seen that virilocal marriages increased dramatically; at the same time, Toushe, Jibeishua, and Longtian women were increasingly marrying out of their natal villages, and women from neighboring Hoklo villages increasingly married in. In spite of the fact that the footbinding ban shifted some gendered expectations away from a Hoklo model—for example, expectations that women would work in the fields increased—other customs changed in accordance with Hoklo notions of gender. Women in Toushe, Jibeishua, and Longtian stopped chewing betel and drinking alcohol (as discussed earlier). Moreover, as we will see, women's willingness to take on roles of public authority diminished because virilocal marriages—brought on by the change in ethnic identity—limited women's options by making them outsiders, even in their natal village, at the same time that Han gender expectations limited their options by narrowing the range of acceptable behavior.

As far as I know, only one recent Hoklo-style custom related to marriages has been prevented, in Jibeishua. In the 1980s, providing strippers' services as gifts at weddings became very common in many parts of Taiwan, including this one (Brown 1993).[50] In Jibeishua, however, strippers were not a part of wedding feasts in 1992. When I inquired about the difference, several people, including the A-li Bu spirit medium, reported that the old women in Jibeishua had gotten together and put a stop to the presence of strippers at weddings. They refused to allow their families to spend money on strippers, either for family weddings or as gifts for the weddings of other families in the village (the latter was common in Toushe). Such action shows that elderly women in Jibeishua maintained some authority. After all, Jibeishua was the natal village of many of these elderly women. Now, however, younger generations of women marry out to other villages and women from other communities marry into Jibeishua, so it is not clear whether women will be able to command the same authority in Jibeishua once the older generation of women passes away.

Hoklo Mortuary Practices

In the 1930s and 1940s—that is, after the change to Hoklo identity—Toushe, Jibeishua, and Longtian residents gave increased attention to grave sites, along the lines of pre-existing Hoklo cultural models. The people I interviewed reported that they began to mark graves more regularly, and they began to perform tomb-sweeping rites annually for three years after a death, a virilocal marriage, or the birth of a son. It is significant that such occasions are times of increased contacts with in-laws: for some years after the initial adoption of tomb-sweeping, residents of Toushe, Jibeishua, and Longtian followed the Hoklo custom primarily at times when their Hoklo in-laws would hear (from the Hoklo bride) whether tomb-sweeping was performed or not. In fact, one Jibeishua woman I interviewed explicitly linked tomb-sweeping to bringing in a daughter-in-law (as discussed above). I interpret the increase in tomb-sweeping (which must have been accompanied by marking graves) as, initially at least, a way of better fitting in with the local Hoklo model, a way of maintaining the newly achieved Hoklo identity.

Over time, however, the practice of tomb-sweeping expanded. By 1992, Toushe, Jibeishua, and Longtian residents were tomb-sweeping every year. Nevertheless, they still did not necessarily sweep all the ancestral graves they could locate. One Toushe family did not present tomb-sweeping offerings at Grandfather Wa's grave in 1992 because, they said, it was in a different graveyard. The graveyard they chose to visit had a more personal tie: the grave of the senior man's late wife, who had died only the year before, was located there. They may have also assumed that other descendants of Grandfather Wa took offerings and swept his grave. This discrepancy may indicate a lag in the adoption of Hoklo ideas regarding ancestral worship—which includes tomb-sweeping duties—since the senior man did remember Grandfather Wa, who was his own grandfather.[51] However, such a lag between the adoption of Hoklo practices and the adoption of Hoklo ideas is more evident with secondary burials.

The common Hoklo custom of secondary burials (after exhuming the body and defleshing the bones) is part of Hoklo ancestor worship. Reburials reflect cosmological beliefs of Taiwanese folk religion that the disposition of ancestors affects the fortunes of their descendants (e.g., Wolf 1974b, Ahern 1973, Weller 1987).[52] A Hoklo family suffering misfortune—in health or finances, for example—may consult a ritual specialist to explore whether they have neglected an ancestor, among other possibilities. Such a consultation may reveal the need to perform a secondary burial for an ancestor.

People in Toushe, Jibeishua, and Longtian did not practice secondary burials at all until very recently. According to interview reports, secondary burials began there some time in the 1980s. One of the few secondary burials in Toushe that I was told about occurred in 1987. Such burials were still rare in 1992, performed only if there were family problems indicating a neglected ancestor, or if a grave had to be moved, for example when a road was widened or put in. One Jibeishua woman told me that she had never even heard of secondary burials and defleshing until late in her life. One Longtian man, who said that secondary burials were still rare in 1992, reported that originally people in the area only exhumed a body and defleshed the bones for secondary burial if something hit the grave, like a plow or a car. He said only later did people start performing secondary burials in response to family troubles. The fact that secondary burials initially occurred in response to practical needs rather than supernatural interpretations suggests that any idea of neglected ancestors punishing their descendants was still relatively rare in Toushe, Jibeishua, and Longtian in the early 1990s, although it appeared to be spreading.

Religious Practices and Gender Issues

The other remaining changes that occurred in Toushe, Jibeishua, and Longtian are related to religious practices. While most of these changes are shifts toward a pre-existing Hoklo cultural model, there are still clear continuities with earlier Aborigine practices (cf. Shepherd 1986). Residents of Toushe, Jibeishua, and Longtian regularly participated in Han folk religion in the 1990s, but these communities also maintained practices worshiping their Aborigine deity—including a large annual festival—at least through 1991. Let us examine the practices of each of the communities in turn.

Jibeishua   In 1991, Jibeishua's worship of A-li Bu appeared to have the least Han influence of the three study communities. The Jibeishua temple to A-li Bu (T., *kong-kai*; see figures 7 and 8) and subsidiary shrines

Figure 7. Main temple (T., *kong-kai*) in Jibeishua, 1992.

Figure 8. Central altar at the main temple in Jibeishua, 1992.

Figure 9. Central altar in Jibeishua at the annual festival, 1991.

(ying) still bore little resemblance to Han temples *(miao)*, other than in the presence of moon-shaped blocks (T., *puah-poe*) for divining the deity's response to petitions or queries. The only recent Han-style change there, as of 1992, was the inclusion of donors' names and the amount of their gifts carved into the walls and altar of the temple built in 1983 (partially visible in figure 8). The Jibeishua annual festival had some Han elements in 1991, including food offerings of the three meats (pork, fish, and chicken) and whole pigs and entertainment offerings of puppet shows and opera performances, but they were not necessarily recent introductions. Other Han elements, however, were notably absent. For example, at Han festivals all the neighboring deities are invited to enjoy the festivities, making for an altar covered with an array of deities. At the Jibeishua annual festival, there were no Han deities on the temple altars (see figure 9). Some Han customs had even been actively suppressed. The Jibeishua A-li Bu spirit medium specifically told me that she regularly removed incense she found stuck in the walls at the temple. She also, when possessed by A-li Bu, cut the electricity to the temple when someone made an entertainment offering of strippers. When the strippers left, "A-li Bu"

restored the electricity. For reasons I discuss further below, I attribute the minimal intrusion of Han elements into worship in Jibeishua as related to gender—specifically to the maintenance of an older woman with some authority as spirit medium.

Toushe   All but one of the changes that have occurred in Thai Tsoo worship in Toushe (as the Aborigine deity is called there) have been toward a Han cultural model.[53] Early in the twentieth century, the role of Thai Tsoo spirit medium was transferred twice from women to men, first at the temple (T., *kong-kai*) near the main settlement and later at the temple farther up in the foothills near one of the satellite settlements.[54] The deity may have even been called A-li Bu by the women spirit mediums (T., *tang-ki*), in which case a change in the deity's name went along with a change in the gender of the mediums.[55] The first transfer occurred before Toushe's identity change to Han, the second at about the time of the identity change. Unfortunately, the first transfer happened early enough that I was not able to reconstruct it. The second transfer—which I reconstruct based on interview reports—links the change in marriage patterns to the gender of the actual holder of the role of spirit medium. Here, then, we see a cultural change that resulted from the change in social experience and identity.

A woman whom I will call Tan A-lien was the last female spirit medium at the satellite temple (see figure 10), and a man whom I will call Lo Kim-hok was the second male spirit medium at the main temple (see figure 11). Tan's daughter and Lo's son were married for a time and then divorced. The two temples worshipped together while the marriage lasted. One villager who discussed this history with me thought that the divorce was related to disputes between Tan and Lo on religious matters. Specifically, Tan refused to teach Lo or his assistant, whom I will call Ong Bun, the important opening power *(kaixiang)* ritual in its entirety. Lo reportedly did not perform a very elaborate version of the kaixiang rite, and Ong's widow explicitly told me that Tan would teach her husband only a little of the rite. Lo and the subsequent male spirit medium later performed an elaborate version of the rite, but they were able to do so only because Ong went to Jibeishua to learn it, from a male relative there who was a spirit medium for the male Aborigine deity A-ka-tuan.

Tan tried to find a woman to take over the role of spirit medium after her but failed. She trained her son instead. Tan had a woman who acted as her assistant. That assistant's daughter-in-law, whom I will call

Figure 10. Toushe female spirit medium, ca. 1932 (probably Tan A-lien). Photograph by Asai Erin; courtesy of SMC Publishing, Inc., Taiwan.

Lim Mui-moe, told me that she herself was an instructor of the songs for the annual festival. Tan had taught her the songs but not how to perform the important kaixiang rite. When Lim volunteered that people thought that the Thai Tsoo spirit medium should be a woman, I asked why Tan had taught her son the kaixiang rite and not her daughter. Lim said that it was because Tan's daughter had married out virilocally and Tan's

TOUSHE

Alternate Names of the Aborigine Deity

Thai Tsoo
Lau Kun (for Tai Shang Lao Jun, in Mandarin)
A-li bu (only by those spirit mediums marked by *)

Spirit Mediums at the Main Temple	*Spirit Mediums at the Satellite Temple*
Ng* (female)	
I* (female)	name unknown (female)
Lo (male)	name unknown (female)
ate raw pig in trance	
Lo Kim-hok (male)	Tan-A-lien (female)
assistant: Ong Bun (male)	wanted to train Lim Mui-moe (female)
ate raw pig in trance	did not eat raw pig in trance
Lo (male, nephew of Lo-Kim-hok)	Ng (male, son of Tan A-lien)
ate raw pig in trance	

JIBEISHUA

Multiple Aborigine Deities

A-li bu (the primary deity, who is female)
An Tsoo (the most important male deity)
A-ka-tuan (a subordinate male deity)

Figure 11. Deity and spirit medium names in Toushe and Jibeishua Villages.

daughter-in-law (who married in virilocally) was not able to learn it. I interviewed Tan's daughter-in-law. She reported that she had wanted to learn the rite but Tan A-lien would not teach her. Given this report, I believe Lim Mui-moe meant that Tan's daughter-in-law *ought* not to learn it, due to her status as a virilocally married woman, rather than that she was not intellectually capable of it.

Tan had wanted to teach Lim the kaixiang rite, but Lim refused. When I asked Lim why she refused, she said that she was not married at the time and she did not know where she would marry; she did not think marrying uxorilocally was a possibility. I asked Lim why she did not reconsider after she married virilocally within Toushe. Lim said she did not want to go out so much for healing rites, another part of the spirit medium's duties, because she had small children. (Tan, by contrast, had become spirit medium when she was in her forties and her children were old enough to be left unsupervised.)

Thus, Lim herself linked virilocal marriages—which were increasing dramatically at that time—both to Tan's inability to pass the role on to her daughter and to Lim's own refusal to take on the role. This link, as well as a reported reduction in women villagers spraying rice wine over betel offerings to Thai Tsoo and the reduction in women chewing betel at all, indicates that local ideas of femininity and gender were changing toward a Hoklo Han cultural model and, in the process, reducing women's authority and the number and status of their roles in Thai Tsoo worship. At the time of the second transfer, Toushe people reportedly still did not think that the Aborigine deity's spirit medium should be a man. Nevertheless, in spite of the persistence of the *idea* across villagers that a woman should be the Aborigine deity's spirit medium, in practice men took over this social role.

Why did women's willingness to take on roles of public authority diminish? Lim Mui-moe initially explained her refusal to take on the role of Thai Tsoo spirit medium in terms of the very real possibility that she might marry out of the village, but the fact that she married within the village and still did not take on the role belies that explanation. Her second explanation was her having children too young to be left alone. In analyzing this reasonable explanation, we must remember that, at the time, Toushe villagers lived in extended families with many people. Why would her children have been alone if she left them? Although Lim did not marry outside the village, as many women in her generation did, like them she did marry virilocally. Thus, she was not an outsider in her husband's village (since it was her own natal village), but she was an outsider in her husband's family. Marrying to her husband's household meant that she would have had to rely on help from her sisters-in-law for child care if she were to take on the role of spirit medium. (Her mother-in-law was Tan's assistant and so she herself would not be home.) I suggest that Lim astutely gauged the probability that her sisters-in-law would not have supported her becoming spirit medium by caring for her children. Had Lim been married uxorilocally, where, as a family insider, she would have been asking her own mother or sisters to care for her children, her decision might well have been different.

According to people I interviewed, most of the Han-style changes in the Toushe main temple occurred in the 1930s, after the second transfer. Many occurred after 1945. In other words, most religious changes occurred after the change to Hoklo Han identity. Here, we see a cultural impact of the identity change: religious content changed. The architecture of the temple was changed (see figure 12), incense burners were introduced, altars were raised, additional vases and a white banner with

Figure 12. Main temple (T., *kong-kai*) in Toushe, 1991.

Han characters on it were introduced (see figures 13 and 14), and annual festival songs were standardized to be like Jibeishua's songs through
writing them down. The Han name "Tai Shang Lao Jun"—the title for
Lao Zi, the (male) founder of Daoism—was introduced as an alternate
name for Thai Tsoo, causing confusion among villagers about Thai Tsoo's
gender. The male spirit medium began practicing self-flagellation. At the
1991 annual festival, local Han deities were placed on the temple main
altar to enjoy the festivities (see figure 15). Finally, in 1991, the spirit medium and his assistant had expanded their services beyond the village—
sometimes traveling an hour or more by car to perform rituals, especially
for healing, and even to establish private Thai Tsoo altars. (In 1992, the
satellite temple did not have any spirit medium at all.)

Only the additional vases and the standardization of songs might be
seen as specifically *not* moving toward a Han model. However, I suggest
they do show Han influence. The additional vases can be interpreted as
mimicking the Han practice of having multiple images of a deity, and the
standardization of songs can be seen as conferring greater status on the
songs by creating a written text. (Writing is considered a fundamental
aspect of Han culture and, indeed, is fundamental to the Han notion of
civilization.) I interpret these changes as fitting within the deliberate efforts by the spirit medium and his assistant to expand Thai Tsoo's and,
by extension, their own influence. Such expansion of influence—including

Figure 13. Main altar at the main temple in Toushe, 1991.

the establishment of new subsidiary altars—is a standard aspect of the Han folk religion (cf. Sangren 1988).

Men also drew on the Han folk religion to consolidate their claim to the role of Thai Tsoo spirit medium. Specifically, they drew on the widespread Han belief in Taiwan that deities (including female deities such as Ma Tsoo) detest the pollution of women's menstrual periods. In 1992, when I asked the Toushe Thai Tsoo spirit medium about female spirit mediums, he explained that it was hard for a woman to do the healing rite (a major part of being a spirit medium), which included the kaixiang rite, because women cannot perform these rites during their menstrual periods. This male spirit medium cannot be seen as totally opposed to female spirit mediums—he did train two different women who lived well outside Toushe as spirit mediums to Thai Tsoo. However, the cultural changes he instituted in the religious practices, in conjunction with his discouraging attitude toward the possibility of a female spirit medium within Toushe, contribute to a consolidation of the role of Thai Tsoo spirit medium as gender.

Why did the acquisition of the role of Thai Tsoo spirit medium by men result in so many changes in religious practices? I suggest that the men may have had a greater sensitivity to the cultural standards of Han

Figure 14. The Thai Tsoo spirit medium singing the opening rite, 1991.

Figure 15. Main altar in Toushe at the Annual Festival, 1991.

religious practice. Not only are Hoklo Han spirit mediums typically men, but the role itself is gendered as male. Thus, from a Han perspective, women are anomalous as the type of spirit medium who are oracles and arbiters (like the Thai Tsoo spirit medium), a type both prestigious and influential in rural areas. "*Tang-ki* are expected to be and do things inappropriate for women, and even though the extraordinary circumstances of a god's demand should make it all right, the sheer incongruity between the expectations of a god's behavior and those of a woman's behavior is enough to create misgivings" (M. Wolf 1992:111). In Toushe, male Thai Tsoo spirit mediums may have been sensitive to comparisons between themselves and the spirit mediums of Han folk religion deities, especially as those male-gendered roles were introduced into their very community. For example, Ong Bun, who served as Lo Kim-hok's assistant in Thai Tsoo worship, was himself spirit medium to a Han deity. Ong strongly influenced both Lo Kim-hok and the man who was Thai Tsoo spirit medium in 1991 (Lo Kim-hok's nephew).

I suggest that the Toushe male spirit mediums adopted so many aspects of Han folk religion because it was possible, at least in theory, for them to achieve the normative social status of Hoklo Han spirit medi-

ums. This possibility existed both because Han folk religion is so syncretic (e.g., Harrell 1974; Weller 1987, 1994) and because—even in the
early twentieth century—these Toushe men were otherwise culturally very
much like the Hoklo. They were right at the border to Han. Choosing
to introduce Han religious practices would—they might have presumed—
push them across that border. Remember that the religious changes were
occurring right around the time that individual villagers were breaking
down the last vestiges of the border by arranging virilocal marriages with
neighboring Hoklo Han. Women spirit mediums—simply because they
were women—could never achieve the social status of male Hoklo Han
spirit mediums. They would always be marked as "other" on the basis
of their gender, so they had no incentive to adopt cultural aspects of the
Han folk religion. Given women's low status in the patriarchal, patrilineal Han social order, one could argue female spirit mediums in Toushe and Jibeishua had reason *not* to adopt Han religious practices. In
other words, I am suggesting that when comparing two stigmatized
groups in the role of ritual specialist—men once considered plains Aborigine and women once considered plains Aborigine—the group that
came closer to the higher-status norm (the men, because that ritual specialist was a male-gendered role to the Han) was more likely to adopt
other markers of the higher-status norm, to try to achieve that status,
than the group that had no chance of ever achieving the higher status
(cf. Brown 1995: chapter 2; n.d.).

The only change in Toushe religious practices that clearly moved away
from a Hoklo cultural model was the introduction of the spirit medium
eating raw pig intestines and blood while in trance during the annual festival. Han are disgusted by the consumption of raw pig's blood and meat,
but judging by the timing of the photography flashbulbs I saw going off
during the 1991 annual festival, it can also fascinate them. My field research suggests that the first male spirit medium at the main temple introduced the practice very early in the twentieth century—that is, well
before the identity change occurred, but when Toushe villagers already
appeared culturally very much like neighboring Hoklo villagers. All the
male spirit mediums were reported to have consumed raw intestines or
blood. In fact, one person criticized the 1991 spirit medium for not consuming as much as his predecessor. There were no reports that any of
the women spirit mediums in memory consumed raw intestines or blood,
and people specifically reported that Tan A-lien did not consume it.

Given the other attempts to practice religious ritual in a more Han
manner, why consume raw pig? The consumption of raw pig may have

been linked to an embrace of a Han stereotype of Aborigines as "savages" (T., *hoan-a*) by the first male spirit medium, precisely because of the sensitivity to how he was perceived by Han standards. If this man felt that he could not meet Han standards—perhaps just by being the spirit medium of an Aborigine deity—he may have chosen to exploit the Han fear of Aborigines and assert a kind of power frightening to Han, by consuming raw meat and even blood.

Such exploitation of the power to frighten can be seen in other examples as well. Shepherd (1986:8) reports that he was told by a Toushe villager that "in the old days human skulls were hung on these staffs" where the pig skulls hang now—a pointed reference to the Han stereotype that all Aborigines were headhunters. Moreover, "one [Toushe] informant told [Shepherd] that when [Han] Chinese referred insultingly to them, plains [A]borigines could, by touching the head of the Chinese, place a hex [*xiang*] on that Chinese which would cause him severe illness" (Shepherd 1986:32–33). Similarly, an old man from the one Han satellite settlement attached to Toushe by the Japanese colonial government told me that people in that satellite settlement did not formerly have much contact with Toushe because they were afraid of Toushe people. He said that Toushe people would tease him about killing him—another reference to head-hunting. One woman I interviewed, who claimed to be the first Han (first-time) bride in Toushe, reported being afraid when she first went there as a bride.

The consumption of raw pig also further consolidated the role of the spirit medium as male. Such consumption not only marks the deity as Aborigine, it also distances both the deity and the role of spirit medium from Han notions of femininity. Women's oral consumption among Han in Taiwan is much more restricted than men's. For example, women are frowned upon for drinking, smoking, chewing betel, and eating dog meat, all common male activities. Thus, the consumption of raw pig both makes Thai Tsoo more masculine—like the Han female deities entertained by strippers—and also makes it less likely that women villagers will aspire to the role of Thai Tsoo's spirit medium.

Thus, the gender of the person who actually held the locally important social role of spirit medium influenced the cultural content for which that role-holder was responsible. In short, the gender of the actual role-holder influenced religious practices and meanings. In Toushe, male role-holders introduced many changes in religious practices toward the Hoklo model including a name change that has created confusion among villagers about the gender of the deity! The consumption of raw pig, another change instituted by men, has probably also contributed to this confusion. In Jibeishua, by contrast, a female role-holder deliberately restricted Han-style religious offerings of incense and stripper performances.

Longtian   Worship of A-li Tsoo or Thai Tsoo (as the Aborigine deity is alternately called in Longtian) has changed so much in Longtian, in the direction of the Han model, that it has become secondary to other forms of worship. The deity is housed in a temple (*miao*, see figure 16). To external appearances, it is a completely Han-style temple dedicated to the founder of Daoism, Lao Zi (Tai Shang Lao Jun), although there were indications in the 1990s that the temple is not entirely what it seems. In front of the anthropomorphic images of Lao Jun (Lao Zi, portrayed as a man with a white beard) on the main altar, there were three ceramic pots which represent the Aborigine deity and, behind them, a flag (similar to the Toushe banner) which names A-li Tsoo and three Aborigine villages from which people were said to have migrated to Longtian (see figure 17). To each side of the main Han-style altar, there were large cisterns of charmed water next to another copy of the flag and a staff with pig skulls and dried flower garlands, the latter worn by dancers in the annual festival to the Aborigine deity (see figure 18). For those who missed these clues, there was a carved plaque near the entrance to the temple giving the town's former name, Fanzi Tian (roughly, Savage Acres), and explaining that plains Aborigines (here using the polite term *pingpu zu*) who worshipped the deity Ali Zu used to live in the town. Finally, in one of the offices, there were photos which show that the temple (*miao*) was built on the site of the former temple (T., *kong-kai*) which had a structure like that of the temple (T., *kong-kai*) in Toushe (see also Liu 1987 [1962]:27–29, 30; Shepherd 1986:80, figure 13; Shi Wanshou 1990:65, 69–71).

There have only been two Longtian spirit mediums in living memory—one in the 1950s and one who began her career in the late 1980s—both women, and both trained by male spirit mediums from Toushe.[56] When I saw the annual festival celebrated here in 1991, it was much more playful than the festivals in Toushe and Jibeishua. The adult women who performed the annual festival songs derived from a plains Aborigine language decided it would be fun to add a mountain Aborigine dance to the festival, so they did, complete with mountain Aborigine costumes. The man who was temple secretary dressed up in robes like a Qing-period Han scholar, creating the delightfully ironic image of a Han scholar taking instructions from a plains Aborigine spirit medium (see figure 19).

Figure 16. Main temple *(miao)* in Longtian, 1991.

Such playfulness helped perpetuate a festival to an Aborigine deity in a Han temple of a now predominantly Han city. The annual festival to A-li Tsoo attracted a small turnout of the immediate community around the temple. By contrast, a Han-style festival on the fourth day of the second lunar month appeared to have the participation of most, if not all, of the residents in that half of the small city. Han visitors at the latter festival must have been surprised to see a young woman in white—the A-li Tsoo spirit medium, who was the primary spirit medium of the temple—in charge at a Han-style temple and festival, but her gender and attire were the only clues at that festival that an Aborigine deity was taking part.

Although ensconcement in a Han-style temple—a community focal point—appears to have saved A-li Tsoo from oblivion in Longtian (cf. Harrell 1974), I think it has only postponed A-li Tsoo's demise there. The image of the deity on the altar is neither Aborigine nor female. While there is a plaque on the temple wall that discusses the Aborigine heritage of Longtian and the Aborigine origins of A-li Tsoo, will A-li Tsoo still be associated with Tai Shang Lao Jun in the years to come? The A-li Tsoo annual festival is a secondary community one, and in 1994 the A-li Tsoo spirit medium took a leave of several years from her role as spirit medium,

Figure 17. Central altar at the main temple in Longtian, 1991.

Figure 18. Pig skulls in the main temple in Longtian, 1991.

Figure 19. The A-li Tsoo spirit medium giving instructions in a trance, 1991.

due to serious illness. Without a spirit medium there to push A-li Tsoo forward, I think it likely that the temple will become completely Han in time, unless perhaps the political aspect of its Aborigine heritage in relation to a Taiwanese national identity keeps the Aborigine deity "alive."

Possible Contributions to Taiwanese Culture

It appears that the people of Toushe, Jibeishua, and Longtian who became the long-route Han have had little influence on local Hoklo cultural models. Marriages and burial rites have shifted toward the pre-existing Hoklo model. Han folk religion has flourished in Toushe, Jibeishua, and Longtian and has influenced religious practices in Toushe and Longtian tremendously. Aborigine elements in Han practice are likely to fade in Longtian without the consistent efforts of A-li Tsoo's spirit medium. Jibeishua has managed to maintain a separate Aborigine-derived religious tradition. However, it is not clear whether it will continue to do so, since the A-li Bu spirit medium did not designate and train a strong female successor before her death in 2001. Like Tan A-lien, the last female spirit medium of Toushe, the Jibeishua A-li Bu spirit medium faced a challenge to find a female successor in the context of the overwhelming change to virilocal, village-exogamous marriages that accompanied the acquisition of Han identity. When asked directly about her successor, the A-li Bu spirit medium assured me that the deity herself would indicate who should be her spirit medium. However, when I visited Jibeishua in 2002, the role of spirit medium (as temple oracle and arbiter) in the village Aborigine-derived religious tradition had passed to a man, who was serving as the spirit medium to An Tsoo, the most important of their male Aborigine deities.

The best possibility for long-route Han contributions of "Aborigine" cultural practices to Taiwanese culture may be the proselytization of Toushe's spirit medium and his assistant in expanding the range of Thai Tsoo's spiritual influence. In 1991–92, I accompanied the Toushe Thai Tsoo spirit medium and his assistant on a number of their trips. They took matters quite seriously and were very sincere in their dedication to bringing Thai Tsoo's aid to those who asked for or needed her help. They set up several private Thai Tsoo altars—I visited one in Gaoxiong city, and one in the mountainous part of Tainan County—but it remains to be seen whether these subsidiary altars, or the main temple at Toushe and Jibeishua, or the A-li Tsoo annual festival at Longtian for that matter, will grow in popularity among Hoklo. If Thai Tsoo becomes perceived as powerful *(ling)* and worship of her spreads in Taiwan, the long-route Han will have succeeded in contributing to larger Taiwanese culture—a potentially significant contribution, depending on how much her worship takes off in religiously observant Taiwan. But will that contribution still be recognizable to older Toushe residents? If it were recognizable to them, would it be appealing to other Taiwanese? By the late 1990s, local religious practices, for all their continuities, could hardly be considered a "contribution" to Hoklo culture, since they had not spread beyond the villages formerly considered plains Aborigine.

The significance of long-route Han contributions for the new narratives of Taiwan's unfolding, however, is immense. Toushe, Jibeishua, and Longtian have been held up to the public eye as "quintessentially" Taiwanese—real cases of Taiwanese villages where local history matches the narrative being constructed of Taiwan's past. An important part of the narrative—important for the nationalistic purpose of distancing Taiwan from the Chinese nation—is that Aborigine contributions have made the Taiwanese significantly different from the Chinese. If, however, Toushe, Jibeishua, and Longtian have contributed little or nothing to Taiwanese culture, then the new narrative itself comes into question. As we shall see in chapters 4 and 5, however, the degree of cultural transformation suggested by the narratives of unfolding does in fact occur.

RECONSIDERATION OF LONG-ROUTE HAN IDENTITY

Toushe, Jibeishua, and Longtian captured media and scholarly attention in the late 1980s and early 1990s. Their maintenance of religious practices, especially the main annual festival to "Ali Zu" (as the Aborigine deity is called in the popular media), provided publicly visible continuities to past Aborigine culture. Given the eclectic and inclusive character of Taiwanese folk religion, worship of an Aborigine deity is neither threatening nor particularly shocking to Hoklo. Moreover, these practices were already sinicized, especially in Toushe and Longtian, and were the only extant continuities with Aborigine culture. Such relatively innocuous cultural continuities combined with contemporary Hoklo identity made Toushe, Jibeishua, and Longtian appear perfect for the role of "quintessential" Taiwanese villages, whose local history matched the new narrative being constructed of Taiwan's past. Ironically, public examination of Toushe, Jibeishua, and Longtian as quintessentially Taiwanese has started to reverse long-route identity change. As I discuss further below, this reversal, by implication, undercuts the new narrative itself.

Outsider Reclassification versus Local Identity

As we have seen, people in Toushe, Jibeishua, and Longtian have some Hoklo patrilineal ancestry and cultural heritage from Hoklo men who married uxorilocally. They also have Hoklo matrilineal ancestry due to the adoption of Hoklo infant girls, and Hoklo matrilineal ancestry and cultural heritage from predominantly virilocal marriages with Hoklo brides since the 1930s. Nevertheless, as the Aborigine part of their ancestry and heritage became public knowledge in the late 1980s and early 1990s, these villages faced an increasing tendency for popular media— including books (e.g., Shi Wanshou 1990), culture tour advertisements, television reports, and newpaper articles (e.g., Duan 1992)—to refer to them as "plains Aborigine" *(pingpu zu).*

Even anthropologists appeared uncomfortable granting them Hoklo status. Scholarly works refer to Toushe, Jibeishua, and Longtian as plains Aborigine villages. Although Toushe, Jibeishua, and Longtian have come to reassert their plains Aborigine identity (beginning around 1996) due to the influences of Taiwanese nationalism, when I did my fieldwork (in 1991–92), these communities did *not* have a plains Aborigine identity, either among themselves or among their Hoklo neighbors. Nevertheless, at the end of a 1992 presentation I gave at the Institute of Ethnology in Taibei, one anthropologist asserted that I must have missed the plains Aborigine identity in those villages for, given their ancestry, they must certainly think of themselves as Aborigine. Similarly, at a conference on Taiwan history and culture in Seattle, a Taiwanese anthropologist placed my paper on "People with Mixed Hoklo and Plains Aborigine Ancestry" on a panel of "Aborigine issues," not Taiwanese or Hoklo issues. Moreoever, anthropologist Stevan Harrell, who has made important contributions to our understanding of identity in China and Taiwan (e.g., 1990a, 1993, 1995a and b, 1996a and b, 2001), took a middle ground, granting that people in these villages were no longer Aborigines but not calling them Hoklo or Han or Taiwanese either—he (1996a:7) called them "Taiwan ex-Aborigines." Such reclassification of long-route Han as plains Aborigine indicates ambivalence over the possibility of recent identity change. As I discuss further in chapter 4, there do not seem to be objections to identity changes occurring in the more distant past, but such is not the case for a recent change like this one.

I want to emphasize that outsiders initiated reclassification of these villages as Aborigine. Locally, Toushe, Jibeishua, and Longtian were still considered Hoklo in the early 1990s. For example, even after discussing the early-twentieth-century identity of Toushe as Aborigine and its change to Hoklo identity, the Hoklo people I interviewed in neighboring Danei were *not* willing to reclassify contemporary Toushe as Aborigine. I also observed Toushe, Jibeishua, and Longtian residents make some efforts to maintain their Hoklo identity. At the 1991 annual festivals which I attended, I overheard tourists calling the local people "plains Aborigine" *(pingpu zu)* on several occasions. Local residents were quick to respond to what they took as insults by saying that they are Hoklo. In Toushe, one tourist pressed the villager who had corrected him, citing worship of "Ali Zu" as evidence of plains Aborigine identity. The Toushe person explained—just as others had initially explained to me— that the Aborigines were gone but Thai Tsoo remains because she belongs to that place. Toushe residents worship her because they live there. This explanation fits within Han folk religion, in which deities such as Di Ji Zu (the spirit of the foundation) also remain in one location to be worshiped by successive residents.[57]

In 1992, a photographer for the Tai Yuan publishing company (which published Shi Wanshou [1990] and sponsored a culture tour for college students to the Jibeishua annual festival in 1991) horrified several Jibeishua villagers by arguing that Taiwanese are not Han but rather a mixture of Han and Aborigine that is significantly different from any cultures in China, including those of Fujian Province where the Hoklo originate. Villagers understood the implications of the photographer's words and they directly responded that they wanted no part in a political agenda to declare Taiwan's independence from China.[58] I think they also understood that they were being held up as examples of "plains Aborigine" culture as part of this agenda—via the books and culture tours of his company— and they were also indirectly responding to such an ethnic reclassification. The National Taiwan University graduate from Toushe who sought me out at the beginning of my fieldwork to say that Toushe is 99-percent Han may have had a similar motivation for his insistence, since he asked me if I wanted to say that Taiwanese are not Han for political reasons. Local people were regularly concerned about their reclassification as plains Aborigine in newpapers—many people I interviewed asked for reassurances from my translators that I was not a reporter.[59]

In the early 1990s, people in Toushe, Jibeishua, and Longtian— including those who discussed their former Aborigine identity with me— thought of themselves as Hoklo Taiwanese. As I have discussed, people presented themselves and their communities to me as Hoklo. It took much effort to get elderly people to discuss their Aborigine heritage, but these discussions were strictly focused on the *past*. That most young people were shocked to hear their grandparents discuss past Aborigine identity suggests that they had never had previous reason to question their Hoklo identity.

Political developments, however, seemed ripe to change local identity. Between August 1992 when I left the field and June 1994 when I returned, two plains Aborigine groups in northern Taiwan became vocal in pan-Aborigine political activism, and one petitioned to be recognized as the "tenth" Aborigine tribe of the Alliance of Taiwan Aborigines (Taiwan Yuanzhuminzu Quanli Cujinhui). Given the media coverage of these events and the obvious pride with which these northern plains Aborigine groups claimed and proclaimed their heritage—and thereby the introduction of the polite term "plains Aborigines" *(pingpu zu;* T., *peN-poo tsoo)* into Minnan—I wondered if people in Toushe, Jibeishua, and Longtian were also beginning to take pride in their Aborigine heritage.

Nevertheless, in response to my inquiries in 1994 about whether any local people were identifying themselves as plains Aborigines *(pingpu zu),* several people made it very clear that they did not. One man in Longtian told me that he does not know of anyone in his community who identifies him- or herself as Aborigine, although he said he could tell who was really Aborigine and indicated his own high cheekbones as an example of physical characteristics that can be used to detect plains Aborigines. This man was one of the most knowledgeable people in Longtian about his and his community's Aborigine heritage and had talked openly with me about both. Nevertheless, when I asked him in 1994 if he would identify himself as plains Aborigine, he shook his head no and even appeared apprehensive until the topic changed. A young woman in Jibeishua reminded me, when I inquired about plains Aborigine identity, that her family is Hoklo, not Aborigine, and brought out a genealogy to show me. She had shown me an old and incomplete copy of her family's genealogy in 1992, but in 1994 she brought out a new copy and told me that after I left the family had copied it from another branch of the family and had added her brothers and their sons to it. The genealogy shows the earliest ancestors as a pair of brothers who traveled from Jiangxi Province on the Chinese mainland to a southwestern Taiwan village identified as Aborigine in historical documents (e.g., Lu 1956, Zhang 1951). Several generations remained in that village until they migrated to Jibeishua, a migration which Liu (1987 [1962]:8) describes as a resettlement of plains Aborigines. A woman from Toushe told me that she now describes herself as *part* plains Aborigine, after she discovered in my interview of her mother that her maternal grand-mother was an adopted daughter of Han origin. She thought that some of the young people in Toushe might also be willing to claim a partial Aborigine ancestry, though none had done so publicly in 1994, but she did not think that the older people in Toushe would ever identify themselves as plains Aborigine because, she said, they are afraid of being called savages (T., *hoan-a*) again.

This generational difference has since proven significant. By 2000, most of the elderly people I interviewed had died. Without them to voice concerns over stigmatization, people in Toushe, Jibeishua, and Longtian have publicly embraced a plains Aborigine *(pingpu zu)* identity. These people belong to generations that do not remember being called savages, and hence the people I spoke with in 2000 were not concerned that a plains Aborigine identity might revert to a more derogatory identity as savages, even when I asked them about it directly. By contrast, such a reversion was a major concern for the elderly people I interviewed in 1991 and 1992. My own concerns derive from the concerns expressed by those elders.

Between 1930 and 1995, the only occasions I am aware of where the term "plains Aborigine" *(pingpu zu)* was used locally were in publicizing the lucrative annual festivals at the end of this period. In 1990, the county government distributed posters advertising the Toushe annual festival as a plains Aborigine festival. In 1991, a member of the Toushe Thai Tsoo temple committee—a committee of a dozen prominent village men who controlled temple finances—asked anthropologist Pan Inghai to help them contact television stations to publicize their annual festival and draw crowds. Pan told me at the time that he had helped them to do so once before, at their request. Similarly, just before Jibeishua's 1992 annual festival, a Jibeishua resident wrote an article for the newspaper *Lianhe Bao (United News)* about the festival songs (Duan 1992). (Jibeishua's annual festival occurs about two months earlier than Toushe's and Longtian's, so its publicity is separate from Toushe's.) Longtian did not publicize its festival at all, to my knowledge, but then its temple had less need of the income. Longtian's largest festival—a Han festival—gets the participation and contributions of about half the small city in which it is located.

There were clear economic reasons for publicizing the annual festivals. The Toushe and Jibeishua annual festivals generate a lot of income for local businesses and for the temples. There are food stalls, games, opera, and puppet shows at each temple. Local people generally invite relatives and coworkers for dinner and hire local companies to set up banquet tables, cook the food, serve it, and clean up afterwards. In 1991, one man told me that his small business served 120 tables the night of the annual festival and that there were 2,000 tables in total served in Toushe that night. A table serves ten to fourteen people and, in 1991, cost about NT$10,000 (New Taiwan dollars), which was about U.S.$380 at the time. Toushe was a village of less than 1,000 people, but there were about 20,000 people there to eat that night! Most people also went to the activities at the temple, and many made small donations. In 1991, the treasurer of the Toushe temple committee reported a net profit of NT$108,685 (about U.S.$4,180). To put this amount in context, it represented over a month's salary at that time for a truck driver, among the highest paid men in Toushe, and more than eight months' salary for those at the other end of the spectrum who relied on agriculture, itinerant wage labor, and home services. In local terms, then, the annual festival brings a large amount of money into the villages. Given the economic benefits of the annual festival, it is hardly surprising that some residents were willing to exploit popular interest in plains Aborigines, even if referring to the festival as "plains Aborigine" *(pingpu zu)* meant risking outside reclassification of the village as a whole as Aborigine.

Economic interests may also have contributed more directly to the turn-of-the-century embrace of plains Aborigine identity. Toushe, which has most aggressively promoted itself as plains Aborigine, has suffered economically from the construction of a new expressway into the central mountains. Before this expressway was built, the road through Toushe was the major county road into the central mountains, and local businesses profited from travelers and truckers who stopped to eat noodles or buy betel chaws. The new expressway is faster not only because it allows higher speeds but also because it avoids the circuitous narrow roads through small villages. For those villages, however, the new expressway has robbed them of much-needed business. These circumstances mean that local businesses must rely even more heavily on revenues generated once a year at the religious festival. More revenue at the annual festivals requires more tourists and thus advertising that will attract more people. In the context of a new Taiwanese national identity that claims a plains Aborigine heritage, it seems that more people in Taiwan will travel longer distances to see a plains Aborigine festival, especially one where the deity consumes raw pig through her spirit medium. Because this advertising plays so heavily on Han stereotypes of Aborigines as savages, the danger exists for plains Aborigines to once again be stigmatized as savages. Indeed, in 2002, I discovered that some scholars and county-level officials had already begun to refer to the villages once again as "savage" *(hoan-a)*. One such scholar, whom I met in Toushe, did not seem to view this further reclassification as problematic, despite my remonstrations.

So What Are They Really?

Viewed in terms of cultural practices today—one major means by which people generally claim ethnic identity, and the means by which Confucianism suggests Han identity ought to be claimed—Toushe, Jibeishua, and Longtian are virtually indistinguishable from nearby Hoklo communities except for part of their religious practices. Viewed in terms of ancestry—the other major means by which people generally claim ethnic identity—many people in these communities have patrilineal Han ancestry through uxorilocal marriages to poor Hoklo men. Most historically documented claims to Han identity rely on patrilineal Han ancestry, so there should be no problem accepting the people of Toushe, Jibeishua, and Longtian as Hoklo. However, when we look at their social and political experience, the factor by which ethnic identity is most often *actually* solidified (regardless of the terms in which it is claimed), we get mixed messages. Until the 1930s, when their classification changed, the social and political experiences of people in Toushe, Jibeishua, and Longtian were different from those of people in the neighboring villages which were classified as Han. Toushe, Jibeishua, and Longtian were treated as "savage" places. Then, from the 1930s through the martial law period, these villages were treated like other Hoklo Taiwanese places. Since political liberalizations began (in 1986), they have been recast as "plains Aborigine" places, leading one Longtian woman to tell me in 2000 that "we plains Aborigines [*pingpu zu*] are the real Taiwanese." What will their experience be in the future? That is what is at stake.

Elderly people I interviewed in Toushe, Jibeishua, and Longtian in 1991 and 1992 were legitimately concerned about the discrimination they and their descendants might face upon return to a classification as plains Aborigine. The senior generation remembered how they were treated in the past, and although the new narrative of Taiwan's unfolding places plains Aborigines in an honored position, other Han values that denigrate non-Han peoples have not changed. One of the people I interviewed brought the issue home to me. He asked me if I knew the Taiwanese term for a pack of matches, which was lying on the table (T., *hoan-a-hoe*, lit. "savage fire"). When I said that I did, he asked if I knew who the "savage" in that term referred to. I laughed and told him that I did—me. (*Hoan-*

a here refers to Westerners—"Western fire.") He responded, "We're all savages" (T., *lan hoan-a*). By using the inclusive-we form (T., *lan*) in his response, he made it clear that he was including me in that we-group. This was the only occasion in my fieldwork when someone referred to himself as "savage" in a present-tense context. However, it should be noted that it was a very unusual occasion because I introduced the term in a present-tense context in reference to myself; he responded in a face-saving way by including us both in the term. I interpret his meaning to be that, because I am also part of a group that the Han have labeled savage, he was comfortable discussing his non-Han heritage with me and that he expected me to bear such prejudice in mind in my use of the information shared with me about his Aborigine heritage. In short, the attitude that non-Han—whether Westerners or Aborigines—are barbaric is still in common-use language, so how will people in these communities be treated now that they have been reclassified as plains Aborigine? Their experience has implications for the new narratives of Taiwanese national unfolding.

ANTIQUITY, AUTHENTICITY, AND NARRATIVES OF UNFOLDING

The insistence of outsiders—ordinary Taiwanese, Taiwanese scholars, and Western scholars—in reclassifying long-route Hoklo as plains Aborigines implies that their plains Aborigine identity is somehow more "authentic." But is it? Just because an identity is recent does not make it less real, in the sense of being meaningful and motivating to people. Hoklo identity was, and I suspect still is, meaningful and motivating to people in Toushe, Jibeishua, and Longtian. For example, in the campaign leading up to the December 1991 elections, many politicians gave political speeches in Minnan (Taiwanese), including then-president Lee Teng-hui in a televised speech. In doing so, politicians were deliberately courting the Hoklo Taiwanese vote. A number of people in Toushe and Jibeishua who discussed these campaigns with me at the time pointed out that these speeches were very powerful statements, especially for older Taiwanese voters who remembered the draconian enforcement of Nationalist policies favoring Mainlanders, including the policy which allowed only Mandarin to be spoken in public places. One Taiwanese woman told me about being fined in the 1970s for speaking Minnan in a private conversation with a friend as they strolled across the campus of National Taiwan University. The political speeches in Minnan in the early 1990s moved the

Toushe and Jibeishua people who discussed them with me in their identity *as Hoklo*—that is, as Han.

If, as this example indicates, recent identities are not necessarily less meaningful, then why view older identities preferentially? The whole point of constructing narratives of unfolding is the presumption—common to nationalistic agendas across cultures—that antiquity confers authenticity. Thus, for example, the PRC—only fifty years old—draws on boundaries from China's imperial past to claim Tibet as part of the Chinese nation (see Karakasidou 1997 for a Macedonian example). Similarly, Mongols and Han dispute each other's claim of Genghis Khan as their symbolic hero (cf. Borchigud 1996: 173–74, Khan 1995).

To the extent that narratives of unfolding allow for change at all—as in the claim by new narratives of Taiwan's unfolding that Taiwanese people are not Chinese—they must make any such changes seem the inevitable culmination of past events, an unfolding of destiny. The problem, as we have seen in this chapter, is that the actual historical development of *recent* identities can be traced. These actual histories show all too clearly that identities are not inevitable, because they are so closely tied to sociopolitical circumstances. In the case of the long-route Hoklo discussed here, it is not clear whether Toushe, Jibeishua, and Longtian would have crossed the border to Han at all if that border had not been forcibly removed by the Japanese colonial government's intervention in banning footbinding. After all, areas still classified as mountain Aborigine at the beginning of Nationalist rule did not cross that border, because they had little contact with Han until after that time and were still visibly different from Han in many ways. Moreover, the choices of individuals—about marriage partners, for example—impact recent changes (cf. Leonard 1992). Think of the first Hoklo first-time bride in Toushe: her father-in-law made the decision to arrange a virilocal marriage to a Hoklo bride for his son, and it took him three years to accomplish that goal. We cannot know whether the change to Hoklo identity would have occurred if he had not been so persistent, but we can see that his actions contributed to that change, probably significantly. The impact of individual choices further undercuts a notion of inevitability because most people can remember having considered or desired someone different as a spouse, for their children or themselves. As a result, the recentness of long-route Han identity change undercuts the sense of destiny which new narratives of unfolding want to create because the historical contingencies that allowed that change to occur can still be reconstructed. This same recentness also allows reconstruction of the actual Aborigine cultural contributions to local Hoklo culture, which do not indicate the contributions claimed in the narratives. Thus, we can understand why people who support the new narratives of unfolding would want to question long-route identity change.

However, questioning long-route Han identity change on the basis of its recentness raises two main problems for narratives of unfolding. First of all, on what grounds should we accept older identity changes? The claim that antiquity confers authenticity appears to be a propaganda tactic designed to rally people around a narrative of unfolding with a nationalistic or ethnic agenda. "Authenticity," then, may arise from antiquity simply because antiquity makes it more difficult to reconstruct what actually happened and hence makes it easier to manipulate what is known of the historical past for political purposes. Viewed in this light, the claim that antiquity confers authenticity does not appear to have any legitimacy.

Even if, for the sake of argument, we accept the claim that antiquity confers authenticity, then we still have the problem of how old is old enough. (I address this issue further in chapter 5.) If an older identity is more authentic, then why should a Taiwanese identity be accepted at all? Taiwanese identity is, after all, relatively recent compared to both Han ethnic identity and Chinese national identity. So although embracing long-route Han as Hoklo Taiwanese might undermine the sense of destiny in the narratives of unfolding, failure to embrace long-route Han as Hoklo Taiwanese creates a worse problem. It undercuts the claim that Taiwanese are not Chinese.

CHAPTER 4

"Having a Wife Is Better than Having a God"

Ancestry, Governmental Power, and Short-Route Identity Change

Between the early seventeenth century, when the Dutch established their colonial mission, and the early eighteenth century, when the Qing regime began to loosen its restrictions on the migration of women and families to Taiwan, Taiwan's southwestern plain transformed.[1] Formerly a territory of networked Aborigine villages, home to a flourishing trading site with Han, Dutch, Japanese, Portuguese, and others at present-day Tainan City, the Jianan plain became a hierarchical system of primarily Han villages and market towns with interspersed Aborigine villages.[2] Huge numbers of Han men migrated to Taiwan throughout this time. I argue that most Han immigrants who were able to marry found brides locally—primarily Aborigine women and the "mixed" daughters or granddaughters of earlier Han men. Intermarriage thus created a "mixed" population—households with both Han and Aborigine members and individuals with both Han and Aborigine ancestry. This mixed population took on a Han identity under the Zheng or, at the latest, in the early part of the Qing regime (i.e., by the beginning of the eighteenth century). The mixed population used ancestry, not culture, to claim Han identity, probably through the use of Han surnames, because they followed many Aborigine cultural practices and could still claim Aborigine identity opportunistically. I call this identity change "the short route to Han" because the identity of these these mixed descendants of plains Aborigines changed before there was much cultural change toward a Han model.[3]

This late seventeenth-century identity change is important to a consideration of new narratives of Taiwan's unfolding for two reasons. First, people in Taiwan today accept this older identity change more readily than the long-route identity change that occurred in the early twentieth century. As discussed in chapter 3, such acceptance may be because people view antiquity as unproblematically conferring authenticity. Alternatively, it may be because people presume that the *process* of identity change was somehow different in the past and that the older process was somehow more authentic. Closer examination, however, indicates that the same processes of intermarriage and political intervention caused identity change in both the seventeenth and twentieth centuries. It was not different processes but merely differences in the *timing* of political intervention and in the *rate* of intermarriage which caused such differences in the claimed basis of identity change and in the accompanying contributions to Hoklo cultural models. Just as in long-route identity change, changes in governmental power ultimately drove identity change. However, where the long route has a low rate of intermarriage and an intervention by a new regime very late with respect to cultural change, the short route has a high rate of identity change and a governmental intervention very early with respect to cultural change.

The second major reason why short-route identity change is important to consideration of new narratives of Taiwan's unfolding is its cultural impact. It appears that short-route identity change, unlike long-route change, did contribute Aborigine cultural influences to local models of Hoklo Taiwanese culture, just as the newly constructed narratives of Taiwan's past suggest. Based on the premise that intermarriage is a primary means for introducing different cultural practices and ideas into a community, I argue such contributions were possible both because there was such a high rate of intermarriage and because identity change occurred so early with respect to cultural change. For both of these points, then, we need to estimate the rate of intermarriage and the timing of relevant political changes.

In this chapter, I reconstruct short-route identity change. Historical references to marriages that occurred between Han and Aborigines in the seventeenth and eighteenth centuries together with evidence of the overwhelmingly male immigration from China and the rapid growth of the Han population in Taiwan suggest that there was significant Han-Aborigine intermarriage, at least through the early eighteenth century. Changes in the ruling regime—first from Dutch to Zheng and later from Zheng to Qing—created windows of opportunity for people of mixed households and ancestry to renegotiate their official classification. These classifications were used, for example, for calculating the types and amounts of taxes owed (see chapter 2). I suggest that discrepancies between Dutch- and Zheng-period census figures not only support that mixed-ancestry descendants of plains Aborigines did indeed take the short route to Han but also imply that changes in governmental power, rather than intermarriage itself, spurred the identity change.

Census discrepancies interpreted in this fashion suggest that intermarriage between Han and Aborigines was quite high during the Dutch and Zheng periods, higher than one might expect from narratives of Taiwan's unfolding (old or new) or from Han disdain of non-Han peoples. The discrepancies also suggest that who was classified as "Aborigine" in the Dutch and Chinese historical records is ambiguous. I consider why individuals might have chosen to marry across ethnic boundaries, since the high intermarriage rate results from many individual decisions regarding marriage partners. Consideration of personal dynamics in a cross-cultural marriage suggests the means by which these short-route Han may have contributed Aborigine cultural ideas and practices to the local model of Taiwanese culture. Finally, I analyze the implications of short-route identity change and the contributions of short-route Han to Taiwanese culture for the new narrative being constructed of the unfolding of Taiwan's past.

MIGRATION AND INTERMARRIAGE

General reports that some Han men married Aborigine women begin in the Dutch period and continue throughout the Zheng period and well into the Qing period (e.g., Campbell 1903:139, 201–2, 551; Chuang 1987: 181, 188; Haguenauer 1977 [1930]:92; Hsu 1980a:17, 25; Meskill 1979:21, 31, 43, 46; Shepherd 1993:84, 152; Huang 1957 [1736] translated in Thompson 1969:120, 122, 137). Unfortunately, these vague references do not give estimates of the numbers of Han-Aborigine marriages that existed. We can, however, get a sense of how much intermarriage must have taken place by examining estimates about migration, the population sex ratio, and the growth of the Han population in southwestern Taiwan based on records of the different regimes. An understanding of both processes of identity and cultural change rests on understanding what can be historically reconstructed about the rate of Han-Aborigine intermarriage.

During the Dutch period, Han women were rare in Taiwan. Even in 1649, there were only 838 women in a Han population of 11,339, ac-

cording to figures from an unpublished letter written by Dutch governor
Verburg and the Council of Formosa to their VOC superiors in Batavia
(Java) on November 18, 1649 (cited in Huber 1990:274n25).[4] Unfortunately, it is not clear how Verburg arrived at this figure—possibly from
poll-tax figures—nor is it clear whether the figure was supposed to be
for Han women only or for all women married to Han men, which would
presumably include most if not all Han women, some Aborigine women,
and probably some women of mixed ancestry. Even if all of these women
were Han immigrants, the ratio of Han men to Han women obtained—
1,353 men to 100 women—shows extreme male bias.

Later in the Dutch period, between 1655 and 1658, the number of
Han women per year who sailed in Chinese ships to Taiwan that were
reported to the Dutch (there were also unreported, "illegal" crossings by
ships to avoid Dutch fees) ranged from 223 to 921 women and constituted between 4 and 12 percent of the total number of passengers; not
all of these Han women remained in Taiwan (Hsu 1980a:19). A 1675
source attributed to Frederick Coyett, the last Dutch governor, estimated
the Han Chinese population in 1661 at 25,000 armed men, not including women and children (Campbell 1903:384).[5] It is not clear whether
Coyett reported the Han population only in terms of men because they
were the labor and fighting power with which he was concerned on the
eve of Zheng Chenggong's invasion—rumors of the coming invasion were
everywhere—or whether he did not consider the women and children to
be unambiguously Han. That is to say, many of the women may have
been Aborigine or mixed, in which case the children would also have
been mixed. Shi Lang, the Qing admiral who defeated the Zhengs in 1683,
estimated Taiwan's Han population under the Dutch as 20,000 to
30,000 (Jiang 1960 [1704]:244, Shepherd 1993:96). It is not clear
whether this figure included such women and children as Shi considered
unambiguously Han.

The Zheng invasion brought 36,000 to 37,000 people from China in
two major waves: 30,000 in 1661 and another 6,000 to 7,000 in 1664.
Assuming that all of these people were Han but taking into account an
estimated attrition of 6,000 soldiers due to disease and the ongoing war
throughout the Zheng regime's control of Taiwan, Shi Lang estimated
the Han population in Taiwan in 1668 at a maximum of 61,000. It is
not clear how many of those who came to Taiwan with the Zhengs were
female. If Shi Lang's figures of the total number of people who went to
Taiwan in 1661 and 1664 include both men and women, then the largest
possible number of women who migrated is the difference between his

estimates of the number of migrants and the number of soldiers: 13,000.[6] If we further assume that each woman estimated represents one marriage, the *minimum* number of men who came to Taiwan in the early Zheng period without wives was 11,000.[7] The addition of at least 11,000 unmarried men would have skewed the population sex ratio even further toward a male bias. In 1668, Shi Lang also estimated that 50 to 60 percent of the Zheng forces (i.e., soldiers)—that is, 9,000 to 10,800 men—were without wives.[8] Thus, *minimally* between 200 and 2,000 Han soldiers were married within a few years after their arrival in Taiwan.[9]

Who married the soldiers? The fact that half the men remaining in Taiwan in 1668 were married does not mean that all their wives accompanied them from the Chinese mainland. Some wives may have accompanied their husbands; other women were kidnapped from the mainland and sold as brides in Taiwan (Hsu 1980a:25; Jiang 1960 [1704]:244, 258; Shepherd 1993:97). In spite of these additional sources of Han wives, a large number of soldiers' wives were probably local women—women who were already living in southwestern Taiwan at the end of the Dutch period. The low proportion of Han women in the population during the Dutch period suggests that most local women were Aborigine or mixed-ancestry women.

CHANGING IDENTITIES

Because Dutch and Chinese historical records generally refer to Han and Aborigine populations—in terms of number of persons, households, and/or taxable heads—but not specifically to a mixed population, most individuals of mixed ancestry and mixed households (with both Han and Aborigine members) must have been classified with one or the other identity label. There were some intermediate categories between Aborigine and Han, such as "those who paid only the [A]borigine head tax but did not give labor service, and those who paid no tax at all yet could not be called wild or untamed" (Shepherd 1993:473n12). Unfortunately, little is currently known about the people in these intermediate categories. In the absence of known records explaining the classification process, we must analyze the historical context to determine how people of mixed ancestry and households with Han-Aborigine marriages were classified. In each period, the identity of the regime in power and its relations with Han and Aborigines are crucial to the social consequences of these different ethnic classifications.

Under Dutch rule, it would *not* have been to the advantage of the mixed population to be classified as Han. Although the Dutch encouraged Han immigration, they were highly suspicious of Han and kept them largely disenfranchised, both politically and militarily.[10] Plains Aborigines, however, had limited access to power under the Dutch—they were allies of the Dutch and, in the 1652 Guo Huaiyi rebellion, were crucial to Dutch control of the large Han population of farmers and laborers. Thus, I think it likely that, before the Zheng invasion, those who could claim Aborigine identity—including people of mixed ancestry—would have done so, except in private transactions with Han.

It is less clear how households with mixed marriages would have been classified under the Dutch. Would a household which contained a nuclear family where the senior male was Han be classified as Han? The Dutch certainly wanted to keep an eye on Han men, but if the Han man converted to Christianity (cf. Campbell 1903:139, 201–202) might they have allowed the household to be classified as Aborigine or in one of the intermediate categories? Would a household which contained an extended, matrilineal Aborigine family where the senior male was Aborigine and the Han man was a son-in-law be classified as Aborigine? We do not know.

After Zheng Chenggong arrived, the situation reversed. It was not merely advantageous for the "mixed" population to be considered Han, in terms of avoiding newly imposed corvée labor duties (see chapter 2), but also disadvantageous to be too closely associated with the Dutch. The Fort Zeelandia daily journal reports that during the siege of 1661–62:

> The Chinese had forced every one [every Aborigine] who bore a Dutch (Christian) name to change this name according to the desire of parents or friends. Severe punishments were threatened if this command were not obeyed. (Translated in Campbell 1903:323)

Certainly the significance of names to the Han was not lost on the people whom the Dutch had classified as Aborigines. It seems likely that at least those who had a Han father or grandfather whose surname they could take—with legitimacy in the eyes of Han if the name was derived patrilineally—would have done so.[11] Thereafter such mixed-ancestry people would likely have been categorized as Han by the Zheng regime and later by the Qing regime.

However they were classified under the Dutch, mixed households that were nuclear families headed by a Han were probably unquestioningly classified as Han under the Zheng and later Qing regimes because of the strong patrilineal, patriarchal assumptions of Han culture. Mixed households where a Han man married uxorilocally were probably open to negotiation—if the Han man was the senior male and/or all the children had his surname, Zheng and Qing officials may have been willing to classify the household as Han.

In short, the regime change from Dutch to Zheng and Qing created a social context in which it was advantageous for the mixed population to change their classification from Aborigine to Han.[12] The Han ancestry of some gave them grounds for claiming Han identity, which were recognized as culturally legitimate within a Han system, and the presence of a Han man probably gave others the means to negotiate a Han status for the household as a whole.

ESTIMATING THE RATE OF INTERMARRIAGE

How many people changed identities in this way? An estimate of Han-Aborigine intermarriage is important because a quantitative difference in the rate of intermarriage—combined with the sociopolitical context of regime change—appears to have changed the chronological order of cultural and identity change for short-route Han. We saw in the long route that a relatively low rate of intermarriage between Han men and Aborigine women led to great cultural change but not identity change. In the short route, by contrast, a relatively high rate of intermarriage led to identity change before there was much cultural change. It looks as though intermarriage led to Aborigine cultural influences on the local model of Taiwanese culture by both direct and indirect means: directly in that mothers passed Aborigine cultural ideas and practices to their children with Han identities (as I discuss further below) and indirectly by allowing identity change to precede most cultural change, so that the new (short-route) Han were still using Aborigine cultural practices and "Han culture" changed by definition.

If many people classified as Aborigines under the Dutch convinced the Zheng regime that they were "really" Han, it would explain the great discrepancy between Dutch- and Zheng-period figures for the Aborigine population.

> The [Z]heng figures for [Zhuluo's] [A]borigine population, 4,516 taxable heads and 2,224 households, seem extremely low when compared with the Dutch census for the same region, which showed 26,047 persons and 5,785 households in 1650. (Shepherd 1993:111)

If the mixed population—and only those who actually had mixed ancestry or lived in mixed households—changed ethnic identities from Aborigine to Han at the beginning of the Zheng period, then these figures would mean that at most 21,531 people, or 83 percent of the population classified as Aborigine under the Dutch, had mixed ancestry or were living in mixed households. If we calculate the mixed population in terms of the discrepancy between the figures for households, however, we get a lower estimate of 61.5 percent of the population classified as Aborigine under the Dutch, roughly 16,019 people, as mixed.[13]

Assuming that the people whom the Dutch considered Han were *not* of mixed ancestry, I calculate the percentage of the total population in 1650 which was mixed—either of mixed ancestry or living in a mixed household—as follows. The Dutch estimated that there were 15,000 Han in 1650, including those paying the poll tax, those exempt, and a few thousand tax evaders (Huber 1990:274). Zhuluo was north of Taiwan County, the core area of Dutch control and Han immigration. If, for the moment, we assume that this Han population estimate covers only the Zhuluo area (the Aborigine figures above are for Zhuluo), then the total Zhuluo population was roughly 41,047. The larger estimate of the mixed population (21,531) is 52 percent of this figure for the total population, while the smaller estimate (16,019) is 39 percent. If, however, the Han population estimate covers a much larger area than Zhuluo (e.g., Zhuluo and Taiwan County and Fengshan), then the mixed population would have been an even larger percentage of the total population of Zhuluo. Given that the Dutch monitored the Han population closely, I think it likely that the Han estimate covers the larger area (and not just the core area in Taiwan County). Thus, I estimate that *at least* 39 to 52 percent of the total population in this area was mixed.

Although this estimate is high, I think it is reasonable given the extreme male bias in the Han immigrant population. Dutch records (e.g., cited in Campbell 1903:118, 127, 128, 133) indicate that some of the Han living in the core area of southwestern Taiwan had integrated themselves into Aborigine communities by 1636. Han living in Aborigine villages even gave rice to the Dutch in 1636 (Campbell 1903:155), suggesting that these Han were settled farmers. Han men—one in 1636 and an unspecified number in 1644—were reported by the Dutch as needing instruction in Christianity because they wanted to marry Christian Aborigine women (Campbell 1903:139, 201–202). As Dutch power grew after 1636 and more Aborigines converted to Christianity, at least nominally, the Dutch policy that Han men who wanted to marry Aborigine women must convert was probably enforced more often. More Han men probably converted, at least in name, which would account for the popular Taiwan frontier saying that "having a wife is better than having a god" (reported in Hsu 1980b:88). These mixed marriages under Dutch rule produced both mixed households and children of mixed ancestry— girls who might become brides of Han men (their Han fathers probably preferred Han sons-in-law) and boys who could claim Han identity patrilineally. Given that the Zheng invasion brought *at least* 11,000 unmarried men to Taiwan, that *at least* 200 to 2,000 of these men managed to marry, and that there were probably far more Aborigine and mixed women available than Han women, a high rate of mixed marriages may well have continued through the end of the Zheng period. These Zheng-period mixed marriages further contributed to the growth of the mixed population, by births of mixed-ancestry children and formation of mixed-marriage households, which could claim a Han identity when the Qing regime took over, if not under the Zheng regime.

John Shepherd (1993:84) suggests that during the Dutch period "a high proportion of [Han Chinese village] traders [as opposed to the immigrant Han Chinese agriculturalists] apparently took [A]borigine wives, a reflection of the relatively high status of the traders in village society and the absence of [Han] Chinese women in Taiwan." Unfortunately, Shepherd does not provide empirical evidence of different rates of intermarriage for traders and farmers. Some Qing period historical records (e.g., Yu Yonghe's 1697 report, translated in Thompson 1964) do comment upon the marriage of village traders or interpreters to Aborigine women yet are silent about the marriages of Han agriculturalists. This silence, however, does not necessarily mean that no marriages were occurring. Consider, for example, a 1787 report by Fukang'an (the Manchu governor-general of Shaanxi and Gansu, whom the Qianlong emperor dispatched to Taiwan to put down the Lin Shuangwen rebellion):

> *In every village I visit, the settlers have families,* and among the refugees [from the Lin rebellion] women and children are especially numerous. These people have already lived in Taiwan for several generations; they could not be ordered back to the mainland. *If the prohibition* [on the migration of women and children to Taiwan] *were reinstituted now, single men arriving in Taiwan could still [find wives and] establish families here;* so no matter how strictly enforced, it would be a prohibition in name only. (Translated in Shepherd 1993:330, emphasis added)

The "settlers" referred to here are probably agriculturalists and, according to Fukang'an, they were finding local wives, whom I suggest includes Aborigine and mixed-ancestry women.

In discussant's remarks (on Brown 1999), Shepherd said that he thinks that an estimate of close to half the total Zhuluo population as mixed is unduly high. I disagree. Let us first examine Shepherd's comments and then analyze the assumptions implicit in them in terms of what is known about the historical context. Shepherd views high mortality rates limiting the natural growth rate (i.e., from births) to such an extent that estimates of the mixed population must come almost entirely from high rates of intermarriage throughout the Dutch and Zheng periods. This view represents a change from his (1993:97) earlier position that the reason "natural increase contributed little to Taiwan's [Han] Chinese population [was] because of the greatly unbalanced sex ratio." Shepherd also views the Aborigine population as so small throughout the Dutch period that such a high intermarriage rate would mean that every Aborigine woman was taken in marriage by Han men. In other words, that *no* plains Aborigine women would have been available for marriages to plains Aborigine men. He suggests that such a high rate of intermarriage in the Dutch period would have been recorded by the Dutch missionaries or their VOC critics and that such a high rate in the Zheng period would have been reported in Chinese sources. Shepherd suggests that Zheng soldiers brought Han brides to Taiwan from the Chinese mainland, possibly years after their initial arrival in Taiwan—in contrast to his remarks elsewhere about a "severe shortage of [Han] Chinese women on the frontier" (1993:386) and "high rates of intermarriage [of Aborigine women] to Han husbands" (1993:526n120). Finally, in his book, Shepherd (e.g., 1993:152, 453n41, 526n120) accepts the occurrence of high rates of intermarriage at various points in the seventeenth and eighteenth centuries.

I am not suggesting that every Aborigine bride who came of marital age was swooped up by Han men, leaving no Aborigine brides for Aborigine men. Nor am I suggesting that every Han man who married had an Aborigine bride. Han women did travel to Taiwan during the Dutch period, albeit in small numbers (4 to 12 percent of reported passengers between 1655 and 1658 [Hsu 1980a:19, op. cit.]). Refugees from the southeast coast of the mainland fled to Taiwan despite Qing efforts to prevent them, and Zheng forces went back and forth to the Chinese mainland after 1661 (cf. Shepherd 1993:96), so there were means for conveying some Han women to Taiwan. Shepherd (1993:97 citing Jiang 1960 [1704]:244, 258) suggests, "The shortage of wives [during the Zheng period] meant that kidnapped women brought a good price in Taiwan. Because of this trade, the number of households on Taiwan 'increased daily.'" Based on Shi Lang's estimates, it appears that some 200 to 2,000 Zheng soldiers found wives. Certainly some Zheng soldiers—and some

Han men earlier under Dutch rule as well—would have been able to bring Han brides over to Taiwan. However, Shepherd appears to assume that most of the 200 to 2,000 requisite brides were stolen from the mainland. By contrast, I think kidnapping procured fewer wives for Han men in Taiwan than did local sources of Aborigine and mixed wives. Why would Zheng soldiers—especially those lower in rank and income—go to the trouble and expense of getting a kidnapped bride if there were other women available locally?

The difficulty, of course, is that we do not have numbers—neither the number of marriages between Han men and Aborigine or mixed women nor the total number of Han women who came from the mainland to live in Taiwan. Both Shepherd and I make assumptions in our analyses of the historical information available. Because we make some different assumptions, we view the possibility of nearly half the total Zhuluo population being mixed in 1650 very differently. I think that there was some growth from births in the mixed population, that there was a larger Aborigine population in the Dutch period than Shepherd thinks, and that there is historical evidence of Han-Aborigine intermarriage occurring during the Dutch period, in spite of missionary disapprobation of it. I suggest that analysis of available data, while not sufficient to definitively calculate the size of the mixed population, supports the assumptions I make leading to a large mixed population estimate as more plausible than Shepherd's assumptions leading to a small estimate.

Consider Shepherd's suggestion that mortality was so high that the mixed population must have come from continuously high rates of intermarriage rather than from the birth and survival of mixed-ancestry children. This suggestion assumes that Han and Aborigines had similarly high mortality rates. However, references to Han falling ill after arrival in Taiwan (e.g., Shepherd 1993:94) and blood and protein studies carried out in the twentieth century suggest that Han were more susceptible to diseases such as malaria than Aborigines were.[14] In this regard, the colonial situation in Taiwan resembled that of Europeans in Africa more than that of Europeans in the Americas: colonizers were more affected by disease than the colonized. Thus, it appears that Han had higher mortality rates than Aborigines. A genetically admixed (mixed-ancestry) population generally has a short-term genetic susceptibility to disease intermediate between its two ancestral populations (in the absence of new selection pressures), so people of mixed ancestry would not have had as high a mortality rate as Han. For mortality in the mixed population to have been high enough to preclude natural growth, the Han mortality rate would have to have been incredibly high—much, much higher than the Aborigine rate—to skew the intermediate rate so much. Figures on longevity from two Fujian lineages which sent sojourners abroad (Wang 1995:211), however, suggest that Han mortality rates in Taiwan were probably intermediate between rates for members of the same lineage in China and in Southeast Asia. It seems unlikely that high mortality would have prevented an increase in the mixed Han-Aborigine population in Taiwan.

The Dutch-period Aborigine population also appears to have been larger than Shepherd suggests. To calculate his estimate of the Dutch period population, Shepherd projects census figures for Aborigines from the late Dutch period—1647, 1650, 1655—onto the early Dutch period. For example, Shepherd (1993:40–41) calculates the average village population in census region 4, which included Zhuluo, as 1,007 in 1647, as 1,012 in 1650, and as 809 in 1655. He (1993:66) appears to rely on these calculations to report the total population of one village in this area as "approximately 1,000" at an earlier point in time—1636 to 1639. Moreover, I understood him, in discussing these figures with me, to accept the 1650 figures as approximately accurate for 1620 through 1650. In other words, Shepherd assumes that the Aborigine population in this area remained fairly constant throughout the Dutch period.

However, some evidence suggests that the Aborigine population dropped in the core area from the early to the late Dutch period. In 1639, VOC governor van der Burgh estimated the number of people per Aborigine village in the core area to be between 1,000 and 3,000 (Campbell 1903:179–80), but the Dutch census surveys of 1647, 1650, and 1655 counted between 800 and 1,000 (Nakamura 1936, 1937, 1951; Shepherd 1993:39–46; Wang 1980; see also Brown, 1996b:48). Unfortunately, none of these sources indicate how many Han are present in those villages. Shepherd (1993:45) himself notes a "curious discrepancy" in population figures, which indicates population fluctuation: Soulang (Xiaolong), a village in the core area where the Dutch had most control (and thus must have had the most reliable figures), reportedly had a population of 2,093 in 241 households in 1650, but four years later had almost 600 fewer people (1,490) yet more households (245). Shepherd (1993:458n91) speculates that this difference is due to high mortality, but, as we will see, the emigration of plains Aborigines and immigration of Han, perhaps linked to uxorilocal marriages, could also explain these figures.

Migration away from their village sites was apparently a common Aborigine strategy for avoiding military threats. Candidius, the first Dutch

missionary to Taiwan, wrote as early as 1628 and 1629 that some of the
people of Sinkan (Xingang), an Aborigine village in the core area which
later became the primary ally of the Dutch, had fled inland in fear of military action by the Dutch (Campbell 1903:96, 99). Moreover, such migration away from their control was a recurrent problem for the Dutch.
Junius, another Dutch missionary, reported four villages using this strategy in anticipation of two Dutch raids in 1635 (Campbell 1903:117, 119–
21, 123–24). According to Junius, writing in 1636,

> Whenever difficulties arose between us and our Sinkandians and other
> villages, and they thereby incurred our displeasure, they were wont to
> say, "We will go to Tevorang [Dawulong, in the foothills], there the Dutch
> cannot and dare not come," and this idea hardened them in their wicked-
> ness. In order to show them that their threat was a futile one, the [Dutch]
> Governor resolved to visit the people of Tevorang. (Translated in Campbell
> 1903:126)

Thus, there was significant movement of Aborigines between the plains,
where Zhuluo is located, and the foothills. As a result, I think it is very
problematic to assume that the late Dutch population figures can be used
for earlier decades. The later Dutch census figures and the 1639 reports
are for populations *after* these known migrations. How do we know that
everyone who fled returned? It is plausible that some Aborigines chose
to stay in the foothills rather than return to Dutch control. Moreover,
the Dutch figures show fluctuations even in the 1650s.

Let us turn now to the matter of Han-Aborigine intermarriage. Occasional Dutch reports of Han men living in Aborigine villages (Campbell 1903:127, 128, 133, 155) suggest that there were Han-Aborigine marriages early in the Dutch period that could have produced mixed-ancestry
children. Moreover, as the passage by Junius quoted above shows, prior
to 1636, the Dutch did not have very strong control of even the Aborigine village which later became their closest ally. In fact, in 1627, the
Dutch were not able to prevent a Japanese captain from transporting sixteen Xingang villagers and two Han interpreters to Japan (Campbell
1903:36, 42, 56–57; Blussé 1984:162; Shepherd 1993:52).[15] Such lack
of control suggests that the Dutch were not able to prevent intermarriage, however much they may have disapproved of it.

Finally, there may have been an unusually high number of Aborigine
women available as brides in the 1640s and 1650s. Upon contact with
the Dutch, Aborigines in the southwest core area limited their population by aborting (through external physical manipulation of the ab-

domen) all pregnancies of women under the age of 30 to 35—some women claimed to have had fifteen or sixteen abortions (e.g., Campbell 1903:19–20, 95; Blussé and Roessingh 1984:70; Shepherd 1993:65–66, 1995). Dutch missionaries strongly discouraged this practice, with increasing success as Dutch control in the area grew throughout the 1630s (Campbell 1903:143, 162, 179, 182–83, 186). A population that had managed to sustain its numbers with such methods of population control must have increased its numbers dramatically as abortions stopped and women began having children fifteen or twenty years younger. If Aborigine men continued to wait decades to marry younger women (e.g., Shepherd 1995:25–26), there may also have been a brief period—probably in the late 1640s or early 1650s—when more Aborigine women were available as brides than there were Aborigine men to marry them. Such a population spike could help explain the occurrence of Han-Aborigine marriages, reported in Dutch missionary records as Han men needing Christian training in order to wed Christian Aborigine women, during the peak of Dutch control (Campbell 1903:139, 201–202). Such dramatic changes might also have affected the age at which Aborigine men married; we do not know whether Aborigine men began to seek marriage at younger ages.

Moreover, Dutch encouragement of early marriage and procreation in combination with Han customs of early marriage and procreation (for women at least) suggest that a short (twenty-year) generation was likely. Given a twenty-year generation, couples marrying in the 1620s and early 1630s would have had adult children by the 1640s and early 1650s and adult grandchildren by the 1660s and early 1670s. Thus, by the Zheng period, the mixed population probably included not only the children of intermarried couples but also some grandchildren.

The apparently differential mortality rate of Han and Aborigines, the possible higher numbers of Aborigines in the early Dutch period, the likely population spike for Aborigines in the 1640s and 1650s, and the consequences of changing to a relatively short twenty-year generation all suggest that the mixed population may have grown naturally (by births) as well as by continued intermarriage. These interpretations of the historical record mean that, contrary to Shepherd's view, not every Aborigine woman had to marry a Han man in order to account for almost half the total population of Zhuluo to have been "mixed" in 1650.

Shepherd suggests that if intermarriage was occurring in large numbers then Dutch and Chinese sources would have recorded them. As I have mentioned, historical sources *do* record that intermarriage occurred.

Unfortunately they fail to give us numbers. Shepherd also argues that, given Dutch factionalism, someone would have recorded large numbers of mixed marriages. VOC administrators, for instance, who were often at odds with the missionaries, would have welcomed the opportunity to show that the missionaries were so ineffective that they could not keep their converts from marrying Han who were presumed to be non-Christian. But there is indirect evidence of such factional jockeying on this topic in the Dutch records. Missionary reports of Han men needing to be instructed in Christianity so that they can marry Christian Aborigine women may have been an attempt to take the sting out of potential or actual VOC criticism about missionaries not preventing intermarriage. If the missionaries could claim that the intermarrying Han men converted to Christianity, then they could not be criticized for the intermarriage; indeed, they could hold these cases up as examples of extending Christianity to Han, who were very difficult to convert.[16]

Chinese sources also reported intermarriage between Han men and Aborigine women. In fact, intermarriage was reported well into the Qing period as sufficiently common to be a source of tension between Han and Aborigines. For example, in 1737, "marriage of Han males to [A]borigine women was prohibited to protect the tribes from depopulation and to eliminate a further source of Han-[A]borigine friction" (Shepherd 1993:453n41). Here, the reference to depopulation suggests that some Aborigine men were going without wives as a result of intermarriage between Aborigine women and Han men. Nevertheless, in 1760 Fujian governor Wu Shigong discussed how "the unfavorable sex ratio among [Han] Chinese migrants [in Taiwan] led to their marrying [A]borigine women (which had been prohibited since 1737) and was thereby disrupting tribal life" (Shepherd 1993:152). Although these reports again do not give numbers, they do demonstrate that intermarriage between Han men and Aborigine women was commonplace at least through 1760—common enough to disrupt tribal life and prompt the imperial government to ban it!

To summarize, I argue that there is historical evidence suggesting that intermarriage between Han immigrant men and local women—that is, women of both Aborigine and mixed ancestry—occurred throughout the Dutch and Zheng periods. Furthermore, there is evidence that the mixed population thus produced—that is, both households with Han and Aborigine members and individuals with Han and Aborigine ancestry—was relatively large by the end of the Zheng period. Specifically, census discrepancies suggest estimates that the mixed population in the Zhuluo area may have been roughly 40 to 50 percent of the total Zhuluo population in 1650. It appears that high rates of intermarriage continued throughout the Dutch and Zheng periods and into the Qing period as well.

CHANGING GOVERNMENTAL POWER

The short-route acquisition of Han identity was extremely fast and unusually easy.[17] The Dutch and Zheng censuses which are so discrepant were only separated by thirty years. I suspect that the mixed population living in the southwestern core at the time of the Zheng invasion probably became "short-route Han" very soon after the invasion—probably in the time it took to establish the tax rolls and policies. The change in social power—that is, the change in regimes which dictated taxes and Aborigine access to power—meant that the mixed population had an incentive to change their identity. I also suspect that this identity change was granted in spite of the continued practice of many or even most Aborigine customs. The demographic condition of an extremely disproportionate male bias to the population meant that Han soldiers and colonists who wanted wives could ill afford to antagonize their potential in-laws by denying their claims to Han identity, and Han colonists who married mixed or Aborigine wives themselves had an interest in granting the children of mixed marriages Han status so that their own children would have Han status.

The window of opportunity for short-route identity changes may still have been open in the early Qing period. The population was still disproportionately male, which can be partly attributed to the fact that for 93 of the first 104 years of Qing rule (most of the period 1684–1788), women and children were not allowed to migrate to Taiwan (Chen 1964, Hsu 1980b:88, Lamley 1981:296–97, Shepherd 1993:143, Zhuang 1964; see also note 2, this chapter). Intermarriage occurred at a high enough rate to be a source of friction between Han and Aborigines, and there were still taxation benefits to being considered Han (see chapter 2). Finally, both Han and Manchu officials of the Qing regime would have considered it legitimate to pass surnames patrilineally and probably also legitimate to pass Han identity the same way.

CHOOSING INTERMARRIAGE

Given the ramifications of intermarriage for cultural and identity change, we might ask why people chose to intermarry. Moreover, from the perspective of late-twentieth-century ethnic tensions worldwide, intermarriage seems a bold choice. But was intermarriage really so bold in seventeenth- and eighteenth-century Taiwan? Han and Aborigines who chose intermarriage then could not foresee all the cultural and identity consequences to follow, even if they might have been able to predict some of them. They made their choices under the influence of their own cultural ideas—Han or Aborigine—and their own perspective on the social and political circumstances in which they lived. Why might so many people of such different perspectives have made the same choice? There are several perspectives from which decisions to intermarry or not must be considered: that of Han immigrant men, that of Aborigine brides and their parents, and that of Aborigine men who saw many of their potential brides marry Han husbands.

For Han immigrant men, the choice to intermarry was probably not much of a choice, if we consider social and cultural factors probably influencing them. (The more surprising choice was the one to immigrate in the first place.) On the one hand, there were cultural reasons not to marry. Han prejudice against non-Han peoples as barbarian undoubtedly meant that most Han men would have preferred a Han wife. More uncomfortably, during the later part of the Dutch period, by which time most Aborigines were at least nominal Christians, Han men wanting to marry Aborigine women had to convert to Christianity. One important reason Han resisted conversion to Christianity was its prohibition of ancestor worship which Han cultural ideas and Confucian moral principles required.

On the other hand, there were countervailing cultural reasons to marry. The predominant Han view of kinship and descent probably made Han men view their own children as Han, regardless of the identity of the children's mother. Furthermore, the Confucian moral imperative to continue the patrilineal descent line (a duty related to ancestor worship) added moral weight to the personal and practical reasons a Han man might have for seeking a wife, such as companionship, sexual desires, and the domestic labor of the wife and any children she bore. Not finding a wife has negative consequences for carrying on a descent line and reproduction.[18]

Reasons to marry would have been augmented by the social practicalities of life in frontier Taiwan. Most Han immigrants would simply not have had the option of finding a Han bride because there were so few Han women in Taiwan. Aborigine women and their families were also tied into Aborigine social and economic networks, which a Han man could use to acquire land or trade goods or to arrange a marriage for other immigrants. Finally, Aborigine women—unlike Han women with bound feet—also performed agricultural labor. Han immigrants trying to improve their lot in life would undoubtedly have appreciated all of these social benefits of an Aborigine wife. The popular Taiwan frontier saying—"having a wife is better than having a god"—succinctly conveys the preferences of many Han immigrant men in this context: having a wife—which was the means to fulfilling personal, social, cultural, and descent goals—apparently made it worth converting, at least nominally, to Christianity.

Women in such a demographically male-biased population would certainly marry, giving women and/or their parents their choice of available men. From their perspective, what were the benefits of having a Han man marry into the family? A Han man had cultural expertise in Han agricultural techniques, and he presumably had some social knowledge about how to deal with or circumvent the Han bureaucratic system, which would have been helpful in the Zheng and Qing periods. Moreover, given Han cultural values, he would likely have been willing to work in the fields. If agriculture did largely remain the sphere of Aborigine women and old men into the Qing period—with young men hunting, driving ox-carts, providing corvée labor service, and occasionally serving in military auxiliary call-ups (see chapter 2)—then we can see the definite attraction of a Han man's agricultural labor to Aborigine women and older Aborigine men with daughters. That labor would reduce the work load of a Han man's wife and parents-in-law and at the same time probably increase their overall yield, due to additional labor and, in some cases, additional expertise and/or a different social status vis-à-vis bureaucrats.

The advantages of a Han husband or son-in-law probably increased with continuing social and political changes in Taiwan—the increasing Han population and the consolidation of political power first by the Zheng then the Qing regime. Han men had ties to various networks—such as native-place ties, temple networks, and same-surname organizations—that could be used for trade or mobilizing labor, they might mediate extortion, and they might get a household's tax status changed by changing the household's ethnic identity to Han. Moreover, with the passage of time, prejudice became a factor—a "mixed" woman's Han father was likely to prefer a Han son-in-law out of ethnic bias as well as for labor reasons.

From the perspective of Aborigine young men, however, the competition from Han men for brides and the presence of uxorilocally married

Han men in the community when they were gone on corvée or military duty—tasks which would not have fallen to a Han man—must not have been attractive. It probably reduced their own chances of marrying by increasing the competition, and it may have increased the uncertainty of paternity even when an Aborigine man was married.[19] Why accept this intermarriage then? One plausible explanation is that young Aborigine men were not in a social position to prevent it, and, as discussed above, Aborigine women themselves as well as older Aborigine men with daughters may have had different interests. Moreover, plains Aborigines had a tradition of women choosing their own husbands (e.g., Thompson 1964:173, 180–81, 191, 192–93; Thompson 1969:76, 81; contra Campbell 1903:18), so perhaps no Aborigine man was in a social position to "prevent" a marriage chosen by a woman.

There is also evidence that plains Aborigine men had a different cultural attitude toward sexual relations than Han. In 1624, two Dutch merchants reported that an Aborigine host had sexual relations with his wife in front of them and then hospitably offered them the opportunity to engage in sexual relations with the woman (Blussé and Roessingh 1984:67, 74). Some Aborigine men apparently even participated in polyandrous marriages with Han men, as this description of the practice of sworn brothers *(fudun)* on the north-central (Zhanghua) part of the western plain in 1722 suggests:

> In Pan-hsien [Banxian] Village many [of the barbarians] have united with Chinese as [*fudun*] . . . that is, "sworn brothers." The Chinese, taking advantage of his means, will utilize the services of a barbarian woman as a go-between, and first come to an agreement with this woman to *present* several pieces of cloth *to the parent of the woman [he covets]*, and to become the [*fudun*] of her husband; [then] he can come and go [in their home] without restriction. In the villages of Mao-erh-kan [Mao'ergan], Tung- and Hsi-lo [Donglo and Xilo], and Ta-wu-chun [Dawujun], they also follow this evil practice, only not to such excess. (Huang Shujing 1957[1736], translated in Thompson 1969:84, emphasis added)[20]

This passage suggests that Aborigine participation in "sworn brotherhood" was primarily decided by an Aborigine woman's parents. The woman's Aborigine husband is not portrayed as having much choice in the matter; the woman's choice is not clear.

Thus, a range of cultural and social factors may have influenced individual choices to intermarry in different ways depending on the perspective from each individual's specific social position. Han cultural beliefs about patrilineal descent combined with the demographic sex-ratio imbalance probably made intermarriage attractive to Han immigrants. Aborigine social organization, which gave women and/or their parents the authority to choose their husbands, suggests that young Aborigine men, who had the most cause to object to intermarriage, would have had relatively little say in preventing individual marriages. Moreover, the labor and economic benefits offered by a Han husband or son-in-law highlights the differences in perspective within Aborigine communities.

CHOOSING MIGRATION

Migration as a cultural strategy for both Han and Aborigines had lasting impacts on Taiwanese society. Han migration, primarily from Fujian, brought Han to Taiwan in such numbers that they overwhelmed the Dutch colonial presence there and encouraged the annexation of Taiwan by the Zheng and then the Qing regime. Aborigine migrations away from areas of Han encroachment set up "colonies" in and near the foothills, whose inhabitants took a much longer path to Han identity. Individuals choosing migration, however, did not have these long-term consequences in mind when they made their choices. Why, then, might they have chosen migration?

For Han men, the risk of having no children to name to their descent line weighed in against the choice to migrate. Han were probably aware that choosing migration to Taiwan might mean difficulty in finding a wife at all (due to the strong male bias in the population) and/or delays in getting married. They would have known that an immigrant looking for a wife would have to establish himself economically before he could successfully arrange a marriage. A man's father (if he was alive) or lineage thus would want some say in the choice to migrate, but poor men without property who wanted to migrate probably had little effective interference from their elders. Han were probably not aware, however, that mortality contributed to this risk. For one Fujian lineage between 1520 and 1750, the average age of death for male immigrants to Taiwan was 43.94 years—lower than for males who migrated elsewhere in China (48.98 years) but higher than for males who migrated to other parts of Southeast Asia (38.82 years) (Wang 1995:211). Moreover, 32.5 percent of males died under forty in China, 46 percent in Taiwan, and 59.7 percent in other parts of Southeast Asia (ibid.). (While men in this lineage probably did not realize the differences in average age at death, they may have had a sense that greater percentages of migrants died early.) Lower average at death combined with later age at marriage meant that men might not survive long enough to get a wife and raise a family. Thus, men choosing to migrate probably faced a greater risk of not continuing their descent line than those who stayed in China.

Why, then, did so many Han men migrate to Taiwan? The above data for Taiwan cover the period 1644 to 1799 (Wang 1995:210), but if we consider a narrower time span, a different picture of the relative risks emerges. From the 1640s to 1680s—that is, from the middle of the Dutch period through the end of the Zheng period—times were incredibly difficult in Fujian and other areas of the southeastern coast, where most of the Han immigrants came from, because of the prolonged war there between Zheng Chenggong fighting for the outgoing Ming dynasty and the consolidating Qing dynasty (e.g., Wang 1995:185). For poor people in Fujian in the mid-seventeenth century (1645–1665), the average chances of making a living in Taiwan may have been the same or better than in Fujian, even given the dangers of the trip itself and of resettlement (starvation, violence, disease). Regardless of whether migrating to Taiwan was actually in the interests of Han peasants in Fujian at that time, many of them probably *perceived* that they had a better chance of getting access to the necessary resources to survive and thrive in Taiwan than in Fujian.

Later, particularly after 1683 when the Qing government had finally taken control of Taiwan and wiped out the last vestiges of Zheng and Ming loyalist resistance to Qing rule in China, why would men in Fujian and elsewhere continue to think it was in their interests for them or their sons to go to Taiwan? Taiwan must still have appeared a great opportunity to poor people in Fujian, which was densely populated and chronically rice-deficient. Under the Qing, Taiwan rice surpluses were sold, and frequently distributed as famine relief, in Fujian (Perkins 1969, Shepherd 1993:163–67). Taiwan was also known for high wages for laborers: in 1717 the Zhuluo gazetteer reported that Taiwan wages were three times the wages on the mainland, and in the early 1730s they were double those on the mainland (Shepherd 1993:167, 485n123). Moreover, there is also a cultural factor involved: Fujian has a long tradition of sending its people overseas (Wang 1995), making Fujianese more likely to perceive migration as a viable option.

In the face of intermarriage and other Han encroachments, some Aborigines also chose to migrate. Migration was a general and recurrent Aborigine solution to threats, both violent and economic. This strategy may have been a useful one in response to head-hunting raids which were common islandwide prior to the intervention of the Dutch, Zheng, and Qing

governments. Because one head may have been enough to satisfy a raid-
ing party (e.g., Campbell 1903:102–103), a strategy of migration in the
face of military threat could save lives. After the threat had passed, villagers could return. This cultural strategy appears to have been passed
on to successive generations, albeit in a slightly different form. Portions
of Aborigine villages periodically migrated (permanently) away from
areas of Han encroachment from the late-seventeenth through the early-
nineteenth centuries.[21] Shepherd (1993:388) suggests that the Aborigines
who chose to migrate were those who were less "successful" at sinicization. He appears to view such "comparative failure" as resulting from
skill differences in language use, in understanding Han business and government practices, and in managing finances in a cash economy, as well
as resulting from choices about intermarriage and subsistence. I see intermarriage as much more important than this view suggests.

The fact that many of these migrations did not involve entire villages,
but only parts of villages, makes sense in the context of conflicting interests between young unmarried Aborigine men, on the one hand, and
Aborigine women and older Aborigine men with daughters, on the other.
The differing interests within Aborigine communities may have been further exacerbated by the high frequency of uxorilocal postmarital residence and, in some places, matrilineal inheritance of property (Shepherd
1993:386). Thus, many Aborigine parents probably expected to be provided for by their daughters and would have been unwilling to be separated from their daughter due to her, or their own, migration. Assuming
Aborigine men did not migrate alone,[22] I think the limitation of permanent Aborigine migrations was largely due to conflicting interests within
Aborigine communities.

CONTRIBUTIONS OF SHORT-ROUTE HAN
TO TAIWANESE CULTURE

The new narrative being constructed of Taiwan's unfolding as a place
that is not Chinese emphasizes the importance of Aborigine cultural contributions to Taiwanese culture, a term which primarily refers to Hoklo
culture in Taiwan. We saw in chapter 3 that long-route Han have contributed little or nothing to Taiwanese culture, instead having taken on
most of the pre-existing Hoklo cultural model. By contrast, short-route
Han do appear to have contributed to Taiwanese culture, or at least to
the southern Hoklo variety of it. Let us first examine evidence of such
contributions and then consider why it was a high rate of intermarriage

in conjunction with an identity change preceding cultural change that allowed such Aborigine "substrate" influence.

Northern Hoklo, southern Hoklo (both on the west coast), and Hoklo on the northeastern coast around Yilan constitute recognizably distinct linguistic and cultural varieties in Taiwan.[23] These Hoklo varieties had different frequencies of minor marriages during the Japanese colonial period, when minor marriage was still practiced in Taiwan (e.g., Chuang and Wolf 1995). (In minor marriage, a girl was given up for adoption, often shortly after birth, and another girl was adopted to be raised as a bride for one of the family's sons.) Most markedly, northern Hoklo had a very high frequency of minor marriages—much closer, in fact, to the high frequencies among northern Hakka than to the very low frequencies of southern Hoklo.

> The lowest frequency of minor marriages in either [predominantly Hoklo] Hai-shan or [predominantly Hakka] Hsin-chu [Xinzhu, in northern Taiwan] was in Tun-p'ing [Dunping] . . . the only [district] in which a few of our subjects were registered as . . . "mountain [A]borigines." What this suggests to me is that the frequency of minor marriages declined when Han men married non-Han women. The obvious reason is that women from more egalitarian traditions were appalled at the idea of giving up their daughters at birth and raising daughters-in-law in their place. This is, I suspect, one of the reasons why minor marriages were rare in southern Taiwan, where the farmers transported by the Dutch and the soldiers accompanying Koxinga [Zheng Chenggong] had little choice but to marry [A]borigine women. (Wolf 1995:54–55)

Here, Wolf argues that southern Hoklo are different from northern Hoklo—as Dunping is different than Haishan and Xinzhu—because of the historical cultural contributions of Aborigines to Han via intermarriage in these regions. Because northern Taiwan was settled largely after the Qing prohibition on women's migration was lifted, many northern Hoklo brought their wives and daughters with them and, thus, had relatively little intermarriage with Aborigines (cf. Wolf 1989). Southern Hoklo are the short-route Han discussed in this chapter and, as we have seen, had high rates of intermarriage.

There was also variation in the frequency of footbinding among the Hoklo. Haishan, a northern Hoklo area, had a higher frequency of footbinding than the Hoklo frequency islandwide: 85.2 percent of Haishan women born between 1891 and 1900 had bound feet in 1905 (Wolf and Huang 1980:265) in contrast to 68 percent of all Hoklo women in Taiwan who had bound feet in 1905 (MNRKC 1908. Shepherd 1993:119,

526n). I suggest that the difference occurs in part because the islandwide census includes the short-route Han, who did not bind their daughters' feet (cf. Brown 1995:155, 1996b:66).[24]

Oral history evidence also suggests that short-route Han maintained some cultural differences from older Hoklo models brought from Fujian. One Taiwanese person whose family was from an old elite family in Tainan City reported that her mother (who was born around 1900) had told her when she was a little girl not to go outside the city walls to play because the people beyond the walls were savages, not Han. Her mother's statement seemed surprising because the people to whom she referred were locally considered Hoklo—thus it was not an accepted identity classification. However, I interpret this attitude as a historical memory of the viewpoint of Hoklo elite in Tainan City (who would have been able to get Han brides in the seventeenth century), according to which people living beyond the city walls behaved differently enough that they were not authentically Han. (In chapter 5, I discuss evidence that outsiders, such as an urban elite commenting on peasants, use culture to classify others while insiders use social experience.) All these differences mean that the model of southern Hoklo culture may well have been influenced by Aborigine culture via the short-route Han, as the new narratives of unfolding suggest.

Why were short-route Han able to change the Hoklo cultural model in southern Taiwan? I argue that intermarriage is a primary means for cultural change.[25] One important consequence of intermarriage is that it places individuals of different cultures in the social role of parent. Thus, descent as a primary line of cultural transmission provides an important mechanism for introducing different cultural ideas and practices into a community. In other words, parents inculcate cultural ideas and practices in their children, and while parents perpetuate their own cultural ideas, they introduce cultural change if their cultural ideas and practices are different from the rest of the local community (e.g., Bruner 1956). Parental roles are influential social roles and the cultural make-up of the individuals who fill them affect the cultural content that their children learn. If one or both parents are culturally different from the rest of the community, then their children have access to a different cultural repertoire than other children in the community.

Consider how a new idea and practice—for example, the adoption of the Han practice of making offerings to one's ancestors—is introduced into an individual household. Why should people who do not already believe in it do it? If there is no violent coercion, the effects of the state or a school text or even some neighbors saying that everyone ought to worship his or her ancestors—as suggested by arguments that depend on prestige- or status-seeking as motivation for adopting Han practices (e.g., Shepherd 1993: 362, 376–83)—are quite different from the effect of a Han immigrant father teaching his children with an Aborigine woman that they must make offerings to him after he is dead or else he will be cold and hungry in the afterworld. In the case of an external authority or neighboring peers espousing the practice of ancestor worship, one is likely at most to practice ancestor worship opportunistically (not on a regular basis) for the sake of prestige. Moreover, there is no guarantee that the practice will mean the same thing to those who adopt it as it did in its original Han cultural context. In the case of a father's instruction, however, the children may well make regular offerings and instruct their own children to do so out of grief and respect for their father and his beliefs—even if they do not believe them. And they may believe them, because their father probably taught them those beliefs.[26]

In one Puyuma mountain Aborigine community in southeastern Taiwan, evidence suggests that ancestor worship was introduced into the Aborigine community by in-marrying Han husbands in the Qing period, though such worship "does not involve boasting of Chinese descent" by the present-day descendants (Suenari 1994:205–206). However, there are indications that, even when inculcated by fathers, practices may be adopted without the meaning they carried for the father. Suenari (1994: 217–18) points out that the post-1945 increase in the Puyuma adoption of ancestor tablets does not constitute outright acceptance of the Han patrilineal pattern of ancestor worship. The Puyuma have modified the custom to be more in agreement with their own traditions. Ancestors of the Tujia (discussed in chapter 5) apparently also modified beliefs and practices relating to ancestral tablets and worship.

The idea that one acquires prestige from worshiping ancestors makes some assumptions about the local social organization and power relations. It implies either that ancestor worship is valued by the larger society, which can refer to either the majority of the population or those with power, or that ancestor worship is valued by the majority or authority of the local community. Different local social organization and power relations can produce quite different effects of the same message along the same line of transmission. The proselytization of one neighboring household, for instance, carries a different weight than the disdain of the majority of the local community's households for not practicing ancestor worship and yet another weight if the single household is in agreement with a distant elite. Similarly, a state edict carries a lighter weight in a community which rarely sees a state official than in a community which houses a garrison of state troops.

When identity labels change on the basis of ancestry claims and with little regard to cultural practices, as in the short route, then the cultural changes which follow take the mixed descendants toward a Han model but at the same time can incorporate substrate—here, Aborigine—values into that Han model. I find footbinding the best example to illustrate this point. Consider the household of a plains Aborigine woman and a Han man in the core area near present-day Tainan City—where the Dutch, Zheng, and Qing governments held their primary military power and where the bulk of the Han immigrants landed. Imagine the reaction of an Aborigine woman to her Han husband who told her he wanted their daughters' feet bound. In the context of a large Aboriginal population early in the Dutch period, one can imagine that were such a thing even suggested it did not go far. As the Han population grew, however, and some Han women with bound feet appeared in the region if not the village of the mixed household in question, pressure from the Han husband might grow. I say it *might* grow because we must also keep in mind that such a man would realize that he would lose the field labor of his daughters if their feet were bound and also that they did not need their feet bound to be marriageable to Han or anyone else, given the sex ratio in that population. Probably his desire for daughters with bound feet would be influenced by whether he could afford to lose their labor—that is, by the need at the household level for labor (see Gates 1996b and 2000 on the need for female labor). The imbalanced sex ratio of the general population was important for quite some time. Another important factor is that, until there were women with bound feet present—immigrants or daughters of Han women with bound feet—there would have been a scarcity of people who knew how to bind feet (cf. Brown 1995:154–55, 455–56; 1996b:65–66).[27] Did the short-route Han ever come to bind women's feet? The fact that only 68 percent of Hoklo women had bound feet in 1905 suggests that, while some descendants of mixed households may have bound feet, others did not. Apparently, the decision to bind feet did not affect people's ability to claim Han status, in spite of oral history accounts to the contrary among the elite.

David Johnson's (1985:62–63) point that women introduce non-elite cultural values up the social hierarchy through marriage further supports the conclusion that short-route Han varied the Hoklo model in southern Taiwan (from the form brought from Fujian) due to influence from

a non-Han or Aborigine cultural substrate.[28] Not only do women appear to have been the agents of changing local Han models, by transmitting to their children non-Han cultural values, but women's relation
to power in a patriarchal, patrilineal Han system also affected mixed
descendants' claims to a Han identity. Short-route descendants had recourse to patrilineal ideology in their negotiation of Han identity because it was primarily Han men who married Aborigine women. At the
beginning of Han colonization of Taiwan, all the Han men marrying Aborigine women must have done so uxorilocally so all of their children (and
many of their grandchildren) would have been in a position to claim Han
identity on the basis of patrilineal ancestry when Taiwan came under
Zheng rule.

COMPARING PROCESSES OF IDENTITY CHANGE

Is short-route Han identity the result of a different process of identity
change than long-route Han identity? And if so, did that older process
produce a somehow more "authentic" identity? The short route and the
long route had different underlying bases for claiming Hoklo identity and
different influences upon the southern Hoklo cultural model in Taiwan.
Nevertheless, I argue that the long and short routes across the border to
Han are not distinct processes, because they are driven by the same two
mechanisms—intermarriage and sociopolitical intervention. Variation in
the rate and timing of these mechanisms leads to different outcomes but
does not fundamentally alter the process of identity change.

Comparing long-route and short-route identity change (as reconstructed in chapters 3 and 4, respectively), we can see clear differences
in the specific historical circumstances of these identity changes. Short-
route identity change would not have occurred without the immigration
of large numbers of Han men to spur high rates of intermarriage with
plains Aborigine women and the subsequent growth of a mixed population. Nevertheless, these circumstances were not sufficient to spark identity change without political intervention. Changes in the political
regime—most importantly from Dutch to Zheng, but probably also from
Zheng to Qing—were necessary to create a window of opportunity for
identity change to occur. It was not simply the change in the status of
Aborigines as reliable allies of the regime which created the opportunity.
After all, this status changed for plains Aborigines over the course of Qing
control of Taiwan without any apparent concurrent large-scale opportunity for identity change. The changeover in power from one regime to

another is what created the opportunity for identity change, because it was then unproblematic to claim that the previous regime had erred in its classification of the large mixed population produced by high rates of intermarriage—especially when the power holders in the previous regime were as culturally different as the Dutch were from the Han of the Zheng regime.[29]

By the same token, even though long-route identity change presupposed the cultural changes spurred by long-term, low rates of uxorilocal intermarriage of poor Han men to plains Aborigine women, these circumstances were also not sufficient to spark identity change without political intervention. A politically mandated shift in the cultural repertoire of the Han toward an Aborigine model—no footbinding—was necessary to allow identity change to occur. It was not simply the change in Hoklo culture vis-à-vis plains Aborigine culture which created the window of opportunity. After all, mountain Aborigines also did not bind women's feet, but they did not change identities. The 1915 mandate to stop binding women's feet created a context in which Hoklo could no longer link footbinding to civilization and thus use it as a marker of non-Han identity. People of Toushe, Jibeishua, and Longtian who were looking to arrange a marriage could then emphasize the many other customs they shared with their Hoklo neighbors, shared due to cultural shifts resulting from long-term intermarriage. Significantly, the mandate to stop binding women's feet only occurred because of the change in political regimes from the Qing to the Japanese and the corresponding cultural change in the power holders.

In spite of the differences between the specific historical circumstances of the short-route and long-route identity changes, these routes are not different processes at a theoretical level. That is to say, the same forces are at work in both routes. Both short-route and long-route identity changes are based upon intermarriage of plains Aborigine or mixed women with Han men who would not otherwise have been able to get wives. In both cases, however, intermarriage was not sufficient. A social intervention of some sort—a change in people's social experience—was required in order for identity change to occur. In both cases, the intervention that occurred—registering a population for tax purposes or banning footbinding to increase female labor capabilities—was necessarily linked to a change in political regimes. Moreover, the change in political regimes was concurrent with a change in the culture of the power holders of the regime. Thus, in both cases, the process by which identity change occurred was intermarriage followed, at some point, by a social intervention enacted by a new political regime which differed culturally from its predecessor.

Why then was identity claimed on different bases by short-route and long-route Han? And why did short-route and long-route Han have such different effects on local Hoklo cultural models? Because the timing and nature of the social interventions and the rates of intermarriage were different, the resultant identity changes were made on the basis of different claims. In the short route, social intervention of new tax registration and policies followed not merely quickly on the heels of much intermarriage—resulting in a large "mixed" population—but also in the context of a continuing high rate of intermarriage. In the long route, social intervention occurred only after two centuries of low rates of intermarriage. Because there was little or no cultural change towards a Han model, short-route Han could claim Han identity only on the basis of ancestry or descent. Those of mixed ancestry almost certainly used patrilineal ancestry. Those of mixed households probably used descent to claim that the presence of a Han man in their household would mean that future generations would have a Han patrilineal ancestor. By contrast, for long-route Han, ancestry would have been more difficult to document and less uniform in the villages. Moreover, it had mattered less than cultural practices to neighboring Hoklo in their classification of Toushe, Jibeishua, and Longtian people as plains Aborigines. With so much cultural similarity in such a context, ancestry must have seemed unimportant to long-route Han and their neighbors.

But the timing of social interventions had a very strong effect upon the cultural contributions that short-route and long-route Han made to local culture. Because short-route Han were granted Han identity while they still retained many Aborigine cultural ideas and practices, and because there were so many short-route Han in southwestern Taiwan due to the immigration of large numbers of Han men and subsequent high rates of intermarriage, the cultural ideas they held and the customs they practiced—regardless of the actual origins of these ideas and practices—were also classified as Han. Thus, Aborigine ideas and practices were "mixed" into the local Hoklo cultural model. In the long route, however, people in Toushe, Jibeishua, and Longtian adopted Hoklo culture as it was presented to them, contributing little or no influence to that cultural model. Their retention of Aborigine identity for so long and their claim to Han identity in terms of culture meant that any differences they exhibited from local Hoklo models were immediately cast as "Aborigine." They had no flexibility in negotiating for the acceptance of even minor differences; they had to conform to what others modeled as Hoklo culture.

To argue, as I do, that the short route to Han and the long route to Han are the same process still allows for significant variation in people's experiences of these routes and the subsequent impact on culture. Because the key mechanisms of the process can vary in rate and timing, a range of outcomes is possible. Recognition that we are dealing with a single process, however, challenges the presumption that older identities— acquired via short-route circumstances—are somehow more authentic on the basis of process, for there is no theoretical reason why differences in rate or timing of mechanisms should somehow convey greater authenticity.

ANTIQUITY AND THE DIFFERENTIAL
APPEARANCE OF AUTHENTICITY

Ironically, with regard to the issue of authenticity, Confucian ideology suggests that the long-route pattern of a cultural claim as the basis of Han identity should be the more "authentic" one. However, as Patricia Ebrey (1996) has noted, in practice, Han people prefer claims on the basis of ancestry—as in the short route. Perhaps Confucian scholars came to prefer cultural (long-route) claims to Han identity because they observed that those who won Han identity on the basis of ancestry had the potential to change Han culture, including Confucianism. Looking at identity strictly in the terms in which it is claimed, however, obscures the underlying similarity of the actual historical processes of long-route and short-route identity change.

Nevertheless, we are left with a puzzle. If the processes of long-route and short-route identity change are essentially the same except for timing, then why does short-route change seem more authentic to people in Taiwan? Consider the implied motivations of those claiming Hoklo identity. Short-route Han claimed ancestry because Han identity was socially (including politically and economically) expedient. The implication is that they *wanted* Han identity itself. Such a desire would seem reasonable to other Han, given Han ideas about the superiority of Han culture, and it may have made Han identity, once achieved, seem more authentic. Long-route Han, by contrast, were granted Han identity by cultural default, as it were, since after the Japanese colonial government intervened to change Hoklo culture towards an Aborigine model of no footbinding, both they and their neighbors could see that they were basically like the

Hoklo majority. The implication is that what long-route Han wanted was *not* to be savages, not to be stigmatized. This negative desire—not to be non-Han—and the fact that they backed into Han identity by default, rather than by any perceived active pursuit on their part, may have made their Han identity seem less authentic to others.

In practice, there was an active pursuit of Han identity by long-route Han—the first Han woman who married into Toushe as a first-time bride reported that it took three years to negotiate the marriage deal. In other words, her Toushe father-in-law pursued the marriage persistently over three years time! However, such pursuit of intermarriage—which can be understood as taking advantage of the window of opportunity created by the footbinding ban—is not immediately apparent to outsiders. Locals might remember it, and researchers might discover it, but most outsiders would only see the achievement of Han identity by cultural default. Such a difference in the understanding of the local processes could explain why there are such different responses to the authenticity of long-route Han identity by those with in-depth local knowledge and those without.

In spite of the lack of theoretical basis for distinguishing between short-route and long-route identity change, we can understand why those constructing the new narrative of Taiwan's past would want to emphasize the short route and ignore the long route. Short-route identity change, after all, does follow the pattern the new narrative suggests—plains Aborigines "disappeared" into the Hoklo Taiwanese population through high rates of intermarriage but nevertheless made their cultural mark, in marriage patterns and perhaps footbinding, for example. By contrast, as we saw in chapter 3, long-route identity change does not follow this pattern. Plains Aborigines did "disappear" through cultural default (made possible by low rates of intermarriage), but they appear not to have had an effect on local Hoklo culture. Moreover, long-route identity change is recent enough that all its arbitrariness and messiness can still be reconstructed, something which detracts from the message of inevitability that narratives of unfolding attempt to convey.

Thus, it is largely a narrative ploy—an ideological strategy—to privilege identities that claim a glorious antiquity as more authentic than recently acquired identities. It is easier to manipulate information about the distant past because it is more difficult for others to provide convincing contradictory evidence. We are fortunate indeed to have as much historical information as we do about short-route identity change. Ideologies, of course, are intended to support present political purposes, not to help us understand what actually occurred in the past. Here is where I think the problem lies.

The clear present-day political purpose of Taiwan's new narrative of unfolding is to distance Taiwanese from Chinese, but the embrace of only short-route Han as authentically Han and the reclassification of long-route Han as plains Aborigines undermines that very purpose. People whose ancestors took the short route to Han are not unique to Taiwan; they can be found throughout China, where they are accepted unquestioningly as Han. If people in Taiwan embrace only short-route Han as authentic, it invites criticism from the PRC that Taiwan's new narrative, although perhaps true, cannot be used for nationalistic goals because it is no different from narratives of other historical, short-route identity changes in China—the Min in Fujian or the Yue in Guangdong, for example. For the Taiwanese not to be simply another "regional" variety of Han, Taiwan's narrative must somehow distinguish the new Taiwanese identity as uniquely different from regional Han identities in China. As we shall see in chapter 5, it is actually the long-route pattern which appears to be unique to Taiwan and which could, then, provide a basis for such differentiation.

CHAPTER 5

"They Came with Their Hands Tied behind Their Backs"

Forced Migrations, Identity Changes, and State Classification in Hubei

Identity and culture changed in China, in ways similar to Taiwan.[1] In the mountainous Enshi prefecture of present-day southwestern Hubei Province, which separates the plains of the Middle Yangzi River region from the Sichuan basin (see figure 20), there have been periodic waves of forced immigration—mostly Han soldiers, farmers and laborers, and exiled convicts *(tu)*—over the last two millennia.[2] These migrations resulted in waves of intermarriage between each new set of immigrants and the "locals" *(tujia)* already in place. The most recent large-scale immigration of Han outsiders occurred in the late 1930s, when the ruling Nationalist Party moved Hubei's provincial capital to the more easily defended Enshi City for the course of the war with Japan. It appears that this new wave of immigrants, like earlier ones, lumped together the descendants of all previous waves of immigrants as the local, if rather coarse, variety of Han. Thus, before 1949, this historically non-Han area had already acquired a Han identity.

Identity change in Hubei before 1949 shows many similarities to short-route identity change in Taiwan. These similarities pose a problem for the new narratives being constructed of Taiwan's past because they show that identity change is not unique to Taiwan. The goal of new narratives of Taiwan's past is to distinguish Taiwanese from Han in China by revealing Taiwanese as a mixture of Han and Taiwan Aborigines. However, descendants of non-Han in many areas of China have intermarried with Han and, over time, come to be considered regional varieties of Han.

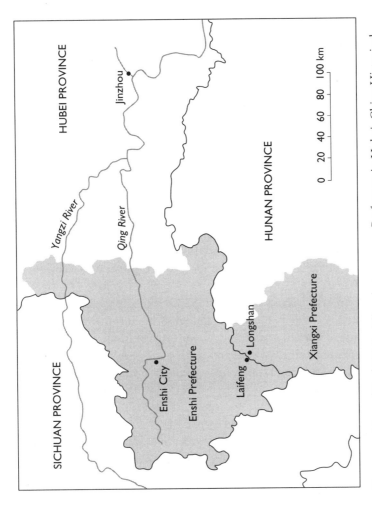

Figure 20. Map of Enshi Tujia-Miao Autonomous Prefecture in Hubei. China Historical GIS Dataset, Version: Pre-release (October 2001).

The same kind of change that Taiwanese claim makes them uniquely different from people in China has in fact occurred in areas that are not contested as Chinese. On what grounds, then, can Taiwan claim not to be Chinese?

With the founding of the People's Republic of China, identity change in Hubei took yet a different turn—undoing short-route identity change. This turn has implications for Taiwan's claims to an independent identity. During the national ethnic identification project *(minzu shibie)*, many "locals" in Hubei were eventually classified as Tujia—one of the 55 officially recognized non-Han ethnic minorities in the PRC.[3] Thus, in spite of local identity as Han, people were forced back across the border to Han. The circumstances of this state reclassification weaken the PRC's stance toward identity and cultural change in Taiwan, because the PRC takes a different position with regard to Taiwan than it did in Hubei. Most notably, officials in Hubei concluded that intermarriage between Han patrilineal ancestors and non-Han matrilineal ancestors led to de-sinicization—Han becoming non-Han—yet the PRC denies that such de-sinicization occurred in Taiwan. Changes in Taiwan have not gone on long "enough" for the PRC to accept them as markers of identity change.

In this chapter, I reconstruct identity and cultural changes among Tujia and their ancestors in Hubei. I begin with the state identification and classification of the Tujia in the 1950s for three reasons. First, interview reports about identities and practices before 1949 are colored by the cultural meanings and social consequences which those identities and practices came to have after 1949. Individuals' official classification underlies all the discussions I had about local identity. Thus, it is helpful to know how individuals wound up in particular categories. Second, this most recent identity change of locals to a non-Han Tujia identity in the state project demonstrates the same driving force that we see in other identity changes described in this book: regime change. In other words, the state identification and classification project shows that identity changes in Hubei as in Taiwan were driven by sociopolitical forces, not cultural ones. Third, officials responsible for the classification of individuals attempted to reconcile what they, as locals, knew about local (sociopolitical) history with the outsider, culturalist perspectives of PRC policies and Confucian ideology. (The influence of Confucian ideology on Communist policies toward ethnic minorities is widespread in the PRC [e.g., Harrell 1995b].)

Keeping the state identification and classification project and other intervening political events in mind, I examine local identities and culture in a village I call Wucun (Fifth Village) from before the founding of the PRC in 1949.[4] People in the area distinguished between "locals" *(bendi ren, or tujia, or tumanzi)* and "outsiders" *(kejia).*[5] These categories of "locals" and "outsiders" do not neatly correspond to the official classifications of Tujia and Han. Moreover, this distinction was *not* strongly linked to any custom—unlike the situation in early-twentieth-century Toushe, Jibeishua, and Longtian, where footbinding drew the border between Han and non-Han. In fact, both locals and outsiders in Enshi appear to have thought of themselves as Han prior to 1949.

Returning to state identification, I suggest that state officials classified locals as non-Han for cultural reasons. As in Taiwan with the reclassification of long-route Han as plains Aborigines, outsiders with little knowledge of local history made assumptions about the relationship between culture and ethnic identity. Ironically, the very cultural basis that PRC officials apparently used to classify Tujia as non-Han in the 1950s suggests that, at the turn of the twenty-first century, Taiwanese should be classified as more Han than most Han in the PRC. The Tujia case informs consideration of whether Taiwan is or should be Chinese by showing that identity and culture in Taiwan and China have diverged due to changes on both sides of the Strait. Ultimately, these divergences are based on sociopolitical differences.

THE STATE CLASSIFICATION OF TUJIA

In the PRC, every citizen is officially classified as belonging to a state-recognized ethnic group *(minzu).*[6] This classification appears on every person's national identity card *(shenfen zheng).* Status as a non-Han minority confers affirmative action benefits in some or all of the following areas: family planning, school admissions, hiring and promotion, and financing and taxation of businesses. Specific preferential policies for ethnic minorities differ across China (Mackerras 1994, Sautman 1998). Additionally, administrative units such as Enshi prefecture, which have large minority populations, get more state funds for economic development projects than Han units. Such differential distribution of funds necessitated the ethnic identification of all PRC citizens.

The nationwide ethnic identification and classification project *(minzu shibie)* began in the 1950s but, because of political campaigns, it was not completed in the Enshi area until the 1980s. Its purpose was to identify all the existing ethnic groups in the PRC and then to classify everyone in the population into one of those groups. State policy required that groups be identified on the basis of what they were, rather than in exclusionary terms (for instance, "not Han" or "not Miao" were not acceptable). Officially, there were four criteria for identifying people into ethnic groups: common language, common territory, common economy, and common psychology as indicated by common culture. (These criteria were originally developed by Stalin for use in the Soviet Union.) They were not applied in classifying the Tujia as a group, however, just as they were not applied in many classifications all over China.

> The minzu identified in the nationalities identification process [minzu shibie], being based on arbitrary objective criteria, and the ethnic groups existing in local society, divided according to people's own perception of their common descent and culture, are in fact two different things. (Harrell 1996b:278)

Officials often ignored the state criteria in favor of Han views of ethnicity (e.g., Brown 2001b, and the case studies in Harrell 1995a and Brown 1996a), although they were careful to present the classification in cultural terms. Officials did use language in their classification of individuals as Tujia or Han, at several points, but the classification still created a distinction in the local population which had not previously existed.

State Identification of Tujia as a Group

In the 1950s, the State Nationalities' Affairs Commission (SNAC) incorporated local people in Enshi—who had so recently been considered local Han by the Nationalists—into the Miao minzu.[7] (Since there were Miao in the region, it was initially identified as a Miao area.) Their identification with the very unsinicized Miao horrified Tujia, who thought of themselves as Han. In 1950, an official who was considered Miao but who considered herself Tujia protested directly to Premier Zhou Enlai that Tujia had been incorrectly identified as Miao.[8] Reportedly, Zhou called in a linguist familiar with the Miao language, asked the Tujia official to speak the Tujia language (which she could do), and then asked the linguist if that language was Miao. The linguist answered that it was definitely not Miao, and so Zhou ordered that the identification of Tujia as Miao be reexamined.[9]

Although the central government and Party supported recognition of the Tujia as distinct from both Miao and Han as early as 1950, the official decision that the Tujia are a separate ethnic group was not announced until January 3, 1957.[10] Even after this recognition, there was a protracted debate in Hunan about whether Tujia should be incorporated into a joint Tujia-Miao autonomous prefecture or established in their own independent autonomous prefecture (see Brown 2002 for more detailed discussion).

In September 1957, while people were still celebrating the founding of the Xiangxi Tujia-Miao Autonomous Prefecture in Hunan, the expansion of the Anti-Rightist Campaign to include ethnic issues made ethnic minority status a liability. It also brought the national ethnic identification project to an abrupt stop. One benefit of this halt was that the classification of individuals was not carried out in Tujia areas. Thus, Tujia who had not spoken out during the investigation period were not identifiable as Tujia, shielding most of them from the extreme ethnic strife found in other parts of China due to the policy of forced assimilation pursued during the Cultural Revolution. In Inner Mongolia, for example, an ethnically based purge "affected the majority of the adult Mongol population" (Khan 1996:141, see also Jankowiak 1988). Although ethnic conflict did occur in Tujia areas in Hunan, it was not as extensive as in Inner Mongolia.

Hunan official Tian Jinggui (1994: 192) claims that in the Hunan-Hubei-Sichuan-Guizhou border region, people did not dare to say they were Tujia, but I found no substantiation of this claim for Hubei. Quite a number of people (officials, scholars, and farmers) assured me that ethnic strife aimed at Tujia during the Cultural Revolution was largely limited to Hunan, with only a small number of cases in Enshi's Laifeng County, which had figured prominently in the Hubei area investigations and had close connections with the Hunan process. (Laifeng in Hubei sits across a small river from the Tujia county of Longshan in Hunan.)

One official in Enshi attributed the general absence of ethnic conflict in Hubei to intermarriage because, according to him, no family *(jia)* was entirely Tujia or Han. I suggest rather that ethnic conflict did not occur in Hubei and was limited in Hunan because local people did not see Han and Tujia as separate ethnic groups, since individuals had not been classified. That is, the pre-1949 conception of all locals as Han continued because the state had not yet made the distinction for them by classifying individuals into separate minzu.

Local Government Classification of Individuals

In December 1978, the Third Plenary Session of the Eleventh Congress of the Chinese Communist Party revived the ethnic classification project (Tian 1994:193). The central government ordered local governments to provide information on ethnic identity (minzu) in the third national census in 1982. State policy decreed that prefectures and other administrative units with large minority populations would receive more state funds for economic development projects than Han units. Thus, a large minority was potentially a boon. Given the previous absence of ethnic conflict, local officials in post-Mao-era Hubei saw their Tujia population as an opportunity to bring in much needed funds. Hubei first established Laifeng and Hefeng as Tujia autonomous counties in 1980. Later, in 1983, they were incorporated into a joint Tujia-Miao autonomous prefecture.

In order to provide the central government with the required ethnic information for use in the third national census and on national identity cards and at the same time to establish Enshi as having sufficient minority population to be a minority autonomous prefecture, the local government in Enshi had to assign an ethnic label to every single individual in the populace. Initially, local officials charged with carrying out the classification relied on surnames only—not the state criteria of language, territory, economy, or culture—and categorized anyone with one of sixty surnames (including Peng, Tian, Xiang, and Tan) as Tujia. They determined specific surnames to be Tujia on the basis of historical references: for example, those surnames assigned to indigenous rulers *(tusi)* or to clans that had migrated from areas that had once been Ba territory.[11]

Relying strictly on surnames produced a large number of minorities, however, and the supervising authorities would not approve so many (see Brown 2002 for an analysis of this refusal). Local officials were directed to revise their classification so that ethnic minorities would constitute between 25 and 40 percent of the total population. Such figures were probably high enough to warrant autonomous prefecture status yet low enough to avoid closer scrutiny or additional Han immigration. In the end, local officials classified about 37 percent of the population as non-Han.[12]

Because surname alone could no longer be sufficient for Tujia status, officials developed a new method of classification using a combination of surname, the identity of a family's local ancestral place, and the timing of migration to the local ancestral place. This approach came closer to (though still did not match) the injunction made in March 1983 at a meeting in the Xiangxi Tujia-Miao Autonomous Prefecture:

> Identify whether each person is Tujia on the basis of ethnic characteristics, ethnic consciousness, blood relationships, and universally acknowledged self reports for three generations before Liberation [1949]. (Reported in Tian 1994:196)

One Enshi official told me that if a family both had a Tujia surname and came from a Tujia area, it could be designated Tujia, even in absence of other evidence. The "identity" of places of origin was derived from a variety of sources. Historical references, genealogies, customs or oral histories of a particular area or clan as reported by selected educated locals, and the language of local place names were all used to classify a particular place as "Tujia."

Local PRC officials relied heavily on former Nationalist officials for such expertise. One official spoke highly of the understanding of local history that former Nationalist officials had. He emphasized their high level of education *(wenhua)*. Given that Han-educated PRC officials sought men (they were all men) who had been well educated in Han schools, both classical and modern, to provide insights on local identity, there should be little surprise that the classification project clearly demonstrates Han influence. The emphasis on patrilineal ancestors—through surnames, through the timing of their immigration, and through genealogies—reflects such a Han perspective on identity rather than the official state criteria for identifying ethnic groups.

Of the four state criteria for ethnic identification, the only one which local government officials often used to classify individuals in Enshi was language. In this case, however, local officials were not interested in the language individuals actually spoke (since everyone spoke Southwest Mandarin), but in the language of place names, which could determine whether a local place was Tujia. For example, one family, I was told, had a surname identified as quintessentially Tujia and lived in a village that was too small to have had historical records. The family had no genealogies preserved after the Cultural Revolution and no oral history about migrations or local origins, but all the local place names in and around the village were derived from the non-Han Tujia language. The official responsible for classifying this family reported his conclusion that, since the place names were Tujia and there was no evidence that large numbers of people with this surname migrated in or out of the area, the family must have been local *(bendi)*, not migrants, and thus were Tujia.

The state criterion of culture *appears* to have indirectly influenced local Enshi officials' classification scheme through their assumptions about the relationship between the number of generations of probable interethnic marriage and the cultural practices of "mixed" descendants. For many people in the Enshi area, the timing of ancestral immigration to the area became crucial to their classification as Han or Tujia. Patrilineal descendants of Han were classified as Tujia if their ancestors arrived before a certain date (different parts of the prefecture reportedly had different cutoff dates). The rationale for such classification was that Han immigrants and their descendants intermarried with locals *(tujia)*. One official volunteered that the characteristic feature *(tedian)* of the Tujia as an ethnic group is that they are easily influenced by outsiders and new things. He viewed assimilative intermarriage *(tonghun)* as a very important part of the process by which outsiders influenced Tujia because both sides *(fang)* bring their culture to a marriage. This official used intermarriage to explain both why Tujia are "sinicized"—they adopted Han culture through intermarriage with Han—and why patrilineal descendants of Han were classified as non-Han Tujia—they adopted local culture through intermarriage. Although such an explanation suggests that the Han, too, were impressionable, they are not generally characterized as being easily influenced, so the official did not discuss this implication.

Officials assumed that the number of generations of intermarriage in a family's past correlates to their degree of Tujia cultural practices today, without verifying this assumption empirically. Officials I spoke with mentioned no evidence linking generations of residence in Enshi and the customs of individual families, and villagers whom I interviewed reported no visits by officials to discuss their identity or customs. I asked one official how he would classify a family whose ancestors had immigrated before the cutoff date but whose customs were completely Han. He replied that such an example is not possible. When a Han family came in, they had to intermarry with local people, so their descendants would definitely manifest local—by which he meant Tujia—cultural and linguistic influence. He volunteered that if there were a family whose ancestors came before the cutoff date and they have some Han customs and some Tujia customs, then its members could be either classification, depending on what they want. He said, "If they say they want to be classified as Han, I don't have the right to say they are ethnic minority [i.e., non-Han]" *(ruguo tamen shuo wo yao dang Han wo mei quanli shuo tamen shi shaoshu minzu)*. In spite of this self-reported deference to people's self-identification, there was no evidence of such respect in actual classifications.[13]

There are two problems with the explanations officials offered for using the timing of ancestral immigration to distinguish between Han and Tujia. First of all, intermarriage occurred not only for early but also for later waves of Han immigrants. Second, if intermarriage sinicized the Tujia and made the Han more like the Tujia, then what is the difference between Han and Tujia? Rather than resolving these problems directly, local officials established a cutoff date for assigning official ethnic identity. In the Enshi City area, they chose 1735, when this area was brought under Qing bureaucratic administration *(gai tu gui liu)*. One official explained this choice as follows: people who immigrated before 1735 had been local people *(tumin)*, in the literal sense of being under the authority of local rulers *(tusi)*. It was also a date before which there are unlikely to be sufficient written records about ordinary people and life in Enshi to contradict twentieth-century assumptions. Officials assumed there had been widespread intermarriage. One told me that most immigrants were Han men who married local women, but even immigrant men who brought Han wives with them would have had to arrange marriages with locals for their sons and daughters. Where immigration—and thus probably intermarriage as well—occurred before 1735, officials decided to classify descendants as Tujia.

Local oral history provides mixed support for officials' view of the widespread occurrence of intermarriage. Many people in Wucun village reported long-term intermarriage between "local" and "outsider" clans, yet some also told me of local sayings warning against intermarriage— for example, "Cattle don't herd with water buffalo; immigrants shouldn't join with locals" *(huangniu buhe shuiniu qun; banjiazi buhe bendiren)*.[14] Because of the reports of intermarriage, I interpret this saying as indicating disapproval of intermarriage that actually went on. It also implies that there may have been other options available. Large numbers of Han immigrants came to Enshi; if many of them came as families, including wives and daughters, as local people claimed, it would have been possible for immigrants in Enshi to marry endogamously (among themselves). If so, intermarriage may not have been as high as in seventeenth-century Taiwan. On the other hand, these claims may reflect invented tradition rather than actual past events. Such invention is not uncommon (Hobsbawn and Ranger 1983). Many people in Taiwan also insisted that their Han patrilineal ancestors brought Han wives with them, for example, even though, as we saw in chapter 4, historical evidence suggests a high rate of intermarriage between Han and Aborigines in the seventeenth century. It is not possible to estimate a rate of intermarriage for Enshi on the basis of currently available information, so it is not clear just how widespread intermarriage was.

In classifying the Enshi population, officials began with a Han perspective on how to determine identity—using surnames and patrilineal ancestors. They also confronted the methodological problem of how to move from a group-level cultural definition of the Tujia to specific guidelines for classifying individuals. The local context of centuries of intermarriage further complicated this problem. Relying only on surname to classify the populace was certainly much easier than analyzing their customs, even if the method glossed over intermarriage by ignoring matrilateral ancestry. Officials' task necessarily became more difficult when their government superiors ordered them to reclassify the population to come up with a smaller percentage of non-Han. This time, they did attempt to make sense of what was known about local history, developing a classification scheme that combined surname, place of origin, and timing of immigration. In doing so, they assumed that patrilineal families that had been in Enshi long "enough," and therefore intermarried with locals long "enough," had had sufficient time to change culturally to Tujia *regardless of the identity of their patrilineal ancestors*. People with "recent" Han immigrant ancestors were assumed not to have changed enough, despite intermarriage, to warrant changing their identity from Han to non-Han. Thus, officials had to set an arbitrary date as a cutoff for long "enough." Officials assumed, without any verification, that the content of cultural practices and beliefs are directly correlated to the length of time people's ancestors have been in a place. Although this assumption appears to incorporate the state criterion of culture into the classification scheme, in fact it does not. As we shall see, these assumptions about intermarriage created a dichotomy between Han and Tujia not empirically supported by cultural practices.

Establishing a Distinction Between Tujia and Han Individuals

I suggest that local officials initially relied on surnames to classify the population not only because it was methodologically easier but also because, as locals themselves, they must have known that there were no cultural markers of ethnic identity used locally on which they could rely (see below, also Brown 2001b). Why, then, do they impute cultural difference to ancestral immigration before and after their cutoff date?

Officials recognized that intermarriage also occurred in Enshi City after 1735, but they listed people whose ancestors immigrated after this date as Han. In explaining their logic to me, officials seemed to assume that these "recent" Han immigrants had been less influenced by local Tujia culture than earlier ones. Did they think that there were greater numbers of Han immigrants after 1735 and thus that the cultural influence of the Tujia lessened? Or did they think that the dominant influence flowed from the post-1735 Han immigrants to the Tujia, rather than the reverse, because more of the Han immigrants were educated? Although not stated directly, the comments of one official on footbinding suggest the latter. He viewed the custom as going hand in hand with *wenhua* (education, civilization) and status.[15]

On the basis of his remarks, I expected footbinding to have been a local marker of ethnic identity—as it had been in Toushe, Jibeishua, and Longtian in Taiwan—but it was not. In the memories of the people I interviewed in Wucun, footbinding, which was practiced through the 1930s, was a sign of wealth and class, not ethnic identity. Regardless of their classification as locals or outsiders, very wealthy women had their feet bound earliest, most compactly, and most permanently. Such binding involved breaking the arch of the foot and often led to the loss of toes. It resulted in the formerly much-lauded three- to five-inch foot (see Levy 1967). Most women in the Enshi area did not experience such an extreme process. Women I interviewed who were first married before 1949 reported having their feet bound when they were between three and eight years old, often as a result of their future mothers-in-law sending the binding cloth as a gift. (Child betrothals were common before 1949.) Although extremely painful, the binding that these women experienced could not have involved breaking the arch of the foot because every woman I spoke with had unbound her feet—some as girls, but most after marriage in order to work in the fields (see Gates 2001 for discussion of the link between footbinding and women's labor). Unbinding could be as painful as binding, for a while, but it was simply impossible if the arch had been broken (e.g., Levy 1967:208, 214–218). Women from both local and outsider families whose standard of living was poor to comfortable reported this less permanent form of binding. Degree of footbinding was not linked to ethnicity.

Culture is supposed to be a major factor in ethnic identity—hence its inclusion in the four state criteria for group identification and in local officials' explanations that the number of generations of intermarriage in a family's past correlates to their degree of Tujia cultural practices today. However, there appears to be no unified Tujia culture. The cultural practices described by Enshi officials and presented to the public and scholars in written and video materials as "Tujia" are practices collected from all over the prefecture. No areas practiced all of these customs, and in some areas most if not all of the locally practiced customs were—in many cases still are—shared with people classified as Han. One official even admitted, in response to one of my questions, that there is not a single "Tujia" custom maintained by Tujia descendants throughout the prefecture. One scholar told me that initially she too would have said there was no such unifying custom, but after giving some thought to the question she decided that perhaps the custom of bridal laments (*kujia ge,* ritualized mournful songs sung by brides) was universal. Bridal laments may well be universal—indeed, given the horrible status of women in this area, particularly before 1949, it is likely—but bridal laments are practiced in Enshi both by people classified as Tujia and by people classified as Han.[16] (In fact, bridal laments are common throughout East Asia and occur in "just about every language in Southwest China" [Stevan Harrell, personal communication 2000].) Another candidate for a custom maintained by Tujia throughout the prefecture is the notion that the dead and the living belong next to each other—that is, the dead should be buried close to their living descendants, an idea I found widespread in my travels around Enshi prefecture. The problem for official group identification and individual classification is that it too is shared by residents generally, those classified today as Han and those classified as Tujia. This notion is quite distinct from Han ideas elsewhere that the interment of the dead should be away from the homes of the living (e.g., Watson 1988: 15–16). Thus, although there are cultural differences—significant by Confucian standards—between people living in Enshi and Han people elsewhere, there are no cultural practices clearly marking differences between Tujia and Han within the Enshi area.

Local officials knew that they were creating an arbitrary distinction between Tujia and Han.[17] Officials could not use cultural practices to classify the population, or else the entire Enshi prefecture would have contained few if any people classified as Han, a result their government superiors would not accept. They rationalized a state-required incorporation of culture into their classification method by assuming that intermarriage led to cultural change in different ways before and after a cutoff date—1735 in the Enshi City area, a date that precludes examining their assumptions directly.

Clearly, the state drove ethnic classification of individuals in the PRC.

The central government ordered the identification of acceptable ethnic categories and then the classification of the entire populace into one and only one of those categories. For people in Enshi, classification—which came in the early 1980s rather than in the 1950s—brought non-Han minority status. But that is not how locals saw themselves.

LOCAL IDENTITY AS HAN

I examine local identity in Wucun in order to show that, like many Hoklo in southwestern Taiwan, people in Enshi were short-route Han prior to 1949. Then, the term *tujia* simply referred to local families. *Tu* (lit., "earth") can mean "local" or "coarse." It is often applied to rural people in a denigrating way, like "hicks" or "hillbillies" in American English. Families officially registered as Tujia today do not directly correspond to those who were once classified as locals, even though the ethnic term "Tujia" is derived from that older classification. Part of the disjuncture is due to the complexity of local identity in the mid-twentieth century, a complexity that derives from viewing a historical pattern synchronically. A series of short-route identity changes spanning millenia meant that the notion of locals was not fixed, neither historically nor at any given point in time. Each wave of Han immigrants merged with locals when a new wave of Han arrived, so that which people were considered locals shifted over time. Additionally, people considered different clans to be locals, depending on the relative timing of their ancestors' immigration to Enshi. One clan might be considered local by a second clan and outsider by a third. As we shall see, such a shifting, contingent identity also meant that no custom strongly marked identity here, as it had for long-route Han in Taiwan before 1915. Before the SNAC arrived to tell them otherwise, people in Enshi saw themselves as Han or, put another way, they had Han consciousness. In fact, many of them continued to insist that they were Han through 1996.

Forced Migrations

The people in the mountainous region of Enshi are descendants of soldiers, farmers, laborers, and exiled convicts forced to migrate there over the course of two millenia. Politically, forced migrations served a range of purposes: occupying a defensible border, providing agricultural and other labor for the local elite, and promoting stability among a population with a reputation for rebellion by bringing in Han (who were viewed as more compliant). The earliest known immigrants came from the state of Chu on the Yangzi plains and the states of Qin and Han in the Yellow River valley—states whose peoples are all considered ancestral to those who later called themselves Han Chinese. The earliest immigrants also included peoples, such as the Ba in eastern Sichuan, who are not considered ancestral to the Han (e.g., Zhang 1995 [1987], Sage 1992, Dong 1999).[18] It is the non-Han Ba whom the SNAC officially designated as ancestral to the Tujia (e.g., Liu 1989, ESMZ 1991, Tian 1994:183, Huang and Shi 1995:188).[19] After the Han dynasty (202 B.C.E.–220 C.E.), Enshi's mountainous location appears to have kept it on the fringes of dynastic struggles until the Yuan dynasty (1276–1368) brought it back into the tribute-paying realm under a system of local or indigenous rulers *(tusi)*. Although imperial soldiers were stationed near present-day Enshi City, the area remained under local authority from the Yuan into the early Qing period (e.g., Hu and Liu 1993). In 1395, under the Ming dynasty, there was an imperial order that all indigenous rulers must learn Confucian principles and the Han writing system, thus promoting Han culture. (There were no Han schools for commoners until after 1735.) Enshi oral histories and genealogies speak frequently of forced migrations during the Ming and Qing dynasties. In 1735, Enshi was removed from local rule and brought directly under Qing bureaucratic administration *(gai tu gui liu)*. This change in administration also brought Han into Enshi in large numbers. The most recent wave of Han immigrants came in the late 1930s and early 1940s, during the war with Japan.

Oral histories in Wucun support this broad historical picture of an area largely populated by forced migrations. Several villagers reported that their ancestors came to the Enshi area "with their hands tied behind their backs" *(kunbang lai de, shuan qilai de, gudao lai de* or *kun qilai de; gudao* is the local dialect for *qianpo* [forced]). A local "just-so" story explained that old people walk with their hands behind their backs because that is how their ancestors came—with their hands (tied) behind their backs. A less common variant of that story says that, because the ancestors came bound, so infants are bound (swaddled) when women work in the fields.

This historical information was accepted locally as a matter of fact. People volunteered that their ancestors were forced to migrate to the Enshi area without apparent embarrassment or shame. Only one man said that he knew other families' ancestors had come like convicts *(tu)*—that is, with their hands tied behind their backs—but that his own ancestors had not. Given that his ancestors came in a migration that many other people described to me as forced could mean he was ashamed, but he could also be honestly reporting family lore. After all, the presence of soldiers was required to force the migrants to come, and such soldiers were not repatriated to Han areas. Nevertheless, even though the accompanying soldiers surely did not have their hands tied, they can hardly be said to have been voluntary immigrants.

Many people in Wucun who considered their own families locals were descendants of people forced to migrate into the area. Although the earliest forced migration reported by villagers dates from 1369 in the early Ming period, there was a large cave near the village which had old carvings claiming a migration during the Northern Song dynasty (960–1127). Much more migration was reported in the Qing dynasty. According to one local scholar, the suppression of rebellions in Sichuan decimated the population there during the Kangxi period of the Qing dynasty (1662–1722), so mass migrations occurred by imperial order. Many people from Hubei were forced to migrate to Sichuan, and many people from Hunan were forced to migrate to the Enshi area.

Not every family's immigration was forced. One man told me that his ancestors had come in the early Qing as refugees from war and famine in their home area *(taonan lai de)*. Another man said that his ancestors came to the mountains of Enshi to escape flooding on the Yangzi plains. Notably, these families came singly. Most voluntary migrants did not come as part of a large group or wave of immigrants.

Migration, both forced and voluntary, was very common in the late eighteenth century after Enshi came under Qing administrative rule and quickly increased the population. Forced migrations, however, are much more important to understanding identity in Enshi: they occurred far more often historically and each one brought a mass or wave of immigrants—large numbers of people arriving at the same time. I suggest that these waves led to the shifting quality of local identity.

Shifting Identity and the Relative Timing of Ancestral Immigration

The relative nature of the conception of "locals" *(tujia)* in Enshi first became apparent to me when one educated man, who came to Enshi with the Nationalists and stayed because he married a local woman, kept referring to everyone whose ancestors came before him as "locals" in conversations with me about local customs. An Enshi scholar confirmed this impression—"the *tu* are old Han immigrants; the Han are recent Han immigrants"—as did a villager who explained "locals and outsiders all came from outside [Enshi] *(bendi ke jia dou waidi laide)*. Locals came earlier, outsiders came later."

Local identity in Enshi was not simply relative, however; it was also contingent and, because it was contingent, shifting. At one end of the continuum were families or clans whom everyone considered outsiders; at the other end were families or clans whom everyone considered locals. Spanning this continuum were families considered locals by those whose ancestors migrated more recently and, at the same time, considered outsiders by those whose ancestors migrated earlier. The shifting and contingent qualities strongly contrast with the fixed nature of official identity as Tujia or Han. Because registered identity is (largely) fixed and local identity was not, it was impossible for Tujia and local identities to correspond neatly. Moreover, even determining which families were local relative to others required knowledge of local social history—whose ancestors came when. This kind of local knowledge was primarily recorded in genealogies and taught to males.

Almost all the men I interviewed, and several of the women, were able to tell me when and/or from where their ancestors had migrated. People talked about migration in terms of the number of generations which had passed since it had occurred—often implicity but also explicitly—linking their family's generational names *(paihang* or *zipai)* to the number of generations the family had been in Enshi. Generational names are a list of between eight and fifty written characters, where each succeeding character is assigned to each such succeeding generation for use in the two-character given name of every male in the generation. (A few families also gave these generational names to females, but most did not.) Families ranging from wealthy to poor commonly had generational names. In response to my question of when his ancestors came to Enshi, one man recited his clan's generational names to the character in his own name, which was the eleventh, and then responded that his ancestors had come eleven generations before. Using a generation length of twenty years and his year of birth (1925), I estimate the date of his ancestors' arrival in Enshi as approximately 1705—before the change to Qing administration.[20] In spite of the fact that his patrilineal ancestors came from the Han area of Jinzhou, he claimed to be both a local and Tujia. Another man, who claimed his ancestors came in 1369, also had the eleventh generational name in a list of twenty. Assuming a twenty-year generation, I estimate that their arrival eleven generations before his birth in 1920 was approximately 1700. If I assume that he was actually in the thirty-first generation since his ancestors came (and the family was on its second time through the list of names since the migration), then I get an arrival estimate of 1300, closer to his claim.

Further evidence that generational names are indeed perceived to indicate ancestral immigration dates came from a man whose claim to be local and Tujia I doubt, not merely because his national identity card listed him as Han.[21] He was anxious to rationalize the apparent discrepancy between his claim and his generational name, which was only his family's seventh generational name. He gave me an elaborate explanation about why generational names did not accurately predict when his particular ancestors came, without questioning their use as general predictors. He explained that, when his ancestors first came to Enshi, they did not bring the generational names with them, but after three generations, they sent someone back to Jinzhou to get them. Thus, even though he has the seventh generational name, he claimed to be the tenth generation in Enshi. Yet he also claimed that his ancestors came at the beginning of the Ming dynasty during the Hongwu reign, 1368–1399! Even with a generous and unlikely thirty-year generation, ten generations yields an estimate of 300 years, reaching back only to the early 1600s. He said that everyone whose ancestors came in the Ming dynasty (1368–1644) are all "local trash" *(tumanzi)* and that outsiders *(kejia)* came later.[22]

People who reported that their ancestors came in the early years of the Ming dynasty stood at one end of the shifting identity continuum in Wucun. They were uniformly considered locals—by themselves and by others. Moreover, they were registered as Tujia. For them, local and Tujia identity did coincide. They viewed almost all of their neighbors as outsiders—families whose ancestors immigrated to Enshi more recently than their own ancestors. They viewed only each other and the few families not known to have migrated at all as locals.

At the other end of the identity continuum in Wucun stood families whose ancestors had come into the Enshi area in one of the most recent forced migrations. They came in a migration from Hunan and were considered outsiders *(kejia),* both by themselves and by others whose ancestors had come earlier. (People who immigrated with the Nationalists in the 1930s, and remained in Enshi, settled primarily in Enshi City, so they were not part of the social context in Wucun.) In Wucun, the most recent immigrants from Hunan probably came between 1790 and 1830.[23] These families considered everyone whose families had come earlier as "locals." Interestingly, the area their ancestors came from in Hunan has been officially designated a Tujia area, and many people told me that people from Hunan were most authentically Tujia *(zhenzhengde tujiazu).*

Even though they arrived after 1735, these families were registered as Tujia. In other words, people generally agreed upon as "outsiders" were officially Tujia. While relative timing of immigration was more important to ordinary people—I will suggest because of sociopolitical experience— the official classification also had to take into consideration place of origin.

Between these two extremes were many people who reported that genealogies or family oral histories said their ancestors came from Jinzhou— a Han area further east in Hubei on the Yangzi River (see figure 20 above). Generational names suggest that their ancestors migrated between seven and nine generations ago. Some people who said their ancestors were from Jinzhou identified themselves as outsiders, but most said they were locals, even when (assuming a generation of twenty years) their ancestors must have come after 1735, the official cutoff date for Tujia status in this area. According to one man, who said his ancestors came early and were from Jinzhou, "People used to call [us] local trash (tumanzi). Before 1949, [we] were really crude (man de hen)."[24] Such terminology is unexpected for a clan tracing its roots to the Han city of Jinzhou, because officially "tumanzi" referred to Tujia in the past (e.g., Huang and Shi 1995:191). To people in Wucun, however, the term referred to locals as determined by the relative timing of ancestral migration, even if such people had Han patrilineal ancestors from Jinzhou. Such families variously considered others from Jinzhou as locals or outsiders, depending on which of the multiple migrations from Jinzhou brought their respective ancestors. One man who identified his clan as outsiders said "most people in this area were outsiders (kejia ren); there wasn't much local trash (tumanzi)." Many people with ancestors from Jinzhou, however, said they were registered as Tujia, and several showed me their identity cards to prove it.

The different reports from people whose ancestors came at different times about which families were locals and which were outsiders suggest two important conclusions. First, the border between locals and outsiders shifted. With each new wave of immigrants, people already there became "locals" to the new immigrants, but they retained their outsider status to those whose ancestors came before theirs did. Thus, the early Ming immigrants were probably outsiders to whomever was here before, they became locals to the next wave, and they were certainly locals to the people who came from Jinzhou in the Qing dynasty. There were several immigrations from Jinzhou, explaining the variety in their classifications of each other, but all Jinzhou people became locals to the people whose ancestors came in the last immigration from Hunan in the Qing dynasty. Even these outsiders from Hunan became locals to those who came with the Nationalists.

The second important conclusion is that knowledge of these historical shifts in identity was preserved in genealogies and oral histories. As a matter of course, males were taught at least rudimentary information about their genealogy—at least when their ancestors immigrated, where they came from, where in Enshi they first arrived, and the list of generational names. Most men I interviewed were also able to say something about whether their neighbors were locals or outsiders, but it is not clear whether they learned this information along with their own genealogies or whether they calculated it based on conversations comparing genealogical stories with neighboring men.

The shifting and contingent character of local identity meant that people with differing kinds and degrees of knowledge might disagree about classifications. One husband and wife whom I interviewed together debated whether their respective ancestors were locals or outsiders. The woman, who knew that her ancestors came from Jinzhou but not when they came, was not sure about their status. Her husband, who knew that his ancestors came from Hunan in the Ming dynasty, said both his and his wife's ancestors were locals. It is no coincidence that the woman in this example lacked crucial genealogical information; most girls were not taught anything about their natal family's history since they would marry out. The woman turned, instead, to a different kind of information that I will take up next—cultural markers. She responded to her husband that they do not celebrate the lunar New Year early and thus, by implication, are not locals. "Those who celebrate the lunar New Year early are real Tujia people, the ones who came to Enshi the earliest" *(zao tuannian shi zhenzheng tujiaren, lai Enshi zuizaode ren)*. Notice that she equated the "real Tujia" with those whose ancestors migrated earliest. Her husband ended the debate by switching to a discussion of official identity. "Locals and outsiders are all in the Tujia ethnic group" *(bendi ke jia dou shi tujiazu)*. Probably because official identification of the Tujia as a group required listing cultural markers, discussion of cultural markers in interviews often led the conversation back to official identities.[25] Discussions about local identity were multileveled and complex. I turn next to the issue of cultural markers before returning to the contrast between unofficial identity and registered identity.

Weak Markers of Local Identity

People I interviewed mentioned cultural markers distinguishing locals and outsiders only occasionally, if at all. As we might expect, given the shifting and contingent nature of local identity, these markers were relatively minor, not particularly visible customs; those who mentioned them often referred to different customs; and the total number of customs mentioned was quite limited. After all, the customs of one family could be viewed as local customs by a second family (whose ancestors immigrated later) and as outsider customs by yet a third family (whose ancestors immigrated earlier). In such a context, markers could not have the classificatory power that the absence of footbinding had for Toushe, Jibeishua, and Longtian people in early-twentieth-century Taiwan. It is important to establish that there were no strong classificatory markers because, as we shall see later, there were striking differences between some beliefs and customs of people in Enshi—both locals and outsiders—and those of Han elsewhere in China. The absence of classificatory markers demonstates that those customs were never used locally to mark identity.

Celebrations for the lunar New Year—often referred to locally as *tuannian*—provide a good example of the weakness of customs as markers of identity. Celebrating the lunar New Year early, on the twenty-eighth or twenty-ninth of the last lunar month rather than on the thirtieth (as Han generally do), was an official characteristic of Tujia culture (e.g., Huang and Shi 1995:189). (Several villagers also mentioned a dish of pork fat and skin, *nianrou,* often served at New Year's, as characteristic of locals and Tujia.) All the villagers who mentioned New Year celebrations as ethnic markers—for example, the woman in the couple who debated whether their ancestors were locals—said that locals celebrate early, except for one man. His patrilineal ancestors came before 1735 from the Han area of Jinzhou, so he identified himself as both local and officially Tujia. He said that *outsiders* celebrated the lunar New Year early, while his own family celebrated on New Year's Eve itself (the thirtieth), thereby showing that his family was local. Was this man deliberately misleading me to strengthen his claim to official Tujia identity, or did he really believe what he told me? The latter is possible—his ancestors' pre-1735 arrival in Enshi would make him legally Tujia, and he may have combined his knowledge of his registration status with his knowledge that celebrating the lunar New Year is an indicator of Tujia identity and mistakenly assumed that his family custom is the one marking Tujia identity. This example also shows much of the complexity involved in reconstructing local identity—official identity on top of shifting and contingent unofficial identities along with the common essentialist assumption that the customs of an ethnic group are whatever customs those with that ethnic label practice. He was officially Tujia, and he was local in relation to neighbors, so—he probably assumed—the customs of his family were local/Tujia. With such shifting and contingent identity, it simply was not possible for customs to definitively mark identity.

Another example of a characteristic mentioned several times as Tujia was *tanshen*, a type of spirit. In one interview, two men and a woman—none of them religious specialists—debated what "tanshen" means. There were three alternatives discussed: altar gods *(tanshen)*, room gods *(tangshen)*, and Tan-surname gods *(Tan shen)*, with altar gods or Tan-surname gods considered most likely. Regardless of the meaning, they agreed that only locals—that is, only those who came earliest to Enshi—have tanshen *(shi dao Enshi lai zuizao de ren caiyou)*. At another time, three men agreed that both Tujia and Han believe in tanshen, although they also agreed that believing in them is not the same thing as having them in one's home. When I asked if tanshen were the same as *jiashen* (lit., family gods), one person said yes, another said no. Locally, "jiashen" referred not to ancestral tablets but to gods (ancestral tablets were called *shenzhu*).[26] The latter man explained that jiashen do not leave a house but tanshen can move to any clan *(jiazu)* member's house. There was also an expensive religious ritual associated with tanshen called *huan tanshen* (repaying the tanshen), formerly conducted by religious specialists called wizards *(wushi* or *duangong)*, which took a day and a night to perform.[27]

The man mentioned above, who went to great lengths to persuade me that his family was tenth-generation instead of seventh-generation and thus local, provided further, if indirect, evidence that no unambiguous marker of local identity exists. He mentioned several cultural markers in the course of giving me different reasons why he should be considered a local, which suggests that there was no established marker of local identity. Had there been such a clear marker, he would surely have invoked it.

We can conclude that no customs incontrovertibly marked any of the various identities in the area—local, outsider, Tujia, or Han—because people contradicted each other about which customs were linked to which identities. Thus, cultural markers of local identity were weak. In other words, Enshi people did not use cultural means to classify themselves and their neighbors. Nevertheless, as we shall see, they thought of themselves and were accepted as Han.

"But We're Really Han"

I have suggested that, with each new wave of immigrants, people already in Enshi became "locals" to the new immigrants. To the wave of Nationalist officials and foreigners that poured into Enshi when it was the provisional provincial capital of Hubei, all people already there were locals. But were they considered Han? For most people, poverty and lack of sophistication was what primarily distinguished locals—and surely farmers and small-town-dwellers elsewhere—from the cosmopolitan Nationalist outsiders. In all of my interviews and informal talks, only one man (quoted above) referred to local people *(bendi ren)* in living memory—and specifically to his own surname lineage in the 1940s—as "barbaric" *(man de hen),* yet I think even he meant it in the sense of "crude," because he was from a wealthy, well-educated branch of his clan. Some local men who had been conscripted by the Nationalists and wound up in Taiwan (as Mainlanders) were surprised, upon their return to Enshi in the 1980s, to discover their relatives classified as a non-Han ethnic minority (Tujia). In short, Nationalist outsiders in the 1920s through 1940s seem to have viewed local identity in Enshi as a Han regional variation, albeit rather coarse *(tu* or *man),* in spite of the fact that local culture varied from more "standard" northern or even southern Han cultural models.

Local people in Enshi still have a strong sense of themselves as Han. At one dinner I attended in 1996, where several families were present, an explanation of my research topic prompted a discussion about Tujia versus Han identity. Over the course of the conversation some local men discussed their personal sense of identity, contrasting it with official classification status. One man said that Han have become like the Tujia *(tujiahua).*[28] Another man agreed, saying that both believe in tanshen (discussed above). The first man went on to discuss the usefulness of having official status as Tujia due to affirmative action benefits for minorities, giving a specific example. A third man replied "In my heart, I don't see my ancestors as Tujia." This statement prompted the first man to agree, pointing out that the names in his family's genealogy are Han. Such discussion of ethnic identity in terms of patrilineal ancestors was common in Enshi.

Examination of people's 1996 reflections on their pre-1949 identity shows that—beyond their struggle to make post-Mao-era ethnic categories fit their earlier social experience—both locals and outsiders were formerly considered Han. One man—whose ancestors were from Jinzhou, who had the ninth of his family's generational names, and whose identity card said he was Tujia—was reluctant to respond to my question about whether his family were locals or outsiders. When someone else present at the interview said that his family were outsiders, he responded: "We should be [considered] outsiders *(yinggai kejia, kehu)*. We were Han in school [a school run through his clan], not Tujia. There were more Han around [then] so we thought we were [Han], but our customs are the same as locals." Here, the speaker imposes post-Mao-era ethnic categories upon pre-1949 events. Significantly, in spite of this imposition, he says that *both locals and outsiders had the same cultural practices and they thought of themselves as Han.* Similarly, a Tujia woman who had grown up in a rural area but lived in Enshi City told me that when she was young and saw local customs, which she now "knows" to be Tujia customs, she thought they were the local Han customs. She said that she did not realize they were the customs of a separate ethnic group (minzu). Even Shen Congwen—an author who became renowned before the founding of the PRC and thus before official ethnic classification designated him Tujia—wrote about the now Tujia area in Hunan where he grew up as an area at the border to Miao territory (1982:116) where most people are "descendants of [the ancient state of] Chu" (1982:107), a designation that conferred ethnic majority (Han or Hua) status.

The pre-1949 identity of locals as Han did not prevent people in the 1990s from seeking minority status. In Enshi, as elsewhere in the PRC, some individuals sought non-Han status for the affirmative action benefits it confers. I was told several times about one young man in Enshi who changed his state-registered minzu identity from Han to Tujia after discovering that his score on the college entrance examination was two points below what he needed to get into the college of his choice. The change in ethnic status gave him the additional points he needed to get into that college, because minorities receive a designated number of extra points on the college entrance exams. (Those with sufficient education to take advantage of this minority benefit are a small percentage of the population.) Such stories abound throughout China.

What is highly unusual in China are the many people in Enshi who have a legitimate basis according to state policies for changing their registration to Tujia but who still want to be listed as Han. This desire shows an extraordinarily strong Han consciousness. The legal way for individuals in the PRC to prove their minority status and change their ethnic classification is by reference to ancestry—an ironic focus, given the state emphasis on culture in identifying groups. The children of intermarried couples can be assigned to either ethnic group, and Han individuals who discover that a grandparent is an ethnic minority can petition to have their identity changed as well. One woman who grew up in Enshi City told me that when she found out the village her parents came from was Tujia she changed her registration from Han to Tujia, but her adult son refused to change his registration. She said she had repeatedly told her son about the benefits of being listed as Tujia, but he considered it a stigma to be listed as non-Han and he adamantly refused. Another man told me that when he changed his family's ethnic registration to Tujia, based on a grandmother's identity as Tujia, his younger brother was very opposed to it, wanting to remain listed as Han instead. (Since the younger brother was a minor, his parents made the decision to change his registration anyway.) Although these individuals accept the state identification of the Tujia as a group, they themselves want to be classified as Han, not as Tujia.

Local people in Enshi made it quite clear to me that they think of themselves as Han. In addition to those who refused legal means to seek Tujia status, several people told me of unsuccessful attempts to change their registration from Tujia to Han. Moreover, even people in Enshi I spoke with who had changed their registration to Tujia wanted me to understand that they too think of themselves as Han. They emphasized that they took Tujia status only for the benefits and went on to state explicitly that their Tujia classification was based on matrilateral ties. They explained that, since their patrilineal ancestors were Han, they were "really" Han, even though they were legitimately non-Han in the eyes of the government. This view of themselves as authentically Han based on their patrilineal ancestry looks like the claims to Han identity through genealogy that Ebrey (1996) describes and also like short-route identity change in Taiwan. It is very much a Han perspective of identity, even though it does not follow Confucian culturalism. It also suggests that, through the 1990s, locals in Enshi were culturally Han enough to think of themselves as Han, and claim identity as Han, in the same way that other Han have for centuries—through patrilineal ancestry. They must have been shocked to have their Han identity revoked.

OUTSIDER RECLASSIFICATION AS NON-HAN

Since locals viewed themselves as Han, why did state officials view them as non-Han? I suggest that, as outsiders, members of the SNAC relied on cultural practices to make their ethnic identification. I argue that the striking differences they found in mortuary practices, ancestor worship, and inheritance of property between local culture and Han culture elsewhere in China led to the initial classification of local people as non-Han in the 1950s, even though these differences were not important locally. The Han demonstrate enormous regional cultural variation (as discussed in chapter 1). However, the late-imperial state promoted standardized versions of several of the aspects of Han culture on which I focus here, thereby greatly reducing variation in these practices, even decades after the last imperial state collapsed in 1911 (Watson 1988, Gates 1996).

The differences between locals in Enshi and Han elsewhere in the 1950s are important to a consideration of Taiwan's new narrative of unfolding for two reasons. First, the simple fact that there were striking differences resulted in the creation of the Tujia minzu (ethnic group), which meant that PRC officials used culture to judge that people with Han ancestors had become non-Han. Second, as we shall see, the very same cultural practices which marked Enshi as non-Han to PRC officials in the 1950s are also markedly different between Taiwan and China at the turn of the twenty-first century. I argue that, in the 1950s, PRC officials used these practices as unstated ethnic markers distinguishing between Han and non-Han identity. Such markers would have remained unstated because, in the official identification process, each ethnic group was supposed to be identified on the basis of its own internal characteristics—language, territory, economy, and culture—not on the basis of characteristics that excluded them from another group. Officials who identified locals as minorities on an exclusionary basis—that is, as non-Han—would not have said so explicitly, since at the time of the identification Han chauvinism (da han zhuyi) was officially discouraged (e.g., Mackerras 1994:145–46).

Coming into the Enhsi area with a knowledge of Han studies, and having been told that culturally Tujia are virtually the same as Han, I was shocked to discover that graves were placed next to houses, that not all ancestors had had ancestral tablets prior to the wide-scale destruction of these tablets during the Cultural Revolution, that ancestors were feasted at New Year's in order to get them to leave their descendants' homes, and that youngest brothers often inherited all the family property.[29] If I was shocked, how much more so must Han from other parts of China have been? I suggest that the Han who came in to identify ethnic groups in the area must have felt that people with such practices could not possibly be Han and thus officially identified them as non-Han (initially as Miao). Although these practices did not serve as markers to Enshi people—I am including both pre-1949 locals and pre-1949 outsiders now as "locals"—they appear to have served as markers to Han from elsewhere in China—the new "outsiders"—responsible for the ethnic identification. What are these strikingly different customs and how are they different from most Han practices elsewhere?

Han Cultural Practices and Beliefs

Local culture in Enshi (as practiced by both pre-1949 locals and pre-1949 outsiders) included many important Han elements, such as language (Southwest Mandarin), marriage practices, and footbinding. However, it did not include several Han elements that carry tremendous moral and ideological weight. As important as they are, the presence of one of these elements alone is not sufficient to mark Han identity.[30] In Enshi, the absence of all of these elements contraindicated Han identity.[31]

Ancestor Worship   Ancestor worship is founded on the assumption that the obligations of filial piety never end, and the Confucian principle of filial piety is derived from the notion that people are obligated to their parents simply for giving them life. Filial piety pervades Han culture in all its variations and, since it extends the filial obligation from parent to ruler, it was strongly supported by the imperial state.[32] Ancestor worship is also a crucial part of the narrative of Han unfolding as a civilization. In addition to Confucian principles emphasizing the reverence of parents, evidence of ancestor worship can be found in the Yellow River valley "cradle" of Han civilization along with the earliest forms of Han writing (e.g., Keightley 1978). The ideological importance attached to this origin gives practices surrounding ancestor worship greater weight as markers of Han identity.

After death, Daoist priests ritually transform relatives into ancestors by installing a new ancestral tablet on the family altar. Descendants must make regular offerings to the dead in order to provide for their well-being. If adequate offerings are not provided to all ancestors, they can cause trouble—illness, financial troubles, and so on—for their descendants. Thus, when Han face domestic difficulties, they often hire a ritual specialist to find out whether an ancestor is punishing the descendants for unfilial treatment. If so, some kind of restitution is settled upon which is supposed to resolve the descendants' troubles. This framework allows for variation across the Han, for example, in what materials are required for a tablet (paper, wood, bamboo), in the quantity and quality of offerings considered "adequate," and in the frequency considered "regular."

Ghost Beliefs   The dead who receive no offerings from descendants become ghosts. The dead may have no offerings because they have no descendants or because their descendants do not provide offerings. The latter can happen for a wide range of reasons. Descendants may not believe in ancestor worship if, for example, they convert to Christianity or Islam. Descendants may not know a relative has died, if he or she dies a long way from home. Other categories of the dead also become ghosts, notably those who have died violent deaths. Although it is not particularly polite to admit it, other people's relatives can also be considered ghosts (e.g., Wolf 1974b:146).

Ghosts are often likened to beggars and bandits—always hungry and ready to prey on anyone within their territory (cf. Wolf 1974b, Jordan 1985, Weller 1987). In short, ghosts are dangerous and threatening. Thus, Han avoid places where the souls of the dead who are not their own ancestors are thought to linger—for example, graves—or where people have died violently or where the corpses of strangers were found. Some Han will not even use the term "ghost" *(gui)* in their speech for fear of attracting their attention, preferring euphemisms instead. Some Han, however, do frequent ghost shrines seeking supernatural assistance (e.g., Harrell 1974, Weller 1994:124–43, 1999:89–90), so ghost beliefs may well be more varied among the Han than other practices and beliefs discussed here.

Mortuary Practices   Standardized Han mortuary practices protect people in a community from the ghosts of their neighbors' ancestors in a variety of ways. Anthropologist James L. Watson (1988) argues that in late imperial China (which he defines as 1750–1920) there was an amazing structural uniformity of Han funerary rites due to state demands of orthopraxy—that people practice uniform rites regardless of whether they believed in them. These mortuary practices largely continued in Han areas after late-imperial times, even though they were no longer state-mandated. In fact, many continued in the PRC until the Cultural Revolution, in spite of official prohibitions (e.g., Whyte 1987: 298). Since the 1980s, with the loosening of punishments for practicing many forms of religion, some of these practices are reportedly reappearing in many Han parts of China (e.g., Whyte 1987: 300–302, Weller 1999: 86). Given these stubborn continuities, Han outsiders in the 1950s would probably have expected locals, if they were "really" Han, to follow these mortuary practices.

Watson (1988:8–9) identifies five features found in Han funerary rites across late imperial China, several of which were not in practice in the Enshi area. (1) Corpse and spirit need to be kept together during the initial stages of death so that the soul does not become disoriented and turn into a wandering ghost. (2) Death does not change a person's social or kin status, thus does not terminate filial obligations. (3) The soul has multiple parts which reside in different locations, so there is more than one location where people have to beware of the souls of their neighbors' ancestors. According to a nineteenth century American missionary who worked in Fujian Province (Doolittle 1865 2:401–402), souls had three parts: one in the afterworld, one in the ancestral tablet, and one in the grave.[33] (4) A balance of the sexes is required even in death, for example, by burying couples closely together or listing their names on the same ancestral tablet. A lack of balance, however, does not preclude the obligation to provide offerings. (5) Reciprocal obligations do not end with death. The living offer food, money, and goods to the deceased and, in return, expect material benefits such as wealth and progeny.

As part of the accepted procedure of Han funerary rites in late imperial China outlined by Watson (1988:12–15), a soul tablet with a written name had to be prepared for the dead and installed on the domestic altar, requiring the services of a literate ritual specialist, often a Daoist priest. The employment of professionals was required both for their expertise in the complex structure of the rites and because someone "had to accept money from the mourners (or the deceased's estate or a public charity) before the corpse could be safely expelled from the community" (Watson 1988:14). The coffin had to be expelled from the community—village, town, or neighborhood—of the deceased. In spite of procedural and sequential standardization, variation existed in the timing and ritual expression of funerary rites as well as in post-expulsion burial rites (Watson 1988:15–16).[34]

Property Inheritance and Parental Authority   Han families *(jia)* are patrilineal, patriarchal, property-holding units, typically run by a senior male member. Gates (1996a:29–30) uses the term "patricorporations" to distinguish them from Western notions of family and argues that these patricorporations are the foundation of a petty capitalist political economy which operates by exploiting the labor of females and immature males within the family. The vesting of corporate "property"—including human labor—under the total control of senior males gave parents an incredible degree of state-sanctioned authority, including the authority to sell children outright and prostitute unmarried daughters (e.g., Gates 1996a:30, Wolf 1995:147–48). Moreover, Gates (1989, 1996a:46–54) links this familial social order to the neo-Confucian revival in the Song dynasty, in which Confucian principles were reinterpreted in even more strongly patriarchal terms. The link to Confucian principles endows this patriarchal and corporate social organization of the family with great moral weight, making it a marker of Han identity.

Families have structural cycles, expanding as children are born, marry, and have grandchildren, and dividing as some of these nuclear units break off and establish their own households (e.g., Cohen 1976, Wolf 1985b). When family division occurs, jointly held property must be divided. For most Han across China in late-imperial times, brothers inherited approximately equal shares of the family property (e.g.,Wolf 1989, Gates 1996a:91–95, Watson 1985:106–107).[35] Ideally, property was not divided between brothers until after the death of both parents, although division often occurred when the senior authority either grew too infirm to manage the household or died. Thus, "dividing property" *(fen jia)* refers to the equal division of property between brothers. As we shall see, the term meant something else in Wucun.

All these elements of Han culture—ancestor worship, ghost beliefs, mortuary practices, and property inheritance—derive from Confucian principles supporting strong parental authority. Like parental authority itself, these cultural practices were widespread, even across Han regional variation, and carried great ideological weight. In the case of mortuary practices, the state even mandated standardization. Thus, I suggest that these elements served as important markers of Han identity.

Non-Han Cultural Practices and Beliefs

Although locals in Enshi shared many Han customs and beliefs found elsewhere, they departed from the widespread Han cultural elements discussed above in some striking ways. (Again, I am using "locals" here to refer to all people in Enshi when the Nationalists arrived. In other words, I include both pre-1949 locals and pre-1949 outsiders here as locals.)

These different practices and beliefs all indicate relatively weak parental authority. Because strong parental authority was the cornerstone of Han society (e.g., Gates 1996a), I argue that these differences constituted clear markers of non-Han identity to the largely Han officials responsible for ethnic identification in the 1950s.

Ancestor Worship   The ideological centrality of ancestors and ancestor worship to Han culture marked the treatment of ancestors in Enshi as strikingly non-Han. In standard Han mortuary practices, death did not disrupt an individual's social or kin status, nor did it terminate obligatory relationships of reciprocity. In Enshi, one local scholar told me that above five generations, people do not consider their ancestors to be relatives, in spite of the fact that many families had genealogies tracing their ancestors back far more than five generations, at least before these genealogies were destroyed in the Cultural Revolution. Moreover, there were a number of substantive ways in which it was clear that, in Enshi, death did terminate relationships of reciprocity—probably because the sense of reciprocity between living parents and children was unusually weak.

The standard Han features of mortuary practices outlined above meant that every deceased person required a soul tablet. People in Wucun, however, told me that ancestral tablets were expensive, so only comparatively well-off families had them made for deceased family members prior to 1949. In other words, not every deceased person had an ancestral tablet. One man in Wucun told me if people have no children, there are no tablets because there are no descendants, but he assured me that having no tablet was not important to what happened to the soul. Elsewhere, before 1949, many Han made every effort to find someone to care for the tablets of people without children, even if the person was not a patrilineal relative of the deceased, because souls without tablets become wandering, hungry ghosts that prey on the living.

In Wucun, offerings at the lunar New Year (through 1996) were intended to encourage the ancestors to leave. People provided offerings for the ancestors at New Year's whether or not they had tablets. One woman told me that they feed the ancestors well at New Year's so that they can leave more happily *(jie laoren tuannian chile hao zoulu)*. When I asked her where these ancestors go when they leave, she said "back to the afterworld" *(hui difu, yinfu)*. Offerings in front of ancestral tablets were relatively few, compared to other parts of China. One man, whose well-to-do family had had many tablets, told me the extent of offerings:

> If there is an illness then [the family] had to worship *(bai)* [the ancestors]
> with incense and paper [spirit money]. [The family] also had to worship
> at New Year's *(guonian)* on the thirtieth [of the last lunar month], the ninth
> [of the first lunar month], and the fifteenth [of the first lunar month].

When I asked whether offerings were presented daily, he explained that
"if there is no illness, then [the family] doesn't worship."

Another man who said that his clan had had more than a thousand
tablets before 1949 suggested slightly more offerings. They offered food
to the ancestors only at New Year's *(tuannian)*. At other times, they would
set off firecrackers, light incense, and the male descendants would kowtow *(ke tou)*.[36]

> It was expensive to have tablets because they had to get incense every day,
> and when other [clan members] came to worship, [the household with the
> tablets] had to feed them [the guests]. So poor people couldn't afford to
> keep them *(lai bu qi)*.

He said that around 1938, when he was just over 10 years old, the tablets
were moved from the youngest branch of the clan *(yao fang)* to his grandfather's house because the youngest branch had gotten poorer and had
had to sell land. The family moved the tablets themselves, without the
assistance of Daoist priests *(daoshi)* or wizards *(wushi* or *duangong)*, indicating no belief that souls reside in the tablets.

A third man whose very poor family nevertheless had four generations of tablets—which a local scholar said was a lot—told me that they
had burned incense, spirit money *(zhi)*, and candles on the first and the
fifteenth of each lunar month. He said those in the clan with money also
worshipped with food *(cai)* at New Year's, implying that his household
had not done so. When asked, he explicitly said that the ancestors' spirits were not in the tablets, that "it's only a written name" *(zhi xie ge
mingzi)*. Moreover, upon further queries, he scoffed at the notion of souls
at all:

> Three souls *(hun)*, seven souls *(po)*—it's wizards and Daoist priests who
> say that to get money out of people *(weile pian qian)*. I don't believe there
> are any spirits. When you're dead, you're dead.

These practices raise another issue. For those who believe in them,
where are the souls of the dead? People in Wucun did not believe that
ancestral tablets contain the souls of the dead. At New Year's, souls had
to travel to their descendants' homes to receive their offerings, indicating that they do not reside in the tablet. I received physical evidence that

people did not believe ancestral tablets contain souls when one man, who
had saved his parents' ancestral tablet from destruction during the Cultural Revolution, brought out the tablet and handed it to me. There were
several people present at the time, but I was the only one who was shocked
by how nonchalantly he handled the tablet and gave it to an outsider.
Elsewhere, tablets are handled only by particular people under special
ritual conditions. One well-educated man explained to me why the soul
(guihun) is not in the ancestral tablet:

> The Daoist priest or the wizard takes it outside the home [in a rite known
> as "leading the way" kailu]; that is why people hire them in the first place.
> The purpose of a funeral is for the Daoist priest to persuade the soul to
> leave (hao zou). Daoist priests are polite (shuo hao). If they cannot get the
> soul to leave, then a wizard is brought in who is fierce and gets rid of it once
> and for all.

Even the ritual specialists I asked—three wizards and one Daoist priest—
agreed that the souls of the dead are not in ancestral tablets.

Tablets were viewed locally simply as memorials made by people with
enough money to do so. Even those who had them did not bother to
provide tablets for all their deceased family members. Tablets were expected to have both husband and wife on them, so men with no wife or
men with more than one wife—meaning a widower who remarried—
could not have tablets. The names of descendants were written on the
back of ancestral tablets too. It was not necessary to have a Daoist priest
write the tablet, as elsewhere. People often wrote the tablets themselves,
if they were literate, or got a literate neighbor or relative to do so. In
fact, there was a local preference to have the tablet written by an elderly literate man who had only married once and had living sons and
grandsons.

When I asked a Daoist priest where souls are, he told me that for the
first three years after death there are three souls: one in the afterworld
(yinjian), one "in the room" (wuli), and one in the grave (fendi). At the
end of three years, a circular grave must be built so the spirit can leave;
otherwise, the soul is imprisoned at the grave. This apparently standard
Han response, however, did not mean what it would have meant elsewhere. When I asked whether people believed souls of the dead resided
in graves, the Daoist priest and wizard told me that people are not afraid
of ghosts there.[37] These ritual specialists said that placement of a grave
close to descendants' houses is better because it is easier for descendants

to take care of it. Moreover, a local scholar explained to me that a soul "in the room" does not mean the soul is in the ancestral tablet, it means the soul is wandering. This explanation seems to correspond to the Daoist priest's explanation that ancestral tablets are simply memorials to the deceased. According to the Daoist priest, neither Daoism nor Buddhism places the spirit in the tablet. He pointed out that the recent practice of using photographs of the deceased as memorials has the same meaning as the practice of making ancestral tablets, although he felt that photographs were better, since people could actually see the deceased.

Some sense of responsibility for the care of the dead was indicated by offerings at lunar New Year's, at an annual grave-lighting ritual (see figure 21), and at *lanshe* rites (graveside rites performed annually for three years after a person's death).[38] (Grave-lighting and lanshe rites are generally *not* part of Han folk religion.) However, explanations of lanshe rites also show that there is no reciprocal relationship between ancestors and descendants, because the dead are cut off from the living. At lanshe, colorful paper lanterns *(baogai)* are taken and placed on the grave (see figure 22) to protect or shield *(baohu, lanjian)* the soul of the deceased, because people in the afterworld *(yinjian)* have arrows shot at them by ghosts *(gui)*. The lanterns give them somewhere to hide *(duoguo)*. However, I was told that living people do *not* bring lanterns because they want to help their relatives—that would do no good in any case because "relatives do not recognize each other after death; they are not part of the clan" *(bushi yi jiazu)*. Rather, living people bring lanterns to make sure that their descendants will help them when they are dead. One man explained, "the living are not compelled to honor the wishes of the dead" *(shengren bumian siren yi)*. Thus, lanshe rites are similar to the carving of descendants names' into tombstones or writing descendants names' on the back of ancestral tablets: they represent a way to encourage the living to care for their ancestors. By practicing lanshe rites, people encourage their children to do so because people practice the customs they see, whether or not they believe or understand them. The man who scoffed at the existence of spirits reported that he still hired a Daoist priest when his father died and still observed lanshe. He did not know any explanation of why people took lanterns as part of lanshe; it was just customary.

The ways in which people attempt to cajole their descendants into caring for them after death suggests that ancestors are dependent on their

Figure 21. Lighting candles at a grave next to a house in Enshi, 1996.

descendants without any reciprocal recourse if their descendants are re-
miss. The need to cajole runs counter to Confucian moral principles that
children are obligated to their parents, even after death. This dependency of the ancestors raises questions about the strength of parental authority in Enshi.

Figure 22. Paper lanterns on a grave in Enshi, 1996.

Ghost Beliefs   People do believe in ghosts in Enshi, and although some
of their beliefs fall within the wide range of ghost beliefs found among
Han elsewhere, other beliefs take them well outside the Han range. A
wizard told me that "ghosts are people who have died but they're not
people without tablets. They're people whose spiritual energy *(qi)* was
not good when they were living. They don't have enough positive spiritual energy" *(yangqi buzou)*. The Daoist priest and wizard who were interviewed together said that people who die without descendants do not
become hungry ghosts.[39] They assured me that the purpose of burning
incense and making other offerings is to be filial *(xiao)*—that is, to show
proper respect—not to take care of the ancestors. These remarks reveal
a concept of filiality greatly at odds with Confucian principles. Gates
(1996a:91) argues that "'filiality' *means* supporting one's parents mate-
rially, as well as submitting to their wishes" (emphasis in original). In
Enshi, "filiality" seems to mean a more distant kind of respect.

I found people in Wucun to be very nonchalant about a number of
things relating to ghosts. People talked easily about ghosts and referred
to them directly as "ghosts" *(gui)*. At one home I visited, an old grave-
stone was used as a stone in the path to the house. Even Daoist priests
were looked down on, not for handling the dead (as elsewhere, see, e.g.,

Watson 1988:115, 117–18) but for cheating people. The annual grave-lighting ritual occurred at dusk, a time when many Han elsewhere worry about ghosts, particularly near graves.[40] Finally, a local scholar told me about an amusement park called Ghost City *(guicheng)* that was built in 1994 or 1995 outside Enshi City. When it first opened, it was so popular that a special bus shuttled between the park and Enshi City, meaning that people got on a bus which said its destination was "Ghost Park" *(guishen daguan)*. This amusement park was undoubtedly capitalizing on the popularity of Fengdu, also called Ghost City, a tourist stop on the Yangzi River before the Three Gorges Dam project. (Interestingly, Fengdu is in a former Ba area of eastern Sichuan, and the Ba are officially designated as ancestral to the Tujia.) Enshi, then, is not alone in such nonchalant attitudes toward ghosts—they are shared by some Han elsewhere—nevertheless, this attitude runs strongly counter to the beliefs of many Han.

Mortuary Practices   The most visible practice showing how Enshi customs differ from those of Han elsewhere was still common in Wucun in 1996—the placement of graves near the houses of the living (see figure 21). A Tujia man in another part of Enshi prefecture put it most bluntly when he said that "the dead and the living should live together." He pointed out that his own descendants still lived near his family's old house site (the house had been destroyed) so that they were near their ancestors. I attended a funeral in Wucun in which the deceased was buried in agricultural land within the village, perhaps 30 yards (or meters) from two houses. Obviously, such placement of graves violates the standard Han mortuary procedure of expelling the corpse from the community. From a "standard" Han perspective, it places ghosts within the community. Thus, graves conveniently accessible to the deceased's home in nearby agricultural land, or worse, adjacent to the deceased's or a neighbor's house, as in Enshi, would be considered dangerous by many Han in other parts of China.

Property Inheritance and Parental Authority   Although people frequently told me in Wucun that brothers inherited property equally, it rapidly became clear that they were speaking of the ideal case, presumably based on knowledge of Confucian principles. People I interviewed reported that, in their families, most if not all of whatever property and ancestral tablets existed was given to the youngest brother *(lao yao)*. This practice violates Han beliefs derived from Confucian principles in two ways: brothers are supposed to share equally, and younger brothers are supposed to defer to older brothers.

Moreover, people reported family division not only as commonly occurring before the deaths of the senior male but as *supposed* to occur then, suggesting that parental authority was not strong enough to hold the family together. One man, who had been well educated in the late-imperial Han fashion which emphasized Confucian teachings, nevertheless explained:

> Once [a man's] first child is born he must quickly establish his own home *(fen jia)* [because] the responsibility of the senior generation ends [with the birth of that child]. Because sons split off at different times, parents must plan ahead and decide what to give whom. The youngest gets a little more than the oldest [because] he doesn't really split off. He's young, so that by the time he marries, his parents are not necessarily alive.

If the youngest son's parents are still alive when he takes a wife, he still does not necessarily establish his own house. "If the relations between daughter-in-law and mother-in-law are not good, then [the youngest son would] split [off from his parents' household]; if they are good, then [the youngest son would] not split [off]."

Another man told me that "if everyone gets along then the family would wait until all the sons were married before dividing *(fen jia)*. Otherwise, each son would split off *(fen chu qu)* as he married." Only one man I interviewed reported five brothers all waiting until after the youngest brother (himself) married before dividing. "There were over 30 people who ate together but in the drought there wasn't enough to eat, so we split up. There was no property to split." That there was only one such case suggests that parent-son relations were often tense. It is ironic that in an area known for its clannishness and clan feuds (e.g., Shen 1982), families were so easily divided.

The unequal distribution of property among brothers in Wucun is not really favoritism of the youngest. Rather, it is a by-product of an even more fundamental break with Confucian principles: parental authority over sons was relatively weak in Wucun compared to most if not all Han parts of China. In Wucun, establishing separate households *(fen jia)* did not mean dividing property among brothers: it meant leaving the parental home and parental authority. Poor men often left their parents' homes as soon as they married; only wealthier people waited until after the first child—boy or girl—was born. One local scholar told me that parents decide what share of the property a man takes with him when he splits off, so they usually give the youngest son more because he takes care of them. The fact that the youngest son winds up with more or even most of the family property is due to the fact that parents give little property to the older sons as each splits off. Parents keep their property for themselves, and the youngest son winds up with it by default.

Although institutional favoritism of the oldest son *(lao da)* was common throughout Han society, it was not in Enshi. The first reports I received of youngest taking all surprised me, but I believed them because others present at the interviews—my Tujia research assistant, a villager appointed to help me contact local families, and family members and sometimes even neighbors of the person being interviewed—did not correct these reports, as they often did other details. I concluded that this practice was commonplace through the accumulation of such reports and through people's ability to articulate a rationale for the custom. For example, one man, whose family was rather well-to-do, reported that his oldest brother split off *before* marrying. When he went off to work, he found a wife himself, with no help from his parents. The other older brother never married. Another man, who was an oldest son himself, reported that he and his wife established their own home without taking any property from his parents. He said that his wife was not on good relations with his parents so they wanted to move out. He claimed that they did not want any property. He pointed out that although his younger brother had considerably more education than his two-and-a-half years—enough for his brother to later become a village-level official—he had a profession (carpentry) which his younger brother did not. He and his wife moved into the Enshi City where he could do carpentry work. Still another man, who was the sixth of seven brothers, split off after his marriage. Initially, he said that there was no property to split because there were too many brothers, so he got a wok as his patrimony. However, it turned out that there was a little bit of land (1–2 *mu,* which is less than 1/75 of a hectare or a third of an acre) and he got none. He said that he did not want it *(meiyao);* he wanted his parents to have it. He admitted, however, that in the end, his younger brother got all the land.

Many people justified the youngest son taking all the property by explaining that he takes care of his parents. In other words, the youngest son feeds his parents in their old age and buries them. This explanation suggests that, for the older sons, filial obligations ended while their parents were still alive. Indeed, the comment that the senior generation's obligation to their children ends with the birth of a grandchild corroborates such an end to filial obligations. The man who made that comment phrased it politely in terms of the end of the senior generation's obligation, but other people's reports about leaving the care of their parents to the youngest son who did not split off strongly suggest that the filial obligation was also thought to end with division. That filial obligation could end at all, let alone during the parents' lifetime, runs strongly counter to beliefs that are central to Confucian principles and thus to Han culture in all its variants as well as to ideological narratives about Han unfolding as a civilization. Moreover, both the idea that filial obligation could end and the rationale that the youngest son got most of the property as a reward for caring for his parents show that local people had a different underlying concept of filiality than Han elsewhere. As stated so bluntly by the Daoist priest who spoke with me, filiality did not include material care of ancestors. Apparently it did not include material care of parents either.

In many practices and beliefs relating to parental authority—such as ancestor worship, ghost beliefs, mortuary practices, and inheritance of property—locals in Enshi differed significantly from Confucian-derived elements of Han culture, elements shared widely across Han regional cultural variation. Thus, in spite of locals' sense of themselves as Han and claims of Han patrilineal ancestry, government outsiders coming in from Han areas to conduct the ethnic identification probably felt strongly that people with such beliefs and practices were not Han.

CULTURE AS OUTSIDER CLASSIFICATION, SOCIAL EXPERIENCE AS LOCAL CLASSIFICATION

Those responsible for identifying ethnic groups in Enshi came in the 1950s and examined locals in terms of culture, not patrilineal ancestry. Whatever else locals in Enshi shared with Han in other parts of China—including language, marriage practices, and footbinding—they were missing practices and beliefs still considered, at that time, fundamental to Han culture and to Confucian-derived notions of what it means to be civilized. I argue these differences made Han outsiders classify the locals as non-Han.

They initially classified the locals as Miao, probably due to the presence of Miao in this region. One anthropologist at the Central University of Nationalities (Zhongyang Minzu Daxue) in Beijing told me in 1995 that the Tujia are just sinicized Miao who do not want to admit their

Miao ancestry. This is really a long-route view. It assumes that Tujia are fundamentally non-Han because of their ancestry but allows that they have begun to become "civilized" by adopting large parts of Han culture. Because locals in Enshi adopted Confucian-derived practices and beliefs related to parental authority either imperfectly or not at all, and because these practices and beliefs served as markers for officials responsible for ethnic identification, these primarily Han outsiders judged Enshi locals as not culturally Han enough to be assigned Han identity. A similar attitude prevailed in southwestern Taiwan toward descendants of plains Aborigines through 1930 or so. Because they did not bind women's feet, they were not considered culturally Han enough to be Hoklo. This outsider, long-route attitude ignores the intermarriage that did occur between Han immigrants and non-Han in both Taiwan and Enshi. By contrast, locals in Enshi saw their identity in short-route terms: they were Han because their patrilineal ancestors were Han, and this ancestry won them social treatment as Han, at least at the local level.

If the ethnic identification project had not begun until after the Cultural Revolution—when no one in the PRC had ancestral tablets and many aspects of standard late-imperial mortuary practices had been eradicated among Han throughout China—Tujia in Enshi might have managed to negotiate a Han status. If locals in Enshi had been accepted as Han, the remaining differences in cultural practices and beliefs might have shifted toward contemporary Han cultural models. Just such a process occurred in Taiwan for long-route Han, who quickly completed their adoption of Hoklo (or local Han) culture after they were finally accepted as Han. Identification of which ethnic groups existed in China preceded the Cultural Revolution, however, and so it was decided that Enshi locals were not Han. They did manage to negotiate a "sinicized" non-Han status as Tujia, instead of Miao, but they could not shake the non-Han designation.

In contrast, I suggest that many people classified as Tujia in Enshi insist that they and their ancestors are "really" Han because of their social experience. Until the 1950s ethnic identification project, they were considered and treated as Han. Before 1949, each succeeding wave of immigrants (outsiders) used culture to evaluate people in Enshi, found no important differences among them, and thus lumped all those already there as "locals." Perhaps because they were more like the Han than the nearby Miao, and because many had Han patrilineal ancestors, those considered locals and those considered outsiders before 1949 all viewed themselves as Han. This self-identification largely continued in the Enshi area through the 1980s, in spite of the official identification of Tujia as non-Han, because individuals were not classified until the 1980s.

To the extent that officials themselves thought about the origins of their cultural basis of classification, they probably did so in anthropological, Stalinist, or Confucian terms, because all these perspectives did influence the PRC ethnic identification project. Western anthropology influenced some scholars in charge of the national identification project at the highest levels (Fei 1981, Chen Yongling 1998 [1989]), Guldin 1994). Stalin's four criteria for ethnic identification, which include culture, were adopted by the PRC. Confucian culturalism views Han identity as based on cultural practices: people are Han if they act Han. Officials clearly privileged these educated perspectives over the self-identification reports of uneducated locals that claimed Han identity in terms of patrilineal ancestry.

A more fundamental origin may underlie the culture-based classification schemes of anthropology, Stalin's criteria, and Confucian culturalism. The schemes of all three of these perspectives represent outsider methods of classification. I propose that outsiders classify others based on culture while locals classify themselves based on social experience (often stated in terms of ancestry).[41] Outsiders, after all, have little or no local social experience on which to draw. While others' social experience is difficult to decipher on the basis of differing and often conflicting reports, cultural practices are much easier to understand because they are more consistently reported and because they can be observed.

Analysis of local officials' classification of individuals in the early 1980s supports my proposal that culture was an external or outsider criterion for classification. There were no consistent cultural differences either between people who had been considered locals and outsiders before 1949 or between people officially classified as Han and Tujia. The relevant Confucian-derived cultural practices and beliefs, on which I argue Tujia identification was originally based, indicated a dichotomy not among Enshi locals but between people in Enshi, on the one hand, and Han elsewhere in China, on the other hand. If local officials had used the Confucian-derived cultural practices and beliefs discussed above to guide their classification of individuals (as they apparently guided identification at the group level), the Enshi population would have been overwhelmingly Tujia, with few if any Han. The government order to classify at least 60 percent of the total population as Han, however, precluded use of such guides. Nevertheless, the assumption linking culture and immigration date allowed local officials to act like locals and clas-

sify the population in terms of surname and timing of immigration—
terms that are locally relevant because they are linked to historical social experience—while at the same time asserting that identity *is* based
on culture, in accordance with the culture-based, outsider classification
schemes of the national identification project. (Where place of origin was
outside Hubei, it disrupted local views—because it referred to nonlocal
classification—yet local officials could not ignore this criterion because
of its use nationally.) In the end, the classification scheme that local officials actually used inverts Confucian culturalism. Rather than assuming
sinicization, it assumes de-sinicization or, as one Wucun person put it, becoming Tujia *(tujiahua)*. The long-route pattern of identity based on cultural transformation—regardless of whether it led to sinicization or de-
sinicization—was assumed to be "authentic" only if it was old "enough."

So how old was old enough? Given the importance of writing to narratives of Han unfolding as a civilization, I think it is no accident that
sufficient time to be authentic was linked to being literally prehistoric—
before there were reliable written records, before 1735 when the area
came under a Han-style bureaucratic system. Such a link was also made
in Taiwan. The authenticity of the short route has not been questioned in
Taiwan, and it is attributed to a time when there are few records on matters of cultural practices written in Chinese. Although the Dutch records
are known to historians in Taiwan, most Taiwanese are unfamiliar with
them. In Enshi, given the existence of many oral and written family histories telling about the arrival of Han patrilineal ancestors as far back as
the early Ming, officials had to set a date as an arbitrary cutoff for long
"enough." The arbitrariness of this temporal marker as the local border
between Han and non-Han should impress upon us the arbitrariness of
all such borders to Han with regard to cultural transformation. However,
this date is significant because it constitutes a change in political regimes,
which resulted in a change in social experience for people in Enshi.

Social experience is crucial to identity. In the PRC, people's officially
assigned ethnic classification determines many aspects of their current
and changing social experience. People in Enshi officially classified as
Tujia in the 1990s include both pre-1949 locals and pre-1949 outsiders,
as do those classified as Han. In the 1980s and 1990s, people's experience of differences between Han and Tujia status was still fairly limited
in Enshi, but as that experience accumulates, Tujia self-identification will
almost certainly develop. Thus, it may *appear* that state, or more generally outsider, classification based on culture overrides local social experience. As one anthropologist at the Central University for National-

ities put it in 1996, "What happens [when official ethnologists make their category decisions] is really this: we tell them what they are, and after a while they get used to it" (Hill Gates, personal communication 2000). However, I suggest that what happens is really this: when powerful outsiders tell locals what they are, after a while the new classification changes local social experience and thus actually changes locals' sense of identity, or ethnicity. (I take up this point again in chapter 6.)

IMPLICATIONS FOR THE "TAIWAN PROBLEM"

What does identity change and state classification in Hubei tell us about the new narratives of Taiwan's unfolding as a non-Chinese domain? If we look no closer to the present than 1949, identity change in Hubei undermines the new Taiwan narratives. It shows that intermarriage with Han immigrants led to Han identity regardless of cultural practices, in Hubei as well as Taiwan. Circumstantial evidence—for example, the ethnic term "Han" can also mean "male" or "husband"—in combination with "regional" Han cultural variation (discussed in chapters 1 and 4) suggests that such short-route changes must have occurred widely throughout China. If, as we consider Taiwan's new narratives, we limit ourselves to viewing identity change in imperial and republican China, then we might well dismiss those narratives as unfounded. From this limited perspective, Taiwanese appear as much Han as locals in Enshi during the 1930s and 1940s.

If we examine China's more recent past, however, we get a different view, for in the 1950s officials decided that locals in Enshi are *not* Han after all. This reclassification of short-route Han (locals) as non-Han appears to have used Confucian-derived, late-imperial standard practices as markers of Han identity. Ironically, if those same standards were applied today, many people classified as Han in the PRC would have to be reclassified as non-Han while most people in Taiwan would be classified as Han. Thus, Taiwan's self-representation as both Han and non-Chinese may not be as far-fetched as it at first appears.

If we continue consideration of official actions in terms of Confucian-derived, late-imperial standards, the PRC fares even worse, for it does not use those standards consistently. Although Confucian culturalism emphasizing the importance of practices apparently guided identification of Tujia as a non-Han ethnic group, this principle did not guide the classification of individuals. After all, people classified as Tujia *and* people classified as Han both buried their dead near the living, failed to provide

ancestral tablets for all their dead, left most if not all family property to
the youngest son, and viewed filial obligations as ending. Instead, PRC
officials only accepted identity change as legitimate if it was linked to
antiquity, violating Confucian culturalism in favor of adopting a common ideological strategy of modern nationalism.

What happened in Hubei provides some insight into the PRC reaction to Taiwan's new narratives. The PRC does not explicitly deny that
de-sinicization is possible. Rather, it reinterprets Taiwan's short-route
claim based on descent as a long-route claim based on culture. It then
denies both that cultural change has gone far enough to warrant a change
to non-Han identity and that the cultural changes that have occurred are
old enough to be legitimate. Insofar as Taiwan itself insists on a non-
Han, plains Aborigine identity for Toushe, Jibeishua, and Longtian, it
agrees with the PRC position denying the legitimacy of recent changes.
If Taiwan would embrace Toushe, Jibeishua, and Longtian as Han *on the
basis of their relatively recent cultural changes,* it could further differentiate itself from China and gain the advantage of consistency in the rhetorical debate. Such a move would prove very difficult to orchestrate, however, because it is not clear whether Toushe, Jibeishua, and Longtian
would want Han status, now that they have themselves claimed Aborigine identity. Furthermore, such a move would certainly not go un-
challenged by the PRC. China cannot afford to allow Taiwan to "secede"
as non-Han, because then how could the PRC justify preventing other
non-Han groups from separating? But what if Taiwan secedes as more
Han than China, according to late-imperial standards? It would still provoke nationalistic fervor in the PRC, but it would not provide a prece-
dent for ethnic separatists within the PRC.

The case studies in the preceding chapters, of identity changes back
and forth across the border to Han and across the centuries in Taiwan
and Hubei, consistently show how culture, power, and migration each
impact identity differently. Ideologies, in the form of narratives of unfolding, overwhelmingly talk about identity in terms of culture, but
people's social experience—derived from their position with regard to
political and economic power—as well as demographic conditions affecting social experience, such as migration, constitute people's sense of
identity, or who they are and how they fit in the world. Why do culture,
social power, and demographic conditions have such different influences?
And how can these theoretical insights guide us through the current political tensions surrounding Taiwan's future? I take up these questions in
chapter 6.

Theory and the Politics of Reunification

Understanding Past Choices and Future Options

The "Taiwan problem"—the question of whether Taiwan should be a part of the Chinese nation or its own independent nation—is a political issue. Moreover, it is fundamentally an issue of identity. These statements are not contradictory, for, as we have seen, identity is political. A specific identity is formed by individuals who share common social experiences because they are classified as members of a single group. Social experience includes political and economic experience. That is, people's social experience derives from their position with regard to political and economic power. Social experience is also influenced by demographic conditions such as migration. However, because identity is ideologically constructed—by political leaders and governments—in terms of culture and/or ancestry, the "Taiwan problem" has unfortunately been debated primarily in these terms, rather than in terms of the sociopolitical basis of actual identities. To understand identity in Taiwan and China, we must analyze the ideological terms of debate as well as actual experiences, for both influence the choices and actions of people and governments. This concluding chapter first examines these influences at a theoretical level and then uses theory to discuss the real-world political implications of the new Taiwanese identity for Taiwan's future relations with the PRC.

Culture, social power, and demographic conditions like migration impact changing identities differently. We must turn to theory to understand why they do so. Theory provides a paradigm for understanding phenomena in the world—a framework guiding what questions we ask and how we seek answers; it explains why and how those answers fit together. My theoretical framework considers culture, social power, and demographic conditions to each constitute a distinct system with its own dynamic for perpetuation and change—that is, for reproducing the system. Human cognition mediates each system and influences the choices of individuals; varying interactions and degrees of influence are possible. As we have seen, political interventions, a form of social power; migration, a demographic condition; and intermarriage, which I suggest is an interaction of social power and culture, have been the primary forces influencing identity changes. In these cases, social power in particular, but also demographic conditions, appears to have greater degrees of influence than culture, which operates primarily in interaction with social power. Debate over such interactions and degrees of influence are at the center of the highly polemical debate between science and postmodernism. To truly understand identity—both as claimed and as actually constructed—we need to examine these influences and interactions. That examination will take us through the fray of current intellectual debate.

Theoretical insights can guide us through "real-world" identity politics. They lead us to distinguish the implications of ideological claims from the implications of people's actual identities, because both actual identities and ideological claims influence the actions of people in Taiwan and China, but in different ways. Theoretical insights suggest that the closer ideologies are to actual identities, the more effective they are in motivating people. Failure to understand this contrast—that is, failure to understand in theoretical terms the actual basis of identity formation as opposed to ideological rhetoric about identity formation—has brought us to the point where the issue of Taiwan's political future impinges on world peace. Such failure has exacerbated identity-based political conflict there—and elsewhere in the world as well—in large part due to unrealistic predictions and policies that fuel tensions rather than damping them.

THEORETICAL BASIS FOR ANALYSIS

When an established theory cannot answer questions raised or when it can no longer explain why particular answers obtain, then researchers—working between empirical cases and theoretical proposals—must develop a new theory, in a process Thomas Kuhn (1962) called a paradigm shift. My theoretical approach synthesizes several perspectives, whose proponents are increasingly antagonistic (e.g., Nader 1988; Shore 1988;

Borofsky 1994a, 1997a, 1997b; Brown 1995, 1997, n.d.). Because no one of these theoretical perspectives suffices to explain the cases of identity change discussed in this book, I propose a new synthesis that distinguishes analytically between the influences of cultural meaning, social power, demographic conditions, and human cognitive structures upon human choices. Of course these influences interact—in narratives of unfolding, intermarriage, and migration—but each of these influences operates by a self-directed process—a process that follows its own dynamic and that can, under certain circumstances, initiate change.

In this chapter, I explain this approach and provide examples from the case studies in earlier chapters which illustrate its explanatory power. I begin with culture, since the ideology of identity uses culture to justify its political claims. After formulating a concept of culture synthesized from several anthropological perspectives, I distinguish culture from social power and discuss their differing but interacting impacts on human beings. Demographic conditions, which I take up next, ultimately involve issues of mortality and fertility, or survival and descent, that impact all living creatures. Yet, finally, humans are distinguished from other living creatures by the cognitive structure of our brain. That cognitive structure mediates the influences and interactions of culture, social power, and demographic conditions through the (not necessarily rational) choices people make and act on. After analytically distinguishing each of these influences, I discuss why this theoretical approach yields a powerful understanding of identity formation, identity changes, cultural change, and ideological rhetoric.

What Is Culture?

A recent exchange in the journal *Modern China* highlights both current interest in and misunderstandings of culture. Historian Philip C. Huang (2000:28) argues that people who are members of both Western and Chinese culture—"biculturals"—have introduced Western practices and ideas into China without "aggression or domination and victimization or subjugation." (In many ways, Huang's biculturals are like the "mixed" peoples I have discussed.) Huang essentially views culture as the lived experiences of people—"the ideas, customs, skills, arts and so on of a given people at a given time" (Huang 2000:4). Historian Prasenjit Duara (2000) disagrees with Huang. He views culture as *interpretations* of lived experience, interpretations strongly influenced by nationalistic ideology. Neither of these positions captures a full anthropological understanding

of culture. Instead, E. B. Tylor's seminal 1871 definition of culture underlies their understanding of culture, as it does the view of many scholars outside of anthropology:

> Culture . . . is that complex whole which includes knowledge, belief, art,
> law, morals, custom, and any other capabilities and habits acquired by man
> as a member of society. (Tylor 1871:1)

This definition is behaviorally based. That is, in addition to beliefs, Tylor
viewed the behaviors—such as the practice of customs and institutions—
as culture. This definition underlies what is commonly meant by "a culture." In other words, when people refer to Chinese culture they generally mean the collection of beliefs, customary practices and social
institutions of Chinese people. This definition also underlies both Huang's
and Duara's views of culture, for all of these—beliefs, customs, and
institutions—are part of people's lived experience.

Contemporary anthropologists, however, define culture as ideational
(cf. Durham 1991:3–8).[1] That is, anthropologists understand culture not
as the customs of a group but as the shared ideas which motivate those
customs. Because they motivate actions, cultural ideas are meaningful.
Throughout most of the late twentieth century, there was widespread
agreement among sociocultural anthropologists that culture was ideational
and meaning-laden. In the 1990s, however, there were challenges to this
consensus.

According to Nicholas B. Dirks, Geoff Eley, and Sherry B. Ortner
(1994:3),

> The notion of culture has recently been undergoing some of the most rad-
> ical rethinking since the early 1960s. Within anthropology, where culture
> was in effect the key symbol of the field, the concept has come under chal-
> lenge precisely because of new understandings regarding power and his-
> tory. . . . [O]ne of the core dimensions of the concept of culture [that Dirks,
> Eley, and Ortner argue is being revised] has been the notion that culture is
> "shared" by *all* members of a given society. (Emphasis added)

Although radical reconsiderations of culture have been promoted from
several perspectives—not simply that of Dirks, Eley, and Ortner, which
focuses on social power—they have not taken over the discipline. Moreover, this portrayal of the older anthropological consensus on culture is
a caricature, a straw man more easily attacked than the actual concept
of culture which still has widespread acceptance. The anthropological
consensus does not claim that any specific cultural idea is shared by every
single member of a society. One of the most basic, though largely un-

stated, things that anthropologists learn from the "worm's eye view" that is fieldwork (to use Stevan Harrell's phrase) is the rich variation that exists in cultural meanings and practices. An idea must be widely shared across a society in order to be considered cultural, but it does not have to be shared by 100 percent of the population.

Analyses of public symbols and meanings that dominate anthropological journals today show that many anthropologists still accept the position most famously articulated by Clifford Geertz (1973) that culture is shared, abstract, meaning-laden, and public. The primary criticism which Dirks, Eley, and Ortner have of Geertz—that "he never confronted the issue of power" (1994:22)—is valid if our goal is to understand human actions and social change, and thus it is important to my theoretical synthesis, but it is not particularly helpful to an understanding of culture because they, like Duara, conflate ideology and culture. Their suggestion that "cultural (read racial, gender, ethnic, religious) categories provide both a source of oppression and a means for empowering groups and communities to contest that oppression" (Dirks, Eley, and Ortner 1994:24) is an excellent description of ideologies. Narratives of unfolding, for example, constitute such ideologies in that they are consciously falsified stories of the past for present political purposes (Harrell 1996b:5n). However, Dirks, Eley, and Ortner (1994:25) go much further to say, "all culture is political." Ideologies are part of culture, but there is more to an anthropological concept of culture as shared, meaningful ideas than ideology.

Consideration of the implications of another aspect of the anthropological concept of culture—that culture is public (external to individuals) because meaning is public (Geertz 1973:12)—is much more useful in refining our understanding of culture. For example, semioticians (e.g., Daniel 1984) demonstrate that the public character of culture leads to an implication of its autonomy or self-directed dynamic. That is, there are ways in which cultural signs and symbols are independent of the people who communicate them. Cognitive anthropologists (e.g., Strauss 1992a, Sperber 1996) also accept culture as public, because it is shared, but they argue, in opposition to Geertz and others, that the implication of this public character of culture is that meaning is mental—internal to individuals and thus subjective (or private). For them, culture is both public and mental. While these perspectives may seem to diverge, I draw on the work of philosopher Karl Popper (1982) to synthesize the older Geertzian consensus on culture with semiotic and cognitive insights.

I argue that there are two different types of cultural meaning: first, logical or semiotic meaning, which is abstract, public, and autonomous; and second, subjective or emotional meaning, which is mental. For example, patrilineal inheritance has both logical and subjective meanings. The semiotic meaning of this concept—that heritable things are transmitted strictly patrilineally—extends from property to surnames to ethnic identity without any conscious intervention necessary. People who hold this idea readily extend it from one heritable thing to another (cf. Strauss and Quinn 1994:291). Thus, the application of the concept of patrilineal inheritance to a relatively recent concept like ethnic identity is "discovered" after the fact rather than deliberately engineered. By contrast, the subjective meaning of the concept—that patrilineal inheritance is a moral good—is both conscious and dependent on experience. Many people in societies which practice patrilineal inheritance do not believe it is moral or good. Thus, feminist social criticism, for example, is possible. Because subjective meaning is idiosyncratically based on personal experience, similar versions of a subjective meaning must be shared for that meaning to be considered cultural (cf. Sperber 1996:82, D'Andrade 1992b:230).

Culture, then, is made up of shared, meaning-laden ideas, some of which are semiotic and some of which are subjective. What percentage of a population must share an idea in order for members of that population and outsiders to consider them part of "the culture" of that population is still not understood (cf. Strauss 1992a, Strauss and Quinn 1994, Sperber 1996, Brown 1997, n.d.).[2] I suggest there is a human cognitive threshold such that, once an idea achieves some critical-mass distribution, people perceive it as part of their "culture." One example of such a threshold, mentioned in chapter 1, pertains to identity. There was a turning point when villages in southwestern Taiwan were no longer perceived as Aborigine villages with Han men living in them and instead became seen as Han villages. At that point, people perceived Han identity as belonging to the majority of the group of villagers and thus as representative of the group or village as a whole. Because the term "a culture" colloquially refers to so many different things—a specific society, customs, beliefs, a disenfranchised minority group within a society—I prefer the term "cultural model" to refer to all the ideas distributed widely enough in a specific population to cross this threshold. (Thus, a cultural model does not include all the ideas extant in a population.)

The ideas in a cultural model interact with each other and also change over time. Recall the example of a uxorilocal minor marriage from Toushe (in chapter 3). There are several reasons to believe that uxorilocal marriages (marriages with postmarital residence at the wife's family's home) were culturally approved—for example, their practice among Taiwan plains Aborigines for at least two centuries and their high frequency in Toushe before 1930. Although minor marriage (in which a girl was adopted and raised to become the wife of one of the adopting family's sons) was culturally approved among Hoklo in northern Taiwan (e.g., Wolf 1995), its rare frequency in Toushe, and indeed in southern Taiwan generally, suggests it was either relatively new or not well accepted or both. The reported acceptance and encouragement of a uxorilocal version of minor marriage in Toushe—where a boy was adopted and raised to marry one of the adoptive family's daughters—shows that these ideas could interact in complex ways. Here, the concept of uxorilocal marriage took precedence over and thereby significantly revised the concept of minor marriage as it was introduced.

Cultural models shape people's worldviews. Meaning-laden ideas affect the perception and understanding, or interpretation, that individuals and groups have of the world around them. The meaning-laden ideas already in people's minds affect the meanings ascribed to subsequent events they experience and ideas they encounter. For example, we saw in chapter 5 that people in Hubei who thought of themselves as Han but sought official ethnic minority status as Tujia on the basis of a maternal relative viewed themselves as "really" Han. In this case, the matrilateral claim to official Tujia identity was subordinated to the idea that kinship and ethnic identity are "really" passed patrilineally.

Additionally, the existing cultural model impacts which new ideas or practices individuals consider acceptable and pass on to others (cf. Brown 1995:28, 35–36). For example, contrast the location of grave sites in Taiwan and Enshi. In Taiwan, where many people believe a spirit of the deceased resides at the grave and can potentially harm the living, graves are well outside of the villages, either in a communal graveyard or outlying agricultural lands. In Enshi, however, where they are not considered dangerous, graves are conveniently accessible to the deceased's home in nearby agricultural land, sometimes even adjacent to the deceased's or a neighbor's house. Consider someone challenging the established custom. In Enshi, it is merely convenient to tend a grave near one's home; there is nothing wrong with placing a grave elsewhere. Such a modification of the local cultural model would be acceptable. In Taiwan, however, placing a grave near houses would be viewed as dangerous and would likely provoke strong objections from neighbors. In this case, the introduction of a new idea to place graves more conveniently within the village would not be accepted, and would probably be actively suppressed, because it contradicts the already existing cultural model.

This anthropological concept of culture explains how shared meaning-laden ideas interact and shape people's worldviews. To understand how some cultural ideas become ideologies, we must first distinguish between culture and social power.

Social Power

What is the difference between society and culture? Huang's (2000:4) definition of culture, like Tylor's (1871), does little to differentiate between culture and society. Some anthropologists suggest there is no difference (e.g., Sperber 1996:9), and yet most anthropologists readily distinguish between British social anthropologists studying social institutions and American cultural anthropologists studying symbols and meanings (cf. Kuper 1999). Some cultural anthropologists have argued, largely based on the work of Michel Foucault, that anthropology must examine "power" (e.g., Dirks, Eley, and Ortner 1994). Duara's (2000) emphasis on ideology and nationalism similarly raises the issue of power.

What is power? And how is it related to society?

> Power in the substantive sense, *"le" pouvoir,* doesn't exist. . . . In reality power means relations, a more-or-less organised, hierarchical, co-ordinated cluster of relations. (Foucault 1980:198, cf. 1980:187–88)

> There is no Power, but power relationships which are being born incessantly, as both effect and condition of other processes. (Foucault 1989:187)

In other words, "power" refers to hierarchical social relations. Moreover, no human society is without hierarchical organization—even supposedly egalitarian hunter-gatherer societies have hierarchies based on age and gender. Thus, "power" and "society" refer to the same thing— hierarchically organized relations between individuals and groups. Since people often think of "social" as simply referring to relationships and "power" as referring to hierarchy, I prefer to combine these terms as "social power" to emphasize that hierarchy is played out socially. Society, or social power, defined as hierarchically organized relations, is different than culture, defined as shared meaning-laden ideas.

I argue (Brown 1995, n.d.) that this difference is important because the dynamics of social power hierarchies are different than the dynamics of cultural models. Social dynamics constitute how an individual person moves about in a specific social system or hierarchy as well as how that system changes. Cultural dynamics, on the other hand, constitute how an idea comes to be widely enough shared to become part of the local cultural model as well as how the introduction of a new idea into the model affects other ideas already present in that model. Part of the reason there is such disagreement over the differences between social and cultural systems is that they interact in myriad ways, both with each other and with cognition.

This interaction, and its importance, is demonstrated by a different sense in which the term "power" is also used—to refer to an ability to direct or manipulate the actions of people. Anthropologists disagree over whether to "locate" power in this sense in individuals or collectivities— that is, whether it is individuals or some collective entity that manipulates people's actions. This disagreement is essentially a debate over agency—the ability to choose and to act—and whether it functions at a collective or individual level. On one side of the disagreement is methodological individualism, which views power as located in individuals and aggregates the actions of individual members of a group to describe collective action (e.g., Elster 1983, Perry 1980, Smith and Winterhalder 1992, Little 1989:245–48). Pitted against this view is collectivism, which views power as located in collective entities—social groups or institutions or semiotic cultural meanings—and describes collective action as beyond the control or the aggregated contributions of individuals (e.g., Comaroff 1985:53; Sahlins 1976a:206, Naquin 1976, 1981, 1985).[3]

Foucault's work, regarded as seminal on the topic of power, does not resolve whether power as an ability to direct actions is derived from the aggregated relations of many individuals or from synergistic relations among collective entities. According to Flynn (1994:34–35), Foucault insists that "'power' does not exist . . . only individual relations of domination and control." Nevertheless, Foucault does not grant agency to individuals in much of his writing—even though he sees individuals as integral to structures, mechanisms, and applications of power (cf. Habermas 1987:274–75; Sangren 1995:9–10, 15–18). Foucault himself (1983: 217) explicitly denied such criticism: "For let us not deceive ourselves; if we speak of the structures or the mechanisms of power, it is only insofar as we suppose that certain persons exercise power over others." However, his published work is replete with individuals without agency and with power operating through collectivities. For example:

> The individual, that is, is not the *vis-à-vis* of power; it is, I believe, one of
> its prime effects. The individual is an effect of power, and at the same time,
> or precisely to the extent to which it is that effect, it is the element of its

articulation. The individual which power has constituted is at the same time its vehicle. (Foucault 1980:98, see also 1980:55, 98, 156)

These power/knowledge relations are to be analyzed, therefore, not on the basis of a subject of knowledge who is or is not free in relation to the power system, but on the contrary, the subject who knows, the objects to be known and the modalities of knowledge must be regarded as so many *effects* of these fundamental implications of power/knowledge and their historical transformations. (Foucault 1979:27, emphasis added)

In other words, power—which is linked to the control of knowledge—is an agent that produces individuals as conscious subjects who "know" only what they are taught. This view does not seem to leave much room for interaction between individual subjects and "power/knowledge." Instead, individuals are acted upon. Nor does it resolve questions about the links between the agency of power, collective entities, and the actions of individuals. Other analyses of power, notably Bourdieu's (e.g., 1977:89, 120; 1990:102), similarly portray humans as automatons; they describe power as acting upon humans—through the ways in which the existing social institutions structure human bodily movements, actions, and thoughts—largely without seeing humans as acting upon those powerful institutions (e.g., Comaroff 1985:5, Strauss 1992a:9, Scheper-Hughes 1994:232).[4]

I resolve these apparently contradictory views of power by synthesizing them with structuralist and cognitive insights (discussed further below), and I suggest that power is located in both individuals *and* collective entities. In this view, collective social action can be described as the aggregate of individual actions. The actions of individuals are affected by social structure, because the actual hierarchical structure of social power relations affects individuals' abilities to act and to move within the system (Brown 1995:31–35, 87; n.d.).[5] Individuals' actions are also affected by their conscious and unconscious choices, and such choices are themselves affected by individuals' *perceptions* about power and social relations. Perceptions—based on idiosyncratic interpretations of the social power hierarchy, personal experiences, and cultural meanings, both semiotic and subjective—may or may not accurately reflect actual social power relations.

Cognitive perception introduces the collective aspect of power through *cultural meanings of social power relations* that guide and constrain individuals' interpretations of actual events and possible future actions (cf. Brown 1995:86–88, n.d.). This is hegemonic ideology at work. Ideologies are constructed by people in power—sometimes by a few individuals, sometimes by a group—to emphasize cultural meanings that support the existing social power hierarchy. For example, narratives of unfolding attempt to make specific cultural ideas selected by people in positions of power especially meaningful to their constituency. If such ideas are already widely shared by this constituency, people more readily embrace these ideological narratives. To the extent that these ideologies become accepted by a populace, the cultural meanings that they tout constitute manipulation of that populace by those in power. However, people may resist ideology where it contradicts their already accepted ideas—unless it offers them a possibility for maneuvering their way up the social power hierarchy.

Narratives of unfolding—especially those for an ethnic group seeking enfranchisement or for an incipient nation-state seeking independence—do offer ways of improving their constituents' standing in the local social power hierarchy. Taiwan's new narratives of unfolding offer the possibility of a Republic of Taiwan. China's narrative of unfolding reinforces already held ideas about foreign imperialism and offers the possibility of acquiring the rich capitalist enclave of Taiwan to add to those of Hong Kong and Macao, which it has already acquired. A populace may have cause to embrace such narrative ideologies even if they are a leap from their previously held ideas. To continue the example of Taiwan, Hong Kong, and Macao, China agreed to a referendum in Hong Kong and Macao to determine whether they would return to the Chinese nation. People in Hong Kong and Macao took such a leap in voting to rejoin China, apparently welcoming the opportunity to be citizens rather than colonial subjects—at least before the massacre at Tiananmen Square on June 4, 1989.

Various kinds of structuralism—including Marxism and Bourdieu's practice theory—posit the existence of an objective, "true" set of social power relations, which are often unconscious to individuals caught in these relations and which can be discovered. This premise is the crux of Foucault's criticism of Marxism (e.g., 1980:84–85) and of Michel de Certeau's (1988 [1984]:59) criticism of Bourdieu. Foucault and de Certeau want to go beyond a structuralist analysis of power—that is, beyond an analysis of power relations in terms of the structure of social hierarchies—to consider how people's subjective experience of these power relations affects their worldviews. Both of these analytic perspectives are important.

The cultural meanings of social power relations do affect people's choices and actions, but so does the actual structure of social power re-

lations, regardless of whether people accurately or consciously understand these relations. Where individuals are located in the existing social power hierarchy—for example, their class or relation to the mode
of production—affects which actions they can carry out and the consequences of those actions. Consequences are influenced, at least in part,
because people perceive the same actions differently depending on who
performs them. Thus, individuals do have agency—we can choose and
we can act. However, that agency—which options we have to choose
from and whether we can successfully carry out a particular action—is
constrained by the actual social power hierarchy in which we live.

For example, consider the village monopoly system instituted by the
Dutch and Aborigine-Han relations, discussed in chapters 2 and 4. A
Han middleman paid a fee for exclusive rights to trade and collect taxes
in a particular village. When this institution began, many Aborigine villages had extensive and close ties with Dutch missionaries, who could
be petitioned to mitigate the more extreme aspects of leaseholders' exploitation, because missionaries frequently disagreed with VOC governing policies and greatly distrusted Han. The monopoly system continued under Zheng and then Qing rule of Taiwan, but under these
regimes there was no mediating group like the missionaries whom Aborigines could use to reduce exploitation. By the early eighteenth century,
abuses of the monopoly system were both rampant and extreme. Some
Aborigine villages sought to reduce the extortion of middlemen by nominating their own people for the position, but nominations had to be
confirmed by Qing officials. Most Qing officials viewed Aborigines as
barbarians but saw identity as patrilineally inherited, so Aborigine villages were more successful in getting the son of a Han father and Aborigine mother—often the daughter of the Aborigine leader—into the role
of middleman.

This example illustrates two important points. First, social power dynamics are historically contingent. In other words, what happens at one
point in time affects the range of possibilities available at another point
in time. The Zheng and Qing regimes continued the monopoly system
set up by the Dutch, albeit with some modification; they did not institute totally new systems of taxation. Second, social power dynamics are
also culturally contingent. In other words, there is some overlap between
the influences of social and cultural systems. The patriarchal values of
those with social power—the Qing officials—constrained the range of
maneuvers Aborigines could make to manipulate the social organization
in their favor. At the same time, intermarriage between Han men and

Aborigine women expanded the range of possible maneuvers by allowing Aborigines to identify their nominees as Han according to the cultural beliefs of the Qing officials themselves.

Even aspiration to specific powerful social roles may depend on cultural beliefs—widely shared public representations—about which categories of people should hold particular roles. The strength of the subjective meaning of this belief to different individuals—is it a historical accident, an honored tradition, a moral law?—affects their aspirations, choices, and actions (cf. Strauss 1992b). Moreover, the holder of an influential role may change the rules about who can hold such roles, thereby changing the dynamics of the local social power hierarchy. A good example is Taiwan's late president, Chiang Ching-kuo. He inherited his position from his father but, before his death in 1988, he instituted reforms leading to democratic elections of officeholders from mayors to the president. He changed the rules about how one achieved office and, thereby, people's expectations about who was likely to hold office and their aspirations to hold office. Chen Shui-bian, elected president in 2000, could not have realistically aspired to that office before the reforms because of his status as a Taiwanese lawyer who defended dissidents.

We can see, then, not only that cultural ideas and social power influence human choices and actions but also that their dynamics often interact. Their interaction, however, plays out in the context of larger demographic conditions which can, under certain circumstances, have a strong influence.

Demographic Conditions

Demographic conditions impact human choice and actions because they are fundamentally matters of survival and descent. For example, migration affects the fertility and mortality of the migrants themselves and also the fertility and mortality of both the population from which the migrants leave and the population(s) with which the migrants interact in their journey and settlement. Certainly the impetus to migrate and the consequences of migration are more complex than just these demographic effects, but the demographic effects should not be discounted. Consider the impact of the influx of some 30,000 mostly male Han immigrants in the course of five years to a population of some 25,000 Han and roughly 60,000 Aborigines, as occurred in mid-seventeenth-century Taiwan (see chapter 4). Even ignoring the concurrent political changes that occurred, we can easily see that the arrival of so many men without wives would affect how marriages were arranged. Moreover, given the sex-ratio imbalance, the fertility rate of the new combined population had to be lower than the fertility rate for the southwestern Taiwan population prior to the influx.

Because fertility and mortality rates are directly linked to natural selection and to concepts of evolutionary viability (the probability of survival), analysis of the influences of demographic conditions takes us into the heart of the polarized debate between science and postmodernism. This major intellectual fissure affects most if not all disciplines in the university today. (See Huang [2000:27] for a discussion of how this debate has affected China Studies.) In anthropology, it has fueled a split over the relevance of natural selection to the actions and cultures of anatomically modern humans.[6] The split has been caricatured by the extreme positions of biological determinism and complete cultural transcendence.[7] However, there is middle ground which recognizes biological influences without yielding to determinism and which recognizes the potential for cultural transcendence without assuming that it always occurs (e.g., Wolf 1995, Brown n.d.). This middle ground is necessarily occupied when the influences of demographic conditions such as migration are considered.

In order to understand the link between fertility and mortality, and thus demographic conditions, on the one hand, and natural selection, on the other, some discussion of the latter is warranted. Natural selection is the environmental culling process that leads to the differential reproduction of individuals with specific genotypes. ("Genotype" refers to the genetic make-up of an individual. Individuals of different phenotypes—external appearances—can have the same genotype, and individuals with the same genotype can have different phenotypes, depending on environmental influences. "Differential reproduction" refers to a combination of fertility and mortality: individuals have different numbers of offspring who themselves survive to have offspring.) For each individual, a child represents a potential genetic descent line, which is at least partially realized when the birth of a grandchild continues the descent line one generation further. In a culling process, a population changes its membership over time through the elimination of some descent lines.[8] In a given generation, natural selection culls out some phenotypes, at the same time allowing a range of varieties to persist. It is better described as the "extinction of the unfit," which leaves behind many variants that merely get by, rather than the "survival of the fittest," an unfortunate phrase, which implies a notion of absolute progress not

part of the neo-Darwinian synthesis used by contemporary evolutionary biologists and geneticists.[9]

Geneticists use technical concepts of "fitness" and "inclusive fitness"
to analyze the effects of natural selection on the behavior of populations.*
In populations where behavioral variants are influenced by an individual's genotype, at least in part, behaviors that have positive inclusive fitness
consequences—that increase inclusive fitness—are expected to spread over
time. In other words, an evolutionary perspective predicts that in populations, such as social insects, where behavior is at least partially dependent
on individual genetic make-up, behaviors that increase inclusive fitness—
possibly through increasing fertility or increasing viability—will be practiced by more and more of the population with each passing generation
because of natural selection. These predictions work very well when analyzing nonhumans, even nonhuman primates with very complex social
power hierarchies.

Consideration of human fertility and mortality in relation to natural
selection is much more complicated and controversial. While the science-
postmodernism divide indicates disagreement over *whether* human fertility and mortality are related to natural selection, scholars on the science side themselves disagree about *how* human fertility and mortality
are related to natural selection. The ultimate cause of this disagreement
is that, in human populations, variation in behavior is not linked to individual genotypes, even though it may be linked to the human genome
(a genetic pattern shared by all humans). For example, while the human
capacity for language is genetically based, which specific language an individual speaks—the behavioral variant—is unrelated to genotype.

Because human behavior is not dependent on individual genotype, even
those who take the position that natural selection influences human behavior must see it as operating on human populations within constraints.
The first important factor which limits natural selection's direct influence
on humans relates to which behavioral practices may be affected by it. Nat-

---

*The absolute fitness of a particular genotype, A, is the expected number of offspring con-
tributed by A individuals to the next generation. Typically, however, population geneticists
use relative fitness, reducing the fitness of one type in the population to 1 and scaling the
others to the same factor (e.g., Maynard Smith 1989:38). Inclusive fitness measures the
relative fitness of an individual not merely from his or her own offspring but by a weighted
aggregation of the fitness of one's surviving genetic relatives, weighted by their degree of
relatedness (Maynard Smith 1989:175–76). Children and full siblings, who share 0.5 of
one's genes on average, are the greatest contributors to one's fitness, followed by half siblings (who share 0.25) and first cousins (who share 0.125).

ural selection works through genetic reproduction, but ideas are not transmitted genetically. Natural selection can only *directly* affect ideas and non-
genetically based behaviors that are transmitted vertically from parent to
child—that is, following the path of genetic transmission (e.g., Cavalli-
Sforza and Feldman 1981:101, 121, 365; Boyd and Richerson 1985:11,
180–81; Richerson and Boyd 1992:78–79; Durham 1991:286, 430–31,
463n). In other words, natural selection can directly influence the perpetuation of ideas and practices that are passed from parents to children. This
influence occurs by the fertility and mortality of individuals who practice
that behavior or hold those ideas. As we shall see, the form of parentally
arranged marriages is a good example of such vertical transmission because parents actually select the marriage form practiced by their children.

The second factor which limits natural selection's effects on humans
is the relative influences of culture and social relations, on the one hand,
and natural selection, on the other. Anthropologist Marshall Sahlins (e.g.,
1976a:57, 102, 208–209; see also 1976b) strongly criticized overemphasis
of natural selection's influence (see also Ehrlich and Feldman 2003).[10]
In doing so, Sahlins made the crucial point that, because the specific cultural logic of a given society drives social and cultural change, inclusive
fitness consequences are relevant to cultural practices only in those rare
cases where viability (probability of survival) is at stake.

In order to synthesize Sahlins's interpretive criticism with an evolutionary perspective, I define a concept called the "descent viability
threshold" which measures the probability of survival of a descent line.
I suggest that, beyond this threshold, inclusive fitness drops off so dramatically that individuals perpetuating a particular behavior are likely
to have no surviving genetic descendants in the course of a few generations (cf. Durham 1991:85, figure 2.2.; Brown n.d., 1995:80–81). This
concept is useful for an analysis of human populations because it distinguishes the relative strength of direct natural selection. In other words,
a particular cultural practice or idea is only likely to be strongly influenced
by natural selection—via fertility and mortality—if continuation of a descent line is at stake. Above a descent viability threshold, natural selection will strongly influence the perpetuation of vertically transmitted ideas
and practices (Durham 1991:368, 450, 451–54). Below this threshold,
natural selection still operates, but it is weak with respect to social and
cultural processes. In other words, the relative strengths of the other processes mean that the relative persistence and/or spread of the various practices are more strongly influenced by social, cultural, and/or cognitive
dynamics than by inclusive fitness consequences.

For example, consider Arthur P. Wolf's work on the Westermarck hypothesis that early childhood association leads to sexual indifference or aversion later in life. At the turn of the twentieth century, Hoklo women in minor marriages in northern Taiwanese families had about 25-percent lower fertility than Hoklo women in major or uxorilocal marriages (that is, who did not come into contact with their husbands until they were adults) (Wolf 1995:120–121). (Through the early twentieth century in Taiwan, brides and grooms were not allowed any voice in the decision of their marriage, thus meeting the criterion of vertical transmission.) Nevertheless, minor marriages constituted 20 to 47 percent of all marriages in one area of northern Taiwan between 1850 and 1920 (Wolf 1995: 42, 51), ending as a common practice only when social changes led to children having more control over whom they married, or more accurately, whom they would not marry (Wolf 1995:47, 222–223). I suggest that the persistence of minor marriages was more strongly influenced by social and cultural processes than natural selection because families whose children had minor marriages did *not* cross a descent viability threshold: Hoklo women in minor marriages still had an average total marital fertility of 5 to 6 children (Wolf 1995:120, 146, 203–205).[11] Wolf's study provides an excellent example of how the human genome can influence human behavior—in terms of reducing fertility and increasing adultery and divorce—but, at the same time, it shows that cultural and social influences can override natural selection effects to maintain a practice that does not cross the descent viability threshold.

I take a middle-ground position that, through demographic conditions, natural selection may influence cultural practices that are passed from parent to child. In order to decide whether natural selection has a strong influence on a particular practice, we must examine the degree to which that practice affects descent viability—the probability of survival of a descent line. In seventeenth-century Taiwan, where Han immigrant men overwhelmingly outnumbered Han women, the choice to avoid intermarriage must have been strongly influenced by natural selection because this choice would have strongly influenced fertility and continuation of a Han man's descent line. This perspective predicts high rates of intermarriage in that circumstance, as we found in chapter 4. This perspective also places humans in the continuum of all living creatures by accepting that we too are subject to natural selection. However, it takes into account the fact that culture mediates the effects of natural selection. I turn next to the mechanism by which culture has this mediating effect—human cognition.

Human Cognition and "Rational" Choices

Anthropologists who advocate the importance of choice (e.g., Boyd and Richerson 1985, Cosmides et al. 1992, Durham 1991, Smith and Winterhalder 1992, Tooby and Cosmides 1992) assume that choices follow principles of rational decision making and individual self-interest, often defined in evolutionary terms, economic terms, or both (as in game theory). This rationalist position is not a new one in the social sciences; it has been known at least since Weber's (1978[1922]) *Economy and Society*. Nevertheless, Huang (2000:25) apparently views the enormous influence acquired by rational-choice theory as a recent attempt to imitate the physical sciences. He (2000:26) suggests, "postmodernist 'cultural studies' . . . [is a potentially] useful corrective to such scientistic tendencies." Huang's position reflects the broader science-postmodernism split in the social sciences over the relevance of human choices in understanding human actions (cf. Elster 1983, Little 1989, Brown 1995:19–23).

Anthropologists who advocate the irrelevancy of choice, however, include both postmodernists (e.g., Bourdieu 1977) and evolutionists (e.g., Dunnell 1992:85). They emphasize the unconscious basis and unintended consequences of many, if not most, human actions. This position is actually the more recent one. It criticizes rational-choice approaches for assuming a rational subject with total understanding of and control over the consequences of his or her actions. Such assumptions are definitely unwarranted. However, the validity of this criticism does not mean that the choices of individuals may not be "rational" in some sense, at some level, nor does it mean that choices are irrelevant.

I combine cognitive, evolutionary, interpretive, and postmodern insights to suggest that choices—conscious or unconscious—are influenced differentially by cultural meaning, social power, the cognitive structure and operation of the brain, and demographic trends (Brown 1995:86–88, n.d.). Actions based on these choices may have intended or unintended consequences, but all choices, actions, and their consequences are constrained by historical contingencies in the specific culture, society, and environment in which the individual decision makers live. In other words, while individuals "choose" their actions, the alternatives available to them are shaped and constrained by the existing cultural meanings, social power relations, and demographic conditions in which they live.

A cognitive anthropological perspective emphasizes the imperfect, variable understanding of the actual social order and the strength of cultural meanings in influencing choices, without throwing out choice and decision making as irrelevant (cf. Strauss 1992a:13, 1992b:217; Sperber 1996:78–79, 135). People understand the social order and how its power relations operate in variable ways because such understanding is *not* straightforwardly transmitted by observation or symbolic communication.[12] An important characteristic of learning, often taken for granted, is that broadcasting of information and internalization of information are separate processes (Brown 1995:36–37, 502–509, figures 9.1, 9.2, 9.3; n.d.). Claudia Strauss (1992a:9–16) makes three points in this regard. First, social information may change, be inconsistent, or be hard to read. Second, the form of information—whether learned as an explicitly stated rule or learned implicitly in practice—and the order of learning affect internalization and subsequent ideas (cf. Strauss and Quinn 1994:286–91). What people learn as children, for example, often carries greater weight than what they learn later in life. Third, acquisition of social information does not automatically affect motivation (cf. Strauss 1992b). In other words, knowing a rule does not necessarily mean that one follows the rule. This variable character of social information influences people's subjective perception, so too do collective cultural meanings. Thus, pre-existing cultural ideas as well as idiosyncratic and/or imperfect understanding of the existing social order may affect a broadcast message, modifying it—in its content or importance—upon reception or even rejecting it completely (Brown 1995:35–36, n.d.).

I add to this cognitive perspective an evolutionary one. Evolutionists (e.g., Boyd and Richerson 1985, Durham 1991, Tooby and Cosmides 1992, Dennett 1995) argue that evolution has shaped the human mind by building into the structure of the human brain various cognitive mechanisms. I suggest that human minds operate as though they have an unconscious goal of fitness enhancement—a sort of "adaptive rationality"— and a derivative goal to manipulate rank and alliances in complex social relations so as to increase one's rank (Brown 1995:67–89, n.d.). Although this position may seem to be an extreme rationalist one, it is not. Drawing on Strauss' points above, I emphasize that *having such goals is not the same thing as achieving them*. The discrepancy between the unconscious goal of an individual's choices and actions, on the one hand, and the actual outcomes of conscious choices, deliberate actions, and unconscious habitual actions, on the other hand, lies in other influences beyond the control of individuals—the influences of cultural meaning, the actual social order, and the environment.

Here the addition of interpretive and postmodern perspectives is crucial. The influence of collective cultural meanings on individual choices and actions (an interpretive point) has already been discussed: such meanings operate through the subjective meanings and perceptions of individuals, coloring their interpretations of the world around them. The influence of the actual social order can be understood by considering that the process determining who within a population actually attains particular powerful roles is not a cognitive process. The cognitive ability to perceive what actions are required to achieve a particular role is not the same thing as the ability to socially carry out those actions successfully. As a postmodern perspective on power reminds us, the latter ability depends upon the social roles themselves—which roles exist and what their relative degree of influence is; upon relative social power, including the position within the existing social organization from which the individual in question begins his or her actions; and additionally, upon the meanings attached to those roles.

How is such a synthesizing perspective applied? Consider the Han Chinese practice of footbinding. For a girl, the risk of death from complications in the binding process (e.g., gangrene) would be a strong factor against a potential decision to bind her own feet, if the decision was hers. However, the decision to bind or not was made by a girl's parents when she was too young to have much influence (e.g., Levy 1967:244–45, Blake 1994:678–79). For parents, the potential juvenile death of a daughter would not necessarily affect their decision to bind that daughter's feet, because it would not necessarily jeopardize their fitness if they had other children, particularly sons whose mortality would not be affected by footbinding. (It would certainly reduce their fitness, but it would not take it below a descent viability threshold.) Empirical evidence suggests that social factors, like whether light labor (e.g., weaving) was lucrative for a daughter, most strongly influenced parents' decision to bind daughters' feet (Gates 1996b, 2001).

Adaptive rationality does not operate independently of the social power hierarchy and cultural meanings. Examination of the existing social order indicates whose decision making plays a role—in the case of Han footbinding, it was parents' decision making that counted. Examination of culture indicates two kinds of meanings related to footbinding (cf. Gates 1989; 1996a: chapter 7; 1996b; 2001). First, women were considered the commodities of their kin, so it was taken for granted that their labor for the family unit and exit from it were manipulated to family's best social advantage, including whether they left as small-footed brides or as natural-footed bond-servants or prostitutes. Second, women believed that binding their feet guaranteed them the better social position of a bride.

As another example, consider migration. There were a variety of factors prompting Han men in Fujian Province to choose to migrate to Taiwan, discussed in chapter 4. In the mid-seventeenth century, war and famine in Fujian may indeed have affected descent viability for poor men. At the very least, given the distribution of Taiwan rice as famine relief in Fujian, it probably appeared to Han men in Fujian that they would fare better in Taiwan. Added to these demographic and cognitive influences was the potential for moving up the social power hierarchy that the higher wages and less rigid frontier society of Taiwan potentially offered. Moreover, Fujian had a long cultural tradition of sojourning and/or migrating overseas. This example shows that the different influences discussed here do not always compete. They can also combine to reinforce practices like migration.

The theoretical synthesis outlined here is an empirically grounded proposal. It provides the framework for my analysis of identity changes throughout this book. This empirical grounding both informed the formulation of the synthesis and allows us to evaluate the extent to which it improves our understanding of identity—how identity is actually formed, how the concept of identity has been used ideologically, and the real-world political implications of the contrast between the two.

FROM THEORY TO POLITICS

Theory can help us better understand what people have done—both as individuals and in collective entities such as societies—and what people may do in the future. In order to understand future actions, we must apply theory to our analysis of the past and arrive at conclusions stated in generalized terms that may be applied to present and future concerns. In chapters 3 through 5, I drew conclusions in terms of the specific case of identity change being discussed—long-route Han, short-route Han, and Enshi locals and Tujia, respectively. For all the cases discussed, however, the combined and sometimes competing influences of cultural meaning, social power, and demographic conditions operated through a human cognitive structure that privileged ideas in the pre-existing cultural model, shaped people's perception of the existing social system and environment, and preferred "adaptively rational" choices insofar as they were perceived at all and perceived as feasible. In this section, I put the conclusions drawn from the case studies in more general, theoretical terms for two purposes: first, to show that this theoretical synthesis *is* the analytical framework of the book, and second, to facilitate analysis of political implications below.

Crossing the Border to Han

In the case of the long route to Han, some plains Aborigines in the seventeenth through nineteenth centuries periodically chose to migrate away from villages on the southwestern plains of Taiwan where Han colonists were so plentiful (chapter 3). The choice to migrate—perhaps influenced by an older plains Aborigine cultural preference to migrate in the face of threat—did not remove the possibility of intermarriage. A significant minority of people in Toushe, Jibeishua, and Longtian continued to choose intermarriage with poor Han men. Intermarriage put these Han men in the important social role of a parent, and they taught their children ideas from the local Hoklo cultural model, a model favored by people higher in the social power hierarchy than the people of Toushe, Jibeishua, and Longtian. However, these cultural ideas were still subject to interpretation in terms of ideas maintained from Aborigine cultural models, thus creating occasional syncretic practices such as uxorilocal minor marriage and ritual consumption of raw pigs' intestines and blood. Moreover, these Han cultural ideas were also subject to the social constraints of poverty. Carved gravestones, for example, were very expensive. In short, migration and intermarriage laid the framework for identity change in Toushe, Jibeishua, and Longtian.

Nevertheless, identity change did not occur without a change in the political regime. In banning footbinding, the Japanese colonial government was operating on a cultural model which condemned footbinding as barbaric—a cultural model very different from the Hoklo one. The Japanese cultural model allowed the colonial government to see footbinding primarily as an impediment to increased agricultural production in Taiwan, rather than as an honored tradition. Economic expedience dictated that they ban the practice, and they did, encouraging women to work in the rice fields. Without this change imposed from a new political regime, the villages of Toushe, Jibeishua, and Longtian did not and could not successfully negotiate a Han identity.

We see similar processes operating in the short route to Han. Han men, primarily from Fujian on China's southeastern coast, found it expedient to migrate in the mid-seventeenth century (chapter 4). Demographic pressures in China—including famines and war—combined with a regional cultural model of sojourning outside China, the relative proximity of Taiwan compared to other locales in southeast Asia, and the fabled rich potential of the Taiwan frontier, all encouraged large numbers of migrants to Taiwan. Continuation of the patrilineal descent line was a strong Han cultural imperative, in addition to being adaptively rational. Because the vast majority of immigrants were men, Han who wanted to marry were primarily forced to seek local wives—either Aborigine women or women of mixed Han-Aborigine ancestry. Aborigine women and parents of daughters may have had self-interested reasons for agreeing to or encouraging intermarriage, and young Aborigine men may not have had the authority in Aborigine social power hierarchies or cultural models to prevent such marriages. Historical records suggest that the rate of intermarriage may have been high enough that close to half the population at the end of the Dutch period (1650) was "mixed."

Nevertheless, we do not see evidence of this mixed population claiming Han identity until after a change in political regimes—from Dutch to Zheng rule, and possibly from Zheng to Qing rule as well—when people could claim that the previous regime had it wrong, they "really" were Han, based on patrilineal ancestry. "Mixed" people knew to claim Han identity on the basis of patrilineal ancestry because their Han fathers or grandfathers would undoubtedly have taught them this primary Han cultural idea. Moreover, officials of the Zheng and Qing regimes—themselves part of a bureaucratic system based on neo-Confucian principles that revered the patrilineal family—would undoubtedly have accepted such claims.

Interestingly, because Han identities were successfully negotiated before much cultural change occurred toward the pre-existing Han cultural model brought from Fujian, it appears that the local Han cultural model in southern Taiwan was modified. After all, Han culture is the culture of those who are Han, so if the local people accepted as Han do not practice minor marriage or even footbinding, who has the authority to say that these practices are necessary parts of Han culture? In southwestern Taiwan, during the seventeenth and early eighteenth centuries, many of those who might have had the authority to say so—Han immigrants from Fujian—had an obvious self-interested reason not to say so: their own families did not practice these customs.

In Enshi, we see a similar process up through 1949. Migrations led to successive waves of immigrants being classified as "locals" by the subsequent migrants. These migrants intermarried with locals, and over time, the local Han cultural model became different from Han cultural models elsewhere—graves are placed near the living and patrilineal inheritance is not shared equally among brothers. Two major regime changes in the area—the establishment of Qing bureaucratic administration and the set-up of the Nationalist provisional provincial government—appear to have solidified consideration of "locals" as Han, in spite of cultural differences.

However, the last major regime change experienced in Enshi—the establishment of Communist rule—impacted identity dramatically. Bureaucrats empowered to classify the local population into ethnic groups *did* have the authority to say that the local practices departed from necessary Han cultural practices. With social authority vested by the PRC government, officials overruled locals' perception of themselves and revoked their identity as local Han. Although locals succeeded in protesting their portrayal as Miao, an ethnic group that was despised as too far from Han, they had to settle for a new official designation as a sinicized ethnic minority, Tujia. This imposed change in identity label by the new regime combined with the subsequent experiences of the Cultural Revolution which eradiated many aspects of local practices—thus changing the local cultural model as it was known to young people because people were so busy simply trying to survive—brought Enshi to the 1980s in a unique position to reinvent locals as an ethnic minority. Those who appear to be making the most of this opportunity are those who stand to gain economically from it—the local government, which receives additional funding because it is a minority prefecture, and businesses involved in ethnic tourism. Ordinary people, however—including many young people—still perceive themselves as "really" Han, whatever their official designation may be. Thus, some ideas in the pre-1949 "local" cultural model appear to have persisted through 1996, in spite of the loss of, or drastic changes in, many cultural practices. With the state shaping people's future social experience as Tujia, however, Tujia consciousness (Tujia ethnicity, a sense of oneself as Tujia) will surely develop for many people.

Understanding Changes

Throughout this book, we have seen that migration and intermarriage combined with changes in political regimes allowed individuals in Taiwan and Enshi to change their identity labels to Han and sometimes led to subsequent changes in the local Han cultural models. The proposed theoretical synthesis allows us to understand why migration and intermarriage are such powerful forces for change. Each of these processes combines different systemic influences in ways that constrain the choices of individuals and affect their aggregate outcomes. Migration brings together the influences of social power and evolutionary viability—social power relations and threatened viability often drive migration from one population, and migration can affect the social power relations and can threaten the viability for groups in the population(s) which migrants enter. Intermarriage between members of different ethnic groups brings together the influences of social power and cultural meaning. It affects the cultural meanings held by parents (an important social role) and thereby serves as an important mechanism of cultural change. At the same time, in the context of sociopolitical changes concurrent with mass migration, intermarriage can be used to change identities.

Narratives of unfolding also combine cultural meanings and social power relations, but in a different way. Here, people in positions of social power deliberately attempt to further a political agenda that maintains or advances their own position by manipulating the cultural meanings of past and present social and political events and cultural ideas. Where narratives of unfolding are largely in agreement with people's actual social and political experience and their existing cultural model, they are readily accepted and easily motivate choices and actions within their framework. Where the cultural meanings advanced by narratives of unfolding do not correspond to existing cultural models and actual social experiences, the reaction to them is much more complex and potentially resistant. Migration and intermarriage are some of these actual social and political experiences, as are the policy enactments of new and continuing regimes. These experiences and people's perceptions of them motivate choices and actions and drive broader social and cultural changes.

POLITICAL IMPLICATIONS: IS REUNIFICATION POSSIBLE?

How can the theoretical perspective outlined above guide us through current political tensions? Identity has been the call to warfare at the end of the twentieth century—in the Balkans, Rwanda, and Kashmir, to name just a few places—and China threatens to make it the call to warfare in the twenty-first century as well. Thus, the need to understand what people and governments may do and why is particularly acute. Theoretical understanding of the contrast between the actual basis of identities and ideological claims about those identities can inform an analysis of the political implications of identities and identity rhetoric

for China and Taiwan. As we shall see, the crucial first step is to realize that there is a difference between the actual basis of identities and
the ideologically claimed basis of identities—that is, to realize that social experience and cultural ideas have different dynamics.

The Actual Basis of Identities in Taiwan and Enshi

Identity formation is based on social experiences, which are more than
the lived experience of individuals. The formation of a group identity requires that members of the group share similar experiences. These experiences do not have to be lived experience, remade anew with each
generation. Social experiences—broadly construed to include political
experiences—are passed down from one generation to the next as oral
history, with events that have been especially important or galvanizing
handed down in more detail and for more generations.

What are the social experiences that have formed the new Taiwanese
identity? Are these experiences significantly different from those that have
formed identities in Enshi? Through 1949, we see the same major forces
influencing identity changes in southwestern Taiwan and in Enshi—
migration, intermarriage, and regime changes.[13] Migrations, especially
migrations as large as Taiwan and Enshi experienced, have the potential
to disrupt descent viability, a potential which is greater when the migrants
are predominantly male. Migrations can also necessitate a readjustment
of the local social hierarchy, as when Zheng Chenggong's troops invaded
Taiwan in 1661 or when Enshi came under the direct bureaucratic administration of the Qing dynasty. Intermarriage served as an important
mechanism of cultural change because it placed immigrants with different cultural ideas in the social role of parents, allowing them to pass on
at least some of their culture to their children. Through intermarriage,
aspects of Han culture were introduced into the local cultural models
but aspects of non-Han culture were also maintained. Local people
achieved Han identity on the basis of patrilineal ancestry, so this amalgamation of Han and non-Han culture came to be considered Han culture, at least locally. Han culture was simply the culture of those considered Han, regardless of whether that culture matched Confucian
standards or Han culture elsewhere.

Why did people want to claim a Han identity? Intermarriage did introduce cultural ideas about the superiority of Han culture and thus could
have introduced a desire to claim Han identity. However, it was changes
in the social power hierarchy that made claiming Han identity impor-

tant. In seventeenth-century Taiwan, regime changes made immediate Han identity desirable for tax reasons. In Enshi, the change to Qing bureaucratic administration strengthened the influence of Han society at the local level because it brought a new wave of migrants that included not only the farmers and ordinary folk of earlier migrations but also many soldiers and a significant number of educated officials to carry out administrative rule. In Taiwan, the Japanese colonial government instituted a change in customs that forced similar practices, and over time social experiences and cultural ideas, onto plains Aborigines and Hoklo.

After 1949, we see a divergence between the experiences of people in Taiwan and people in Enshi, which led to critical differences in identity. The experience of people in Taiwan is not so drastically different from previous historical experiences. Rather, we still see migration, intermarriage and subsequent changes in the power structure strongly affecting identity changes. As in Enshi prior to 1949, all Han who were in Taiwan when the Nationalists arrived—Hoklo and Hakka, including short-route and long-route Han—were locals, that is, Taiwanese *(taiwan ren* or *bensheng ren)*. Only mountain Aborigines were distinguished from Han Taiwanese. Initially, there were low rates of intermarriage, because so many Mainlander men were able to bring their families, but there was some intermarriage, especially among people at the very bottom of the social power hierarchy—Mainlander foot soldiers without wives, a small proportion of the very poorest Taiwanese women, and a large proportion of mountain Aborigine women. With time, however, intermarriage increased—many second- and third-generation Mainlanders, especially those who had learned to speak Minnan, married Taiwanese people.

A series of major sociopolitical experiences shared by most Taiwanese solidified "ethnic" Taiwanese identity. (Although major, these experiences were not drastically different in character from those of earlier eras. The Zheng invasion, for example, must have been at least as galvanizing as the 2:28 Incident.) Virtually overnight, the national language was changed from Japanese to Mandarin. Many Taiwanese people lost jobs because they could not speak the new language. Taiwanese grievances against Mainlander treatment of them culminated in the 2:28 Incident. Many if not most Taiwanese had a relative or friend affected by the crackdown, since the families of people executed or imprisoned were under suspicion for decades. The 2:28 Incident effectively suppressed the immediate political challenge to the Nationalist Party, but it solidified an ethnic identity which galvanized Taiwanese for decades to come. In fact, the political forces that ultimately pushed the way to democratization—including the illegal Taiwan Independence Movement—were derived from Taiwanese reaction to the 2:28 Incident.

The experience of people in Enshi since 1949—because they are part of the PRC—is so drastically different that it demonstrates the increased difference between China and Taiwan generally. In contrast to Taiwan—where Han cultural ideas and practices, including patrilineal inheritance, were encouraged by the Nationalists, and the folk religion suffered relatively little interference—Enshi and the rest of the PRC experienced major upheavals as part of Communist efforts to restructure and re-educate the Chinese populace. The economic realignments of 1950s land reform had dramatic effects on the local social power hierarchy in Enshi, but they did not strongly affect cultural ideas and practices. People reported hiring Daoist priests to bury their dead well into the 1950s. In 1957, however, things changed dramatically. China began its spiral into social chaos, first with the Anti-Rightist Campaign, later with the Great Leap Forward—which resulted in the "excess" deaths of at least 23 million people (beyond the normal mortality rate), many from starvation—and then with the Cultural Revolution.

The devastating personal impacts of these years came home to me in the course of my fieldwork, even though I did not interview people about these political events specifically. In talking about the marriages and funerals in their families, people referred to events of that period. Most people had at least one relative who starved to death as a result of the Great Leap Forward. Reports about diet show that Wucun in the 1930s and 1940s—during the war—was economically much better off than Toushe, Jibeishua, and Longtian in Taiwan at that time. People in Wucun ate meat regularly—even poor people there could afford to slaughter pigs at least once a year. In Toushe, by contrast, most people could not afford to slaughter pigs and many people could not even afford to slaughter their own chickens. The Great Leap Forward and Cultural Revolution so devastated the local economy in Enshi that in 1996, after over a decade of economic reforms and boom, standards of living in Wucun had still not caught up to Toushe, the poorest of the villages where I interviewed in Taiwan.

Further political crackdowns in China—not just the June 4, 1989, massacre of demonstrators in Tiananmen Square, but also the subsequent suppression of any organizations which could potentially foment political opposition to the CCP—continue to assail ordinary people's views of their government. In the aftermath of its fear over the growing popularity of the quasi-religious organization Fa Lun Gong, the Chinese government even began to try to suppress the very popular quasi-religious, quasi-medical, quasi-exercise Han practice of *qi gong*. Such attacks continue the Cultural Revolution legacy of destroying Confucian cultural traditions, especially those related, even peripherally, to religion. Ironically, by crippling indigenous religion, the CCP is paving the way for foreign religions it is at least as suspicious of—such as Christianity—to enjoy a success in proselytizing that was impossible when Han folk religion was strong.

The lengths to which the Chinese government has gone in political crackdowns over the years is reflected in the attitudes of Chinese citizens. During the 1996 war games in the Taiwan Strait, one person asked me whether I thought that China was deliberately trying to provoke a war with the U.S. in order to decrease the surplus population in China. Such cynicism seems to reflect a belief that the People's government cares little about the ordinary people of China. At the very least, decades of capricious political crackdowns have led many people to distrust their government and to always be on edge. Politically, people do not know what to expect.

By contrast, Taiwan has been very stable politically since the 2:28 Incident. There were some capricious political crackdowns in the 1950s, but these were primarily aimed at Mainlanders as Chiang Kai-shek consolidated his control of the Nationalist Party. Taiwanese did experience the martial-law period as very repressive, but they knew what to expect. The only major unexpected event was a liberalizing one—the 1986 decision by then-president Chiang Ching-kuo *not* to crack down on those who had illegally formed an opposition party. In fact, this decision essentially led to a regime change in Taiwan because it set in motion political changes that moved Taiwan to a full electoral democracy over the next ten years. Amazingly, democratization has been peaceful and economically stable.

Democratization constitutes a regime change. Like previous regime changes, it has spurred identity change—this time the development of a new, inclusive, and national Taiwanese identity—and led to a series of galvanizing events for the people of Taiwan. They have now directly elected their government. Americans may take this privilege for granted, but people I have spoken to about it in Taiwan do not. They are cognizant of the empowerment it gives them. Moreover, because of Taiwan's democratization, the PRC has embarked upon a series of threats peaking before each of the presidential elections. In March 1996, before the first presidential elections, war games with live ammunition were held in the Taiwan Strait. The PRC was strongly opposed to the election of Lee Teng-hui, who had previously been appointed president, but Lee won with strong voter support. In February of 2000, a month before the second presidential elections, the PRC put out a white paper adding a third reason it would consider legitimate grounds to invade Taiwan to the two it had previously declared (Taiwan declaring its independence and Taiwan being invaded by another country). The PRC announced it would be equally justified in invading Taiwan if Taiwan merely delays negotiating their reunification with the PRC indefinitely. On March 16, 2000— two days before the second presidential elections—China's prime minister, Zhu Rongji, warned the people of Taiwan not to elect "people who favor independence," (reported in Rosenthal 2000a), referring to the Democratic Progressive Party candidate Chen Shui-bian. Chen had explicitly endorsed Taiwan independence earlier in his career, although in the campaign he said he would not seek a referendum on the issue unless China attacked Taiwan. Chen won the three-way election.

These political threats are precisely the kind of sociopolitical events that consolidate identity (cf. Chang 2000:68). Moreover, rather than bringing Taiwan's people into line with PRC sentiment, they consolidate the identity of all people in Taiwan—ethnic Taiwanese (Hakka and Hoklo), Mainlanders, and Aborigines—as a single group, thus reinforcing the very Taiwanese national identity that the PRC wishes to undercut. Nor are these threats the only way that the PRC governmental policy has contributed to the formation of a national Taiwanese identity. Beginning in 1987, first Taiwan Mainlanders and then anyone in Taiwan were allowed by the government of Taiwan to visit the PRC. PRC policy was to treat all these visitors—Mainlanders and ethnic Taiwanese alike—as "Taiwan compatriots" *(taiwan tongbao),* with largely the same combination of ingratiation and suspicion. Threats of invasion and bombing similarly fail to recognize the heterogeneity of Taiwan's population. Ren Hai, who is from the PRC, reports that, during his 1994 visit to Taiwan, mountain Aborigines asked him to inform his government not to bomb the Aborigines when they bomb the Han (Ren 1996:79). They were reacting to the PRC's treatment of people in Taiwan as a single group. Such treatment runs precisely counter to PRC goals by directly contributing to Taiwanese national identity, for sociopolitical treatment of people as members of a group promotes those people's identity as a group.

Observations about the enduring devastation wrought by the Cultural Revolution has also contributed to the new Taiwanese identity. For one thing, people from Taiwan who visit China are struck by the poverty there, by the apparent sense among Chinese that those who escaped the Cultural Revolution owe them restitution in the form of material goods, and by the apparent loss of a Confucian work ethic (e.g., Hsiao and So 1996). They realize that people in China were often persecuted during the Cultural Revolution for practicing Han customs still common in Taiwan. Moreover, the political suppression and chaos of the Cultural Revolution actually makes Nationalist martial law rule in Taiwan, as repressive as it was, look good. In the 1950s, there was a joke that circulated among Taiwanese: "The Japanese were lucky because the Americans only dropped atomic bombs on them; Americans dropped Chiang Kai-shek on us." Now, it appears that Taiwanese feel they were not as unlucky as they might have been.

The clear differences in sociopolitical experience between Taiwan and China since 1945—differences resulting from two regime changes, first, the founding of the PRC in 1949 and, second, the realization of full electoral democracy in Taiwan in 1996—along with the PRC's treatment of everyone in Taiwan as a single group have formed a very real national identity for the people of Taiwan. A 1998 poll sponsored by the Taiwan government found that "only 18 percent of the people on Taiwan say they want to reunify with the mainland, even in the long run" (Kristof 1998). Taiwan national identity is real in the sense that it is meaningful and motivating to people of Taiwan: people in Taiwan act—collectively and individually—on the basis of this identity. They have already, by electing Lee Teng-hui president in 1996 and Chen Shui-bian president in 2000 against the wishes of the PRC. One voter said, leaving the polling booth on March 18, 2000, "We are not obliged to take any advice from China" (Eckholm 2000c).

Past attempts to suppress Taiwan national identity have only strengthened it; any future attempts are likely to do the same. Taiwan national identity is here to stay, and that fact is part of the huge problem facing any political negotiations over Taiwan's future. The PRC does not appear to accept this fact, nor to understand that many of the actions it takes actually strengthens this identity. However, the reality of this identity should come as no surprise to the PRC, since the PRC, like imperial regimes before it, has forced Han to migrate to troublesome non-Han areas—such as Lhasa (Tibet), Urumqi (Xinjiang or Chinese Turkestan) and Hohhot (Inner Mongolia)—and has encouraged intermarriage between Han and non-Han by allowing the children of mixed marriages to be registered as non-Han. Such tactics suggest that the PRC government recognizes, at some level, that migration and intermarriage are compelling means of changing identities over the long-term.

The Rhetorically Claimed Basis of Identities in Taiwan and China

The various PRC white papers on Taiwan are classic narratives of unfolding in many ways. For example, in the February 21, 2000, white paper, the PRC claims that the Chinese nation has been in existence for five thousand years (TAIOISC 2000), even though the concept of a nation-state did not exist prior to the seventeenth century. This claim asserts the unity of a contemporary political domain since antiquity, a common feature of narratives of national unfolding. Some of Taiwan's new narratives of unfolding similarly claim unity since antiquity. *Island Nostalgia* (Liu 1991), for example, does so by claiming the migrations of Aborigines to Taiwan ten to fifteen thousand years ago as Taiwan's ultimate origin as a nation. The competing narratives put forward—officially by the PRC government and unofficially by Taiwanese in the popular media—are both selective in their construction of history, which is a standard feature of narratives of unfolding. The competition lies not in the fact that a selection occurs but in which events are selected and which are excluded.

More recently, and semi-officially, Taiwan's government and political leaders have been pushing a more politically based narrative of unfolding. In July 1999, then-president Lee Teng-hui said that Taiwan would only continue negotiations with China on a state-to-state basis. This statement sent Taiwan government officials into a series of meetings to clarify whether it indicated a change in policy. It did.

> "We believe there is one nation and two countries," said Chen Chien-jen (Chen Jianren), Taiwan's chief spokesman, speaking in English in an interview. . . . Invited to say the same thing in Chinese, Chen paused and then replied, again in English: "We are still looking for the right words." (Faison 1999)

In the 2000 presidential elections, all three leading candidates—Chen Shui-bian (DPP), Lien Chan (Lian Jan, GMD), and James Soong (Independent)—agreed that Taiwan is sovereign in practice (Eckholm 2000a). In its subsequent white paper, the PRC responded to this position, denying that Taiwan has been a separate state since 1945: "Chinese territory and sovereignty has not been split, and the two sides of the Straits are not two states" (TAIOISC 2000).

Taiwan appears to be trying to push the rhetoric towards a discussion of politics rather than culture. Reporters discussing the difference between "nation" and "country" in English focused on the frequent translation of both terms into Chinese as the same word *(guojia)*. In English, "nation" usually refers to a nation-state, but it can also refer to a politically activist ethnic group—for example, Native American tribes often refer to themselves as nations, using the double meaning of ethnic group and political entity. China itself invokes this same double meaning by translating *minzu*, the term for ethnic groups, as "nationalities." If "nation" is translated "minzu" and "country" is translated "guojia," then Taiwan appears to be claiming both Han nationality and non-Chinese statehood. The difficulty with such a translation into Chinese, however, is that the PRC refers to China as *Zhonghua Minzu*—a term that most Taiwanese, Overseas Chinese, and China scholars view as referring to a Han ethnic nation rather than the multiethnic PRC (cf. Borchigud 1996:160).

Ideological narratives can and do affect people's perceptions of the past and present and thus affect their choices and actions. The closer ideological narratives are to actual identities—that is, identities actually experienced socially and politically by their members—the more powerfully these narratives can motivate people to act. In Taiwan, ideological claims about identity are generally coming into line with people's actual identities. Taiwan's new narratives of unfolding claim that Taiwanese are a mixture of plains Aborigines and Han, genetically and culturally. Historical evidence from the seventeenth century indicates that this rhetoric has a strong basis in actual social experiences (chapter 4). Ethnographic evidence from the first half of the twentieth century paints a more complex picture. In spite of intermarriage, long-route Han adopted Han culture, having little if any effect on it (chapter 3). Moreover, long-route Han have been reclassified by Taiwanese as Aborigines or non-Han. Identification of the long-route Han as Han is so important because it would further Taiwan's position that Taiwanese are, in a sense, more Han—or at least more Confucian—than Han in China. Such a move would reinforce, in yet another way, the actual experiences of people from Taiwan who were shocked about the loss of so much Confucian cultural influence in the PRC in the aftermath of the Cultural Revolution. It would continue to closely link Taiwan's claimed and actual identities, making both stronger.

What about the PRC's narrative of Taiwan's unfolding as a Han Chinese domain? In Taiwan, this narrative is laughable because it is so far removed from people's actual identities, from the actual experiences of people in Taiwan today. Taiwanese know they are not Chinese—they are not treated as Chinese in China and many have experienced for themselves that Taiwan is not China.

But what about in China? People in the PRC have no experience of contemporary Taiwan, so they have only ideological narratives to give them an understanding of Taiwan's relation to China and to them as individuals. This vacuum of actual social experience of Taiwan on the part of the Chinese people is another major factor in the Taiwan problem. China's ideological narratives about Taiwan tap into China's narrative of its own national unfolding. Taiwan is portrayed as the last piece of China ripped away by foreign imperialists and accepted by corrupt domestic regimes—first the Qing dynasty and then the Nationalists—that has not been returned. This link to foreign imperialism and to the corrupt regimes that failed to protect China from that imperialism brings Taiwan into the realm of the actual experiences of the Chinese populace. They remember—many still by personal experience and many more through family lore—the Japanese invasion of China and the Nationalist accommodation of that invasion. For the vast majority of Chinese, there is no more recent, more direct experience of Taiwan—and precious little direct contact with Taiwanese in China—to counter the associations invoked by China's ideological narratives.

Moreover, this link of the PRC's narrative of Taiwan's unfolding to China's national narrative of colonial humiliation *(bainian guochi)* also invokes a common but unofficial resentment about the Great Leap Forward and the Cultural Revolution. Why did China's people have to suffer through those eras? Such resentment is directed broadly. For example, I have experienced resentment by Chinese, who expressed a belief that if the U.S. had not cut off diplomatic relations with the PRC then the Cultural Revolution could not have occurred. If such resentment is readily directed at Americans, how much more must Chinese resent the people of Taiwan—Nationalist Mainlanders who were important enough to be taken to Taiwan and ethnic Taiwanese who had been part of the hated Japanese empire? They were not only spared the turmoil of these eras, but the U.S. allied itself with them.

Additionally, as we saw among the Tujia, many people in China have themselves experienced the shock of having the PRC government classify them in contradiction to their actual identity (chapter 5; see also Cheung 1996, Harrell 1996b). Why should they object to their government doing so to Taiwanese? The difference, however, is that, within China, these classifications become the basis of new social and political experiences, which reinforce the state-designated identity and can subsequently change actual identities (e.g., Harrell 1996b). As one Chinese ethnologist put it, "We tell them what they are and after a while they get used to it" (Hill Gates, personal communication, 2000). Because the PRC does not control Taiwan—a fact made embarrassingly clear by the results of the last two presidential elections there—the PRC government cannot institute sociopolitical experiences which would reinforce the identity it has designated for Taiwan.

What If? Reunification versus Independence

Analysis of the underlying identity issues in the "Taiwan problem" shows how difficult it will be to work out the political impasse over Taiwan's future. As we have seen, identity is the negotiated product of the interaction between what people claim for themselves and what others allow them to claim. The PRC white paper threatening to invade if Taiwan delays too long in negotiating reunification shows just how desperate the PRC is. At some level, PRC officials must be aware that Taiwan's actual identity is being solidified as a national identity. The longer that Taiwan remains a democracy, the less actual social basis there is for reunification. Moreover, with the passage of time, and the deaths of those generations of Chinese who remember the Japanese invasion, the Civil War, and the Cultural Revolution, sentiment within China may change as well.

What would be required for Taiwan to identify with China? Taiwan officials and ordinary citizens have said that the PRC would have to become a democracy before Taiwan will choose reunification. This position is not simply rhetoric. Because people in Taiwan have experienced democracy, they are very unlikely to identify with an authoritarian regime. The actual social experiences of people in a democracy are just too far removed from those of people in an authoritarian regime. Based on their experience of democracy, Taiwanese are developing an identity closer to the U.S. or Japan than to China, in spite of sharing a cultural heritage with China. In the early 1990s, a number of Taiwanese expressed their shame to me over the many fistfights in Taiwan's newly elected Legislative Yuan, as politicians disagreed with each other bluntly and publicly for the first time. These Taiwanese explicitly compared themselves to the U.S., noting that the U.S. Congress does not have such fisticuffs. They were greatly relieved when I assured them that there is a U.S. law which forbids discharging guns within the Capitol building because congressmen once used to do so to punctuate their arguments. If the U.S. Congress could be so indecorous in the early years of American democracy, these Taiwanese felt there was hope that the Legislative Yuan would also become more dignified as democracy matures in Taiwan.

In fact, democracy has matured in Taiwan. Leading up to the March 2000 elections, a Taiwanese cable television program, called "An Interview with the Chairman," broadcast biting satires of the three main presidential candidates and of Lee Teng-hui every night (Eckholm 2000b). People in the PRC go to prison for less than that. Moreover, by electing Chen Shui-bian, an opposition candidate, Taiwan's voters set up perhaps the most important indicator of a maturing democracy: a peaceful transfer of power from one political party to another. This event was as unimaginable in Taiwan in 1980 as it still is in the PRC today.

Given all these ways in which Taiwanese identity is and continues to become more and more different from Chinese identity, the people of Taiwan would most likely rise up and prevent any attempted reunification with an undemocratic PRC—probably using democratic methods like challenging the policy in court, popular demonstrations, and removing those responsible from office. However, I can think of little else that might lead to a military coup in Taiwan than a deal to return to the PRC prior to democratization in China.

Then what can the PRC do? There are at least three options, none of which is likely to be favored by the PRC government. A first option is, as the PRC has threatened, to go to war. One benefit of war to the Communist Party is that it might rally the citizens of China and relieve current pressures to reform corruption in the government and the party. If the Communist Party feels it is faced with a real threat to its hold on power, then this awful step seems more possible. It may be that the PRC stepped up the pressure on Taiwan in February 2000 because of a behind-the-scenes struggle for control of the Communist Party and the government of the PRC. Then-president Jiang Zimin might have felt the need to appear tough on Taiwan in order to maintain the support of hardliners in the military.

On the other hand, China may have been testing the reaction of ordinary Chinese to a war over Taiwan. Although PRC government polls released the week before Taiwan's 2000 election claimed that 95 percent of Chinese approved using military force to prevent Taiwan's independence, reporter Elisabeth Rosenthal (2000b) presented signs that ordinary Chinese are ambivalent about such a fight. One young woman who only gave her surname said, "We strongly believe that Taiwan should return to the motherland; after Hong Kong and Macao, it is the only one left. . . . But we don't support the use of force. That wouldn't be good for anyone" (Rosenthal 2000b). A middle-aged store manager who gave his complete name said, "Ordinary [Chinese] people just want to get on with their lives, and whether Taiwan becomes independent has no effect on them," although he did accept the inevitability of force—if Taiwan "takes steps toward independence, we'll surely just have to give them a beating" (Rosenthal 2000b). The problem for the PRC is that there is no guarantee it would win a war against Taiwan. In fact, a number of Western analysts predict that they would not win such a war (e.g., Smith 2000). This is a dangerous possibility. On the one hand, if the PRC lost, it would effectively reduce the power of military hardliners. On the other hand, not only would a loss be a source of international embarrassment to China, but it might also create a nationalistic backlash that would sweep the Communist Party out of power, an issue of much more pressing concern to PRC officials than Taiwan.

A second option is to proceed with political reforms that might actually lead to democratization in order to draw Taiwan in. Anthropologist Robert P. Weller (1999) has argued that China's current informal associations provide the potential for a peaceful transition to democracy, similar to that of Taiwan in the martial law period; Hill Gates (1996a: chapter 10) also sees a return in the PRC to the petty capitalist mode of production and patriarchal stratification familiar to many Taiwanese. Thus, it appears that democratization along Taiwanese lines may indeed be possible for China. Democratization is not good news to the Communist Party, however, for it would mean losing power.

A third option is to accept that Taiwan will not return to China. This course has no direct benefits to the Communist Party, although it maintains the political and economic status quo. The problem is how to reconcile the Chinese people to such a course so that the Communist Party is not perceived as accommodating continuing imperialism of China. The threat of such perceived accomodation is that it could shake Communist control of the PRC. Here, the PRC government must face the very rhetoric that it has stirred up. Can the PRC create a way for the Chinese populace to experience Taiwan as different? If so, then Chinese might well accept a separate Taiwanese identity. It is very unlikely that Chinese who might visit Taiwan are going to view it as sufficiently culturally different to be outside the realm of Chinese—or even Han—variation. China has so much internal cultural variation that Chinese can easily visit places within the PRC which are at least as culturally different from their own community as Taiwan, if not more so. Thus, we return to experiencing sociopolitical differences. Can the PRC allow enough of its citizens to observe Taiwanese democracy that it will affect popular opinion about a separate Taiwan without committing itself to democracy? On the other hand, can they prevent news of Taiwan's democracy from reaching PRC citizens?

Ultimately the Taiwan problem is about the new Taiwanese identity forged in the 1990s. Although we have examined several instances of it, changing identities is not easy. Such changes may be contested even years after the fact—as in Toushe, Jibeishua, and Longtian in Taiwan and Enshi in China. In the end, all of these identity changes come down to changes in political regimes. Thus, I expect that whether Taiwan can succeed in negotiating a new non-Chinese identity for itself—making the claim and getting that claim accepted by China—will come down to whether the PRC accepts that a regime change has occurred in Taiwan. Perhaps the change in the political party governing Taiwan will spark such acceptance. The January 2002 announcement that Taiwan entered the World Trade Organization one month after the PRC suggests that there is growing international acceptance of their political differentiation.

What are Taiwan's options? Taiwan's government in the 1990s accepted the new Taiwanese identity as a real part of the political landscape. In 1999, it finally started to talk about that identity in terms of the social and political experience of its constituents—terms that resonate with voters in Taiwan. The problem now is how to make that message resonate elsewhere—in China and internationally—for if Taiwan can negotiate a separate identity in either realm, it has leverage for its negotiations in the remaining realm.

I suspect that Lee Teng-hui did not seek re-election in 2000 in part because he saw the opportunity to pursue international support for Taiwan's sovereignty as a retired elder statesman. Doubly retired, from the presidency and the chair of the Nationalist Party, he could get visas as a private citizen to the U.S., Japan, and elsewhere. Moreover, he has the stature in these democratic countries of being the man who oversaw Taiwan's transition to democracy, the first democratically elected president of Taiwan, and the first head of state to willingly hand over power to the opposition in at least two millenia of Han history. Current president Chen Shui-bian does not appear to have used Lee in this regard, though he has demonstrated willingness to work with other senior Nationalists to promote Taiwan's stability (for example, he appointed Tang Fei, Chairman of Taiwan's Joint Chiefs of Staff under Nationalist rule, as his first premier, thereby securing the neutrality of Taiwan's military during the political turnover).

Such strategic cooperation across party lines is essential, because even with democracies sympathetic to Taiwan's goal of sovereignty, Taiwan's leaders have their work cut out. They must persuade the international community that the new Taiwanese identity is not only reasonable and justifiable but real, in the sense that it will motivate the actions of Taiwan's people. The international community must be persuaded not merely that supporting Taiwan is the morally correct thing to do, but that it is economically necessary. The international community is slow to act for moral reasons—for example, in Rwanda, Bosnia, and Kosovo—and quick to act for economic reasons—for example, in Kuwait. Taiwan is wealthy but has not yet learned how to use its wealth successfully. Lee's 1995 offer to buy a UN seat for several million dollars fell flat. Ironically, Taiwan's huge investment in China—$24.8 billion in 1998, according to the U.S. State Department—probably gives it the most international leverage, for it is China's objections that prevent most countries from recognizing Taiwan. If Japan, Taiwan, and the U.S.—the top three investors in China—were to coordinate economic pressure on the PRC, it could be effective, as long as other steps had been taken to prepare the people of China for a change in Taiwan's status.

What can Taiwan do to affect the experience and perception of Taiwan for people in China and to influence the PRC's choices regarding its options? Certainly, Taiwan's military capabilities influence the decisions of many governments, including the PRC. These moves influence governments, though, not ordinary people. Much more important at the level of ordinary individual experience are the myriad contacts from economic investment there. Taiwanese who travel to the PRC have an advantage over other foreign investors—they can speak directly with people in China without going through an interpreter. Thus, they can—and undoubtedly do—discuss Taiwan and the ways it is different from China, including the political differences. The proposal (announced in January 2002) to allow PRC businesspeople to live and work in Taiwan, following China's and Taiwan's admission to the WTO, promises that at least some PRC citizens will directly experience Taiwan's sociopolitial differences from China.

It is possible that, with time, such ordinary contacts can change Chinese public opinion. There are even small signs of such influence already.

After Taiwan elected Chen Shui-bian president in 2000, reporter Elisa-beth Rosenthal (2000b) quoted a Beijing University student as saying, "I think both sides will have to make adjustments to their policies. Af-ter all, Taiwan is democratic now, and the people have exercised their own right to choose a president." If such acceptance of the new Taiwanese identity and its social and political basis spreads in China, it bodes well for Taiwan's future.

Notes

1. For an overview of China's and Taiwan's official position on "one China" and the eventual reunification of China and Taiwan, see Chai (1999).

2. "Aborigine" is the preferred English appellation of the Alliance of Taiwan Aborigines. *Yuanzhumin* (original inhabitants) is their preferred appellation in Mandarin Chinese. These English and Chinese terms do not carry a pejorative meaning in Taiwan. I capitalize "Aborigine" to indicate the equivalence between this term and "Han" as ethnic designations.

3. Nations, and some ethnic groups, also claim a territory, but since territorial claims are typically justified in terms of ancestry and/or culture as well, I do not deal with territory separately.

4. However, the fact that Hong Kong and Macao have decided their own fates by referendum has raised expectations that Taiwan should do so as well. China counters that Taiwan is not entitled to a referendum, because it is not currently separated from China because of a colonial status; it was returned to Chinese rule in 1945. "The issue of national self-determination, therefore, does not exist" (TAOIOSC 2000: section IV).

5. Some historians discuss what I call narratives of unfolding as "collective memory," based on work done in the 1920s by French sociologist Maurice Halbwachs (1980). I thank Mona Siegel for bringing this point to my attention. Other historians discuss it in terms of the "invention of tradition" (e.g., Hobsbawm and Ranger 1983).

6. The Mandarin Chinese term "minzu" is officially translated in the PRC as "nationality," although some scholars (e.g., Fei 1981:60) translate it as "ethnic group."

7. The application of these criteria even to the classification of non-Han

peoples is questionable. For example, the Hainan Muslims are classified as part of the Hui minzu, even though they have clearly different territory, language, and culture than the other people classified as Hui (Pang 1996:190–91).

8. I use the term "Hoklo" for Taiwanese who are native speakers of Min- nan. These are the same people often referred to as "Hokkien" in scholarly lit- erature about Taiwan.

Guang and *fu* refer to the administrative unit of the origin of a person's pa- trilineal ancestors (Guangdong Province and Fujian Province, respectively). They are often used as ethnic indicators because Hoklo came exclusively from Fujian and many Hakka came from Guangdong. However, a significant number of Hakka came from Fujian, so we cannot assume that everyone listed in the reg- isters as fu is Hoklo. I thank Chuang Ying-chang and Lim Khay Thiong for clar- ifying this method of coding for me.

See Wolf and Huang (1980:16–33) for a detailed description of the house- hold registers in Taiwan. Note that because the classifications in these registers are written with Chinese characters, I refer to them here by their Mandarin Chi- nese pronunciation, even though the same characters are pronounced differently in Japanese.

9. Although the recent, more polite designations of *pingpu zu* (plains tribes) and *gaoshan zu* (mountain tribes) are ostensibly geographic categorizations, in fact they still refer to the same groups historically distinguished by their relation to Han culture—*shufan* (cooked barbarians) and *shengfan* (raw barbarians) re- spectively (cf. Brown 1996b:38). For example, the Ami who live on the eastern plains of Taiwan and the Yami who live on Orchid Island are today categorized as "mountain" Aborigines; both were historically classified as shengfan.

10. Estimates of the number of executed Taiwanese range from 8,000 to 22,000 (Lai, Myers and Wei 1991:160, Chang 2000:70n33).

11. "Inside the province" and "outside the province" are allusions to Tai- wan as a province of China, which the Nationalist government still claimed to rule. The National Assembly in Taiwan, through 1991, and the Legislative Yuan, through 1992, were made up of "representatives" of provinces in mainland China who had been elected in the late 1940s.

12. "Mainlander" has been used as an ethnic distinction at least since Gates' (1981) article on ethnicity in Taiwan, but only by non-Han ("foreign") scholars. Chang (1996) reasserts the standard position that Han in Taiwan have always insisted on: that the political construction is important. Chang (2000:69) accepts "an 'ethnic' divide between Mainlanders and the Taiwanese" only because of their self-definitions. However, when we understand that ethnic groups *are* po- litical constructions, not cultural or descent groups despite claims to the con- trary, then considering Mainlanders as an ethnic group does not ignore the pol- itics involved.

13. At the end of 1998, the provincial-level government was dismantled, elim- inating the fiction of Taiwan as a province of China. This move, spearheaded by then-president Lee Teng-hui, has been variously interpreted as a move toward independence and as a tactic to weaken the power base of James Soong (Song Chuyu), a popular GMD Mainlander and provincial governor at the time. (Soong was later expelled from the GMD and founded the People First Party.)

14. Lee did include Aborigines and their descendants as part of the new Taiwanese, at least in an October 1998 speech (Lee 1999:193), but his focus was always on bridging the divide between the two main categories of Han, because Lee's public endorsement of such an identity was intended to boost ethnic Taiwanese voter support for the Mainlander GMD candidate, Ma Ying-jeou (Ma Yingjiu), who won the election (Lee 1999:191–192).

15. "Lived experience" and "social experience" are not the same thing. Lived experience refers to the actual experiences of specific individuals; social experience refers to negotiations over power positions. Thus, people's social experiences are broader than their lived experiences and influence their lived experiences. For example, the passage of a law—the U.S. Civil Rights Act, say, or Title IX (which requires equity in funding of men's and women's sports by educational institutions)—may not be part of someone's lived experience, if he or she born after the law was passed. Nevertheless, the law is part of the social experience of everyone whose subsequent lived experiences are affected by the law, such as African American voters and women athletes.

16. Sperber (1996:78) defines mental representations as "internal, . . . patterns in the brain . . . which represent something for the owner of that brain," and offers personal memories as an example. He defines public representations as "external, . . . material phenomena in the environment of people . . . which represent something for people who perceive and interpret them." (For fuller discussions of mental and public representations, see Sperber 1996; Brown 1997, n.d.)

17. Bringing a notion of power into her analysis of identity, Ortner (1998) suggests that ethnic and "racial" identities are the speakable aspect of unspeakable class identities. While I completely agree that power is relevant to identity formation and ethnic identities, I see three main problems with Ortner's suggestion. First, her distinction between ethnic identity and racial identity is misleading. Ethnic and racial identities are constructed in the same way—claimed in terms of ancestry and/or culture, yet solidified in terms of common sociopolitical experience. Thus, "race" is a special kind of ethnic identity—one with an *assumed* biological basis—not a totally different type of identity. Second, it may have been the case in the U.S. that ethnic identities were so often linked to class identities that the former came to represent the latter. However, the visibly growing number of ethnic minorities in the upper-income brackets in the U.S. indicates that this link is changing. Indeed, I suggest that recent movements in the U.S. to abandon affirmative action programs—for example, the 1996 California initiative Proposition 209—derive from the increasing disconnection between class and ethnic identities. Third, Ortner's suggestion does not apply at all in Taiwan and China, and thus cannot be taken as universally true. In Taiwan and China, the unspeakable was not class but ethnic identity. People constructing patrilineal genealogies frequently traced their ancestors to Han peasants rather than to non-Han rulers *(tusi)* (e.g., Ebrey 1996:23). Thus, we have to find a different way to incorporate a notion of power into an analysis of identities.

18. Sperber (1996:145, emphases in original) goes on to say: "Racial classification may be a mere cultural domain, based on an underlying competence that does not have any proper domain. The initialization of an *ad hoc*

template for racial classification could well be the effect of parasitic, cultural input information on the higher-level learning module, the function of which is to generate *ad hoc* templates for genuine living-kind domains such as zoology and botany. If this hypothesis is correct—mind you, I am not claiming that it is, merely that it may be—then no racist disposition has been selected *for* . . . in humans. However, the dispositions that *have* been selected for make humans all too easily susceptible to racism, given minimal, innocuous-looking cultural input."

19. Although racial differences are described as biologically based, that assumption is actually a cultural idea. Races are defined socially, *not* biologically. The genetic variation within any group classified as a race is as great or greater than the variation between groups classified as different races (e.g., Cavalli-Sforza and Cavalli-Sforza 1995: chapter 5). Moreover, "humans show only modest levels of differentiation among populations when compared to other large-bodied mammals, and this level of differentiation is well below the usual threshold used to identify subspecies (races) in nonhuman species" (Templeton 1998:646, see also his figure 1, p. 634). Classifying people in terms of race is a hegemonic attempt to make the social, economic, and political differences between people who are classified differently appear naturally (that is, biologically) based and thus justified and immutable. Understanding that a race is actually an ethnic group reminds us that race, like ethnicity, is really about politics (cf. Shanklin 1994).

20. Such fluidity also raises an ontological question: Are these borders real? I would say that they are abstract; that is, they exist in the minds of those making such classifications. The borders themselves do not exist in the material world, but they are real in the sense that they influence what happens in the material world (cf. Popper 1982; Brown 1997, n.d.).

21. Anthropologist David Schneider (1980 [1968], 1984) criticized the anthropological focus on kinship as an ethnocentric artifact of European and North American researchers, reflecting their cultural preoccupation with sexual relations. Although he seems to have understood that the primordial nature of kinship is only a perception (a perception of anthropologists, he suggests), he missed the importance of kinship terms for understanding how social relations are carried out.

22. Marriage between first cousins is now illegal, both in Taiwan and the PRC, on the basis of principles of genetic inbreeding.

23. Liu 1991:115–120. Ren (1996:88–89) discusses these verses. I primarily use his translation, although I have modified the last verse quoted here.

24. See Harrell (1996b:276–77) for a discussion of how "minzu" and "zhonghua minzu" have been used to discuss ethnic groups and the nation.

25. In countries such as the U.S., where the name of the national language (English) derives from a former colonial power (England), the term for the national language does not coincide with the term for the politically and economically dominant ethnic group (White Anglo-Saxon Protestants or WASPs). Nevertheless, the dominant ethnic group and the national language are historically linked. Borchigud (1996:164, 166) also discusses the assumed importance of language in classifying other people's identities.

26. The term "Big Brother" comes from George Orwell's *1984*. The idea that "some animals are more equal than others" comes from *Animal Farm*. Both novels are commentaries on Leninist-Stalinist totalitarian regimes.

27. Uneducated people in China today will still say *"wo meiyou wenhua"* ("I have no wenhua"). This statement can mean "I am illiterate," but a common alternate meaning is "I am not well educated." I suggest this alternate meaning derives from the meaning of *wenhua* (lit., transformed by literature) as "cultured" or "civilized." Culture and civilization are seen as going hand-in-hand with literacy and education.

Farmers and laborers in Hubei who were at least literate enough to read a newspaper, which is quite literate in rural China, frequently told me "wo meiyou wenhua" at the beginning of interviews. Until word spread that I also interviewed illiterate people—mostly women—many people found it difficult to believe that I would want to interview them if I knew they had little education.

28. "Han" remains the most common term in the PRC and in scholarly literature on China. However, people outside these areas, including in Taiwan, increasingly use the term "Hua."

29. Johnson's argument applied specifically to late imperial Chinese society. I would not expect to be able to generalize his conclusion to other societies because women are unlikely to be the primary transmitters of popular, "substrate" culture without the presence of two crucial factors: (1) the illiteracy of the majority of the population and most women, including elite women, and (2) the practice of hypergamy—women marrying up the social hierarchy.

CHAPTER 2. WHERE DID THE ABORIGINES GO?

1. There were some migrations of plains Aborigines away from areas of Han colonization. However, as Shepherd (1993:2, 358) notes, these migrations were not the origins of the mountain Aborigines, nor did these migrations push all the plains Aborigines into the mountains. Many plains Aborigines did not migrate; of those who did, many migrated only a short distance from their original villages (cf. Ferrell 1969, Brown 1996b:56). See Pan Ying (1992) for a more general discussion of plains Aborigine migrations.

2. Campbell (1903), Huber (1990), Hsu Wen-hsiung (1980a), and Shepherd (1993) use the English term "Chinese" to translate Dutch record references to the immigrants. Since historical references about language, culture, and place of origin of the immigrants suggests they were Han, and since I am reserving the term "Chinese" to refer to national identity, I refer to the immigrants as "Han." Not all were Han though—Lan Dingyuan, for instance, an official from Fujian who came to Taiwan later, was a sinicized She minority.

3. VOC records indicate that Han were living in Soulang and Mattau by 1636 (e.g., Campbell 1903:132, 133, 154), including Han sugarcane farmers in Mattau (Campbell 1903:117, but see Campbell 1903:306, where it is suggested that Mattau is free of "the bustle and turmoil of the Chinese"), and there are other references to Han farmers living in Aborigine villages in 1636 (Campbell 1903:155) and later in 1660 (Campbell 1903:410, Shepherd 1993:83).

4. The Dutch missionaries fined Aborigines for such things as not attending the Christian schools, and issued other punishments (flogging, exile, or imprisonment) related to "idolatry" or to "debauchery." They fined Han for such things as working or going without shoes on Sunday. See, for example, Campbell (1903:186–87, 209, 214, 296, 316), Huber (1990:278), and Shepherd (1993:66, 68–69, 73, 77, 79, 84).

5. Dutch governor Verburg reports in December 1650, "the ten Chinese cabessa's [sic] [headmen and merchants] of Tayouan [the area immediately surrounding Fort Zeelandia] . . . are indeed the principal promoters of the sugar cultivation" (translated in Huber 1990:277). Encouraging sugarcane production was probably a more reliable way for the merchants to profit on their investment, because the cane had to be turned into sugar before it could be shipped or it would rot. If the merchants monopolized the local sugar mills, then the farmers would have to bring all their cane to the merchants for processing, and the merchants could take their profit out of what they paid the farmers. This method would have been much easier than collecting rents or interest on grains which farmers could process by hand. See Ka (1995) for a discussion of sugar production in Taiwan during the late-Qing and Japanese periods.

6. The rebellion is known as the Guo Huaiyi rebellion, but VOC records report that Guo Huaiyi (whom they refer to as Faijit) was only one of four leaders; the others are recorded as Sinco Blackbeard, Laueeko (or Louequa), and Tsieko (Huber 1990:283–84). The ethnic identity of these men is not clear.

7. Zheng Chenggong had Portuguese mercenaries among his troops who laid siege to the prefectural capital of Zhangzhou, Fujian, in 1652 (Huber 1990:287), and among his troops who landed in Taiwan in 1661 there were two companies of "'Black-boys,' many of whom had been Dutch slaves" (Campbell 1903:421) and who may have been African (Hsu Wen-hsiung 1980a:22).

8. The Zhengs can be said to have extracted more labor because Han farmers were involved in labor-intensive land-clearing and rice cultivation (sugarcane was less labor intensive), Han soldiers were subject to be called up for military duty, and Aborigines were subject to a corvée labor tax that they had not been subject to under the Dutch (see Brown 1995:179–181).

9. Shepherd (1993:80 based on Campbell 1903:230, 248–49) suggests that Aborigines began adopting Han agricultural techniques under Dutch impetus. VOC records written at Batavia (in Java) suggests that in 1650 "the Soulangians have already become fairly well acquainted with the art of ploughing, and are beginning to understand the use of cars or wagons" (translated in Campbell 1903:249). Records written in Taiwan refer to the Dutch buying surplus grain from two villages—Mattau and Soulang—in 1648 (Campbell 1903:230). However, there were Han living in these villages (see note 3 above). Shepherd also seems to assume that eight villages in Fengshan had a strictly Aborigine population, in spite of his own (1993:168) remark that Chinese settlers had moved south toward Fengshan and north toward Zhuluo along the plains. We do not know—for any of these villages—whether it was Aborigines or Han, or people of mixed descent, or all of the above, who plowed and/or produced the surplus rice or grain.

10. Aborigines outside the core area—both plains and mountain peoples—

adopted agriculture at different times, and under different conditions, right up through the twentieth century.

11. Gates (1996a:29–30) suggests that the family (patricorporation or *jia*) was the basic unit of petty capitalist production in China. Families, run by senior men, turned a profit by exploiting women and immature males (using or selling their labor or selling the individuals outright). Gates' analysis provides insight into the hegemonic Han ideology that surplus production fulfilled an obligation to family—this ideology provided moral justification for the exploitation of female and immature male family members.

12. A basic theme in Shepherd's (1993) volume is that land tenure is significant both in Qing frontier policy and in Han-minority relations in Taiwan. He documents in convincing detail the fluctuations in Qing policy on Aborigine land rights, in terms of taxes due and rents collectable, and the relation that these rights had to Aborigine military service and Qing control of Taiwan.

13. The Qing initially divided Taiwan into three counties: Fengshan in the south, Zhuluo in the north, and Taiwan, the core southwest area around present-day Tainan city.

14. Shepherd (1993:522n23) counters that Shi "underestimates the role of overhunting in the decline of the deer trade and exaggerates both the ease with which male [A]borigine hunters could become farmers and their desire to do so."

15. Lan Dingyuan came to Taiwan from Fujian in 1721 as secretary to his cousin, Lan Tingzhen, a military commander in the imperial forces that helped suppress the Zhu Yigui rebellion. Lan Dingyuan was prolific and outspoken in his arguments that the best route to Qing control of Taiwan was aggressive Han Chinese colonization. Lan Tingzhen's scheme to reclaim Aborigine lands makes the extremity of Lan Dingyuan's procolonization stand suspect, and the revelation that the Lans were not Han but She (a non-Han minority in Fujian) makes his pro-Han, anti-Aborigine views puzzling. (See Shepherd 1993:17, 138, 149, 234, 498n64.)

16. Land cultivation in Taiwan generally followed a three-tiered system: a large-rent *(dazu)* holder, a small-rent *(xiaozu)* holder, and the actual cultivator. For further discussion of this system, see Ka (1995:16–35), Chen (1994), and Shepherd (1993).

17. Shepherd (1993:473n12) notes that there were some intermediate tax categories between Aborigine and Han. Could these be people of "mixed" ancestry or mixed (i.e., intermarried Han-Aborigine) households that were officially recognized for some reason? (See chapter 4.)

18. See Harrell (1990b) and Lamley (1981) for further discussions of ethnic feuds *(fenlei xiedou)*, and Meskill (1979) for a historical example of a lineage caught up in it. See Shepherd (1993) for a more detailed discussion of Aborigine land rights.

19. Although migrations did occur in the 1660s, in the early Zheng period, the bulk of the migrations appears to have occurred after the huge influx of Han immigrants to Taiwan in the mid-Qing period, when the ban on family migration was lifted for eight years (1732–40). This apparent concentration in the mid-Qing period may be due simply to more limited information about population and population movement during the Zheng period, but increased migration af-

ter the 1730s would make sense, because of the much higher density of Han settlers in the area, the continued intermarriage, and the possible reduction in official identity changes related to a change in tax status.

20. To end opium addiction in Taiwan, which Davidson (1988 [1903]:614) estimates afflicted 7 percent of the population, the Japanese monopolized opium production, licensed opium sellers, registered all habitual opium users, and issued them certificates entitling them (and only them) to purchase the drug. One woman I interviewed, whose father-in-law had smoked opium, told me that the Japanese weaned opium smokers of their habit, issuing them less and less of the drug over time. Davidson mentions nothing of such weaning; instead, he suggests that the Japanese plan was to maintain current opium smokers until their deaths but to regulate opium so that no new addicts would appear. The unlicensed import, production, sale, or purchase of opium was severely punished.

21. In 1988, I interviewed several elderly people in a mountain Aborigine village in the Puli basin who reported that they had not seen or heard news of siblings and other relatives since their forced relocation by the Japanese police some 50 years before.

22. Many of those I interviewed either served, or had male relatives who served, in the Japanese Imperial Army. Most of these men were drafted and thus were porters and laborers, not soldiers. Only one man told me that he had enlisted as a soldier. Two women, whose husbands never came back, were never notified of the fate of their husbands or recognized in anyway for their loss. Another man, who served as a laborer repairing the runways on a south Pacific island which took heavy American bombing, told me that after the surrender, the Japanese army pulled out and abandoned all the laborers there. It was the Americans who fed them and, a few months later, shipped them home. Of the 200,000 from Taiwan who served, 30,000 died (*Free China Journal* August 5, 1984:1, cf. Chang 2000:62, 70n29).

23. For example, the battle for Shanghai, from August to October of 1937, cost the Chinese as many as 250,000 casualties and the Japanese 40,000 or more; in the seven-week reign of destruction and terror after the Japanese took Nanjing in mid-December 1937, foreign observers estimated 20,000 female rape victims (many of whom died after repeated assaults), 30,000 fugitive soldiers killed, and 12,000 murdered civilians; the city was left in ruins (e.g., Spence 1990: 447–48).

24. American military commanders were well aware of the differences in how the GMD and the CCP treated subordinates and civilians. They accurately predicted that Mao's CCP would win the civil war, but they wound up blacklisted in the McCarthy era. See Tuchman (1972 [1970]) for an introduction to the American military perspective on the Chinese civil war.

25. "A 1949 inflation rate of around 3,400 percent was reduced to 306 percent in 1950, 66 percent in 1951, and from 1952 onward dropped slowly to an annual rate of 8.8. percent. By 1961 it had been forced down to 3 percent" (Spence 1990:668).

26. The Korean War (1950–53) had dramatic effects on the region. China's participation in the war led to staggering losses—between 700,000 and 900,000 people—and to China's realizing the need for a modern, well-equipped army to

face the West (Spence 1990:530–31). The war increased the suspicion and distrust between the U.S. and China—leading the U.S. into McCarthyism and China into isolationism. China forced most of the Westerners who had remained there after 1949 to leave, hunted for domestic spies and enemy agents, and ordered mass campaigns against everyone who had had long contact with the GMD or with foreigners.

27. I thank Chang Mao-kuei for bringing this remark and its implications to my attention.

28. Such lack of UN representation can have very real consequences: in August 1999, when Taiwan was struck by a major earthquake (7.6 on the Richter scale) and many large aftershocks, the UN could not send in aid—including urgently needed search-and-rescue teams—without first getting permission from the PRC. Although individual countries, including the U.S. and Japan, sent aid without waiting for such approval, UN aid was delayed a crucial day or so. Similarly, in March 2003 the World Health Organization (WHO) could not share much-needed information about the SARS (Severe Acute Respiratory Syndrome) epidemic with Taiwan, since it was not a WHO member. Taiwan had to get its information on SARS from the U.S. Centers for Disease Control.

CHAPTER 3. "WE SAVAGES DIDN'T BIND FEET"

1. Parts of this chapter were originally published in Brown (1996b), Brown (2001a), and Brown (2003).

2. See Brown (1995: chapter 6) for a more complete discussion of these communities. See the preface of this book for the number of people interviewed in each community.

3. High or long noses and round eyes are physical characteristics attributed both to Aborigines in Taiwan and to Westerners. In fact, one common Taiwanese term for Westerners is *a-tok-a*, meaning "high noses." These and other comments by villagers indicate linkages between notions of ethnicity and physical characteristics (see Brown 1996b:38–39). I do not take up the complex issue of how perceptions of physical characteristics are linked to perceptions and concepts of race in Taiwan. Dikötter (1992) discusses concepts of race in China, both before and after contact with the West.

4. Few people over 60 spoke Mandarin so, in each community, I worked with a local woman who translated for me between Minnan and Mandarin. Even after my Minnan improved, I continued working with these translators because I found their presence reassuring to the elderly people I interviewed and found their local knowledge immeasurably helpful to my research.

5. Japanese census data for 1935 report the entire population of Toushe, including the Han satellite settlement, as 1,092 people, of whom 709 (64.9 percent) were categorized as plains Aborigine; these 1935 data also give the total Jibeishua population as 1,138, of whom 865 (76 percent) were categorized as plains Aborigines (Shepherd 1986:5). Earlier census data report the plains Aborigine population in 1911 as 796 in Toushe and 830 in Jibeishua (Pan 1989a:125).

6. Copies of the household registers for these communities are located at the Program for Historical Demography, Tsai Yuan-pei Research Center for Hu-

manities and Social Sciences, Academia Sinica. Chuang Ying-chang, Arthur P. Wolf, and Pan Inghai kindly allowed me to examine these registers.

7. There were both "open" and "dead" registers. Open registers had a living head of the household. When an individual who was not head of a household died, a red line was drawn through his or her name in the register for the household, but the register itself remained open. When the head of a household died, however, the entire register became "dead." All names were crossed out, the physical copy of the register was transferred to storage, and the information for all living members was transcribed into one or more new registers (depending on whether the old household also divided) under one or more new heads.

8. There were also seven Japanese living in the village. They are not included in the village population figures.

9. Interestingly, 6 of these 37 people had both their mother and a grandmother in the registers who were listed as plains Aborigine. Here is a hint that intermarriage recurred over generations, though given nineteenth-century mortality rates, grandmothers were rare in the registers, so an estimate of the frequency of recurring intermarriage cannot reliably be calculated.

10. By contrast, men listed as Hoklo were almost certainly raised by their natal families, since Hoklo only rarely gave boys up for adoption.

11. Most people I interviewed were between 70 and 85 (though they ranged between 60 and 95), and most had married between 18 and 25. Thus, my figures for the generation of people I interviewed concentrate on marriages that occurred between 1925 and 1947, and figures for their parents' and grandparents' generation concentrate on marriages that occurred roughly between 1875 and 1925.

12. I classified a person as known Hoklo only if the interview subject knew for certain that the person's mother had bound feet—the local marker of Hoklo identity. If the interview subject was certain that a person's mother did not have bound feet, then he or she was classified as plains Aborigine. If the interview subject was uncertain whether a person's mother had bound feet, then that person was classified as having unknown or mixed ancestry. People known to have one socially Hoklo parent and one plains Aborigines parent were also included in the mixed or unknown category. For children adopted as infants, I used the bound foot status of the adoptive mother to classify the child (as discussed later in the text). This method probably yields an overestimate of people classified as plains Aborigine. A person whose mother was plains Aborigine and whose father was Hoklo might be classified as plains Aborigine because the interview subject would not necessarily be certain that the Hoklo father's mother had bound feet. Also, Hoklo men who married uxorilocally would probably not be remembered as Hoklo after two or three generations.

13. Cultural meaning is relevant only insofar as it correlates to social experience. As we shall see, people in Toushe, Jibeishua, and Longtian accepted that not binding women's feet made them less than Han, made them "savages." The acceptance of this categorization does indicate an acceptance of the cultural meaning of footbinding, but I suggest that this acceptance of meaning followed people's social experience of discrimination. There is evidence (which I discuss later in this section) that changes in meanings often followed changes in practices, and I suggest that it may be a general pattern.

14. In late imperial China, Taiwan and the southeastern coast of the Chinese mainland were characterized by a strong petty capitalist mode of production and a relatively weak state tributary mode of production (Gates 1996a:73). Although Qing-period Aborigines participated in the tributary mode of production by paying taxes, they did not fully participate in the petty capitalist mode of production until they became involved in commercial agriculture.

15. Pan (1989a, 1989b, 1994) suggests that migrations of several different Aborigine villages from the plains (Xiaolong, Madou, Xingang) joined a preceding group (Dawulong) in one of my field sites (Toushe), while a second of my field sites (Jibeishua) was populated largely in a single migration (from Xiaolong). The Dutch names for these villages were Sinkan (Xingang), Soulang (Xiaolong), Mattau (Madou), and Tevorang (Dawulong).

16. Following a phonological evaluation of Toushe, Jibeishua, Longtian, and Danei, David Prager Branner concluded that all use the common Tainan accent of Taiwanese, which is part of the greater Zhangzhou-style Minnan Chinese found in Taiwan and part of Fujian (Branner 1995: personal communication; see also Branner 1990, Brown 1995:375). There is no linguistic analysis of the Minnan used in this area during the early 1900s.

17. Although they are commonly referred to as "dialects," there are seven or eight Chinese languages which are mutually unintelligible (e.g., Ramsey 1987, Norman 1988) in the way that Romance languages are mutually unintelligible— a native speaker of one language might understand a few words of another language here and there, but that is all. The Austronesian languages spoken by Aborigines in Taiwan are in a different language family than Chinese languages, making Chinese and Austronesian languages as mutually unintelligible as, for example, German and Arabic.

18. In Minnan, *peh* is commonly used to indicate the vernacular or even secret languages (see, for example, Douglas 1899:364), and *a* is a diminutive; *oe* means "speech;" and *kin-chiu* is clearly "banana," although it is not clear which character represents *kin* (D. Branner 1995: personal communication). Thus, *kin-chiu peh-a-oe* can be translated as "banana slang." The rules for generating banana slang are similar to the rules for generating words in the "secret" language of pig latin used by American children. Linguist Paul Li (1985b) has described banana slang, which he learned as a child in another part of Taiwan (see also Y. R. Chao 1931 and Branner's analysis presented in Brown 1995:375–78). A few of the "Austronesian" words elicited by Japanese linguists around 1900 were actually banana slang (see the word lists in Tsuchida et. al. 1991).

19. Dessication and above-surface preservation appear to have ended by 1685, based on Lin Qiangguang's report (translated in Thompson 1964:181). Imperial Censor Huang Shujing reported a wide variety of funerary and burial practices among Aborigines in Taiwan in 1722, but in the core-area villages and some villages north and west of there—including what I believe to be present-day Toushe, Jibeishua, and Longtian—the custom was to "encoffin" the corpse (in a coffin or a large pottery jar) inside a separate burial hut for a year in the core area, for three months in areas north of the core, and for one month in areas west of the core (Thompson 1969:54, 60–61, 76).

20. In the ethnological literature, postmarital residence is generally referred

to under the heading of different types of marriages, because they correspond to different types of marriage rights and rites. I speak of these differences in terms of residence because the historical information (e.g., from Huang Shujing) generally describes residence not marital rights. Thus, we have Qing-period documentary evidence about when postmarital residence changed but not when marital rights changed.

21. I think it likely that the Dutch did not have a preference with regard to postmarital residence, given that I have not found any preference recorded by the Dutch, that the Netherlands fall into the neolocal area of Europe, and that Dutch men who married Aborigine women lived in or near their wives' natal villages (e.g., Campbell 1903:85, 101, 179, 324).

22. Chuang and Wolf use first marriages because they are interested in minor marriages, a virilocal form of marriage that only occurs with first marriages. Since I am interested in postmarital residence, I include both first marriages and later marriages in my figures.

23. Chuang and Wolf work from a computerized database of the Japanese-period household registers. At the time of their publication, the database was configured in such a way that it did not allow ethnic classification as a basis of analysis below the village level (Arthur P. Wolf 1995: personal communication). According to my manual count, 28.6 percent of the people in Toushe were categorized as Han in the 1905–10 household registers (see table 1). Most of the Han lived in a single Han satellite settlement, where many of the women had bound feet—a characteristic which local people accepted as marking Han identity. However, by Chuang and Wolf's categorization, these Han people's predominantly virilocal marriages show up in the "Aborigine" category, thus reducing the apparent frequency of uxorilocal marriages among "Aborigines." Such uniform categorizations of broad areas are frequent in the literature—for example, the categorization by administrative units in Pasternak (1985: table 13.3) and by prefecture in Shepherd (1989, figure 8)—even though lumping together such broad categories can mask considerable variation.

24. In northern Taiwan, virilocal remarriage for widows was viewed by Hoklo people with great scorn (e.g., Wolf and Huang 1980:227–28).

25. There may have been other children who died as infants or juveniles, or who lived but married out of the village before the Japanese household registers opened and before the people I interviewed were born.

26. Two of the men (one Hoklo and one plains Aborigine) were dead by the time the Japanese began the household registers. I inferred their ethnic classification from their children's listings, based on the rule used by the Japanese government classifying an individual by his or her biological father's classification. However, for the man presumed Hoklo, note that the married-in Han wife of one of his grandsons reported him to me as Aborigine, not Hoklo. Note also the periodic "mistakes" (in terms of the Japanese rule) in classifications in the register (ethnic registration is indicated in figure 6). Thus, it is not clear whether the grandson's wife made a false assumption or whether the household register was wrong.

27. The same pattern also obtained in Chungshe, a village in southern Taiwan which Pasternak (1972, 1983, 1985) describes as Hoklo. Elsewhere (Brown

1995:235–42), I suggest that Chungshe—like Toushe, Jibeishua, and Longtian—may have been considered Aborigine in the early 1900s and only recently taken on a Hoklo identity.

28. The link between surname and property inheritance was not as solid in Hoklo areas near Toushe as it apparently was in Hoklo areas of Haishan (Brown 1995:360–61). Stevan Harrell (personal communication, 2000) points out that there was also a loose correlation between property and surname in Ploughshare, the Haishan village where he conducted field research in the 1970s (see Harrell 1982). It would be interesting to ask whether Ploughshare had some Aborigine influence, since it is located in a valley where John Shepherd (1993:12) has found contracts from 1778 and 1816 in which plains Aborigines sold land rights to Han.

29. I use data on adopted children who were in the same generation as the people I interviewed not only because the time period corresponds, but also because the people I interviewed were more likely to know if their siblings were adopted (or given up for adoption) than if their parents or grandparents were.

30. Why did families in Toushe adopt daughters at a rate so much higher than that of Jibeishua, Longtian, or even the Haishan Hoklo? I have no mortality figures by village, but given the greater poverty and very large number of premature deaths reported there, especially for boys and men, my impression is that it probably had a higher child mortality rate. In an area where adoptions are linked to the loss of a child, we should expect higher adoption rates with higher mortality rates. Some scholars (e.g., Tsuchida et al. 1991, Pan 1989a, 1989b, 1994) suggest that the Aborigine heritage of Toushe is different from that of Jibeishua and Longtian, so the different adoption rates might reflect a different valuation of daughters and women. My impression, however, is that women were more highly valued in Jibeishua than in Toushe, so I do not think that this cultural explanation of the frequency difference is as likely as the demographic explanation.

31. Although others (e.g., Wolf and Huang 1980:242 ff., Pasternak 1985:122) have reported "leading in" a son (i.e., causing the adoptive mother to give birth to a boy) as a frequent motive in the adoption of girls, only two people of all those I interviewed (including Hoklo in Toushe, Jibeishua, Longtian, and Danei) mentioned it as a motive for adoption.

32. I found several cases of marriages between stepsiblings—where both husband and wife were remarrying and both had children from their first marriages, they would often have one child from each first marriage marry, especially where there was property involved (e.g., Brown 1995:369).

33. Betel "nut" is the seed of the palm, *Areca catechu*, which is chewed as a stimulant in the Malaysian archipelago, Taiwan, and some other parts of Southeast Asia, in combination with lime (calcium oxide, not the citrus fruit) and leaves of the betel pepper plant, *Piper betle*. This combination produces a red liquid which stains the teeth, lips, and gums. Like a tobacco chaw, a betel chaw is not swallowed; it is chewed for a time, then spit out. The earliest description I have found of a betel chaw in Taiwan is from 1771 (translated in Campbell 1903:525).

34. According to one Toushe man, however, the reason why a lot of women in his grandparents' generation smoked tobacco, drank mijiu, and chewed betel

but women in his own generation did not was that the Japanese said it was un-
healthy. While the Japanese may indeed have discouraged such practices, they
did not *enforce* the end of these practices as they did with footbinding, so I think
the decreasing frequency of these practices is more related to identity (as I discuss further in the text).

35. I knew of only two women who chewed betel while I was there. Both were
spirit mediums for an Aborigine deity who accepted betel chaws as offerings.

36. Shepherd (1993:385) suggests that the "marking of burial sites of parents with gravestones in the [Han] Chinese style" occurred very early, citing the
marked "graves of prominent tribal leaders from 1806 and later." The examples
which Shepherd cites are for Aborigine tribal leaders, who probably had more
interaction with Han and may even have had a Han son-in-law or two. In the
communities where I interviewed, these examples do not represent the practices
of most residents even in the early 1900s.

37. Shepherd's (1993:385) report of prominent tribal leaders having gravestones would lead one to expect that Grandfather Wa had one. He was prominent, wealthy, and had several uxorilocally married Han sons-in-law. One family member did claim that Grandfather Wa's grave had once had a marker and
that it had been stolen, but other reports suggest that there may not have been
any marker at all.

38. Seven people out of the twenty-nine interviewed in Jibeishua, and two
out of the fifteen interviewed in Longtian, reported seeing a marked grave. Unfortunately, I did not ask this question systematically in Toushe because I did not
think to ask about gravestones until the Qingming festival, when I saw the local
cemetery, after I had completed my interviews in Toushe.

39. Hoklo worshiped ancestors, providing regular offerings of incense, food,
and spirit money. Many Hoklo believed that ancestors supernaturally interceded
in their lives, positively when properly propitiated and negatively when neglected.
Ghosts were also worshiped, symbolically bought off from harming the living.
(There are many fine works on Taiwanese folk religion, e.g., Ahern 1973, Wolf
1974a and b, Weller 1987, Sangren 1987. See also chapter 5.)

40. In Toushe, a few older residents suggested that the deity may have once
been called A-li Bu, but people generally referred to the deity as Thai Tsoo. Only
one ritual specialist there regularly used the name Lau Kun. In Jibeishua—although
many of the small A-li Bu vases which people keep in their homes have "Tai Shang
Li Lao Jun" inscribed on one side and "An Zu Da Gongjie Ali Mu" on the other—
I never heard anyone refer to A-li Bu as (Li) Lau Kun. An Zu is a different, male,
deity, unique to Jibeishua, called An Tsoo in Taiwanese. In Longtian, older residents who talked with me about their Aborigine heritage generally called the deity Thai Tsoo, their children generally referred to A-li Tsoo, and recent immigrants
to Longtian generally referred to Lau Kun.

41. The introduction of Lao Zi's name for a female Aborigine deity has had
extremely interesting ramifications, including a growing uncertainty across the
generations as to the gender of the local deity (and one set of surprised pilgrims
from Taibei who were touring Daoist temples islandwide). The vast majority of
the elders I interviewed, as well as the ritual specialists, agreed that this deity,
however named, is female; thus, I refer to the deity as female.

42. The religious practices of Ali Zu, as she is generally referred to in the literature, have been the object of anthropological and, more recently, popular attention and thus are more fully described elsewhere. See, for example, Liu Pin-hsiung (1987[1962]), Pan Inghai (1989a, 1989b, 1994), Shepherd (1986), Shi Wanshou (1990), Brown (1995: chapter 6), Yan and Liao (1988), and Duan (1992). Shepherd (1986:30), following Liu (1987 [1962]:23, 28, 30–31, 58), accepts Thai Tsoo and A-li Bu (and A-li Tsoo) as alternate names of the same deity, in spite of variation in worship. Pan (1989a:189–93, 1994:243–47) argues that the deities are different. My own data indicate that 1990s A-li Tsoo worship in Longtian is historically derived from Thai Tsoo worship in Toushe but are ambiguous regarding Toushe and Jibeishua religious practices (Brown 1995:256–62).

43. Unlike in the West, where Christianity insisted on orthodoxy (a standard set of *beliefs*), orthopraxy—a standard set of *practices*—was emphasized in late imperial China (Watson 1988) and continued in Japanese-period Taiwan. It was important to worship one's ancestors—provide certain offerings and observe certain rites—but no one cared whether people believed that those ancestors could really act to affect their lives. Thus, even though many Hoklo have always been agnostic, ancestor worship was still commonly practiced.

44. Footbinding constituted the border locally at least, where there were no Hakka. Although they were Han, Hakka did not practice footbinding. I do not know what, if anything, constituted the boundary in Hakka areas, and I fear that we are rapidly losing any opportunity to know, since there are fewer and fewer people old enough to remember when Hoklo women in Taiwan had bound feet. Intriguingly, Jerry Norman (1989 [1986], 1988b) suggests on the basis of linguistic evidence that the Hakka are sinicized She—the She are a non-Han group in Fujian and Guangdong. In other words, it appears that the Hakka are short-route Han. If Norman is correct, it means that the absence of footbinding may be a more general historical marker of non-Han ancestry.

45. The Japanese colonial government intially discouraged footbinding in 1905, apparently because it considered footbinding barbaric, but with little effect. More importantly, however, the practice interfered with their economic plans for the colony of Taiwan, because it kept women from many types of heavy labor. Thus, the colonial government instituted a prohibition on the practice in 1915. One Hoklo woman who married into Toushe—the first Hoklo woman to do so, in fact—told me that her mother had had bound feet but that the Japanese had insisted her mother unbind them so that she could work in the fields. People I interviewed in Danei whose mothers had had their feet unbound by the Japanese also reported that the Japanese explicitly stated they were unbinding women's feet so that women could work in the fields.

46. Although dictionaries translate "po" as "woman" or even "wife," the term was used in Toushe, Jibeishua and Longtian to refer to women old enough to be grandmothers.

47. I do not give numbers for children's generation (except in Toushe) because, after discovering that virtually all marriages in the children's generation were virilocal, I did not systematically ask about marriages of children, in order to use the interview time for other subjects.

48. Since the data for women's marriages outside the study communities are from reports of the marriages of siblings, I consider them fairly reliable.

49. A number of sources (e.g., Shi 1990:25, 90) refer to the spirit mediums for the Aborigine deity, even the man in Toushe, with the feminine term *ang-i* (T., "witch"), an exclusively female category of spirit medium in the Han folk religion who communicate with the dead (thus with ghosts, not deities). On one occasion, I referred to the Jibeishua spirit medium for the Aborigine deity A-li Bu as *ang-i* in her presence, and she informed me that she is a *tang-ki*—the male category of spirit medium who serve as oracles for temple deities—not an *ang-i*. Moreover, local people in these communities call the spirit mediums for the Aborigine deity *tang-ki*.

50. Strippers at weddings did not remove all clothing; they stripped to bikini tops and G-strings.

51. Hoklo have been reported to follow such details of the ancestral cult as tomb-sweeping only for ancestors whom the senior generation remembers (e.g., Groot 1897:1061 and Freeman 1966:120, but see Ahern 1973:166).

52. "Han folk religion" refers broadly to aspects of folk religion shared across regional Han varieties, "Taiwanese folk religion" refers to the Han folk religion as practiced in Taiwan, and "Hoklo folk religion" refers to the folk religion as practiced by Hoklo. Nevertheless, all these forms are broadly understandable to Han who participate in them. (Han in the PRC often do not participate in the folk religion any more.)

53. Even the name is more Han-like. "Thai Tsoo" is an entirely (Minnan) Chinese term, and it is commonly used for other figures of worship in Han folk religion and ancestor worship. "A-li" is a Minnanized derivation of an Austronesian term and has no Han equivalent. "Bu" is the Minnan word for "mother."

54. Pan (1989a:175) places the transition to male spirit mediums in the nineteenth century. Reconstructing the historical sequence of previous female spirit mediums was difficult, since people often did not know or remember women's surnames. To further complicate matters, several women spirit mediums married men with the same surname as the maiden name of the earliest recalled female spirit medium. I conflated two of the female spirit mediums until the woman whom the last female spirit medium wanted to train as her successor (whom I call Lim Mui-moe, and discuss further in the text) explicitly corrected me. Based on her correction, I place the transition to male spirit mediums for the main temple in the early twentieth century.

55. Only a few Toushe villagers reported the use of "A-li Bu" by women spirit mediums there, and others did not remember that name being used in Toushe. Such a change would constitute another move toward a Hoklo cultural model.

56. When Thai Tsoo worship was revived in Longtian in the 1950s by a woman who married from Toushe into Longtian with help from ritual specialists from Toushe, the new female spirit medium also drank pig blood and ate raw pig. The young woman who was spirit medium in Longtian in 1991–92, however, never consumed raw pig, even though she and her father (whose mother was from Jibeishua) were also instructed in Thai Tsoo worship by Toushe ritual specialists.

57. I thank Rob Weller for pointing out the similarity to Di Ji Zu.

58. The man was visiting the village to photograph an annual ceremony at one of the subsidiary shrines *(ying)*. After the conclusion of the ceremony, he, several villagers, and I chatted. One villager asked the photographer point blank if he was a member of the DPP (Democratic Progressive Party), which in 1992 supported Taiwan's declaring itself independent of China. In response, the photographer denied that he belonged to the DPP but was nevertheless informed that Jibeishua was GMD (Nationalist) not DPP. (This statement accurately reflected the reported Jibeishua majority vote in the December 1991 elections.) Conversation virtually stopped after that exchange, and the photographer left the village shortly afterwards.

59. By contrast, visibly Western anthropologists in Taiwan are usually more likely to be asked whether they are missionaries than whether they are reporters.

CHAPTER 4. "HAVING A WIFE
IS BETTER THAN HAVING A GOD"

1. Parts of this chapter were originally published in Brown (1996b).

2. Women and families were allowed to migrate in 1732–40, 1746–48, 1760–61, and again after 1788.

3. Individual descendants of southwestern plains Aborigines may have taken the short route—taking on a Han identity before taking on most of Han culture—after the early Qing period. Certainly, the short-route process occurred later in northern, eastern, and mountainous central Taiwan, where extensive contact with Han came later as well. Nevertheless, I believe that the bulk of short-route identity change in southwestern Taiwan, around the core area of Han immigration, occurred by the early Qing period.

4. Between 1636 and 1649, Han migration to Taiwan was both high and encouraged by the Dutch, in large part because Han farmers would produce agricultural surpluses for taxation and export, which Aborigines would not (see chapter 2). Most Chinese immigrants went to Taiwan on smaller Chinese fishing and trading ships (Hsu 1980a:16; Shepherd 1993:85). "An estimated 100 to 400 Chinese ships left the mainland for the island annually after 1625. After 1636, more junks [ships] arrived as a result of the efforts of Su Ming-kang [Su Minggang, "Captain China" at the Dutch colony at Batavia], the peace in the straits, and the subjugation of the [A]borigines near Tainan. The Chinese ships sailing to Taiwan in 1637, for example, numbered 491 (188 trading junks and 303 fishing boats). . . . In 1642, despite the company's complaint that its trade with China was declining and Chinese fishing activities were slackening, approximately two hundred Fukienese [Fujianese] fishing boats still sailed to the island. Six years later, some seven or eight thousand famine-stricken Chinese on the coast of Fukien [Fujian] went to Taiwan, but most of them returned after the famine was over. After Kuo Huai-I's [Guo Huaiyi's] revolt in 1652, however, fewer Chinese arrived" (Hsu 1980a:16–17). Although the Dutch themselves transported few Chinese farmers to Taiwan, they did other things to encourage migration. In 1649, "[i]n order to encourage Chinese colonists to settle their families in Taiwan, anyone who brought a woman from the mainland with him was granted exemption

from the poll-tax for three persons" (Huber 1990:274n25). However, in 1652, after the Guo Huaiyi rebellion, the Dutch reversed this position, including women in the poll tax (Huber 1990:289).

5. Hsu Wen-hsiung (1980a:17) projects this figure to 40,000–50,000 Han men, women, and children, while Shepherd (1993:86) estimates 35,000–50,000. These estimates assume that most of the Han men have wives and that all those wives are Han.

6. I assume that none of the soldiers were women. Calculation: (30,000 + 7,000) migrants - (20,000 + 4,000) soldiers = 13,000 women. See chapter 2 for sources of the estimated numbers of soldiers and migrants.

7. The assumption that each woman represents one marriage allows us to be confident that we have not underestimated the number of married men, because it is likely that some of the women were polygamously married and that some were unmarried relatives of other immigrants. Calculation: 24,000 soldiers - 13,000 married men = 11,000 unmarried men.

8. Calculations: 50 percent × (24,000 immigrant soldiers - 6,000 soldiers estimated to have died) = 9,000 soldiers; 0.60 × (24,000 - 6,000) = 10,800.

9. Calculations: 11,000 unmarried men who arrived in 1661 and 1664 - 10,800 men still unmarried in 1668 (the second percent estimate calculated above) = 200 men who found wives; 11,000 - 9,000 (the first percent estimate calculated above) = 2,000.

10. However, wealthy Han merchants such as Su Minggang (see note 4, this chapter) cooperated with the Dutch and thus must have had at least some political leverage.

11. Ostensibly, this claim would be legitimate only in the case of patrilineal descendants of intermarriage. However, claims by matrilineal descendants may also have been acceptable. In the nineteenth and twentieth centuries, Hoklo in Fujian and Taiwan often assigned one or more children of uxorilocal marriages the mother's patrilineally derived surname, in cases where there were no sons to carry on the surname. If this practice was as commonly accepted in Fujian in the seventeenth century as it was in the nineteenth century, then matrilineal descendants of mixed marriages might also have been able to claim a Han surname with some legitimacy in the eyes of Hoklo immigrants, because Han immigrant men in Taiwan could easily be argued to have married uxorilocally.

12. Although the Qing imperial family and a substantial proportion of the highest levels of the ruling elite were Manchu not Han, nevertheless the Qing dynasty adopted Confucian principles to legitimate its rule. Moreover, they preserved the examination system which required candidates to have a classical Confucian education in order to achieve bureaucratic office. Thus, it is not unreasonable to expect Qing officials—whether Han or Manchu—to have accepted Han patrilineal, patriarchal cultural assumptions that were morally sanctioned by Confucian teachings.

13. Because a figure for taxable heads does not include people who were not subject to a head tax, such as women and children, it is not clear how many people present in the population and definitely categorized as "Aborigine" were left out of the taxable head figure. Thus, household figures provide a more conservative estimate. I thank John Shepherd for suggesting use of this estimate. Note, how-

ever, that this calculation also assumes that everyone in a household had the same identity.

14. This conclusion is based on Brown (1990), which analyzes data from Blackwell et al. (1969), Dewey et al. (1967), Fong (1974), Huang (1970), Ikemoto et al. (1966), Ting-chien Lee et al. (1963), Ming-ta Lee et al. (1970), Lin (1975), Motulsky et al. (1965), Nakajima et al. (1967), and Nakajima et al. (1971).

15. The Japanese captain hoped that these villagers would present Taiwan as a gift to the Japanese shogun. It was in response to Dutch retaliation for this trip that the people of Xingang fled in 1629 (cf. Shepherd 1993:52).

16. By contrast, Shepherd (1993:84) interprets one such report (Campbell 1903:201–202) as evidence that "[Han] Chinese imperviousness to the [Christian] message of salvation rankled the missionaries and embarrassed them in front of the [A]borigines."

17. The Zheng-period southwestern plain is not the only time and place in which a Han identity was taken on in a single generation, however. During the nineteenth century, descendants of intermarrying Han and plains Aborigines in the Puli basin of central Taiwan adopted a Han identity within twenty years (Hsieh 1979b:45).

18. Biological reproduction can certainly occur outside of marriage, and some Han men probably did father children in the biological sense without getting married. Such children would have continued a man's biological line but not carried his surname, and Han thought of descent in terms of patrilineal surnames (cf. Ebrey 1996). Moreover, I believe that the adult population imbalance was a limiting factor that greatly reduced the frequency of extramarital reproduction because many men simply did not have the opportunity.

19. Huang Shujing remarked on sexual license in plains and mountain Aborigine villages in 1722 (Thompson 1969:54, 60, 67–68, 76, 84, 87, 94, 102, 110, 119–20, 137). Shepherd (1993:116, 288, 386, 474n41) cites sources which refer to Han men seeking sexual favors of Aborigine women; in some cases, these advances are reported to have led to Aborigine revolts (see chapter 2 and Thompson 1964:195–96).

20. I consider this polyandry, not merely licentiousness, because Huang also noted that in many Aborigine groups, grooms' families gave gifts to the brides' families (Thompson 1969:54, 60, 68, 76, 83, 87, 94, 101, 141). Moreover, an 1869 contract for a polyandrous marriage in Taiwan (translated in Ebrey 1981:235) provides further evidence of polyandry in the cultural repertoire, although the ethnic identity of the participants is not stated. Gates (1987:192) also provides an interesting report of several cases of polyandry in twentieth-century Taiwan.

21. In the late seventeenth century, a group of Siraya plains Aborigines reportedly migrated from the Tainan area east to the foothills, then further south in the foothills, and finally in the early 1700s further into the mountains (Ferrell 1971:225). In the Zheng period, two tribes near Tainan moved a few miles east toward the foothills when a Zheng military colony (village) was established near their original village sites (Shepherd 1993:94, 469n23). Under the Qing, Han harassment also caused Aborigines to migrate (Shepherd 1993:242, Pickering

1898:116). Starting in the 1750s, people from Xingang and other Aborigine villages near present-day Tainan established "colonies" in the foothills (Pickering 1898:116, Shepherd 1993:388). In 1804, over 1,000 one plains Aborigines from ten villages migrated to Yilan (Hsu 1980:73, Shepherd 1993:357–58). Between 1823 and 1831, in the largest and best known of the migrations, plains Aborigines used Confucian rhetoric in their petition for Qing permission to settle the Puli basin and to exclude Han migration there (Hsieh 1979a, 1979b; Shepherd 1993:391–93).

22. Even if they were going to already established Aborigine villages, it is unlikely that a large group of young, unmarried men would have been welcomed by the men of that village.

23. As discussed in chapter 2, the so-called "regional" variation in China actually refers to mutually unintelligible language differences, as well as other cultural differences. For example, differences between Hoklo and Hakka (both of whom live in Taiwan as well as China) would be glossed as "regional" Han variation in China. The variation among Hoklo in Taiwan is not so great, however. Language differences, for example, are mutually intelligible "accent" differences and reflect linguistic differences between the Minnan language as spoken in Zhangzhou and Minnan as spoken in Quanzhou, both of which are in Fujian (David Prager Branner, 1995, personal communication; cf. Branner 1990).

24. There were probably additional factors contributing to this difference. The census data are not limited to women born between 1891 and 1900, some women classified as Hoklo in the registers had no doubt been adopted as infants and raised by Aborigines, and some Hakka women whose patrilineal ancestors came from Fujian are also included in this figure.

25. Hsieh (1979b) and Yuan (1971) also discuss the importance of intermarriage to cultural change in Taiwan, in the cases of plains Aborigines in the Puli basin moving toward a Han cultural model and of Han immigrants on the east coast moving toward an Ami Aborigine model, respectively.

26. Aborigine customs may also be passed in this way. Here I am considering the transmission of a Han custom. Also, while it is often the wife or daughter-in-law who performs the ritual obeisances, it is not exclusively a female practice. I presume that in the household of a Han husband and Aborigine wife, the Han husband would be the primary performer of these obeisances.

27. The binding of a girl's feet was usually carried out by her mother or grandmother (e.g., Levy 1967, 26, 224, 234, 246, 247, 249–51; Blake 1994:682).

28. Tannen's (1982) work on continuities with Greek culture among English-speaking Greek Americans provides examples of a similar process in a different context.

29. By contrast, a Qing official who claimed that earlier Qing officials had erred in their classifications would have initiated legal review and possible prosecution of the earlier officials responsible. In the meantime, some of those officials would likely have moved up to more powerful positions in the imperial bureaucracy, so most officials would not want to stir up trouble by making such a claim, even if they were persuaded that an error had been made (cf. Kuhn's [1990: 230–232] discussion of the ordinary practices of average bureaucrats).

CHAPTER 5. "THEY CAME WITH
THEIR HANDS TIED BEHIND THEIR BACKS"

1. Parts of this chapter were originally published in Brown (2001b) and Brown (2002).

2. Today, this region is part of the Enshi Tujia-Miao Autonomous Prefecture, of which Enshi City is the capital. The prefecture was called the Exi Tujia-Miao Autonomous Prefecture from 1983 to 1993, drawing on classical and historical references to western Hubei as Exi. For a more general discussion of Tujia, see Dong, Brown, and Wu (2002).

3. The term *tujia* has two distinct but related meanings which I distinguish by capitalization: "tujia" is the older term, meaning "locals"; "Tujia" is the more recent term, meaning a specific officially recognized ethnic group.

4. In 1995–96, I conducted research with Chinese colleagues. In five counties in the Enshi Tujia-Miao Autonomous Prefecture in Hubei and in two counties with Tujia populations in Hunan, we met with local officials, collected books, were accompanied to museums and sites of ethnohistorical interest, and interviewed one or two people—often retired officials or scholars—familiar with local history. Near Enshi City, we interviewed at three villages and selected one, to which I give the pseudonym Wucun (Fifth Village), where we conducted more in-depth research. We lived there for two months, interviewing 33 village people who were not officials, participating in and observing mortuary rituals, the lunar New Year's festivities, and marriage rituals, and visiting local officials. We also interviewed five ritual specialists, three of whom lived outside the village. People in the Enshi City area spoke a local *(tu)* version of Southwest Mandarin Chinese.

5. In Guangdong, Fujian, and Taiwan, "Kejia" (lit., guest families) refers to a Han regional variety and language, called Hakka in that language. In Enshi, the term is not associated with that Han group or language in any way. It simply means "outsiders."

6. The term *minzu* is officially translated into English as "nationalities" in the PRC, due to the eventual equation of the term with the Soviet Russian term *natsionalnost*. See Harrell (1996b:276–77) for a discussion of the ambiguities in the term.

7. I am simplifying somewhat here. A number of different minzu were identified in this mountainous region, including the Miao and Dong. I did not visit Miao areas, so I do not know how people still classified as Miao thought of themselves before 1949.

8. Huang and Shi (1995: 187) and Tian (1994:178) give more complete versions of this story and its influence on the identification of the Tujia. Huang and Shi do not mention Zhou Enlai's role in the story at all, and Tian does so only obliquely. Many scholars and officials I talked with in Hubei and Hunan, however, mentioned Zhou by name and attributed the identification of the Tujia as a separate minzu from the Miao to his intervention.

9. In Hunan, in 1996, my colleagues and I talked with two men in their sixties who could speak the Tujia language, which they reported was used as a native language in only one remote township *(xiang)*. Elsewhere in Hunan and

Hubei, Tujia exclusively speak a local form of Southwest Mandarin. Little work has been done on the Tujia language (but see Shih 2001:75, 76); it is only broadly classified, as a remote language on the Tibetan side of the Sino-Tibetan language family (Liu 1989:4). For a discussion of Tujia in Hunan Province, see Tian (1994), Dong (1996, 1999), Shih (2001), and Sutton (2001).

10. In China, the "Party" refers to the Chinese Communist Party (CCP), which has different administrative levels—central, provincial, prefectural, and so on—just like the government.

11. Reportedly, so many surnames were Tujia because of dialect differences in the past. One official explained that at the time names were being recorded—probably in the Tang, Song, and Yuan dynasties—if Han ran into two people speaking different Tujia dialects but saying the same name, they recorded them as two different surnames—that is, as two different written characters. Similarly, speakers of different Chinese languages (such as Minnan and Mandarin) might record the same Tujia name with different characters.

12. According to Huang and Shi (1995:191), Tujia were 36.44 percent of the Enshi population in 1982. My sources in Enshi told me that the figure was 37.2 percent. This difference may result from what each considered the "Enshi area" in 1982, since Enshi was not an autonomous prefecture then.

13. There are discrepancies between government records and the national identity cards of individuals (see Brown 2002). I am sure that there are further discrepancies between what people's identity cards said and what they sometimes reported to me and my colleagues in interviews. For the sake of consistency, and because my information on government records was very limited, all mention of official registration in the text is based on a combination of what people self-reported and what was listed on their identity cards (most people were willing to show me their identity cards).

14. Although I have recorded the saying here as it was said to me, with the polite term *bendi ren,* I believe that the original saying used the pejorative term *tumanzi* for "locals."

15. Lei (1994) also links sinicizing cultural changes among Tujia and their ancestors to attempts to gain prestige.

16. One example of women's low status before 1949 is that many daughters were never named. Some were called "little sister" *(xiaomei),* some "dead branch" *(yatou).* One woman I interviewed spoke highly of Western missionaries who came to the area with the Nationalists because they always gave proper names to girls in their orphanage.

17. Elsewhere (Brown 2002), I discuss discrepancies *which local officials knew about* between classifications listed in local government records and those listed on individuals' identity cards. I suggest these discrepancies indicate that local officials managed the likely concerns of ordinary individuals to avoid unwanted state attention to local ethnic consciousness as Han.

18. The Ba were a multiethnic confederation of peoples in the first millennium B.C.E.

19. For differing scholarly views on whether the Ba are the primary ancestor of the Tujia, see Dong (1999) and Huang Baiquan (1999). I thank Wu Xu for bringing this debate to my attention.

20. I use a twenty-year generation length because one elderly Wucun woman told me that she got her period when she was 14 years old and that, at the time, most girls did. Unfortunately, I was not able to get systematic information about menses for the elderly women I interviewed in Wucun.

21. This man was the only person I interviewed who claimed that officials had come to his home to discuss his ethnic classification. In doing so, he claimed a number of very unlikely things: he said the officials came in the 1950s, he referred to them as from the *minwei*—the government office which took over the area in 1984—and he claimed that he had said he was Han *(da hanzu)* but the officials wanted to increase the number of Tujia and told him he was Tujia. (Before 1984, the local government was run by the *tongzhan bu,* a branch of the Communist Party.)

22. "Tumanzi" is a very disparaging term. Very few people I spoke with used it. It combines *"tu,"* which can mean "earth" or "local" or "coarse," with *"man,"* which means non-Han barbarians. I translate "tumanzi" as "local trash" to convey the degree to which the term was a slur.

23. People reported this migration as variously five or six generations before they were born. Most people I interviewed were born between 1910 and 1930. Thus, assuming a twenty-year generation length, I estimate the migration occurred between 1790 and 1830.

24. I translate this man's references to his own surname or clan as "us" and "we" rather than giving a pseudonym, so as not to stigmatize any surname in Enshi. If I use "A" to represent his own surname, he actually said "People used to call the As *(xing* A *de)* local trash. Before 1949, the As (A *xing*) were really crude."

25. In fact, sources on ethnic minorities give lists of traits "characteristic" of Tujia culture and the Tujia people. Some sources (notably Ma 1994 [1989]) but not others (e.g., Liu 1989, Huang and Shi 1995) include cremation and other customs that I never heard of during my field research in Enshi—neither in my travels around the prefecture interviewing people about Tujia culture, nor in my conversations with local officials and scholars familiar with the Tujia. Perhaps cremation was practiced in a Tujia area somewhere in Hunan, Sichuan, or Guizhou, but I think it highly unlikely that it was practiced in Hubei.

26. The gods were represented by a large red sheet of paper or cloth, located high on the wall in the main room, on which was written "Heaven, Earth, King, Family, Teacher are seated here" *(tian di jun qin shi wei).*

27. Scholars at the Hubei Minzu Xueyuan produced a video of such a ritual in the early 1990s. One of the participating wizards *(duangong)* told me that, because the wizards were in their seventies and eighties, they performed the ritual over three days, so the elderly men could take rests, instead of for twenty-four hours straight as it used to be performed. The people in the discussion described in the text agreed that those with tanshen had to have this ritual performed periodically or else family members would become ill, either physically or mentally. By contrast, local scholars explained that this ritual established a family's ancestors as deities, thus apparently viewing tanshen as a family's ancestors. See Lei (1995) and Tian (1995) for further discussion of tanshen.

28. For a further discussion of "becoming Tujia" *(tujiahua),* see Dong (1992:55, 1999).

29. One case of levirate marriage—where a widow marries one of her late husband's brothers—was even reported to me! In some cultures, levirate marriage is required if a widow is still young, but in Han culture elsewhere levirate marriage is strongly prohibited as incestuous. In this particular case, an elderly woman told me that, after a typhoid epidemic decimated the family, her grandmother arranged a marriage between her mother and her father's surviving younger brother whose wife had also died. There were three children from the original marriages who survived the epidemic—herself and two cousins. The voluntary self-report of such a case, with no signs of embarrassment (though much grief), shows underlying beliefs about the relationships between brothers and their wives very different from those of Han elsewhere.

30. The Yi in Panshihua (in Sichuan), for example, practice the funerary rituals described below (Stevan Harrell, personal communication 2000).

31. It is not clear whether (a) the absence of only one of these markers would be sufficient to contraindicate Han identity or (b) the presence of all of them would be sufficient to indicate Han identity in the absence of other cultural elements such as language.

32. See Ebrey (1993) for a translation of Confucian principles at an introductory level and Wolf (1995:215–217) for a discussion of the connections between filial piety, parental authority, and state authority.

33. For a more complete discussion of the Han concept of soul, see Harrell (1979:521–23).

34. While there was an accepted ritual sequence for treatment of the dead and for funerals, there was no commensurate standardization for Han burial practices: "As long as the sealed coffin was removed from the community in the accepted fashion, mourners were free to dispose of the corpse according to local custom" (Watson 1988:16). For example, in Fujian, Guangdong, and Taiwan, secondary burial is practiced. (A specialist exhumes the remains and prepares them for secondary burial by scraping any undecomposed flesh from the bones.) In contrast, secondary burial is not practiced in northern China. In fact, this practice often horrifies northern Han. Some northerners, however, may horrify southern Han by maintaining a sealed coffin above ground for decades until the deceased's spouse dies and they can be buried together (Watson 1988: 15–16).

35. Rubie Watson (1985:106–111) cites a wide range of evidence supporting a general rule that brothers inherited property equally in many parts of China, from late-imperial times through the twentieth century. However, she goes on to document that brothers did not always share equally in Ha Tsuen, New Territories, Hong Kong. In very poor families, younger sons often received no inheritance. Similarly, in very wealthy families, sons of a man's mistresses often received no inheritance. Although these cases break the general rule about sons inheriting property equally, the preference enjoyed by older sons and sons of recognized wives is in accordance with Confucian principles.

36. Locally, people explained a kowtow as a kneeling bow, sometimes with only a single knee on the ground. Elsewhere, a kowtow required not only kneeling but pressing the forehead to the floor.

37. This answer begs the question of whether souls are located in the grave.

These ritual specialists very patiently responded to my questions, but they did not always have answers. At one point, the Daoist priest explained to me that, when he was learning his trade, apprentices were not allowed to question their master; they could only learn what their master taught.

38. Lanshe is performed on or around the lunar date of *shere*, which falls at different places in the lunar calendar each year. In 1996, it fell on March 22, which was the fourth day of the second lunar month in the Year of the Rat. People annually purchase a lunar almanac to know when such dates fall. I was not present for the Qingming tomb-sweeping festival, but it too may not be what Han would expect. One woman reported that her family does not have any daughters so they do not tomb-sweep at all. She informed me that tomb-sweeping "is the responsibility of daughters and sons-in-law" *(shi guniang nuxu de shi)*. For Han elsewhere, tomb-sweeping is a patrilineal responsibility. She also reported that tomb-sweeping is performed for three years on or around *shere*, not during the Qingming festival.

39. In response to my concern about hungry ghosts, this Daoist priest and wizard assured me that there are rites—the Buddhist Ghost Festival rite and parts of some ordinary funerals—devoted to "wild ghosts." See Weller (1987) for an in-depth examination of the Ghost Festival rite.

40. Tomb-sweeping celebrations are held in the bright light of day, even though people are dealing with their own ancestors, perhaps because of the presence of other people's ancestors in cemeteries.

41. Ancestry is probably a good indicator of social experience in societies with little social mobility (Brown n.d.).

CHAPTER 6. THEORY AND THE POLITICS OF REUNIFICATION

1. Anthropologists in the nineteenth and early twentieth centuries were far from unified on how to define culture. In 1952, A. L. Kroeber and Clyde Kluckholn (1952)—two giants of mid-century American anthropology—compiled the anthropological definitions of culture of the previous century and filled 217 pages. Today, in the United States, the discipline of anthropology includes a wide range of researchers—sociocultural anthropologists who study contemporary societies and cultures; linguistic anthropologists who study languages, often in interaction with culture; archaeologists who study historic and prehistoric human societies; biological anthropologists who study human evolution and genetics. The contemporary consensus on ideational cultures is found primarily among sociocultural anthropologists. It has not spread to many of those with interests in evolution, for instance (but see Cronk 1999).

2. Neuropsychological research on numerical abilities supports the idea of such a threshold regarding the perception of countable but not-actually-counted groupings: "numbers *qua* symbols enter into objective relations, and to talk of a subjective scale of *number* is absurd. However, if numbers can be transformed into a mental representation of quantities, and thereafter be treated just like other physical quantities [as several studies suggest], then it is no more absurd to talk of a subjective scale of *numerical magnitude* than to talk of subjective scales of weight, area, etc." (Dehaene 1992:24, emphases in original).

Unfortunately, anthropological inquiries do not generally include information about actual distributions of public representations—for example, how many people in a group actually label themselves as Han. Mass media may provide one means of projecting an idea as "shared" by the majority, regardless of its actual distribution. However, anthropological studies on mass media and "public culture" also do not document the relation between representations in mass media and the distributions of similar representations among individuals in a population. Without empirical evidence on where such a critical mass threshold may lie—at a distribution of 40 percent? 60 percent? 80 percent? at varying distributions?—anthropological designations of a concept as shared or "cultural" must currently be considered arbitrary (Brown 1997).

3. Collectivists often refer to methodological individualists as "positivists," "reductionists," "vulgar materialists," etc. (e.g., Dirks, Eley, and Ortner 1994:36; Comaroff 1985:53, 125–26; cf. Roscoe 1995).

4. For example, Jean Comaroff, whose own analysis (e.g., 1985:54–60) draws strongly on Bourdieu, remarks: "In his effort to correct what he perceives to be a subjectivist bias in prevailing views of human practice, Bourdieu goes so far in the other direction that his actors seem doomed to reproduce their world mindlessly, without its contradictions leaving any mark on their awareness—at least until a crisis (in the form of 'culture contact' or the emergence of class division) initiates a process of overt struggle" (Comaroff 1985:5).

5. These effects have been analyzed in widely varying terms, for example, the practices of everyday life and embodied learning (Bourdieu 1977, 1990), political-economic constraints (Gates 1996a), and evolutionary dynamics operating in the social realm (Boyd and Richerson 1985:187; Durham 1991:181; Brown 1995, n.d.).

6. This theoretical disagreement was so polemical that it caused the Department of Anthropology at Stanford University to split into two departments in 1998—a Department of Cultural and Social Anthropology and a Department of Anthropological Sciences (cf. Gibbs 1998).

7. Sociobiologist E. O. Wilson's infamous comment that "genes hold culture on a leash" is often used to represent biological determinism. However, Wilson (1978:167) allows for some unspecified degree of cultural transcendence: "The leash is very long, but inevitably [ethical] values will be constrained in accordance with their effects on the human gene pool." A more extreme example of biological determinism is David Barash's (1977:293) suggestions that specific cultural ideas and practices—such as a gender double standard on sexual activity—are direct expressions of genetic "whisperings within" (Barash 1979). See Durham (1991:17–20, 156–59) for a criticism of sociobiology from an evolutionary perspective.

Following the work of David Schneider, Sylvia Yanagisako and Jane Collier (1994[1987]:195) provide an equally extreme example, this time of cultural transcendence: "there are no 'facts,' biological or material, that have social consequences and cultural meanings in and of themselves. Sexual intercourse, pregnancy, and parturition are cultural facts, whose form, consequences, and meanings are socially constructed in any society, as are mothering, fathering, judging, ruling, and talking with the gods. Similarly, there are no material 'facts' that can be treated as precultural givens. The consequences and meanings of force are socially constructed, as are those of the means of production or the resources upon which people depend for their living."

8. Theoretically, viewing selection as a culling process implies that the generation of variation in a population and the natural selection of environmentally favored phenotypes are not separate processes (Brown n.d.).

9. Elsewhere, I (Brown 1995, n.d.) use the term "selection" broadly to refer to any culling process that leads to differential transmission of information. However, for clarity's sake, I reserve the use of "natural selection" to refer to the differential transmission of genetic information through the differential reproduction of individuals. I find the concept of a culling process—as opposed to the concept of a replication process used by many evolutionists (e.g., Richerson and Boyd 1992, Flinn 1997)—useful both in understanding natural selection and in examining analogies drawn between natural selection and transmission of nongenetic information.

10. Sahlins began his anthropological career as an evolutionist (e.g., Sahlins and Service 1960), but later in his career moved to a strongly interpretive perspective (e.g., Sahlins 1976a, 1976b).

11. Based on an examination of fertility in relation to age at adoption with some control of confounding variables, Wolf (1995:205) predicts that "where association beginning before age 2 reduces fertility by something more than 40 percent, association beginning after age 3 has no appreciable effect." However, even women adopted before age 2 had total marital fertility rates of around 5 children (Wolf 1995:203–204). Wolf (e.g., 1995:257) attributes this fertility to social, economic, and religious motivations.

12. Nevertheless, among evolutionary perspectives—perspectives which deal with how culture is perpetuated in terms of individual choices—there is a tendency to model transmission as replication, that is, like a "fax line from the public social order to individuals' psyches" (Strauss 1992a:8). This tendency persists in spite of recognition that replication is an inadequate model of social and cultural transmission (e.g., Cronk 1995a, 1995b; Dawkins 1982:112; Sperber 1996: 101–103; *contra* Richerson and Boyd 1992:64; cf. Brown n.d.).

13. Chang (2000) argues that the divergence of Taiwanese and Chinese social experiences began in 1895 and that Taiwanese identity was already very different from Chinese identity by 1945. The specific social experiences of Taiwanese under Japanese colonial rule certainly differed from those of Chinese, but I see strong similarities between Japanese colonial annexation of Taiwan, Han colonial annexation of non-Han areas throughout Chinese imperial history, and even Nationalist solidification of power in Taiwan after 1945. In my view, the sharpest divergence came after the founding of the People's Republic of China in 1949.

References

Ahern, Emily Martin.
   1973. *The Cult of the Dead in a Chinese Village.* Stanford, Calif.: Stanford
   University Press.

Barash, David P.
   1977. *Sociobiology and Behavior.* New York: Esevier.

   1979. *The Whisperings Within: Evolution and the Origins of Human Nature.*
   New York: Harper & Row.

Barth, Fredrik.
   1969. *Ethnic Groups and Boundaries.* Boston: Little, Brown and Company.

Bentley, G. Carter.
   1987. Ethnicity and Practice. *Comparative Studies in Society and History* 29,
   no. 1: 24–25.

   1991. Response to Yelvington. *Comparative Studies in Society and History*
   33, no. 1: 169–75.

Bhabha, Homi.
   1990. Introduction. In *Nation and Narration,* ed. H. K. Bhabha, 1–7. London: Routledge.

Blackwell, R. Q., B.-N. Blackwell, L. Yen, and H-F. Lee.
   1969. Low Incidence of Erythrocyte G-6-P D Deficiency in Aborigines of Taiwan. *Vox Sanginis* 17, no. 4: 310–13.

Blake, C. Fred.
   1994. Foot-binding in Neo-Confucian China and the Appropriation of Female Labor. *Signs: The Journal of Women in Culture and Society* 19, no.
   3: 676–712.

Blussé, Leonard.

1984. Dutch Protestant Missionaries as Protagonists of the Territorial Expansion of the VOC on Formosa. In *Conversion, Competition and Conflict,* ed. Dick Kooiman, Otto van den Muijzenberg, and Peter van der Veer, 155–84. Amsterdam: Free University Press.

1990. Minnan-jen or Cosmopolitan? The Rise of Chen Chih-lung alias Nicolas Iquan. In *Development and Declines of Fukien Province in the Seventeenth and Eighteenth Centuries,* ed. E. B. Vermeer, 245–64. Leiden: E. J. Brill.

Blussé, Leonard and Marius P. H. Roessingh.

1984. A Visit to the Past: Soulang, a Formosan Village Anno 1623. *Archipel* 27: 63–80.

Borchigud, Wurlig.

1996. Transgressing Ethnic and National Boundaries: Contemporary "Inner Mongolian" Identities in China. In *Negotiating Ethnicities in China and Taiwan,* ed. Melissa J. Brown, 160–82. Berkeley: Institute of East Asian Studies, University of California.

Borofsky, Robert.

1994a. Diversity and Divergence Within the Anthropological Community. In *Assessing Cultural Anthropology,* ed. Robert Borofsky, 23–28. New York: McGraw-Hill, Inc.

1994b. Rethinking the Cultural. In *Assessing Cultural Anthropology,* ed. Robert Borofsky, 243–49. New York: McGraw-Hill, Inc.

1997a. Cook, Lono, Obeyesekere, and Sahlins. *Current Anthropology* 38, no. 2: 255–82.

1997b. Aumatangi's Question. Paper presented at the 96th annual meeting of the American Anthropological Association, Washington, D.C., November 19–23, 1997.

Bourdieu, Pierre.

1977. *Outline of a Theory of Practice.* Cambridge: Cambridge University Press.

1990. *The Logic of Practice.* Stanford, Calif.: Stanford University Press.

Boyd, R. and P. J. Richerson.

1985. *Culture and the Evolutionary Process.* Chicago: University of Chicago Press.

Boyer, Pascal.

1998. Cognitive Tracks of Cultural Inheritance: How Evolved Intuitive Ontology Governs Cultural Transmission. *American Anthropologist* 100, no. 4: 876–89.

Branner, David Prager.

1990. The Quanzhou and Zhangzhou Accents in Fujian Minnan. Master's thesis, Department of Asian Languages and Literature, University of Washington.

Brown, Melissa J.
    1990. Issues of Genetic Admixture in Taiwan. Unpublished manuscript.

    1993. Sexuality, Exploitation and Gender Roles in Rural Taiwan. Paper presented at the 92nd annual meeting of the American Anthropological Association, November 17–21, 1993.

    1995. "We Savages Didn't Bind Feet"—The Implications of Cultural Contact and Change in Southwestern Taiwan for an Evolutionary Anthropology. Ph.D. dissertation, Department of Anthropology, University of Washington.

    ed. 1996a. *Negotiating Ethnicities in China and Taiwan.* Berkeley: Institute for East Asian Studies, University of California.

    1996b. On Becoming Chinese. In *Negotiating Ethnicities in China and Taiwan,* ed. Melissa J. Brown, 37–74. Berkeley: Institute of East Asian Studies, University of California.

    1997. Articulating Collectivism and Individualism: Choices at the Border to Han. Paper presented at the 96th annual meeting of the American Anthropological Association, Washington, D.C., November 19–23, 1997.

    1999. Changing Taiwanese Identities: People with Mixed Plains Aborigine and Hokkien Ancestry. Paper presented at the fourth annual Conference on the History and Culture of Taiwan, August 20, 1999.

    2001a. Reconstructing Ethnicity: Recorded and Remembered Identity in Taiwan *Ethnology* 40, no. 2: 153–64.

    2001b. Ethnic Classification and Culture: The Case of the Tujia in Hubei, China. *Asian Ethnicity* 2, no. 1: 55–72.

    2002. Local Government Agency: Manipulating Tujia Identity. *Modern China* 28, no. 3: 362–95.

    2003. The Cultural Impact of a Gendered Social Role: Changing Religious Practices in Taiwan. *Journal of Anthropological Research* 59, no. 1: 47–67.

    n.d. Meaning, Power, Cognition, and Evolution: A Multiple Inheritance Systems Synthesis. Manuscript in progress.

Bruner, Edward M.
    1956. Primary Group Experience and the Processes of Acculturation. *American Anthropologist* 58, no. 4: 605–23.

Buck, John Lossing.
    1937. *Land Utilization in China: A Study of 16,786 Farms in 169 Localities, and 32,256 Farm Families in Twenty-two Provinces in China, 1929–1933.* Nanking: University of Nanking.

Bureau of Statistics.
    1992. *National Conditions of the Republic of China (Summer 1992).* Taibei: Republic of China Executive Yuan, Bureau of Statistics.

Campbell, William.
    1888. *The Gospel of Saint Matthew in Sinkang-Formosan, Dutch, and English,*

282   References

edited from Gravius' edition of 1661. London: Kegan Paul, Trench, Truber and Co., Ltd.

1903. *Formosa Under the Dutch.* London: Kegan Paul.

Cavalli-Sforza, L. L., and F. Cavalli-Sforza.

1995. *The Great Human Diasporas: The History of Diversity and Evolution.* New York: Addison-Wesley Publishing, Inc.

Cavalli-Sforza, L. L., and M. W. Feldman.

1981. *Cultural Transmission and Evolution: A Quantitative Approach.* Princeton: Princeton University Press.

Certeau, Michel de.

1988 (1984). *The Practice of Everyday Life.* Berkeley: University of California Press.

Chai, Winberg, ed.

1999. Relations Between the Chinese Mainland and Taiwan. *Asian Affairs* 26, no. 2: 59–76.

Chang Mao-kuei.

1994. Toward an Understanding of the Shen-chi Wen-ti in Taiwan: Focusing on Changes After Political Liberalization. In *Ethnicity in Taiwan: Social, Historical, and Cultural Perspectives,* ed. Chen Chung-min, Chuang Ying-chang, and Huang Shu-min, 93–150. Taibei: Institute of Ethnology, Academia Sinica.

1996. Review of "Taiwan: National Identity and Democratization." *Bulletin of Concerned Asian Scholars* 28, no. 3–4: 78–81.

2000. On the Origins and Transformation of Taiwanese National Identity. *China Perspectives* 28 (March–April): 51–70.

Chao, Y. R. (Zhao Yuanren).

1931. Fanqieyu bazhong (Eight Types of Phonetic Languages). *Zhongyang Yanjinyuan Lishi Yuyan Yanjiuso Jikan (Bulletin of the Institute of History and Philology)* 2 (April): 3.

Chen Chiu-kun.

1994. State, Proprietary Rights, and Ethnic Relations in Ch'ing Taiwan, 1680–1840. In *Ethnicity in Taiwan: Social, Historical, and Cultural Perspectives,* ed. Chen Chung-min, Chuang Ying-chang, and Huang Shu-min, 25–39. Taibei: Institute of Ethnology, Acadamia Sinica.

Chen Chung-min, Chuang Ying-chang, and Huang Shu-min, eds.

1994. *Ethnicity in Taiwan: Social, Historical, and Cultural Perspectives.* Taibei: Institute of Ethnology, Academia Sinica.

Chen Gengjin.

1986. *Taizhong Xian Anlishe Kaifashui (The Developmental History of Anli She in Taizhong County).* Taizhong: Taizhong Xianli Wenhua Zhongxin.

Ch'en, Jerome.

1992. *The Highlanders of Central China: A History 1895–1937.* New York: M. E. Sharpe, Inc.

Chen Shaoxing.
    1964. *Renkou pian (Population)*. Vol. 2, part 1: Renmin zhi. Taibei: Taiwan Sheng Wenxian Weiyuanhui.

Chen Yongling.
    1998 [1989]. The History of Ethnology in China. In *A Collection of Chinese Ethnological Studies: A Dream of Ethnic Unity, Equality and Prosperity*, 1–72. Taibei: Hong-Yih Publishing Co.

Cheng K'o-ch'eng.
    1990. Cheng Ch'eng-kung's Maritime Expansion and Early Ch'ing Coastal Prohibition. In *Development and Declines of Fukien Province in the Seventeenth and Eighteenth centuries*, ed. E. B. Vermeer, 217–44. Leiden: E. J. Brill.

Cheung, Siu-woo.
    1996. Representation and Negotiation of Ge Identities in Southeast Guizhou. In *Negotiating Ethnicities in China and Taiwan*, ed. Melissa J. Brown, 240–73. Berkeley: Institute of East Asian Studies, University of California.

Chuang Ying-chang.
    1987. Ch'ing Dynasty Chinese Immigration to Taiwan: An Anthropological Perspective. *Bulletin of the Institute of Ethnology, Academia Sinica* 64: 179–203.

Chuang Ying-chang and Arthur P. Wolf.
    1995. Marriage in Taiwan, 1881–1905: An Example of Regional Diversity. *Journal of Asian Studies* 54, no. 3: 781–95.

Cohen, Myron L.
    1976. *House United, House Divided: The Chinese Family in Taiwan*. New York: Columbia University Press.

Comaroff, Jean.
    1985. *Body of Power, Spirit of Resistance: The Culture and History of a South African People*. Chicago: University of Chicago Press.

Corcuff, Stéphane.
    2000. Taiwan's "Mainlanders": A New Ethnic Category. *China Perspectives* 28 (March–April): 71–81.

Cosmides, Leda, John Tooby, and Jerome H. Barkow.
    1992. Introduction. In *The Adapted Mind: Evolutionary Psychology and the Generation of Culture*, ed. Jerome H. Barkow, Leda Cosmides, and John Tooby, 3–15. New York: Oxford University Press.

Cronk, Lee.
    1995a. Comment on: Gene-Culture Coevolutionary Theory, by Kevin N. Laland, Jochen Kumm, and Marcus W. Feldman. *Current Anthropology* 36, no. 1: 147–48.

    1995b. Is There a Role for Culture in Human Behavioral Ecology? *Ethnology and Sociobiology* 16, no. 3: 181–205.

    1999. *That Complex Whole: Culture and the Evolution of Human Behavior*. Boulder, Colo.: Westview Press.

Crossley, Pamela Kyle.
  1990. Thinking about Ethnicity in Early Modern China. *Late Imperial China*
  11, no. 1: 1–34.
D'Andrade, Roy.
  1992a. Schemas and Motivation. In *Human Motives and Cultural Models,*
  ed. Roy D'Andrade and Claudia Strauss, 23–44. Cambridge: Cambridge
  University Press.
  1992b. Afterword. In *Human Motives and Cultural models,* ed. Roy D'Andrade and Claudia Strauss, 225–32. Cambridge: Cambridge University
  Press.
Daniel, E. Valentine.
  1984. *Fluid Signs: Being a Person the Tamil Way.* Berkeley: University of California Press.
Davidson, James W.
  1988 (1903). *The Island of Formosa Past and Present: History, People, Resources, and Commercial Prospects—Tea, Camphor, Sugar, Gold, Coal,
  Sulphur, Economical Plants, and Other Productions.* Taibei and Oxford:
  Southern Materials Center, Inc., and Oxford University Press.
Dawkins, Richard.
  1982. *The Extended Phenotype.* Oxford: Oxford University Press.
Dehaene, Stanislas.
  1992. Varieties of Numerical Abilities. *Cognition* 44, no. 1–2: 1–42.
Dennett, Daniel C.
  1995. *Darwin's Dangerous Idea: Evolution and the Meanings of Life.* New
  York: Simon & Schuster.
Dewey, William J., Joseph D. Mann, C. E. Jackson, William Bouman, H. Samuel
  Noordhoff, T. C. Wu, and Harvey Doorenbos.
  1967. Xg Blood Group Frequencies in some Further Populations. *Journal of
  Medical Genetics* 4, no. 1: 12–15.
Dikötter, Frank.
  1992. *The Discourse of Race in Modern China.* Stanford, Calif.: Stanford Uni-
  versity Press.
Dirks, Nicholas B., Geoff Eley, and Sherry B. Ortner, eds.
  1994. *Culture/Power/History: A Reader in Contemporary Social Theory.*
  Princeton, N.J.: Princeton University Press.
Dong Luo.
  1992. Tujia fengsu jiangou jiexi (An Analytic Outline of Tujia Customs).
  *Zhongnan Minzu Xueyuan Xuebao, Zhexue Shehui Kexue Ban (Journal
  of the South-Central Nationalities College, Philosophy and Social Sciences
  Edition)* 57, no. 6: 54–58.
  1996. Nanbu fangyan qu tujiazu yuanlin tanxi (Analyzing the Origins of the
  Southern-Dialect-Area Tujia). *Nanfang Minzu Yanjiu Luncong (Southern
  Ethnological Research Forum)* 2: 58–70.

1999. *Ba feng Tu yun—Tujia wenhua yuanliu jiexi (Ba manners, Tu charm—An Analysis of the Origins of Tujia culture)*. Wuhan: Wuhan Daxue Chubanshe.

Dong, Luo, Melissa J. Brown, and Xu Wu.
2002. Tujia. In *Encyclopedia of World Cultures Supplement*, ed. Carol R. Ember, Melvin Ember, and Ian Skoggard, 351–54. New York: Macmillan Reference USA.

Doolittle, Justus.
1865. *The Social Life of the Chinese*. New York: Harper and Brothers, Publishers.

Douglas, Carstairs.
1899. *Chinese-English Dictionary of the Vernacular or Spoken Language of Amoy, With the Principal Variations of the Chang-chew and Chin-chew Dialects (corrected edition)*. London: Publishing Office of the Presbyterian Church of England.

Duan Hongkun.
1992. Jibeishua de shengqu (Jibeishua's Holy Songs), parts 1 and 2. *Lianhe Bao (United News)*, January 6, p. 25, and January 7, p. 25.

Duara, Prasenjit.
1995. *Rescuing History from the Nation: Questioning Narratives of Modern China*. Chicago: University of Chicago Press.

2000. Response to Philip Huang's "Biculturality in Modern China and in Chinese Studies." *Modern China* 26, no. 1: 32–37.

Dunnell, R. C.
1992. Is a Scientific Archaeology Possible? In *Metaarchaeology*, ed. Lester Embree, 75–97. Amsterdam: Kluwer Academic Publishers.

Durham, W. H.
1991. *Coevolution: Genes, Culture and Human Diversity*. Stanford, Calif.: Stanford University Press.

Ebrey, Patricia.
1981. *Chinese Civilization and Society: A Sourcebook*. New York: The Free Press.

1993. *Chinese Civilization: A Sourcebook*. Second edition. New York: The Free Press.

1996. Surnames and Han Chinese Identity. In *Negotiating Ethnicities in China and Taiwan*, ed. Melissa J. Brown, 19–36. Berkeley: Institute of East Asian Studies, University of California.

Eckholm, Erik.
2000a. Opposition Candidate in Taiwan Won't Push China on Independence Issue. *New York Times on the Web*, January 31, http://www.nytimes.com/library/world/asia/013100taiwan-china.html.

2000b. In Weighty Times, an Island Lampoons Its Jitters. *New York Times on the Web,* March 17, http://www.nytimes.com/library/world/asia/ 031700taiwan-china-election.html.

2000c. As Taiwan Votes in Close Race, a Weak Government is the Likeliest Outcome. *New York Times on the Web,* March 18, http://www.nytimes .com/library/world/asia/031800taiwan-election.html.

Ehrlich, Paul, and Marcus Feldman.
2003. Genes and Cultures: What Creates Our Behavioral Phenome? *Current Anthropology* 44, no. 1: 87–107.

Elster, Jon.
1983. *Explaining Technical Change: A Case Study in the Philosophy of Science.* Cambridge: Cambridge University Press.

Engelen, Theo, and Arthur P. Wolf.
Forthcoming. *Marriage and the Family in Eurasia.* Stanford, Calif.: Stanford University Press.

ESMZ.
1991. *Enshi Shi Minzu Zhi (Enshi City Nationalities Journal).* Enshi Shi: Minzu Chubanshe.

Faison, Seth.
1999. Taiwan's New Doctrine Unintelligible in Chinese. *New York Times on the Web,* July 21.

Fei Xiaotong (Fei Hsiao Tung).
1981. *Toward a People's Anthropology.* Beijing: New World Press.

Ferrell, Raleigh.
1969. *Taiwan's Aboriginal groups: Problems in Cultural and Linguistic Classification.* Acadamia Sincia Monograph no. 17. Taibei: Institute of Ethnology, Academia Sincia.

1971. Aboriginal Peoples of the Southwestern Taiwan Plain. *Zhongyang Yanjiuyuan Minzuxue Yanjiuso Jikan* 32: 217–35.

Flinn, Mark V.
1997. Culture and the Evolution of Social Learning. *Evolution and Human Behavior* 18, no. 1: 23–67.

Flynn, Thomas.
1994. Foucault's Mapping of History. In *The Cambridge Companion to Foucault,* ed. Gary Gutting, 28–46. Cambridge: Cambridge University Press.

Fong, John M.
1974. The Distribution of the Polymorphic Groups of Blood, Serum Protein, and Red Cell Enzyme among the Three Endogamous Groups of Takasago in Taiwan. *Bulletin of the Osaka Medical School* 20, no. 2: 35–45.

Foucault, Michel.
1979. *Discipline and Punish: The Birth of the Prison.* New York: Vintage Books.

1980. *Power/Knowledge: Selected Interviews and Other Writings, 1972–77.* New York: Pantheon Books.

1983. The Subject and Power. In *Michel Foucault: Beyond Structuralism and Hermeneutics,* second edition, ed. Hubert L. Dreyfus and Paul Rabinow, 208–226. Chicago: University of Chicago Press.

1989. *Foucault Live: Interviews, 1966–1984.* Ed. Sylvere Lotringer. New York: Semiotext(e).

Freedman, Maurice.
1971 (1966). *Chinese Lineage and Society: Fukien and Kwangtung.* London School of Economics Monographs on Social Anthropology no. 33. London: Athlone Press.

Gates, Hill.
1981. Social Class and Ethnicity. In *The Anthropology of Taiwanese Society,* ed. Emily Martin Ahern and Hill Gates, 241–81. Stanford, Calif.: Stanford University Press.

1987. *Chinese Working-Class Lives: Getting by in Taiwan.* Ithaca, NY: Cornell University Press.

1989. The Commoditization of Chinese Women. *Signs: Journal of Women in Culture and Society* 14, no. 4: 799–832.

1996a. *China's Motor: A Thousand Years of Petty Capitalism.* Ithaca, N.Y.: Cornell University Press.

1996b. On a New Footing: Footbinding and the Coming of Modernity. Paper presented at the Center for Chinese Studies, University of California. University of California, Berkeley, October 18.

2001. Footloose in Fujian: Economic Correlates of Footbinding. *Comparative Studies in Society and History* 43, no. 1: 130–148.

Geertz, Clifford.
1973. *The Interpretation of Cultures.* New York: Basic Books.

Gibbs, James L., Jr.
1998. Stanford's Anthro Department Splits. *Anthropology Newsletter* 39, no. 7: 21.

Goffman, Erving.
1963. *Stigma: Notes on the Management of Spoiled Identity.* Englewood Cliffs, N.J.: Prentice-Hall, Inc.

Gold, Thomas.
1986. *State and Society in the Taiwan Miracle.* Armonk, New York: M. E. Sharpe.

1994. Civil Society and Taiwan's Quest for Identity. In *Cultural Change in Postwar Taiwan,* ed. Stevan Harrell and Huang Chun-chieh, 47–68. Boulder, Colo.: Westview Press.

Gramsci, Antonio.
1992 (1971). *The Prison Notebooks.* New York: Columbia University Press.

Greenhalgh, Susan.
1984. Networks and their Nodes: Urban Society on Taiwan. *China Quarterly* 99: 528–52.

Groot, J. J. M. de.
  1897. *The Religious System of China,* vol. 3. Leiden: E. J. Brill.
Guldin, Gregory Elihu.
  1994. *The Saga of Anthropology in China: From Malinowski to Moscow to Mao.* Armonk, New York: M. E. Sharpe.
Habermas, Jürgen.
  1987. *The Philosophical Discourse of Modernity: Twelve Lectures,* trans. Frederick Lawrence. Cambridge: MIT Press.
Haguenauer, Charles.
  1977 (1930). Formose depuis son origine jusqu'au son annexion par le Japon (Formosa from Its Origin to Its Annexation by Japan). In *Etudes choisies de Charles Haguenauer (Selected Works of Charles Haguenauer),* ed. P. Akamatsu et al., 45–100. Vol. 3: Les Ryukyu et Formose, études historiques et ethnograhiques. Leiden: E. J. Brill.
Halbwachs, Maurice.
  1980. Historical Memory and Collective Memory. In *The Collective Memory,* trans. Francis J. Ditter, Jr., and Vida Yazdi Ditter, 50–87. New York: Harper & Row.
Harrell, Stevan.
  1974. When a Ghost Becomes a God. In *Religion and Ritual in Chinese Society,* ed. Arthur P. Wolf, 193–206. Stanford, Calif.: Stanford University Press.
  1979. The Concept of Soul in Chinese Folk Religion. *Journal of Asian Studies* 38, no. 3: 519–28.
  1982. *Ploughshare Village: Culture and Context in Taiwan.* Seattle: University of Washington Press.
  1990a. Ethnicity, Local Interests, and the State: Yi Communities in Southwest China. *Comparative Studies in Society and History* 32, no. 3: 515–48.
  1990b. From Xiedou to Yijun: The Decline of Ethnicity in Northern Taiwan, 1885–1895. *Late Imperial China* 11, no. 1: 99–127.
  1993. Linguistics and Hegemony in China. *International Journal of the Sociology of Language* 103: 97–114
  ed. 1995a. *Cultural Encounters on China's Ethnic Frontiers.* Seattle: University of Washington Press.
  1995b. Introduction. In *Cultural Encounters on China's Ethnic Frontiers,* ed. Steven Harrell, 3–36. Seattle: University of Washington Press.
  1996a. Introduction. In *Negotiating Ethnicities in China and Taiwan,* ed. Melissa J. Brown, 1–18. Berkeley: Institute of East Asian Studies, University of California.
  1996b. The Nationalities Question and the Prmi Problem. In *Negotiating Ethnicities in China and Taiwan,* ed. Melissa J. Brown, 274–96. Berkeley: Institute for East Asian Studies, University of California.
  2001. *Ways of Being Ethnic in Southwest China.* Seattle: University of Washington Press.

Hobsbawm, Eric and Terence Ranger.
  1983. *The Invention of Tradition.* Cambridge: Cambridge University Press.
Hsiao, Hsin-huang Michael, and Alvin Y. So.
  1996. The Taiwan-Mainland Economic Nexus: Sociopolitical Origins, State-Society Impacts, and Future Prospects. *Bulletin of Concerned Asian Studies* 28, no. 1: 3–12.
Hsieh, Jih-chang Chester.
  1979a. Pingpuzu zhi hanhua (The Sinicization of the plains Aborigines). *Zhongyang Yanjiuyuan Minzuxue Yanjiuso Jikan (Bulletin of the Institute of Ethnology, Acadamia Sinica)* 47: 49–72.
  1979b. *Structure and History of a Chinese Community in Taiwan.* Academia Sinica Monograph no. 25. Taibei: Institute of Ethnology, Academia Sinica.
Hsu Cho-yun.
  1980. The Settlement of the I-lan Plain. In *China's Island Frontier: Studies in the Historical Geography of Taiwan,* ed. Ronald G. Knapp, 69–86. Honolulu: University Press of Hawaii.
Hsu Wen-hsiung.
  1980a. From Aboriginal Island to Chinese Frontier: The Development of Taiwan Before 1683. In *China's Island Frontier: Studies in the Historical Geography of Taiwan,* ed. Ronald G. Knapp, 3–29. Honolulu: University Press of Hawaii.
  1980b. Frontier Social Organization and Social Disorder in Ch'ing Taiwan. In *China's Island Frontier: Studies in the Historical Geography of Taiwan,* ed. Ronald G. Knapp, 87–105. Honolulu: University Press of Hawaii.
Hu Nao and Liu Donghai.
  1993. *Exi tusi shehui gailue (A Synopsis of Society under Local Rulers in Western Hubei).* Chengdu: Sichuan Minzu Chubanshe.
Huang Baiquan.
  1999. Tujiazu zuyuan yanjiu zonglun (A Review of Research on Tujia Ancestral Origins). In *Tujia zu lizhi wenhua lunji (A Colloquium on Tujia History and Culture),* ed. Huang Baiquan and Tian Wanzheng, 25–42. Enshi, Hubei: Hubei Minzu Xueyuan.
Huang Guangxue and Shi Lianzhu.
  1995. *Zhongguo Minzu Shibie (China's Ethnic Identification Project).* Beijing: Minzu Chubanshe.
Huang Huanyao.
  1986. Qingji Taiwan fanren dui difang zhi'an de gongxian: Yifan jiqi gongneng de tantao (The Contributions of Barbarians to the Maintenance of Local Order in Qing-Period Taiwan: A Discussion of Loyalist Barbarians and Their Function). *Taibei Wenxian* 75: 131–97.
Huang Min-chuan.
  1970. Studies on the Distribution of Blood Types among Various Racial Tribes in Formosa. *Journal of the Formosan Medical Association* 69, no. 9: 439–54.

Huang, Philip C.
   2000. Biculturality in Modern China and in Chinese Studies. *Modern China* 26, no. 1: 3–31.

Huang Shujing.
   1957 [1736]. Tai hai shi cha lu (A Tour of Duty in the Taiwan Sea). *Taiwan Wenxian Congkan* 4. Taibei: Taiwan Yinghang.

Huber, Johannes.
   1990. Chinese Settlers Against the Dutch East India Company: The Rebellion Led by Kuo Huai-i on Taiwan in 1652. In *Development and Declines of Fukien Province in the Seventeenth and Eighteenth Centuries*, ed. E. B. Vermeer, 265–96. Leiden: E. J. Brill.

Ikemoto, Shigenori, Chuan-tsun Ming, Natsuko Haruyama, and Tanemoto Furuhata.
   1966. Blood Group Frequencies in the Ami Tribe (Formosa). *Proceedings of the Japan Academy* 42, no. 2: 173–77.

Jankowiak, William.
   1988. The Last Hurrah? Political Protest in Inner Mongolia. *Australian Journal of Chinese Affairs* 19/20: 269–88.

Jiang Risheng.
   1960 [1704]. Taiwan waiji (Unofficial Record of Taiwan). *Taiwan Wenxian Congkan* 60. Taibei: Taiwan Yinghang.

Johnson, David.
   1985. Communication, Class, and Consciousness in Late Imperial China. In *Popular Culture in Late Imperial China,* ed. David Johnson, Andrew J. Nathan, and Evelyn S. Rawski, 292–324. Berkeley: University of California Press.

Jordan, David K.
   1985. *Gods, Ghosts, and Ancestors: Folk Religion in a Taiwanese Village,* second edition. Taipei: Caves Ltd.

Ka, Chih-ming.
   1995. *Japanese Colonialism in Taiwan: Land Tenure, Development, and Dependency, 1895–1945*. Boulder, Colo.: Westview Press.

Karakasidou, Anastasia N.
   1997. *Fields of Wheat, Hills of Blood: Passages to Nationhood in Greek Macedonia, 1870–1990*. Chicago: University of Chicago Press.

Keightley, David N.
   1978. The Religious Commitment: Shang Theology and the Genesis of Chinese Political Culture. *History of Religions* 17, no. 3–4: 211–24.

Kelliher, Daniel.
   1992. *Peasant Power in China: The Era of Rural Reform, 1979–1989*. New Haven: Yale University Press.

Keyes, Charles F.
   1981. The Dialectics of Ethnic Change. In *Ethnic Change,* ed. C. F. Keyes, 3–30. Seattle: University of Washington Press.

Khan, Almaz.
    1995. Chinggis Khan: From Imperial Ancestor to Ethnic Hero. In *Cultural Encounters on China's Ethnic Frontiers*, ed. Stevan Harrell, 248–77. Seattle: University of Washington Press.

    1996. Who Are the Mongols? State, Ethnicity, and the Politics of Representation in the PRC. In *Negotiating Ethnicities in China and Taiwan*, ed. Melissa J. Brown, 125–59. Berkeley: Institute of East Asian Studies, University of California.

Kristof, Nicholas.
    1998. President of Taiwan Seeks Separate Identity. *New York Times on the Web*, September 2, http://www.nytimes.com/library/world/asia/090298china-taiwan.html

Kroeber, A. L., and Clyde Klukhohn.
    1952. *Culture: A Critical Review of Concepts and Definitions.* Cambridge: Harvard University Printing Office.

Kubler, Cornelius.
    1985. *The Development of Mandarin in Taiwan: A Case Study of Language Contact.* Taipei: Student Book Co., Ltd.

Kuhn, Philip A.
    1990. *Soulstealers: The Chinese Sorcery Scare of 1768.* Cambridge, Mass.: Harvard University Press.

Kuhn, Thomas S.
    1970 (1962). *The Structure of Scientific Revolutions,* second edition, enlarged. Chicago: University of Chicago Press.

Kuper, Adam.
    1999. *Culture: The Anthropologists' Account.* Cambridge, Mass.: Harvard University Press.

Labov, William.
    1972. Hypercorrection by the Lower Middle Class as a Factor of Linguistic Change. In *Sociolinguistic Patterns*, ed. W. Labov, 122–42. Philadelphia: University of Pennsylvania Press.

Lai, Tse-han, Ramon H. Myers, and O. Wei.
    1991. *A Tragic Beginning: The Taiwan Uprising of February 28, 1947.* Stanford, Calif.: Stanford University Press.

Lamley, Harry.
    1981. Subethnic Rivalry in the Ch'ing period. In *The Anthropology of Taiwanese Society,* ed. Emily M. Ahern and Hill Gates, 282–318. Stanford, Calif.: Stanford University Press.

Lee, Ming-ta, Ming-chuan Huang, Koji Okura, Hachiro Nakajima, and Kwei-mei Hsu.
    1970. A Survey of ABO, MN, Q, Rh Blood Types in Inhabitants of the Kaohsiung District of Taiwan. *Journal of the Formosan Medical Association* 69, no. 10: 489–94.

Lee Teng-hui.
  1999. *The Road to Democracy: Taiwan's Pursuit of Identity*. Tokyo: PHP Institute, Inc.

Lee, Ting-chien, Ling-yu Shih, Pai-chi Huang, Chi-chuh Lin, Boon-nam Blackwell, R. Quentin Blackwell, and David Yi-yung Hsia.
  1963. Glucose-6-Phosphate Dehydogenase Deficiency in Taiwan. *American Journal of Human Genetics* 15, no. 2: 126–32.

Lei Xiang.
  1994. Tujia Tianshi kaolue—jian ping "zaopu" xianxiang (Examining the Tian Clan of the Tujia—A Critical Review of the Phenomenon of Fabricating Genealogies). *Hubei Minzu Xueyuan Xuebao, Shehui Keuxue Ban* 12, no. 3: 12–17.

  1995. Huan tanshen tanyuan (Exploring the Origins of Repaying Tanshen). *Hubei Minzu Xueyuan Xuebao, Shehui Kexue Ban* 13, no. 4: 40–41.

Leonard, Karen Isaksen.
  1992. *Making Ethnic Choices: California's Punjabi Mexican Americans*. Philadelphia: Temple University Press.

Levy, Howard S.
  1967. *Chinese Footbinding: The History of a Curious Erotic Custom*. New York: Bell Publishing.

Li, Paul Jen-kuei.
  1985a. The Position of Atayal in the Austronesian Family. In *Austronesian Linguistics at the 15th Pacific Science Congress*, ed. Andrew Pauley and Lois Carrington, 257–80. Pacific Linguistics Series C, no. 88. Potts Point, New South Wales: Australian National University.

  1985b. A Secret Language in Taiwanese. *Journal of Chinese Linguistics* 13, no. 1: 91–118.

Lin, Jing Y.
  1975. The Distribution of the Polymorphic Groups of Blood Serum Protein, and Red Cell Enzyme of the Taiwanese. *Journal of the Anthropological Society of Nippon* 83, no. 2: 203–11.

Little, Daniel.
  1989. *Understanding Peasant China: Case Studies in the Philosophy of Social Science*. New Haven: Yale University Press.

Liu Huixiong.
  1991. *Dao Lian: Taiwan shishi (Island Nostalgia: The Epic of Taiwan)*. Taibei: Qianwei chubanshe.

Liu Liyu.
  1989. *Tujia zu*. Beijing: Minzu Chubanshe.

Liu Pin-hsiung (Liu Binxiong).
  1987 (1962). Taiwan nanbu diqu pingpuzu de Ali Zu xinyang (The Ali Zu Worship of Southern Taiwan Plains Aborigines). *Taiwan Fengwu* 37, no. 3: 1–62.

Lu Jiaxing.
    1956. Tainan xianxia gufanshe diming kao (An Examination of Old Barbarian Village Place Names in Tainan County). *Nanying Wenxian* 4, no. 1: 1–13.

Ma Yin, ed.
    1994 (1989). *China's Minority Nationalities*. Beijing: Foreign Languages Press.

MAC (Mainland Affairs Council).
    1999 (1994). ROC white paper, "Relations Across the Taiwan Straight" (concluding statements). *Asian Affairs: An American Review* 26, no. 2: 93–99.

Mackerras, Colin.
    1994. *China's Minorities: Integration and Modernization in the Twentieth Century*. Oxford: Oxford University Press

Maynard Smith, John.
    1989. *Evolutionary Genetics*. Oxford: Oxford University Press.

Meskill, Johanna Menzel.
    1979. *A Chinese Pioneer Family: The Lins of Wu-Feng, Taiwan, 1729–1895*. Princeton, N.J.: Princeton University Press.

MNRKC.
    1908. *Meiji sanchū-hachi nen rinji kokō chōsa: Kekkahyō (1908 Provisional Household Census: General Statistical Tables)*. Tokyo.

Motulsky, A. G., Ting-chien Lee, and G. R. Fraser.
    1965. Glucose-6-Phosphate Dehydrogenase (G6PD) Deficiency, Thalassaemia, and Abnormal Haemoglobins in Taiwan. *Journal of Medical Genetics* 2, no. 1: 18–20.

Nader, Laura.
    1988. Post-Interpretive Anthropology. *Anthropological Quarterly* 61, no. 4: 149–59.

Nakajima, Hachiro, Koji Ohkura, Min-chuan Huang, Ryusuke Saito, and Takashi Seto.
    1971. The Distribution of Several Serological and Biochemical Traits in East Asia: IV. The Distribution of the Blood Groups in the Taiwanese Mountain Aborigines. *Japanese Journal of Human Genetics* 16, no. 2: 57–68.

Nakajima, Hachiro, Koji Ohkura, Yu-zen Shen, Zan Siw Chow, Su-pei Lee, Yozo Orita, Yu Masuda, Sigeo Takahara, Yoshiko Hayashida, and Sachiko Tanaka.
    1967. The Distribution of Several Serological and Biochemical Traits in East Asia: I. The Distributions of ABO, MN, Q, Lewis, and Rh Blood Groups in Taiwan. *Japanese Journal of Human Genetics* 11, no. 4: 244–51.

Nakamura Takashi.
    1936. Ranjin jidai no bansha kokō hyō (The Dutch Period Barbarian Census, 1650). *Nanpō Dozoku* 4, no. 1: 42–59.

    1937. Ranjin jidai no bansha kokō hyō (2) (The Dutch Period Barbarian Census, part 2, 1655). *Nanpō Dozoku* 4, no. 3: 182–96.

1951. Sen roppyaku yonjū shichi nen no Taiwan bansha kokō hyō (The 1647 Census of Taiwan Barbarians). *Yamato Bunka* 31: 91–110.

Naquin, Susan.

1976. *Millenarian Rebellion in China: The Eight Trigrams Uprising of 1813.* New Haven: Yale University Press.

1981. *Shantung Rebellion: The Wang Lun Uprising of 1774.* New Haven: Yale University Press.

1985. The Transmission of White Lotus Sectarianism in Late Imperial China. In *Popular Culture in Late Imperial China,* ed. David Johnson, Andrew J. Nathan, and Evelyn S. Rawski. Berkeley: University of California Press.

Nelson, Erik-Lars.

1999. Washington: The Yellow Peril. *The New York Review of Books* 46, no. 12: 6–10.

Norman, Jerry.

1988a. *Chinese.* Cambridge: Cambridge University Press.

1988b. The She Dialect of Luoyang County. *Zhongyang Yanjiuyuan Lishi Yuyan Yanjiuso Jikan* 59, no. 2: 353–67.

1989 (1986). What is a Kejia Dialect? In *Proceedings of the Second International Conference on Sinology, Academia Sinica,* 323–44. Taibei: Academia Sinica.

Ong Jok-tik (Wang Yude).

1999. *Taiwan kumen de lishi* (The Suffocating History of Taiwan). Taibei: Qianwei.

Ortner, Sherry B.

1998. Identities: The Hidden Life of Class. *Journal of Anthropological Research* 54, no. 1: 1–17.

Pan Inghai (Pan Yinghai).

1989a. "A Study on the Pragmatics of Human Understanding: Ritual Processes in a Southern Taiwanese Village." Ph.D. dissertation, Department of Anthropology, University of Oregon.

1989b. Toushe cun de juluo fazhan yu zuqun guanxi (The Ethnic Relations and Settlement Development of Toushe Village). Paper presented at Zuqun guanxi yu quyu fazhan (Symposium on Ethnic Relations and Regional Development). Institute of Ethnology, Academia Sinica, Taiwan, September 1–2.

1994. Wenhua hecheng yu hechange wenhua—Toushe cun Tai Zu niandu jiyi wenhua yihan (Cultural Recombination and Recombinatory Culture: The Implications of the Taizu Annual Festival of Toushe Village). In *Taiwan yu Fujian shehui wenhua yanjiu lunwenji (Collected Essays on Research on Taiwan and Fujian Society and Culture),* ed. Chuang Ying-chang and Pan Ying-hai, 235–56. Taibei: Institute of Ethnology, Academia Sinica, Taiwan.

2000. "Pingpu" Consciousness in Today's Taiwan: On History and Ethnicity. *China Perspectives* 28 (March–April):82–88.

Pan Ying.
   1992. Tan Taiwan pingpuzu de qianxi (A Discussion of the Migrations of Tai-
      wan Plains Tribes). *Taiwan Wenxian* 43, no. 4: 277–301.

   1993. Pingpuzu shilue (A Short History of Plains Tribes). *Taiwan Wenxian* 44,
      no. 1: 113–53.

Pang Keng-fong.
   1996. Being Hui, Huan-nang, and Utsat Simultaneously: Contextualizing
      History and Identities of the Austronesian-speaking Hainan Muslims. In
      Negotiating Ethnicities in China and Taiwan, ed. Melissa J. Brown, 183–
      207. Berkeley: Institute of East Asian Studies, University of California.

Pasternak, Burton.
   1972. *Kinship and Community in Two Chinese Villages.* Stanford, Calif.: Stan-
      ford University Press.

   1983. *Guests in the Dragon: Social Demography of a Chinese District, 1895–
      1946.* New York: Columbia University Press.

   1985. Causes and Demographic Consequences of Uxorilocal Marriage in
      China. In *Family and Population in East Asian History,* ed. Susan B. Han-
      ley and Arthur P. Wolf., 309–34. Stanford, Calif.: Stanford University
      Press.

Perkins, Dwight H.
   1969. *Agricultural Development in China, 1368–1968.* Edinburgh: Edinburgh
      University Press.

Perry, Elizabeth J.
   1980. *Rebels and Revolutionaries in North China 1845–1945.* Stanford, Calif.:
      Stanford University Press.

Pickering, William A.
   1898. *Pioneering in Formosa: Recollections of Adventures Among Mandarins,
      Wreckers, and Head-hunting Savages.* London: Hurst and Blackett, Ltd.

Popper, Karl.
   1982. *Unended Quest: An Intellectual Autobiography.* La Salle, Ill.: Open
      Court Publishing Company.

Pulleyblank, E. G.
   1983. The Chinese and their Neighbors in Prehistoric and Early Historic
      Times. In *The Origins of Chinese Civilization,* ed. David N. Keightley, 411–
      66. Berkeley: University of California Press.

Ramsey, S. Robert.
   1987. *The Languages of China.* Princeton, N.J.: Princeton University Press.

Ren, Hai.
   1996. Taiwan and the Impossibility of the Chinese. In *Negotiating Ethnici-
      ties in China and Taiwan,* ed. Melissa J. Brown, 37–74. Berkeley: Institute
      of East Asian Studies, University of California.

Richerson, Peter J. and Robert Boyd.
   1992. Cultural Inheritance and Evolutionary Ecology. In *Evolutionary Ecol-*

ogy and Human Behavior, ed. Eric Alden Smith and Bruce Winterhalder, 61–92. New York: Aldine de Gruyter.

Roscoe, Paul B.

1995. The Perils of "Positivism" in Cultural Anthropology. *American Anthropologist* 97, no. 3: 492–504.

Rosenthal, Elisabeth.

2000a. China Fires Off Warning to Taiwan Voters. *New York Times on the Web*, March 16. http://www.nytimes.com/library/world/asia/031600china-taiwan-warn.html.

2000b. Deep Feeling That China Owns Taiwan is Put to Test. *New York Times on the Web*, March 20. http://www.nytimes.com/library/world/asia/032000taiwan-china.html.

Sage, Steven F.

1992. *Ancient Sichuan and the Unification of China*. Albany: State University of New York Press.

Sahlins, Marshall.

1976a. *Culture and Practical Reason*. Chicago: University of Chicago Press.

1976b. *The Use and Abuse of Biology: An Anthropological Critique of Sociobiology*. Ann Arbor: University of Michigan Press.

Sahlins, Marshall and Elman R. Service, eds.

1960. *Evolution and Culture*. Ann Arbor: University of Michigan Press.

Sangren, P. Steven.

1987. *History and Magical Power in a Chinese Community*. Stanford, Calif.: Stanford University Press.

1995. "Power" Against Ideology: A Critique of Foucauldian Usage. *Cultural Anthropology* 10, no. 1: 3–40.

Sautman, Barry.

1998. Preferential Policies for Ethnic Minorities in China: The Case of Xinjiang. In *Nationalism and Ethnoregional Identities in China*, ed. William Safran. London: Frank Cass.

Scheper-Hughes, Nancy.

1994. Embodied Knowledge: Thinking with the Body in Critical Medical Anthropology. In *Assessing Cultural Anthropology*, ed. Robert Borofsky, 229–239. New York: McGraw-Hill, Inc.

Schneider, David.

1980 (1968). *American Kinship: A Cultural Account*, second edition. Chicago: University of Chicago Press.

1984. *A Critique of the Study of Kinship*. Ann Arbor: University of Michigan Press.

Shanklin, Eugenia.

1994. *Anthropology and Race*. Belmont, Calif.: Wadsworth Publishing Co.

Shen Congwen.

1982. *Recollections of West Hunan*. Trans. Gladys Young. Beijing: Panda Books.

Shepherd, John Robert.

1986. Sincized Siraya Worship of A-li-tzu. *Zhongyang Yanjiuyuan Minzuxue Yanjiuso Jikan* 58: 1–81.

1988. Plains Aborigines and Missionaries in Ch'ing Taiwan, 1859–1895. Paper presented at Taiwan tuzhe zongjiao jiyi yanlunhui (Conference on the Religious Practices of Taiwan Natives). Institute of Ethnology, Academia Sinica, Taibei, May 27–28.

1989. Marriage Mode and Marriage Market. Unpublished manuscript.

1993. *Statecraft and Political Economy on the Taiwan Frontier, 1600–1800.* Stanford, Calif.: Stanford University Press.

1995. *Marriage and Mandatory Abortion Among the Seventeenth Century Siraya.* American Ethnological Society Monograph no. 6. Arlington, Va.: American Anthropological Association.

Shi Lang.

1958 (1685). *Qing hai ji shi (Record of Pacifying the Seas).* Taiwan Wenxian Congkan 13. Taibei: Taiwan Yinghang.

Shi Tianfu.

1990. Qingdai Taiwan "fanli bu'an gengzuo" de yuanyou (The Causes of the Lack of Agricultural Skills among Aborigines in Qing Taiwan). *Zhongyang Yanjiuyuan Minzuxue Yanjiuso Jikan* 69: 67–92.

Shi Wanshou.

1990. *Taiwan de baihu minzu (The Ethnic Groups of Taiwan that Worship Vases).* Taibei: Taiyuan Chubanshe, Xiehe Taiwan Congkan 15.

Shih, Chih-yu.

2001. Ethnicity as Policy Expedience: Clan Confucianism in Ethnic Tujia-Miao Yongshun. *Asian Ethnicity* 2, no. 1: 72–88.

Shore, Bradd.

1988. Interpretation Under Fire. *Anthropological Quarterly* 61, no. 4: 161–76.

Smith, Craig S.

2000. China's Threat to Taiwan: Likelihood of Attack Deemed Low. *New York Times on the Web,* March 7. http://www.nytimes.com/library/world/asia/030700china-taiwan-assess.html

Smith, Eric Alden and Bruce Winterhalder, eds.

1992. *Evolutionary Ecology and Human Behavior.* New York: Aldine de Gruyter.

Speidel, W. M.

1976. The Administrative and Fiscal Reforms of Liu Ming-ch'uan in Taiwan, 1884–1891: Foundation for Self-Strengthening. *Journal of Asian Studies* 35: 441–59.

Spence, Jonathan D.

1990. *The Search for Modern China.* New York: W. W. Norton and Company.

Sperber, Dan.

1996. *Explaining Culture.* Oxford: Blackwell Publishers.

Stockard, Janice E.
  1989. *Daughters of the Canton Delta: Marriage Patterns and Economic Strate-gies in South China, 1860–1930*. Stanford, Calif.: Stanford University Press.
Strauss, Claudia.
  1992a. Models and Motives. In *Human Motives and Cultural Models,* ed. Roy D'Andrade and C. Strauss, 1–20. Cambridge: Cambridge University Press.

  1992b. What Makes Tony Run? Schemas as Motives Reconsidered. In *Human Motives and Cultural Models,* ed. Roy D'Andrade and Claudia Strauss, 197–224. Cambridge: Cambridge University Press.
Strauss, Claudia and Naomi Quinn.
  1994. A Cognitive/Cultural Anthropology. In *Assessing Cultural Anthropology,* ed. Robert Borofsky, 284–97. New York: McGraw-Hill, Inc.
Suenari Michio.
  1994. Becoming Chinese? Ethnic Transformations and Ancestral Tablets among the Puyuma of Taiwan. In *Perspectives on Chinese Society: Views from Japan,* ed. Michio Suenari, J. S. Eades, and Christian Daniels, 199–219. Tokyo: Institute for the Study of Languages and Cultures of Asia and Africa, Tokyo University of Foreign Studies.
Sutton, Donald S.
  2000. Myth Making on an Ethnic Frontier: The Cult of the Heavenly Kings of West Hunan, 1715–1996. *Modern China* 26, no. 4: 448–500.
Taiwan jinkō dōtai tōkei (Taiwan: Vital Statistics of the Population).
  Annual Publication, 1905–42. Taibei: Sōtokufu.
Tannen, Deborah.
  1982. Ethnic Style in Male-Female Conversation. In *Language and Social Identity,* ed. John J. Gumperz, 217–31. Cambridge: Cambridge University Press.
TAOIOSC (Taiwan Affairs Office and the Information Office of the State Council).
  1999. PRC White Paper. *Asian Affairs* 26, no. 2.

  2000. PRC White Paper: The One-China Principle and the Taiwan Issue. http://newtaiwan.virtualave.net/white.htm.
Templeton, Alan R.
  1998. Human Races: A Genetic and Evolutionary Perspective. *American Anthropologist* 100, no. 3: 632–650.
Thompson, Laurence G.
  1964. The Earliest Chinese Eyewitness Accounts of the Formosan Aborigines. *Monumenta Serica* 23: 163–204.

  1969. Formosan Aborigines in the Early Eighteenth Century: Huang Shu-ching's Fan-su liu-k'ao. *Monumenta Serica* 28: 41–147.
Tian Jinggui.
  1994. Queding yu huifu Tujiazu minzu chengfen de qianqianhouhou (Defining and restoring Tujia ethnic status once and for all). In *Wenshi ziliao xianqi*

128: *jianguohou shiliao zhuanqi (Compilation of Cultural History Materials 128: Special Collection of Post-1949 Historical Materials)*, 177–204. Beijing: Zhongguo wenshi chubanshe.

Tian Wanzhen.
1995. Enshi "huan tanshen" de yuanshi zongjiao xinyang yicun chutan (A Preliminary Analysis of the Remaining Original Religious Beliefs of "Repaying Tanshen" in Enshi). *Hubei Minzu Xueyuan Xuebao, Shehui Kexue Ban* 13, no. 4: 45–47.

Tooby, John and Leda Cosmides.
1992. The Psychological Foundations of Culture. In *The Adapted Mind: Evolutionary Psychology and the Generation of Culture*, ed. J. Barkow, L. Cosmides, and J. Tooby. New York: Oxford University Press.

Tsuchida Shigeru, Yamadea Yukihiro, and Moriguchi Tsunekazu.
1991. *Linguistic Materials of the Formosan Sinicized Populations I: Siraya and Basai*. Tokyo: Department of Linguistics, University of Tokyo.

Tu Wei-ming.
1991. Cultural China: The Periphery as Center. *Daedalus* 20, no. 2: 1–32.

Tuchman, Barbara W.
1972 (1970). *Stilwell and the American Experience in China, 1911–1945*. New York: Bantam Books.

Tylor, Edward B.
1871. *Primitive Culture*. London: John Murray.

Wang I-shou.
1980. Cultural Contact and the Migration of Taiwan's Aborigines: A Historical Perspective. In *China's Island Frontier: Studies in the Historical Geography of Taiwan*, ed. Ronald Knapp. Honolulu: University Press of Hawaii.

Wang Lianmao.
1995. Migration in Two Minnan Lineages in the Ming and Qing Periods. Trans. Steven Harrell. In *Chinese Historical Micro-Demography*, ed. Stevan Harrell, 183–213. Berkeley: University of California Press.

Wang Yude. See Ong Jok-tik.

Watson, James L.
1988. The Structure of Chinese Funerary Rites: Elementary Forms, Ritual Sequence, and the Primacy of Performance. In *Death Ritual in Late Imperial and Modern China*, ed. James L. Watson and Evelyn S. Rawski, 3–19. Berkeley: University of California Press.

Watson, Rubie.
1985. *Inequality Among Brothers: Class and Kinship in South China*. Cambridge: Cambridge University Press.

Weber, Max.
1978 (1922). *Economy and Society: An Outline of Interpretive Sociology*. Ed. Guenther Roth and Claus Wittich. Berkeley: University of California Press.

Welch, Holmes.
  1967. *The Practice of Chinese Buddhism, 1900–1950*. Cambridge, Mass.: Harvard University Press.

Weller, Robert P.
  1987. *Unities and Diversities in Chinese Religion*. Seattle: University of Washington Press.

  1994. *Resistance, Chaos and Control in China: Taiping Rebels, Taiwanese Ghosts and Tiananmen*. Seattle: University of Washington Press.

  1999. *Alternate Civilities: Democracy and Culture in China and Taiwan*. Boulder, Colo.: Westview Press.

Westermarck, Edward.
  1922. *The History of Human Marriage*. Fifth ed., vol. 2. New York: Allerton Book Company.

  1934. Recent Theories of Exogamy. In *Three Essays on Sex and Marriage*, 127–159. London: Macmillan.

Whyte, Martin K.
  1988. Death in the People's Republic. In *Death Ritual in Late Imperial and Modern China,* ed. James L. Watson and Evelyn S. Rawski, 289–316. Berkeley: University of California Press.

Williams, Brackette.
  1989. A Class Act: Anthropology and the Race to Nation Across Ethnic Terrain. *Annual Review of Anthropology* 18: 401–44.

Wills, John E. Jr.
  1984. *Embassies and Illusions: Dutch and Portuguese Envoys to K'ang-hsi, 1666–1687*. Cambridge, Mass.: Council on East Asian Studies, Harvard University.

Wilson, Edward O.
  1978. *On Human Nature*. Cambridge, Mass.: Harvard University Press.

Wolf, Arthur P., ed.
  1974a. *Religion and Ritual in Chinese Society*. Stanford, Calif.: Stanford University Press.

Wolf, Arthur P.
  1974b. Gods, Ghosts, and Ancestors. In *Religion and Ritual in Chinese Society,* ed. Arthur P. Wolf, 131–182. Stanford, Calif.: Stanford University Press.

  1985a. Fertility in Prerevolutionary Rural China. In *Family and Population in East Asian History,* ed. Susan B. Hanley and Arthur P. Wolf, 154–85. Stanford, Calif.: Stanford University Press.

  1985b. Chinese Family Size: A Myth Revitalized. In *The Chinese Family and Its Ritual Behavior,* ed. Hsieh Jih-Chang and Chuang Ying-chang, 30–49. Taibei: Institute of Ethnology.

  1989. The Origins and Explanations of Variation in the Chinese Kinship System. In *Anthropological Studies of the Taiwan Area,* ed. K. C. Chang, K. C.

Li, A. P. Wolf, and A. Yin, 241–60. Taibei: National Taiwan University, Department of Anthropology.

1995. *Sexual Attraction and Childhood Association: A Chinese Brief for Edward Westermarck*. Stanford, Calif.: Stanford University Press.

Wolf, Arthur P. and Chieh-shan Huang.

1980. *Marriage and Adoption in China, 1845–1945*. Stanford, Calif.: Stanford University Press.

Wolf, Margery.

1992. *A Thrice-told Tale; Feminism, Postmodernism, and Ethnographic Responsibility*. Stanford, Calif.: Stanford University Press.

Yan Xingzhu and Liao Jiazhan.

1988. Women de jia, women de buluo, women de mingyun (Our Family, Our Tribe, Our Destiny). *Renjian Zazhi*, January: 72–85.

Yanagisako, Sylvia, and Jane Collier.

1994 (1987). Gender and Kinship Reconsidered: Toward a Unified Analysis. In *Assessing Cultural Anthropology*, ed. Robert Borofsky, 190–203. New York: McGraw-Hill, Inc.

Yelvington, Kevin A.

1991. Ethnicity as Practice? A Comment on Bentley. *Comparative Studies in Society and History* 33, no. 1: 158–68.

Young Yi-rong.

1995. Education Reform in Present-day Taiwan: Problems and Prospects. Paper presented at the Taiwan on the Eve of the Twenty-First Century conference. University of Washington, Seattle, September 6–8.

Yuan Chang-rue (Changrui).

1971. Takangkou hanren de Ameihua (Acculturation of Ami and Han Chinese in Takang'kuo). *Zhongyang Yanjiuyuan Minzuxue Yanjiuso Jikan* 31: 47–64.

Zhang Yaoqi.

1951. *Pingpuzu sheming duizhao biao* (A Comparative Name List of Plains Tribes Villages). Vol. 2, no. 1–2. Taibei: Wenxian zhuakan.

Zhang Zhengming.

1995 (1987). *Chu Wenhuashi (Chu Cultural History)*. Shanghai: Shanghai Renmin Chubanshe.

Zhuang Jinde.

1964. Qing chu yanjin yanhai renmin toudu lai Tai shimo (A History of Early Qing Prohibitions on Crossing to Taiwan), parts 1 and 2. *Taiwan Wenxian* 15, no. 3: 1–20.

Character List

Unmarked terms are in Mandarin Chinese, according to pinyin romanization. Terms used in Taiwan and in imperial and republican China are given in traditional characters, while terms used in the PRC are given in simplified characters.

Minnan terms, also called Hoklo or Taiwanese, are indicated by "T." Romanization of Taiwanese terms is the Church romanization in Douglas (1899). Note that, following Douglas, I use "ts" where current Church romanization uses "ch." However, following current Church simplification, I use "oo" where Douglas uses a character something like θ'. It sounds like an English "aw."

One Kejia term is indicated by "K." "?" indicates unknown or nonstandard characters from local dialects.

a-tok-a　阿凸仔
Ali Mu (see A-li Bu)
Ali Zu (see A-li Tsoo)
A-li Bu (T.)　阿立母
A-li Tsoo (T.)　阿立祖
An Tsoo (T.)　案祖
An Zu Da Gongjie Ali Mu　案祖大公界阿立母
ang-i (T.)　尪姨
Ba　巴
bai　拜
bainian guochi　百年国耻
baogai　宝盖
baohu　保护
bendi　本地
bendi ke jia dou shi tujiazu　本地客家都是土家族
bendi ke jia dou waidi laide　本地客家都外地来的

bendi ren 本地人
bensheng ren 本省人
Bingshe 丙社
bushi yi jiazu 不是一家族
cai 菜
Chikan (Saccam) 赤嵌
Chu 楚
Chungshe 中社
da han zhuyi 大汉主义
Danei 大内
dangwai 黨外
daoshi 道士
Dawulong (Tevorang) 大武壠
dazu 大租
Dingcun 丁村
duangong 端公
duoguo 躲过
Enshi 恩施
Enshi Tujia-Miao Autonomous Prefecture 恩施土家苗族自治州
Exi 鄂西
Exi Tujia-Miao Autonomous Prefecture 鄂西土家苗族自治州
fan 番
fang 方
fanzi po (see *huan-a-pho*)
Fanzi Tian 番仔田
fen chu qu 分出去
fen jia 分家
fendi 坟地
fenlei xiedou 分類械鬥
fu 福
fudun 副遯
Fujian 福建
gai tu gui liu 改土归流
gaoshan zu 高山族
guan hoan-a bo pak-kha (T.) 我們番仔沒綁腳
guan tian 官田
Guantian 官田
guang 廣
Guangdong 廣東
guangfu 光復
gudao lai de ?到來的
gui 鬼
guicheng 鬼城
guihun 鬼魂
guishen daguan 鬼神大观
guo 国/國
guojia 国家/國家

guomindang 國民黨
guonian 过年
Hakka (K.) 客家
Han 漢/汉
han ren 漢人/汉人
hanhua 漢化
hanyu 汉语
haozou 好走
Hefeng 鹤峰
Hok-kien (T.) 福建
Hok-lo (T.) 福佬
hoan-a (T.) 番仔
hoan-a hoe (T.) 番仔火
hoan-a oe (T.) 番仔話
hoan-a pho (T.) 番仔婆
Hua/*hua* 華/华
huan tanshen 还坛神
huangniu buhe shuiniu qun; banjiazi buhe bendiren 黄牛不合水牛群 搬家子不合
本地人
huaqiao 華僑/华侨
huaren 華人/华人
Hubei 湖北
hui difu, yinfu 回地府, 阴府
hun 魂
jia 家
Jiashe 甲社
jiashen 家神
jiazu 家族
Jibeishua 吉貝耍
jie laoren tuannian chile hao zoulu 接老人团年吃了好走路
Jingzhou 荆州
kailu 开路
kaixiang 開向
ke (T.) 家
ke tou 磕头
kejia/Kejia 客家
kejia ren 客家人
kin-chiu peh-a oe (T.) ?蕉白仔話
kong-kai (T.) 公界
kujia ge 哭嫁歌
kun qilai de 捆起来的
kunbang lai de 捆绑来的
Laifeng 来凤
lan (T.) 我們 (你和我)
lan hoan-a (T.) 我們番仔
lanjian 拦箭
lanshe 拦社

lao da 老大
Lao Jun (see Lau Kun)
lao yao 老幺
Lao Zi 老子
Lau Kun 老君
li 里
ling 靈
Longshan 龙山
Longtian 隆田
Ma Tsoo (T.) 媽祖
Madou (Mattau) 麻豆
man 蛮
man de hen 蛮的很
Mattau (see Madou)
meiyao 没要
miao (temple) 廟
Miao (ethnic group) 苗
mijiu 米酒
Min 閩
Minnan 閩南
minwei 民委
minzu 民族
minzu shibie 民族识别
mu 畝
nianrou 年肉
paihang 派行
peN-poo tsoo (T.) 平埔族
Peng 彭
pingpu zu 平埔族
po (woman) 婆
po (soul) 魄
poah-poe (T.) 賭筶
putonghua 普通话
qi 气
qianpo 强迫
Qing 清
Qingming 清明
ruguo tamen shuo wo yao dang Han wo mei quanli shuo tamen shi shaoshu minzu
如果他们说我要当汉我没权利说他们是少数民族
Saccam (see Chikan)
shenfen zheng 身份证
sheng 生
shengfan 生番
shengren bumian siren yi 生人不勉死人意
shenzhu 神主
sheri 社日
sheshang 社商

shi dao Enshi lai zuizao de ren caiyou 是到恩施来最早的人才有
shi guniang nuxu de shi 是姑娘女婿的事
shu 熟
shuan qilai de 拴起来的
shufan 熟番
shuo hao 说好
si tian 私田
Sinkan (see Xingang)
Siraya (see Xilaya)
Soulong (see Xiaolong)
Tai Shang Lao Jun 太上老君
Tai Shang Li Lao Jun 太上李老君
Tai Zu (see Thai Tsoo)
Taibei 臺北
Tainan 臺南
Taiwan 臺灣
taiwan guomindang 臺灣國民黨
taiwan ren 臺灣人
taiwan tongbao 台湾同胞
taiwan wenti 台湾问题
Tan 谭
Tan shen 谭神
tanshen 坛神
tangshen 堂神
tang-ki (T.) 乩童
taonan lai de 逃难来的
tedian 特点
Tevorang (see Dawulong)
Tian 田
tian di jun qin shi wei 天地君亲师立
Thai Tsoo (T.) 太祖
tonghun 同婚
tongyi duominzu de guojia 同一多民族的国家
Toushe 頭社
Tsoo Su Kong (T.) 祖師公
tu (convicts) 徒
tu (earth, local) 土
tuannian 团年
tuhua 土话
*tujia/*Tujia 土家／土家
tujiahua 土家化
tumanzi 土蛮子
tumin 土民
tusi 土司
waisheng ren 外省人
wang tian 王田
weile pian qian 为了骗钱

wenhua 文化
wo meiyou wenhua 我没有文化
Wucun 午村
wuli 屋里
wushi 巫师
xiang (hex) 向
xiang (township) 鄉/乡
Xiang (surname) 向
Xiangxi Tujia-Miao Autonomous Prefecture 湘西土家苗族自治州
xiao 孝
Xiaolong (Soulang) 蕭壠
xiaomei 小妹
xiaozu 小租
xiedou 械鬥
Xilaya (Siraya) 西拉雅
xing . . . de 姓 . . . 的
Xingang (Sinkan) 新港
yangqi buzou 阳气不足
yao fang 幺方
yatou 丫头
yijun 義軍
ying 營
yinggai kejia, kehu 应该客家, 客户
yingpan tian 營盤田
yinjian 阴间
Yishe 乙社
yuanzhumin 原住民
zao tuannian shi zhenzheng tujiaren, lai Enshi zuizaode ren 早团年是真正土家人,
　来恩施最早的人
zhenzheng 真正
Zheng Chenggong 鄭成功
zhenzhengde tujiazu 真正的土家族
zhi 纸
zhi xie ge mingzi 只写个名子
zhongbie 種別
Zhongguo 中國/中国
zhongguo ren 中國人/中国人
zhonghua minzu 中華民族/中华民族
Zhongyang Minzu Daxue 中央民族大学
Zhongyang Yanjiuyuan 中央研究院
zhongzu 種族
Zhuluo 諸羅
zipai 字派

Index

Aborigine cultural ideas, different than Han, 83–84, 86–88, 92–94, 152, 216–17, 232, 233

Aborigine cultural practices: invisible differences in, from Hoklo, 67, 75, 78, 88, 92–93; similarities to Hoklo practices, 74–88, 91–94

Aborigine culture (cultural models), 102, 124, 126, 232, 263n30, 264n40, 270n25. *See also* Austronesian languages; Hoklo cultural models, contributions of Aborigine culture to

Aborigine deity, worship of, 56, 68, 126; in Jibeishua, 105–8, 118, 123, 128, 264n40, 265n42, 266n49; in Longtian, 118–23, 128, 264n40, 265n42, 266n56; sinicization of, 102–3, 105, 111–13, 116, 117, 124; in Toushe, 108–18, 123–24, 126, 128–29, 264n40, 264n41, 265n42, 266n49, 266n55. *See also* festivals, to Aborigine deity; folk religion, Hoklo, comparison to; opening power ritual; pig skulls; religious offerings; spirit mediums; temples; *names of Aborigine deities*

Aborigine-Han social relations, 42–43, 48–51, 222, 269n21

Aborigine identity: ability of researcher to discuss, 68–69, 130–31; advantages and disadvantages of, 16, 43, 48–53, 74, 139, 160 (*see also* plains Aborigine identity, claiming); changes in, 18, 36, 65, 66, 216 (*see also* Aborigines, disappearance of); claimed on basis of ancestry, 125, 127–28; physical markers of, 68, 96, 127, 259n3. *See also* footbinding, as cultural marker of Aborigine identity

Aborigine labor. *See* Aborigines, exploitation of; corvée labor

Aborigine land rights, 43, 46, 49–51, 54, 257n12, 257n18. *See also* land

Aborigine militia, 37, 43, 48, 50–53, 151, 152, 257n12. *See also* rebellions

Aborigine population, estimating, 37, 136, 140–46, 148–49, 223, 256n9, 259n5, 268n13. *See also* Aborigines, disappearance of; abortions, among Aborigines

Aborigines: Alliance of Taiwan (Taiwan Yuanzhuminzu Quanli Cujinhui), 127, 251n2; classification of, 8–10, 66, 70–73, 88, 92, 136, 141, 162–63, 260n12 (*see also* reclassification, as Aborigines); disappearance of, 10, 21, 36, 65, 68, 164 (*see also* Aborigine identity, changes in; Aborigine population, estimating; Hoklo identity, acquisition of); exploitation of, 8, 36, 39, 40, 46–50, 222, 256n8, 269n19; stereotypes of, 68, 117; stigmatization of, 48, 95–96, 151, 164, 222 (*see also* plains Aborigine identity, stigmatization of; savages);

Aborigines *(continued)*
terminology for, 10, 68, 251n2,
252n9. *See also* mountain Aborigines; plains Aborigines
Aborigine villages, 125, 134, 255n3,
270n22; under Dutch regime, 37–
39, 222; identity change in, 16,
66–68, 74–75; migration of, 145–
46, 261n15, 269n21; under Qing
regime, 44, 47, 49, 222
Aborigine women: agriculture done
primarily by, 38, 44, 151 (*see also*
women, labor of, in agriculture);
choosing their own husbands, 152–
53 (*see also* intermarriage, Han-
Aborigine; intermarriage, Hoklo-
Aborigine; mixed ancestry, women
of; mixed marriages); interests of,
different than Aborigine men, 151–
53, 155, 233
abortions, among Aborigines, 146–47
Academia Sinica, xiv, xv, 35–36, 125,
259n6
acculturation, 30, 33. *See also* assimilation; cultural ideas, spread of;
sinicization
actions. *See* agency; choices; collectivism;
methodological individualism
adaptive rationality, 229–31, 233. *See
also* choices; cognition; evolutionary
perspective
adopt, decision to, 72, 84–85, 87–88.
See also choices
adoption, 71, 72, 75, 81–88, 93–94,
125, 217, 263n30, 263n31, 270n24.
See also fertility; demographic conditions; Han kinship; mortality of
children
affirmative action for PRC minorities, 15,
17, 169, 171, 172, 188–90. *See also*
PRC official identity
affinal ties. *See* in-laws, relations with
agency, xi, 132, 212, 215, 218–23, 228,
229–31, 235, 243, 276n4, 276n5.
See also A-li Bu, actions attributed
to; choices; collectivism; historical
contingency; intermarriage, pursuit
of; social authority
agricultural practices, Aborigine, 37–38,
44–46, 256n9, 256n10
agriculture, commercial, 37–39, 44–46,
75, 256n9, 261n14, 267n4. *See also*
farmers and laborers, Han; sugar
Ahern, Emily Martin, cited, 105, 264n39,
266n51
A-ka-tuan, 108, 110. *See also* Aborigine
deity

alcohol, consumption of. *See* women,
alcohol consumption of
A-li Bu (Ali Mu), 105, 123, 265n42;
actions attributed to, 107–8,
123; names for, 91, 110, 264n40,
265n42, 266n53; representation of,
91, 265n40; use of name, in Toushe,
108, 110, 264n40, 265n42, 266n55.
See also Aborigine deity; spirit
mediums, to Ali-Bu
A-li Tsoo (Ali Zu), 124, 265n42; Aborigine identity of, publicized, 118,
119, 124, 126; names for, 91, 118,
119, 264n40, 265n42; representation of, 91, 118, 119; worship to,
kept alive, 119–23. *See also* Aborigine deity; spirit mediums, to A-li
Tsoo
altars: domestic, 192, 194, 273n26; in
temples, 91, 106–7, 111–12, 113,
114, 115, 118, 120, 123
American-born Chinese (ABCs), 25,
33. *See also* Chinese Americans;
overseas Chinese; Taiwanese
Americans
Ami, 10, 252n9, 270n25. *See also*
mountain Aborigines
An Tsoo (An Zu), 110, 123, 264n40.
See also Aborigine deity
ancestor worship, 104–5, 150, 157–59,
191, 205, 264n39, 265n43, 266n51,
266n53; adoption of Han practices
of, 104–5, 157–58, 265n43; association with Han identity, 23, 24, 29,
158, 192, 196; in Enshi, 196–200.
See also folk religion; mortuary
practices; souls
ancestral tablets (*shenzhu*), 158, 187, 191–
92, 194, 196–99, 201–2, 206, 209
ancestry, in relation to identity, xi, 2, 5,
10, 24, 69–70, 170, 176, 207, 211,
275n41. *See also* Aborigine identity,
claimed on basis of ancestry; descent,
as a primordial aspect of identity;
mixed ancestry, manipulation of
identity possible with; PRC official
identity, criteria for; PRC official
identity, legally changing
ang-i (T., witch), 266n49. *See also* spirit
mediums
anthropology, discipline of, 125, 212–
15, 218, 219, 224, 228, 275n1,
275n2, 275n6. *See also* cognitive
perspective; evolutionary perspective; interpretivism; Marxism; postmodernism; structuralism; *names of
anthropologists*

Index   313

colonial intervention. *See* footbinding
ban; imperialism; social power
colonial regimes. *See* Dutch regime; Han
imperialism; Japanese colonial regime
Comaroff, Jean, cited, 219, 220, 276n3,
276n4
Communist Party. *See* Chinese Communist Party
Confucian culturalism: concept of, 24,
29, 31, 92, 130, 163, 190, 208 (*see
also* sinicization); PRC usage of, 7,
28, 168, 178, 205–6, 207, 209–10;
Taiwan's usage of, 33–34, 243
Confucian principles, 23, 150, 180, 233,
236, 268n12, 274n32, 274n35; loss
of, 239, 241. *See also* filial obligation; parental authority
consciousness (cognitive). *See* choices;
cognition; unconscious processes
consciousness (ethnic). *See* Han identity,
personal sense of; identity, personal
sense of; *names of specific identities*
cooked Aborigines (*shufan*), 8, 9, 10, 70,
252n9. *See also* Aborigines; plains
Aborigines
Corcuff, Stéphane, cited, 10, 60
corvée labor, 41, 46–49, 139, 151, 152,
256n8
Cosmides, Leda, cited, 228, 229
Coyett, Frederick, 137. *See also* Dutch
regime
critical mass threshold, 16, 216, 275n2.
See also cognitive processes
Cronk, Lee, cited, 275n1, 277n12
Crossley, Pamela, 30
culling process, 224, 277n8, 277n9. *See
also* evolutionary perspective
cultural change, 213, 226; intermarriage
resulting in, 73, 135, 140, 155–60,
161–64, 174–75, 177–78, 205–6,
236–37, 243, 270n25 (*see also*
cultural models, effect of intermarriage on; cultural practices, intermarriage and; cultural transmission,
intermarriage and; intermarriage,
cultural system and); reasons for,
116, 232, 272n15; social experience
and, 95, 108, 234–35. *See also*
cultural ideas, cultural practices
changing before; cultural ideas,
manipulation of; cultural models,
modification of; cultural practices,
spread of; footbinding, as a cultural
impact of short-route identity
change; identity change, cultural
change not sufficient for
cultural ideas (cultural beliefs, cultural

meanings), 2, 215–16, 219, 220,
223, 230; cultural practices changing before, 67, 92–94, 104 (*see also*
cultural change); distinct system of,
xi, 212–13, 215, 218–19, 226–27,
228, 231, 235 (*see also* cultural
system); interaction of, 216–17,
218, 219, 221, 222–23, 229, 230–
31; interpretation of, 216–18, 223,
229, 232 (*see also* interpretivism;
meanings); manipulation of, 158,
220–21, 222–23, 229, 235 (*see also*
cultural change); social experience
and, 95, 216, 217, 229, 260n13;
spread of, 84, 93, 105, 135, 216,
217–18, 219, 229 (*see also* Confucian culturalism; cultural change);
variation in, 94, 215, 223, 230–31
cultural markers. *See* cultural practices,
as ethnic markers
cultural meanings. *See* cultural ideas
cultural models, 216–18, 219, 235; effect
of intermarriage on, 140, 162–63,
233–34, 236 (*see also* cultural
transmission, intermarriage and;
Hoklo cultural models); modification of, 216–18, 229, 233, 234 (*see
also* cultural change)
cultural practices, 213–14, 217; as ethnic
markers, 23, 94, 130, 186–87, 190–
92, 196, 206, 209, 234 (*see also*
ancestor worship; classification by
outsiders; Confucian culturalism;
footbinding, as cultural marker of
Aborigine identity; Han identity,
cultural markers of; local identity
in Enshi, cultural markers of; PRC
official identity, criteria for; surnames,
as cultural markers of identity; *Tanshen*); effect of natural selection on,
225–27; intermarriage and, 98–99,
135, 157, 162, 233–34 (*see also* cultural change, intermarriage resulting
in); spread of, 84, 93, 135, 213, 217,
226 (*see also* cultural change, social
experience and). *See also* cultural
ideas, cultural practices changing
before; state influence, on cultural
practices; *names of specific practices*
Cultural Revolution: current political
implications of, 244–45; disrupted
ethnic identification project, 171,
206; eradicated late-imperial Han
practices, 173, 191, 193, 196, 198,
206, 234, 238–39; political suppression and economic impact of, 171,
238, 241

fertility, xiii, 142, 144, 147, 213, 223–27, 277n11. *See also* abortions, among Aborigines; adoption; demographic conditions; family planning; menarche; mortality, of children

festivals, Hoklo, 56, 62, 119, 128, 275n39. *See also* folk religion; Qingming festival

festivals, to Aborigine deity, 56, 105, 123, 126; comparison to Han festivals, 107–8, 112, 116, 118–19, 122 (*see also* folk religion); content of, 91, 107–8, 112, 115, 116, 118, 122 (*see also* songs); economic benefits of, 128–29. *See also* Aborigine deity

feuds (*xiedou*). *See* ethnic feuds and conflicts

filial obligation (filial piety, filiality, *xiao*), 24, 192, 194, 200, 201, 204–5, 210, 274n32. *See also* Confucian principles; Han kinship; parental authority; social authority

fitness, 225–26, 229, 230. *See also* descent viability; evolutionary perspective; genetic relatedness; natural selection

Flinn, Mark V., cited, 277n9

Flynn, Thomas, cited, 219

folk religion, 266n52; Han, adoption of, 115–16; Han, comparison to, 199, 205, 209–10; Han, practice of, 56, 90–91, 92, 105, 119, 123, 193, 238–39, 266n52, 275n39; Hoklo, comparison to, 67, 88, 90–91, 92, 102–3, 105, 107–8, 111–24, 126, 130, 266n52, 266n53; Taiwanese, 56, 62, 104–5, 124, 126, 238, 264n39, 266n52. *See also* Aborigine deity; ancestor worship; festivals; ghost beliefs; lanshe rites; mortuary practices; Qingming festival; religious practices; ritual specialists; spirit mediums; strippers; *names of deities*

Fong, John M., cited, 269n14

footbinding, 177, 230, 270n27; absence of, in Aborigines, 69, 88, 94, 95, 161, 163; absence of, in Hakka, 265n44; as civilized, 69, 92, 94, 96–97, 101–2, 177, 192, 206, 260n13; as class marker, 177; as a cultural impact of short-route identity change, 159, 164, 233; as cultural marker of Aborigine identity, 66, 67, 69, 70, 71, 88, 92, 94, 95, 97, 102, 161, 260n12, 262n23; decision to practice, 230

(*see also* choices); discouragement of, prior to ban, 56, 265n45; frequencies of, 88, 156–57, 159; by locals in Enshi, 177, 192, 205; and marriageability of women, 96–97, 101, 151, 159, 164, 177, 230–31; not a cultural marker of Tujia identity, 169, 177, 186; recorded in household registers, 54, 95; recorded in household registers, 54, 95; visibility of, 67, 70, 75, 88, 91, 92, 94, 96; women's labor and, 103, 151, 159, 161, 177, 230, 232, 265n45

footbinding ban, 56, 66, 95, 161; enforcement of, 56, 95, 263n34; linked to regime change, 161–62, 232; resulting in identity change, 67, 95–97, 102, 132, 161, 163–64, 232; resulting in change in social experience, 98, 101–2

Formosa, 41. *See also* Dutch regime; Taiwan

Foucault, Michel, 218, 219–20, 221. *See also* postmodernism; subjectivism

French invasion of Taiwan, 52, 53. *See also* war

Friedman, Edward, 11

fu (Hoklo), 8, 70, 252n8

Fujian, 32, 41, 44, 68, 165, 256n7, 265n44, 267n4, 268n11, 270n23, 271n5, 274n34; Han cultural model from, 126, 157, 159, 194, 233; migration from, 19, 35, 153–54, 231, 232, 252n8

funerary rites, 77, 92, 193–94, 198, 202, 238, 261n19, 274n30. *See also* mortuary practices

gaoshan zu (mountain tribes), 10, 252n9. *See also* mountain Aborigines

Gaoxiong, 11, 123

Gates, Hill, cited, xiv, 9, 10, 32, 38, 59–62, 159, 177, 191, 194–96, 201, 209, 230, 245, 247, 252n12, 257n1, 261n14, 269n20, 276n5

gazetteers, 44, 46, 75, 76, 154. *See also* Chinese records

Geertz, Clifford, 215. *See also* anthropology; interpretivism

gender, 116, 117, 218. *See also* religious practices, effect of spirit medium's gender on; spirit mediums, gender of; Thai Tsoo, gender of; women

gendered expectations, 88–89, 103–4, 111, 115, 117, 263n34. *See also* spirit mediums, to Thai Tsoo, transferring the role from women to men

Huang Min-chuan, cited, 269n14
Huang, Philip C., 213–14, 218, 228; cited, 224
Huang Shujing, cited, 44, 46, 75, 78, 136, 152, 261n19, 261n20, 269n19, 269n20. *See also* officials, Qing
Huang Shu-min, cited, 35
Hubei, xii, 64, 166, 171, 172, 188, 217, 271n2, 271n4. *See also* Enshi Tujia-Miao Autonomous Prefecture
Huber, Johannes, cited, 37–41, 137, 141, 255n2, 256n4, 256n5, 256n6, 256n7, 267n4
Hunan, 171, 173, 181, 183, 185, 189, 271n4, 271n8, 271n9, 273n25

ideas. *See* cultural ideas
identification, self. *See* identity, personal sense of; self-identification
identity, 13–19, 74, 131–33, 211–12, 231, 235–36; actual, 2, 13–14, 27, 211–12, 231, 235–36, 243, 245 (*see also* real); borders of, 3, 5, 13, 17–18, 28, 94, 254n20; changeability of, 5, 16–17, 170, 217, 234; choices about, 5, 13, 14, 132, 211; and culture, 163, 216, 233; culture as basis of claims to, 5, 10, 17, 24, 27, 69–70, 210, 211; culture not basis for, xi, 2, 94; as fixed, 5, 13, 16–17, 18, 74, 132, 182; fluidity of, 5, 16–17, 66, 216, 234, 254n20 (*see also* Jibeishua; Longtian; mixed ancestry, people of; Toushe); group, 5, 6, 10, 13–19, 27, 177–79, 211, 216, 236, 240 (*see also* villages, identity of); ideological construction of, 2, 5, 13, 27, 163, 210, 211–12, 231, 235, 243, 252n12; linked to language, 5, 8, 10, 27, 68, 70, 170, 173, 254n25, 255n2; as negotiated, 13–19, 140, 185, 206, 222–23, 233, 245, 248; personal sense of, 2, 3, 13–14, 100–101, 131, 170, 171, 208–9, 210; political implications of, 2, 15, 16, 25–26, 33, 138, 211–12, 231, 234, 235–36, 241; recent, as problematic, 125, 131–33, 164, 168, 176–77, 210; shifting, 16–18, 65, 179, 182, 185, 216 (*see also* historical contingency; local identity in Enshi); social experience as basis of, 2, 13–15, 18–19, 27, 100–101, 132, 206, 207–9, 211–12, 236, 240, 243–44, 245; social experience as basis of, mentioned, xi, 5, 10, 130, 210, 253n17; variability of, 17–18.

See also authenticity; classification; classification by outsiders; identity change; mixed ancestry, manipulation of identity possible with; narratives of unfolding; state influence, on identity; *names of specific identities*
identity change: cultural change not sufficient for, 17, 74, 92, 94, 140, 233, 234; cultural influence on, 33–34, 210, 211–12, 231; effect of demographic conditions on 16, 18, 65, 128, 210–12, 213, 231; effect of outsider classification on, 168, 208–9, 234; effect of social experience on, 100–101, 208–9, 236–42; formation, 2, 3, 5, 13–15, 211–12, 213, 231, 236; impact on culture, 102, 108, 116, 140, 155–56, 160, 162–63, 206, 232–34, 236 (*see also* footbinding, as a cultural impact of short-route identity change; mortuary practices, Han, adopting; religious practices, effect of spirit medium's gender on); intermarriage contributes to, 18, 160, 232, 235, 241–42; intermarriage not sufficient for, 66, 69–74, 161–62, 232; intermarriage used to justify, 15–16, 17, 134, 135–36, 139–40, 149, 189–90, 212, 233, 237, 268n11; as label change, 16–19, 102, 159, 216, 234; migrations contribute to, 16, 18, 162, 172, 174, 181, 188, 210, 212, 235–37, 242; migrations not sufficient for, 160, 232–34; not unique to Taiwan, 3, 165–68, 209; process of, 3, 16–19, 135, 160–63, 168, 212, 213, 216, 232–35, 248. *See also* Aborigine identity, changes in; classification by outsiders; cultural change, identity change and; de-sinicization; footbinding ban, resulting in identity change; Han identity, acquisition of; Hoklo identity, acquisition of; identity label change; identity, shifting; local identity change in Enshi; long-route identity change; mixed ancestry, manipulation of identity possible with; reclassification; short-route identity change; sinicization; social power, drives identity change
identity label change: leads to changes in social experience, 33, 101–2, 128, 129–31, 208–9, 244–45 (*see also* identity, social experience as basis of); leads to changes in personal

social roles, 18, 32, 157, 223, 230, 232, 235, 236. *See also* social transmission; spirit mediums to Thai Tsoo, transferring the role from women to men; women, authority of; women, as transmitters of culture

social structure. *See* social power; Structuralism

social transmission, 158–59, 222–23, 229, 277n12. *See also* cultural transmission; social power; Transmission of information

sociopolitical forces. *See* social power

society, 216, 218–19, 226, 228. *See also* social power

sojourning, 145, 154, 231, 233, 264n4. *See also* migrations

songs, used in annual festival to Aborigine deity, 91, 109, 112, 114, 118, 128. *See also* bridal laments; festivals, to Aborigine deity

sons, 82, 85, 203, 268n11, 274n35. *See also* filial obligation

Soong, James (Song Chuyu), 242, 252n13

Soulang (Xiaolong), 38, 145, 255n3, 256n9, 261n15. *See* plains Aborigine villages

souls (*guihun*), 90, 92, 193, 194, 196, 197–99, 217, 274n33, 274n37. *See also* ancestor worship; ancestral tablets; ghost beliefs; *Qi*; *names of deities*

sovereignty, 1–2, 4, 5, 13, 64, 242, 248, 249, 251n4. *See also* independence from China

Speidel, W. M., cited, 52

Spence, Jonathan D., cited, 41, 258n23, 258n25, 258n26

Sperber, Dan, 15; cited, 93, 215–16, 218, 229, 253n16, 253n18, 277n12. *See also* cognitive perspective

spirit mediums: to A-li Bu, 103, 107–8, 123, 264n35, 266n49, 266n55; to A-li Tsoo, 118–19, 122, 123, 264n35, 266n56; to An Tsoo, 123; consumption of raw pig by, 110, 116–18, 129, 232, 266n56; gender of, 91, 108, 111, 112–16, 117–18; terms for, 91, 108, 115, 266n49; to Thai Tsoo, 91, 266n49; to Thai Tsoo, comparison with spirit mediums to Han deities, 112–17; to Thai Tsoo, transferring the role from women to men, 108–11, 113, 117, 123 266n54, 266n55; to Thai Tsoo, spreading

influence of, 102, 112–13, 123–24, 129, 266n56. See also *pseudonyms of individual spirit mediums*

spirits. *See* souls

spying, accusations of, 25–26, 258n26

Stalin, Joseph, 9, 170, 207

Stalinist criteria for ethnic identification, 7, 170, 172, 191, 251n7. *See also* PRC official identity, criteria for

state (government) influence, on cultural practices, 157–58, 159; democratic, 245–46; Dutch, 44–45, 77, 141–42, 146–47, 154–55, 256n9, 267n4; Japanese, 55, 56, 258n20, 263n34 (*see also* footbinding ban); Nationalist, 59, 131, 237; PRC, 25, 191, 206, 234, 238–39; Qing, 73, 75, 154, 157–58, 159, 191, 192–95, 222, 257n12, 265n43 (*see also* intermarriage, Han-Aborigine, prohibitions against); Zheng, 44–45, 139, 154–55. *See also* intermarriage, effect of social context; migrations to Enshi, forced; parental authority, state-sanctioned

state (government) influence, on identity, 5, 23, 27, 135–36, 208–9, 211, 221, 234, 240, 244–45. *See also* footbinding ban; Chinese nationalism; classification by outsiders, in Enshi; ethnic identification project; ideological rhetoric; migrations to Enshi, forced; narratives of unfolding; PRC official identity; PRC state, official classification of individuals by; regime change; social power; Zheng regime change

State Nationalities Affairs Commission (SNAC), of the PRC, 170, 179, 180, 190. *See also* ethnic identification project

state tributary mode of production, 32, 261n14. *See also* petty capitalism; taxation

stigmatization, 116. *See also* Aborigines, stigmatization of; plains Aborigine identity, stigmatization of; racial classification and racism

Stockard, Janice, cited, 32

Strauss, Claudia, 229; cited, 13, 215–16, 220, 223, 277n12. *See also* cognitive perspective

strippers, 103–4, 107, 117–18, 266n50. *See also* folk religion

structuralism, 220, 221–22. *See also* anthropology; social power

Su Minggang (Su Ming-kang), 267n4, 268n10

intermarriage; marriage market; migrations to Taiwan, of Han women;
migrations to Taiwan, of women;
sex ratio; spirit mediums
World Trade Organization, 248
World War II, 56, 57–58, 258n22,
258n24. *See also* Japanese invasion
of China
writing, 23, 112, 180, 192, 208. *See also*
education; *wenhua*
Wu Shigong, 148
Wu Xu, cited, xv, 271n2, 272n19
Wucun (Fifth Village; pseudonym), xiii,
169, 238, 271n4, 273n20. *See also*
Enshi Tujia-Miao Autonomous Prefecture; locals in Enshi

Xiangxi Tujia-Miao Autonomous Pre-
fecture, 171, 173, 271n4, 271n8,
271n9. *See also* Enshi Tujia-Miao
Autonomous Prefecture; Hunan
Xiaolong. *See* Soulang
Xingang. *See* Sinkan

Yan Xingzhu, cited, 265n42
Yanagisako, Sylvia, cited, 276n7

Yelvington, Kevin A., cited, 14
Yuan Chang-rue, cited, 270n25
yuanzhumin (original inhabitants), 68,
251n2. *See also* Aborigines

Zhang Yaoqi, cited, 69, 71, 127
Zhang Zhengming, cited, 180
Zhangzhou, 51, 256n7, 270n23. *See also*
Fujian
Zheng Chenggong, 40–41, 137, 139,
154, 156, 236, 256n7
Zheng invasion, 20, 40, 137–38, 139,
142, 149, 237. *See also* war
Zheng regime, xix, 40–42, 43, 134, 154–
55; change to, 135, 140, 151, 160,
233; classification under the, 16,
135–36, 139–41, 161
zhonghua minzu, 22, 243, 254n24. *See
also* narratives of China's unfolding
Zhou Enlai, 170, 271n8
Zhu Rongji, 240
Zhu Yigui rebellion, 257n15. *See also*
rebellions
Zhuang Jinde, 43, 149
Zhuluo, 140, 141, 143–49, 154, 256n9,
257n13

Compositor:	Integrated Composition Systems
Text:	10/13 Sabon
Display:	Sabon
Printer and binder:	Sheridan Books, Inc.